T0310993

THE OUTER EDGE
OF ULSTER

DONEGAL, 60 YEARS AGO.
A True
Historical Narrative
By Hugh Dorian

Contents

THE OUTER EDGE
OF ULSTER

A memoir of social life in nineteenth-century Donegal

HUGH DORIAN

Edited by Breandán Mac Suibhne and David Dickson

UNIVERSITY OF NOTRE DAME PRESS

Do Anne, Brendan agus John Óg Hiúdaí Neidí
i gcuimhne ar
Eibhlín Ní Chnáimhsí

Introduction and editorial matter copyright © David Dickson
and Breandán Mac Suibhne, 2000

All rights reserved. No part of this publication
may be reproduced in any form or by any means
without the prior permission of the publisher.

First published in North America 2001 by
UNIVERSITY OF NOTRE DAME PRESS
Notre Dame, Indiana 46556, USA
http://www.undpress.nd.edu

First published in Ireland 2000 by
The Lilliput Press
in association with
Donegal County Council

A record of the Library of Congress Cataloguing-in-Publication Data
is available upon request from the Library of Congress.

1 3 5 4 2   1 3 5 4 2

ISBN 0 268 03712 4 (cloth)
ISBN 0 268 03711 6 (paper)

Frontispiece: Table of contents to Dorian's Narrative
(St Columb's College, Derry)

Set in Sabon by Marsha Swan

CONTENTS

ACKNOWLEDGMENTS

The editors are grateful to the Rev. John Walsh, president of St Columb's College, Derry, for permission to publish this edition of Dorian's Narrative, and to An tOllamh Séamas Ó Catháin for permission to photocopy the photostat of the text held in Roinn Bhéaloideas Éireann, Coláiste na hOllscoile, Baile Átha Cliath.

The staff of the following libraries and archives kindly allowed us to consult materials in their care: National Archives of Ireland, Dublin; National Library of Ireland, Dublin; Irish Architectural Archive, Dublin; Trinity College, Dublin; Roinn Bhéaloideas Éireann, Coláiste na hOllscoile, Baile Átha Cliath; Linenhall Library, Belfast; Donegal County Library, Letterkenny; Hesburgh Library, University of Notre Dame. For permission to reproduce the photographs of the third earl of Leitrim and Massmount Church, we would like to thank the Hon. Hedley Strutt, and Prof. Alistair Rowan (*Buildings of Ireland* Archive).

We are very much indebted to Professor David W. Miller of Carnegie Mellon University for preparing the explanatory maps and for his general support of the project.

A number of other people assisted in various ways; they include Stephen Ball, National Library of Ireland; Charles Doherty, Dublin; Paul Ferguson, Trinity College, Dublin; Paul Gorry, Gorry Research; Billy Kelly and Peter Walker, University of Ulster at Magee; John Logan, University of Limerick; Tim O'Neill and Willie Nolan, University College Dublin; Peter McQuillan, Jay Walton and Kevin Whelan, University of Notre Dame; Tarlach Mac Giolla Bhríde, Linenhall Library, Belfast; Dónall Ó Baoill, Queen's University, Belfast; Lillis Ó Laoire, University of California at Los Angeles; Liam Ronayne, Donegal

County Library; and Dermot Francis, Derry City Council. We would like to thank them all for their help. We would also like to place on record our great appreciation of Brendan Barrington and all the editorial team at The Lilliput Press.

Tá muid buíoch fosta do Údarás na Gaeltachta, is go háirithe do Dhonnchadh Ó Baoill, a chuir cuidiú airgid ar fáil leis an inneács a chur leis an téacs.

Preface to the North American edition

In summer 1845 *phyophthora infestans*, potato blight, reached Europe from the Americas. The disease attacked ripening plants, turning the food of many countries' rural poor into black mush. In Ireland three million of the country's eight and a half million people were dependent on potatoes. The blight's effects were devastating. One third of the 1845 potato crop was lost and the scarcity of seed potatoes and recurrence of blight resulted in paltry harvests over the next three years.

Ireland was then part of the United Kingdom, the most developed economy and state system in Europe, but a malign conjuncture of political economy, providentialism and prejudice created an ambivalence to the fate of the Irish poor that eclipsed moral responsibility. The state's response was wantonly inadequate. Debilitated by hunger, young and old fell victim to disease, and deaths multiplied. By the end of the decade, over one million people had perished and two million more had emigrated.

These years of famine transformed rural Ireland within a generation. Young people deferred marriage and increasing numbers never married. Fathers ceased to subdivide their land, passing it intact to a favourite son. Emigration removed the landless: the youngest in many families knew their elder siblings only through occasional letters from the steel towns of Pennsylvania or the mining communities of Montana. As population dwindled, the conservative values of the large farmer and the townsman achieved a new hegemony. And a "great silence" fell across the country. In some districts, households composed of monolingual Irish-speakers in the 1840s were made up of monolingual English-speakers by the 1880s; in such households, parents can scarcely have had a meaningful conversation with their children.

Silence, however, was never absolute. In the smallholders' cabins of Ireland and the immigrant slums of America, the remnants of obliterated communities recalled *an droch-shaol* [the bad life] and *am an ghorta* [the time of the hunger]. They remembered forestalling farmers and shopkeepers, the theft of food supplies, and family and friends buried without shroud or coffin. But they also recalled houses leveled by bailiffs with police escorts, and ships sailing from Irish ports with cargoes of grain. And remembering those things, they blamed Britain for the cataclysm.

Recovering lower-class experiences of those years is difficult. Those who died and those who suffered but survived left few written records, and for much of the twentieth century historians deemed second-hand memories suspect. Written accounts by people of a different class and culture—philanthropists, priests and ministers, poorhouse officials, policemen and other social bookkeepers—became the sources of an often antiseptic history. The men and women who worked on government roads and stood in line for rations of watery soup were seen but not heard.

*

Hugh Dorian's Narrative contains the most extensive lower-class account of the Great Famine. Dorian wrote the Narrative in 1889–90 as he and his family staggered into alcohol-numbed poverty. His purpose was not to write a history of the great hunger itself but to explain why the rural poor of the 1880s sporadically resorted to violence for political ends. A conviction that a multi-layered colonialism had deformed Ireland's development underlies that explanation. The Narrative opens with the author surveying the rugged Donegal hills he knew as a boy. His eye falls on a ruined building. "The mind takes an ungovernable flight and carries the imagination backwards half a century; a cloud of events and of rapid changes rushes upon the memory which for a little bewilders one's ideas until they are calmed down by reflection ..." As he reflects on his youth, the intrusion of the extraordinary into the everyday foregrounds Ireland's subjection to Britain: rabbits were plentiful in the sand dunes but their meat was never tasted at home, being shipped away to "satisfy the appetites of those living in Liverpool or distant London." Other seemingly incongruous aspects of everyday life—the Irishman mocked for speaking Irish in Ireland, differences in the dress and physical appearance of Catholics and Protestants, the extra rent charged a tenant who had improved his holding—illuminate broader social and cultural inequalities that contributed to political unrest. For Dorian, the horrors of the past are inscribed in a landscape made up of the "rich lands of the plantation" and the "mountain, the bog and the seashore" inhabited by the "Celt." "The Donegal peasant has got all the historical learning he requires; he has his ancestors' history open before him every day he rises; it is exhibited in the large characters—the ocean, the mountain, and his own state of poverty—and if he reads anything he must read how it is that he is there and why."

Detailing the lives of ordinary people in an extraordinary time and place, the Narrative moves to the catastrophe of 1845–52. Horror is described vividly but with restraint: "in a very short time there was nothing but stillness; a mournful silence in the villages; in the cottages grim poverty and emaciated faces showing all the signs of hardships." The picture of starvation is stark but authentic: "the cheek bones became thin and high, the cheeks blue, the bones sharp, and the eyes sunk ... the legs and the feet swell and get red and the skin cracks ...". And then came "the dispersion ... to places which their fathers never heard of and which they themselves never would have seen, had the times not changed." "No one," he writes, "can measure the distance of the broad Atlantic speedier and better than a father whose child is there."

Here Dorian articulates a nationalist analysis, blaming Britain for the calamity. Public work schemes in particular are identified as the point where "government advisers dealt out the successful blow—and it would appear premeditated—the great blow for slowly taking away human life, getting rid of the population and nothing else." That analysis, however, frames a more intimate history, and his assessment of the Famine's effects is unsettlingly callous:

> Arising from death, emigration and dispersion to all parts, the population soon dwindled away. And indeed I hope it will not be any uncharitable to say it, but with the multitude also disappeared many turbulent and indifferent persons and characters who were only a disgrace to the good, the honest, and the well-doing, and if there was poverty, there was peace too.

But Dorian was himself a disgrace to "the good, the honest, and the well-doing": he drank and brawled through his adult years, his intimacy with "turbulent and indifferent persons" landing him in trouble with priests and policemen. His cold words, therefore, serve as a sharp reminder that the Famine was not simply an event in Anglo-Irish relations. They are a reminder too that men, women and children are not simply receptacles of food or members of a social class: they belong to households and kin-groups and have cultural and political bonds, and such filiations and affiliations can make the difference between life and death. For Dorian, the Almighty may have sent the blight and Britain—in the long term and the short—made the Famine but, within that general context, everyday attachments and animosities determined the fate of many.

Still, it is the pulse of feeling as much as the political analysis that makes Dorian's Narrative so compelling. A sense of loss, closer to bereavement than nostalgia, is threaded through the text: it is a lament for the might-have-been—the future as imagined before the Famine—rather than the actual past. The phrase "mournful silence" that recurs in his treatment of the Famine's impact is first used to describe school-children paralyzed with fear by an irate schoolmaster. The final and last-ing image is of trauma without recovery: the wise-men who had sat late into the small hours debating politics in the years before the Famine congregated in the after years but sat in silence, "their subjects ... lack-ing words."

*

Dorian gave these people voice when few wanted to listen. By the 1890s tensions within rural Catholic communities had been buried in an alliance for land reform and limited home rule for Ireland. At the same time, a literary revival was constructing the west of Ireland as the hearthstone of Irish identity and nationhood: here, in the imagination of the cultural nationalist, Irish-speaking "peasants" had escaped the full effects of colonialism and the national character was preserved in amber; national recovery would come from the outer edges. Dorian's Narrative was a discordant testimony. He portrays the western poor as reduced and degraded as any other; "downtrodden ... in oppression and cruelty," they are consumed with self-interest and greed, slavishly vying for the favor of landlords and bailiffs. Rather than Dorian's poverty or whiskey-drinking, it is this discordance that best explains his failure to find a publisher. The publication of the Narrative one hundred and fifty years after the Great Famine allows the totality of that calamity to be seen from the cabin with the empty pot and the crying child, and from the hard road taken by the anonymous emigrant.

B. Mac S., D. D., February 2001

THE OUTER EDGE
OF ULSTER

INTRODUCTION

The inhabitants of Inishowen state that Fánaid extends from Rathmeltan to Mulroy Lough, but the natives of the parishes of Killygarvan, Tully and Aughnish, who consider themselves civilized, deny that they themselves are of the 'men of Fánaid' so that when civilization advances northwards and encroaches on the savage mountains, Fánaid will gradually move towards the sea, and perhaps in the course of some years, lose its very name and precipitate itself into the ocean. However, I entertain strong hopes that as long as Saint O'Woddog keeps the rats and cuckoos out of it, it will retain its name to the glory of MacSweeney.

John O'Donovan to Thomas Larcom, 1835[1]

In the years before the blight, Fánaid—the peninsula forming the western shore of Lough Swilly—was beyond the frontier of respectability. From the perspective of the barracks and the big house, its inhabitants were 'a rude people'; 'a most bigoted and superstitious race'; 'a lawless and turbulent body'; 'ill-disposed'; 'uncivilised'; 'outrageous'; even 'evil'.[2] As one pioneer lawman explained in 1820, it was the last part of Donegal to which a stranger 'could have any good discoverable motive for resorting and none at all for remaining in it—a district which has

1. Ros na Cille (Rosnakill), 3 Sept. 1835, J. O'Donovan to T. Larcom, in M. O'Flanagan, ed., *Letters containing information relative to the antiquities of the county of Donegal collected during the progress of the Ordnance Survey in 1835* (Bray, 1927), pp. 24–6.

2. Rathmullan, 31 Aug. 1835, J. O'Donovan to T. Larcom, in ibid., pp. 21–3; National Archives of Ireland, Outrage Papers 1841/7/13177, Memorial of the Inhabitants of the Parish of Clondevadock, 19 Aug. 1841; 1846/7/36551, Rathmullan House, 10 Dec. 1846, T. Batt to H. Laboucher; State of the Country Papers I 1565/34, Derry, 7 May 1814, J. Burnett to P. Carey; C. Otway, *Sketches in Ireland descriptive of interesting and hitherto unnoticed districts in the north and south* (Dublin, 1827), p. 101.

I

always been considered more lawless than any other of the county'.[3] Only two landowners, Capt. Humphrey Babington of Greenfort and Robert Patton of Croaghan, resided in the peninsula; tithe- and cess-collectors regularly required armed support; a 'spirit of insubordination' prevented peace officers from serving warrants and police constables found it virtually impossible to procure information about seemingly insignificant offences.[4] Investigations of serious infractions, particularly those with a socio-political dimension, frequently reached the formulaic conclusion that they were the work of 'a person or persons unknown'. The odium attached to informers was general: the authorities first learned of the killing of Betty Thompson when Joseph Forster of Ballinafad and Moses Hay of Aghadreenan uncovered her body in the 'highest state of preservation' while footing turf in Ballykinard Bog in August 1840; a deep wound on her throat was clearly evident; she had disappeared in May 1812 when she informed on Owen Sweeney, her husband, for stealing sheep. Sub-Inspector Alexander Fox observed that the Sweeneys were 'a numerous and wicked faction' and, although there could be no doubt as to her identity, those who recognized her would 'only swear to the best of their knowledge'.[5]

Fánaid's silence as the earth gave up the dead reinforced a well-established reputation for violence. In neighbouring parishes, the townspeople of Rathmullan, Rathmelton, Kilmacrenan and Milford had long blamed the 'men of Fánaid' for riots and brawls at their fairs and markets. In the peninsula itself, disputes between kin-groups—Sweeneys, Shiels, Friels, McAteers and Carrs being the largest 'connections'—and the ruthless punishment of those who transgressed customary codes of

---

3. N.A.I., S.O.C. I 2187/9, No. 34 Blessington St., 6 Mar. 1820, W. C. Major to C. Grant; Fannet Glebe, 22 Mar. 1820, Rev. H. Maturin to S. Carter.

4. W. Lancey, 'Parish of Clondavaddog, county Donegal, statistical report ... April 1835', in A. Day and P. McWilliams, eds, *Ordnance Survey memoirs of Ireland, vol. 38: Parishes of county Donegal I, 1833–5: North-east Donegal* (Belfast, 1997), p. 18; S. Lewis, *A topographical dictionary of Ireland* (London, 1837), vol. I, p. 355; N.A.I., S.O.C. II Box 164 [1813 M-W], Abstract of reports received from general officers and brigade-majors of yeomanry in Ireland on the state of their respective districts and counties during the month of March 1813; Strabane, 31 Mar. 1813, J. Burnet to the Chief Secretary. The Babington and Patton families, the family of the Rev. Henry Maturin, and the Bartons, Hays, Borelands and Dills formed 'a very pleasant circle of society' in early nineteenth-century Fánaid: see Rev. J. R. Dill, *Autobiography of a country parson* (2nd ed., Belfast, 1892), p. 8.

5. N.A.I., Outrage Papers 1840/7/15531, Rathmelton, 26 Aug. 1840, A. K. Fox to Inspector General; 1840/7/15673, Rathmelton, 31 Aug. 1840, A. K. Fox to Inspector General. The following year, another woman's body was found in Glenalla Bog in the nearby parish of Aughnish: see Outrage Papers 1841/7/7645, Rathmelton, 27 May 1841, A. K. Fox to C. Plunkett; Milford, 28 May 1841, Statement of J. Baldurk M.D.; Rathmelton, 29 May 1841, C. Plunkett to Under Secretary.

behaviour confirmed outsiders' impressions of an implacable hostility to the law. During the hungry winter of 1836–7, an oath-bound 'confederacy', regulated by a 'board', repeatedly posted threatening notices fixing the local price of potatoes; when some farmers sold at a higher price, people dressed in white coverings torched their outhouses, crops and turf stacks. The authorities suspected that the 'combinators' were 'a few of the lower order who are engaged in purchasing potatoes ... and conveying them, generally in boats, to the adjacent markets to sell at an advanced price'. The number of police constables in Tamney, a hamlet whose barracks and post office made it the peninsula's administrative centre, was doubled to ten; large rewards were offered for information, and Dr Patrick McGettigan, the Roman Catholic bishop of Raphoe, descended on Fánaid threatening excommunication. Few broke *omertà* and the 'midnight regulators' prevailed.[6]

Violence was not only a weapon of the weak. Faced with a deep antipathy to outside authority, landowners and their agents devolved the day-to-day management of their estates to dominant figures in the local 'connections'; in effect, many 'bailiffs' were the headmen of kin-based mafia who mediated between owners and occupiers.[7] Customary and contractual roles intertwined, and in pursuit of ostensibly 'modern' ends—the enforcement of owners' legal claims—they called on the brute muscle of their factions. Hugh Blaney of Ballykinard, for instance, was both head-bailiff on several small estates and a headman with a considerable 'backing'. In February 1840 Blaney failed to prevent men employed by Dr James Watt Fullerton of Tamney from removing furniture which he, as bailiff, had intended distraining for unpaid rent. Blaney immediately gathered a 'number of the meanest tenantry on the

6. N.A.I., Outrage Papers 1836/7/112, Rathmelton, 24 Dec. 1836, J. L. Rogers to Inspector General; 1837/7/32, Rathmelton, 10 Mar. 1837, J. L. Rogers to Inspector General; Rathmelton, 8 June 1837, J. L. Rogers to Inspector General; 1837/7/42, Rathmelton, [Apr. 1837], J. L. Rogers to Inspector General; Information of John Diver, Carron; Rosnakill, 4 Apr. 1837, J. Taylor to Inspector General; 1837/7/45, Rathmelton, 19 Apr. 1837, J. L. Rogers to Inspector General; 1837/7/70, Rathmelton, [May 1837], J. L. Rogers to Inspector General; 1837/7/71, Rathmelton, 3 Jun. 1837, J. L. Rogers to Inspector General. Guns were ubiquitous in Fánaid: in 1843 when a bailiff and two assistants seized some property of Edward Doherty, a cottier to Patrick Gallagher of Glenfannet, for non-payment of a debt, Gallagher and four relatives attacked them with guns and stones to recapture the seizure, which they claimed as rent; noting that the constabulary had confiscated five guns, the investigating magistrate reported that there was 'scarce a house' in Fánaid without firearms: see Outrage Papers 1843/7/3651, Rathmullan, 21 January 1843, C. Plunkett to E. Lucas.

7. Headmen also mediated between occupiers and the authorities. In August 1840, for instance, Hugh Blaney, a headman discussed below, informed the constabulary that Nelly Doherty of Fanavolty was rumoured to have committed infanticide: see N.A.I., Outrage Papers 1840/7/14387, Rathmelton, 8 Aug. 1840, A. K. Fox to Inspector General.

3

estate', and Tamney became 'one scene of confusion and riot' that lasted from about nine at night until nine the following morning; houses where the doctor's men had lodged his goods were smashed open, his men were attacked with sticks and stones, teeth broken and heads cut.[8]

Such incidents were not Fánaid's only rebuffs to reason and respectability. Few features of its social and cultural life failed to provoke the condescending horror of outside observers. They denounced rundale—the open-field arrangements in which most land was held—as a 'vicious system'; wrote in exasperation of 'thick villages' of 'mean and dirty' houses, 'huddled and packed together in the most incomprehensible confusion!'; and blamed the area's economic dependence on illicit distillation of *poitín* for 'disorder and distress'.[9] The symbols and substance of older beliefs that pervaded popular Catholicism also attracted scorn. The Rev. Caesar Otway, the evangelical writer who visited in the mid-1820s, dismissed the peninsula's Catholics as 'given-up to ... saint-adoration' and 'addicted to well-worshipping and sundry absurd superstitions', and even John O'Donovan, a more sophisticated if sometimes cynical commentator, scoffed at the grip which prophecies ascribed to Colm Cille, the west Ulster patron, had on smallholders' imagination: why, he wondered, if the saint had prophesied that gun emplacements would be erected at Muckamish, had he not foretold their name rather than composing a cryptic verse that was open to a variety of interpretations?[10] Irish, the most widely spoken language in the peninsula, was yet another marker of backwardness and resistance to modernity. Even the very landscape could disturb the outsider.[11]

Perceptions of Fánaid were, in part, a product of environment. Peninsulas have something of the character of islands and, in this

8. N.A.I., Outrage Papers 1840/7/2687, Letterkenny, 15 Feb. 1840, A. K. Fox to Inspector General.

9. Lancey, 'Clondavaddog, 1835', pp. 6–9; Rev. H. Maturin, 'Replies ... to queries of North West Farming Society, July 1825', in Day and McWilliams, *North-east Donegal*, p. 10; Lord G. Hill, *Hints to Donegal tourists* (Dublin, 1847), p. 14.

10. Otway, *Sketches*, pp. 101, 112; Rathmullan, 31 Aug. 1835, J. O'Donovan to T. Larcom, in O'Flanagan, *Letters*, pp. 21–3.

11. On a visit to north Donegal in 1837, the American novelist Charlotte Elizabeth wrote: 'What a glorious land is this ... where every prospect pleases, and only man is vile! ... As in the music of the Irish, and in their national character, so it is in the natural scenery of their country. Some unexpected trait of the softest beauty continually steals upon you in the midst of what is dark, stern, and wild; something of the latter breaks in, where seemingly it has no business, just to remind you that what you are contemplating is Irish. The grandeur of this mountain tract of Donegal is really savage; yet I am mistaken if the sky of Italy looks down on anything so softly, so enchantingly lovely as this Lough Salt': C. Elizabeth, *Letters from Ireland, 1837* (London, 1838), pp. 396–7.

instance, proximity to an advantaged, heavily Protestant district to the south cast cultural difference in sharp relief.[12] Fánaid, however, changed in the mid-nineteenth century, making an accommodation with respectability and, more ambiguously, outside authority. There were straws in the wind before the blight—swearing to the best of one's knowledge was a change from not swearing at all—but it was in the latter half of the century that the district underwent a profound transformation. Consolidated holdings replaced rundale plots; landlords more regularly received rents; the chapel and catechism replaced the *tobar beannaithe* (holy well), the *turas* (pilgrimage), and the *tairngreacht* (prophecy) as the touchstones of popular devotion; *poitín*-making decreased; social unrest subsided and Irish-speaking retreated from the town and farm to the most marginal smallholdings until it all but disappeared when the heather and the rushes finally recaptured them in the late twentieth century; with the demise of the language, the vestiges of a once highly developed oral culture foundered and were lost.

And yet O'Donovan was right to sniff at the notion that 'civilisation' would inevitably advance on the 'savage mountains' and erode the perception of difference. For all that Fánaid changed, outsiders continued to regard the district as separate and distinct, its inhabitants hidebound in tradition or backwardness, clannish, rough and ready, or simply rough. Even today, people from Rathmullan still protest too much when it is suggested they are 'really from Fánaid'; 'put a coat on a brush and send it to Fánaid', they say, 'and it is sure to come back with a woman'. Around Milford a person who has gone 'out of this world and into Fánaid' is in a very remote place indeed, and in the few Irish-speaking homes left in the western and always more genteel peninsula of Ros Goill, '*Ordógaí Fhánada!*' (clumsy Fánaid oaf!) remains the choice rebuke to the awkward and the ungainly.[13]

12. Similarly circumstanced districts had comparable reputations. In County Donegal, Glenswilly, a predominantly Catholic valley opening into the Presbyterian Laggan, and Townawilly, an impoverished and inaccessible area just north of the Episcopalian farmland that fringed Donegal Bay, were also dubbed the 'most lawless' in the county while, in a provincial context, south Armagh's place beyond the physical and proverbial pale is well known. For an insider's account of Glenswilly, see M. Wall, *Glenswilly: A talk on her native glen* (Dublin, 1973). For an outsider's impressions of south Armagh, see T. Harnden, *Bandit country: The IRA and south Armagh* (London, 1999).

13. For the expression 'out of this world and into Fánaid', see M. Traynor, *The English dialect of Donegal: A glossary incorporating the collections of H. C. Hart, M.R.I.A. (1847–1900)* (Dublin, 1953), p. 97. The song *Brón Dhónaill i ndiaidh Mhánais* (Dónall's pining for Mánas) also expresses the notion that Fánaid is far away; the song concerns Dónall and Mánas, two brothers, who lived together in Gortnalaragh in Termon, outside Kilmacrenan; Mánas married '*sladaí mná … nach nglacann comhairle*' (a trampish thieving woman who

*

In 1890 Hugh Dorian (1834-1914), a native of Fánaid working as a writing clerk in Derry, completed a 'true historical narrative' of the transformation of his home-place in the mid-nineteenth century. In doing so, Dorian recreated the world of his childhood and his young adult years. As a text, the Narrative is quite exceptional. Its distinctive conversational style, heavily influenced by the author's bilingualism, is an intimate yet coded history of a single isolated community, written with passion but detachment. Anecdotal, analytical, polemical, it is a polychromatic narrative without literary pretension.

Although clearly intended for publication, the Narrative was never published in Dorian's lifetime. A manuscript copy ended up in the library of St Columb's College in Derry and photostats were deposited in the Irish Folklore Commission and National Library of Ireland in 1946; the original manuscript itself appears to have been lost. Although consulted for a handful of works in social and cultural history, the Narrative has remained unknown to all but a privileged few.[14]

I

Fánaid[15] juts into the Atlantic from the north-west coast of Ulster. Its glacier-hewn and sea-carved landscape is a patchwork of jagged cliffs and low hills, windblown sand dunes and lake-dotted bog; pockets of sandy soil that require frequent fertilizing are the only areas of arable.

---

heeds no one) and brought her to live with them; Dónall left home in protest and went to live in *íochtar Fhánada* (the bottom of Fánaid); in the song he presents himself as a forlorn exile and promises to return to Termon only when Mánas is 'released': see É. Ó Muirgheasa, eag., *Dhá chéad de cheoltaibh Uladh* [Two hundred Ulster songs] (Baile Átha Cliath, 1934), pp. 148–9. The political career of Neil T. Blaney has caused Fánaid to be associated with a 'machine'-style politics that outsiders have conceived as 'traditional'; for an analysis of the Blaney 'machine', see P. M. Sacks, *The Donegal mafia: An Irish political machine* (New Haven, 1976).

14. Dorian's Narrative has been cited in a small number of social and cultural histories: see M. Mac Néill, *The festival of Lughnasa* (Oxford, 1962); K. H. Connell, 'Illicit distillation', in idem, *Irish peasant society* (Oxford, 1968), pp. 1–50; C. Woodham-Smith, *The Great Hunger: Ireland, 1845–49* (London, 1962).

15. Fannet or Fanad are the common English spellings; the district is coterminous with the civil parish of Clondavaddog.

In the early 1800s, a seventeenth-century template could still be discerned with deceptive ease in linguistic and settlement patterns and, more importantly, in a virulent sectarianism that infused social relations. Fánaid was polarized into two communities—*Gaeil* (Gaels; Catholics) and *Albanaigh* (Scotsmen; Protestants, especially Presbyterians)—neither of which could find comfort in sectarian head-counting. Catholics outnumbered Protestants by about four to one in the peninsula itself, but the ratio was reversed in much of the rich flax country between Kerrykeel and Letterkenny.[16] Encircled in the 'respectable' villages of Tamney, Glinsk and Rosnakill, local Protestants regarded Catholics with feelings of distrust and disdain. Castles built by the Sweeneys, the preplantation élite, were an uncomfortable reminder of the 'civilization' of the anterior order, while folk memory of atrocities—the disinterment of corpses in Killygarvan and the sacking of Rathmelton church in 1641—recalled 'barbarity' and stirred a different type of unease.[17] Catholics, meanwhile, raked the ashes of *am na caorthaíochta* (the time of the cattle-raiding, the early penal era)—a vividly remembered if sometimes vaguely periodized cycle of events—and rekindled an acute sense of physical and cultural loss. They talked about Protestants laying claim to Catholics' land, rustling their livestock, disrupting their masses and hunting their priests. In particular, they talked about *na trí Sheán* (the three Johns)—Cunningham, Sproule and Dunlop—whose casual cruelties had come to a sanguinary end when a Catholic crowd killed all three of them. *Poll Uí Gheamaill* (Gamble's Hole), *Ard an Albanaigh* (The Scotsman's Hillock) and other heights and hollows had associations with sectarian savagery and, while fireside tales melded, they still cast the shadows of communal trauma: *Scoilt an Duine* (The Person's Cleft), an inlet in Ballyhoorisky, was pointed out by some as the place where Catholics had slaughtered the last of na trí Sheán and by others as the spot where priest-hunters had butchered a man fleeing an interrupted mass at *Lag na hAltóra* (The Altar Hollow).[18]

16. For confessional data, see Fannet Glebe, 15 March 1835, Rev. H. Carre to W. Lancey, in Day and McWilliams, *North-east Donegal*, p. 10. For the continued use of *Gael* and *Albanach*, see E. Evans, 'A vocabulary of the dialects of Fanad and Glenvar, co. Donegal', *Zeitschrift für Celtische philologie*, Band 32 (1972), 178, 217–18.

17. W. Lancey, 'Parish of Killygarvan ... statistical report, November 1834', in Day and McWilliams, *North-east Donegal*, pp. 41–2; idem, 'Parish of Tullyaughnish ... statistical report, 1834', in ibid., p. 87.

18. Roinn Bhéaloideas Éireann, 705, 427–31 (Tomás Ó Siadhail, 55, An Sean-Bhaile, Baile Uí Bhorascaidhe, 8 Iuíl 1940); 718, 5–14 (Padaí Ó Canainn, c. 68, Tuaim, Baile Láir, 25 Meán Fómhair 1940); 740, 23–5, 42–3 (Brian Mac Giolla Cearra, 85, An Tóin Bhán, 13 Nollaig 1940). These stories were collected by Seán Ó hEochaidh of the Irish Folklore Commission in 1940; the narrators had heard them from their parents or *na sean-daoine* (the old people).

Critically, the monochrome oppositions which these narratives sustained were new or, more accurately, newly sharpened after 1800. In the latter half of the eighteenth century, social and cultural differentiation within both the Catholic and Protestant blocs had helped to dissipate sectarian animosities and, with the rise of the Volunteers, there had been signs of a new dispensation in Irish society—the possibility of an inclusive national identity displacing older attachments. This process had been particularly pronounced in north-west Ulster, a region characterized by a high level of commercialization, a bristling tension between politically advantaged Episcopalians and numerically superior Presbyterians and also a substantial Catholic community with which 'union' was desirable for stability and sustained commercial growth. Locally, St Columba's, Fánaid's first chapel, was erected about 1785 on a site at Massmount provided by Andrew Patton, lieutenant of the local Volunteer company, for a peppercorn rent; it was one of no fewer than sixteen chapels built with Protestant support in the diocese of Raphoe in the mid-1780s, and although now construed as 'a monument to a tenacious faith', its erection was an optimistic act of nation-building.[19] In the late 1790s many of the peninsula's Catholics and Presbyterians displayed a high level of commitment to the United Irishmen's republican project. Thus when Dr William Hamilton, the local rector and an active magistrate, supported by a party of Manx Fencibles, detained republican leaders in January 1797, some eight hundred croppies laid siege to the glebe-house for two days in an attempt to force their release. The attempt failed when reinforcements arrived from Letterkenny; but Hamilton was assassinated a few weeks later and Fánaid was one of the few districts in north-west Ulster where the military expected 'much trouble' in the bloody summer of 1798.[20]

Retreat from the politics of inclusion after the failed rising was a rapid affair, expedited by the government's discrediting of the national

19. A. Coyle, *Collectanea sacra, or pious miscellany in prose and verse in six books* (Strabane, 1788), quoted in E. Maguire, *A history of the diocese of Raphoe* (Dublin, 1920), pt. I, vol. II, pp. 285–6. On Massmount, see Lancey, 'Clondavaddog, 1835', p. 4, and A. Rowan, *The buildings of Ireland. North-west Ulster: The counties of Londonderry, Donegal, Fermanagh and Tyrone* (London, 1979), p. 478. Inclusion is also evident in the local Presbyterian congregation's published acknowledgment of contributions received towards rebuilding their meeting-house in 1783; they expressly excused an Episcopalian minister for not making a donation on account of his involvement in fund-raising for a Catholic chapel in Derry: see *London-Derry Journal*, 1 April 1783.

20. For the context of these events, see B. Mac Suibhne, 'Up not out: Why did north-west Ulster not rise in 1798?', in C. Póirtéir, ed., *The great Irish rebellion of 1798* (Cork, 1998), pp. 83–100.

republican leadership and its encroachments on the 'free press'. By the 1830s the Volunteers and 'Unites' were perceived as an aberration in the dominant Catholic and Protestant narratives of their past, proof only of the mendacity of the reconstructed 'other'.[21] The pull of the old politics had been almost irresistible in the early 1810s, years of escalating tension at regional and provincial levels, punctuated by sectarian rioting at fairs and markets and by widespread trouble when newly formed Orange lodges initiated coat-trailing marches through Catholic districts on the 12th of July. In north Donegal there had been major disturbances in July 1810 when Orangemen from Rathmelton and Milford, armed with guns, pistols and swords, had attempted to parade through Letterkenny, 'a populous town chiefly inhabited by Catholics'. The following month, the Raphoe Yeomanry disobeyed orders and attempted, again unsuccessfully, to march through the town.[22] Ribbon societies, a Catholic lodge-network strongest in south and mid-Ulster, were now organized in the district, and there was a whirlwind of violence between Letterkenny and Milford as sectarian gangs (distinguished by coloured ribbons and other emblems) contested for dominance of public space. Flickering along a sharp sectarian interface, violence assumed a tit-for-tat dynamic: Fánaid and Ros Goill Catholics might be accosted at fairs in Rathmelton or Milford and Protestants then beaten at the pig-markets of Rosnakill or Carrigart, or vice versa. Partisan policing by the yeomanry exacerbated the situation; the Milford Rangers, for instance, shot and bayoneted at least three Catholics when clearing the town fair in May 1811.[23] The worst single incident—which threatened to spark a conflagration across a much wider district—occurred in May 1813 when five men died in an affray at Ranny, outside Kerrykeel. Its genesis had an already dreary familiarity: two Catholics who attacked John Williamson, a young Protestant, for sporting an Orange lily on the way home from Milford Fair were themselves severely beaten by their victim's friends; Fánaid Catholics threatened revenge against Protestants if they attended the next fair in Kerrykeel; on the fair day, seven or eight armed Protestants, including Williamson, assembled on a hill overlook-

---

21. For a Presbyterian minister's reflections on his ancestors' involvement in the United Irishmen, see Rev. J. R. Dill, *The Dill worthies* (2nd ed., Belfast, 1892), pp. 98–102.

22. N.A.I., S.O.C. I 1276/4, Letterkenny, 17 Sept. 1810, Sir H. C. Montgomery to W. W. Pole; 1383/38, Letterkenny, 19 June 1811, J. Mansfield to ——.

23. N.A.I., S.O.C. I 1383/41, Ards, 24 June 1811, J. Stewart to J. O. Vandeleur; S.O.C. II Box 162 (unsorted), Fortstewart, 23 Jan. 1811, J. Stewart to Sir C. Saxton; Report by Brigade Major Gibson respecting the disturbances which took place at the late fairs of Milford and of Carrykeel, Barony of Kilmacrenan, County of Donegall, Londonderry, 20 June 1811.

ing the town; Williamson displayed himself to the Catholic crowd at about four o'clock and 'several hundreds' then pursued the party into Ranny; the Protestants fired, killing two Catholics and wounding another before barricading themselves in a house; the Catholics burned the building, killing three Protestants as they tried to escape the flames and then ransacked the village until sunset.[24]

By this stage, the most assiduous forces for change were already evident. Commercialization had long insinuated new ideas and expectations, elaborating the advantages of bilingualism and literacy and illuminating the interaction of politics and economy as stealthily as it opened local markets for tea and tobacco, sugar, second-hand clothes and shop-goods. From the mid-eighteenth century, Fánaid had been involved in the regional livestock market—rearing cattle to be sold for fattening—in herring-fishing, and in the cultivation of flax, the spinning of yarn and weaving of linen. By the early nineteenth century there were also networks for the production of bent hats, shoes and kelp; smallholders collected *slata mara* (sea rods), burned them in lime-kilns and sold the dark granular residue to agents of Rathmelton iodine companies.[25] *Poitín*, however, was king: the bulk of the peninsula's barley crop was distilled and shipped across Lough Swilly into Inishowen, the whiskey warehouse for north Ulster.[26] Efforts by the Revenue to suppress the illicit industry were frustrated by its very scale—most townlands had a number of malt- and still-houses—and the profits tapped by kiln-owners, millers and middlemen.[27] Indeed, the hide-and-seek game played out by distillers and 'gaugers'—a term subsequently used for social welfare inspectors—contributed in no small part to the formation of Fánaid's attitude to authority: loose talk could lead to the discovery

24. N.A.I., S.O.C. I 1537/40, Rathmullan, 28 May 1813, J. C. Gibson to J. Burnet; S.O.C. II Box 164 (1813 M-W), Letterkenny, 29 May 1813, F. Mansfield to R. Peel.

25. Lancey, 'Clondavaddog, 1835', pp. 1–9; Maturin, 'Replies, 1825', pp. 10–11; R. Montgomery, 'Account of Lough Swilly, county Donegal, 1823', in Day and McWilliams, *Northeast Donegal*, pp. 126–30; responses by Dean Peter Gallagher, parish priest, in the appendices to *The first report of the commissioners for inquiring into the conditions of the poorer classes in Ireland*, H.C. 1835, vol. XXXII; *Congested Districts Board for Ireland: Base-line report – District of Fanad, 18 August, 1892* (n.p., n.d.) (hereafter *Base-line report, Fanad*), pp. 1–13.

26. N.A.I., S.O.C. I 2085/1, Grouse Hall, 12 Jan. 1819, T. D'Arcy to W. Gregory; 2085/6–14, Weekly Reports of the Detail of Duty of the Chief Magistrate, the Chief and Sub-Constables, the General State of the Barony and the Number of Outrages Committed in the Proclaimed Barony of Ennishowen, 29 March to 13 June 1819. For a discussion of the *poitín* industry in the north-west, see D. Dickson, 'Derry's backyard: The barony of Inishowen, 1650–1800', in W. Nolan, L. Ronayne and M. Dunlevy, eds, *Donegal: History and society* (Dublin, 1995), pp. 425–9.

27. For the ambivalence of Fánaid's 'respectable' families to illicit distillation in the 1820s and 1830s, see Dill, *Autobiography*, pp. 8–10.

of a still or the seizure of kegs, resulting in fines, gaol sentences and financial ruin. By the 1820s, however, the domestic shoe and linen industries were in decline, the herring shoals had moved far away from the Donegal shore, and *poitín*-makers were coming under increasing pressure from the state and, to a lesser extent, the Catholic Church. Unable to replace their fathers at the loom or to support their own families on shrinking holdings without a cash income, weavers' sons gambled more on *poitín* or travelled each year to Scotland to work as reapers and tattie-hokers at the harvest; others became day-labourers at home. Women's work, rearing hens and bartering eggs with local dealers, increasingly balanced domestic budgets and, to get hard cash and be rid of hungry mouths, young children were sent to the 'rabbles' or hiring fairs of Milford, Letterkenny, Derry and Strabane to be employed as herds and labourers for six-month terms.[28]

All the while, the world of the potato facilitated rapid demographic growth. The population was probably no more than 4,000 in 1766; by the turn of the century it was in the region of 6,000; twenty years later it was 8,846, and in 1831 it was 9,596 and still rising.[29] Two generations saw snug farms frittered into beggarly patches: in one instance a holding of 37 acres—one third of them bog—that had supported a single family in 1781 was divided among the occupier's six children; by 1823 these six holdings had become thirteen, and they were supporting 91 persons.[30] The human cost was 'poverty and misery': the average size of holdings fell to about four acres, lazy beds stretched onto moor and mountain previously set aside for rough pasture, and barren expanses of exhausted bog presented a stark and ominous contrast with the teeming rundale 'villages'. In the mid-1820s the Rev. Henry Maturin, Church of Ireland rector from 1797 to 1842, reported that the average holding was 'barely sufficient to supply the family with necessaries', while rent, tithe and cess were reducing diet and clothing to 'the very lowest state'. About the same time, Robert Montgomery, a surveyor with considerable experience in Fánaid, believed that the population was 'numerous beyond the extent and capability of the tillable land to produce food for their support'. Ten years later, Lieut. William Lancey, a Royal Engineer

28. Lancey, 'Clondavaddog, 1835', p. 6.

29. Of 748 families in Fánaid in 1766, 121 were Episcopalians, 89 were Dissenters and 538 were Catholics: see J. B. Leslie, *Raphoe clergy and parishes* (Enniskillen, 1940), p. 53. For the population in 1821 and 1831, see *Census of Ireland, 1831*, H.C. 1833, vol. XXXIX, pp. 32, 246–7.

30. Montgomery, 'Lough Swilly, 1823', p. 127.

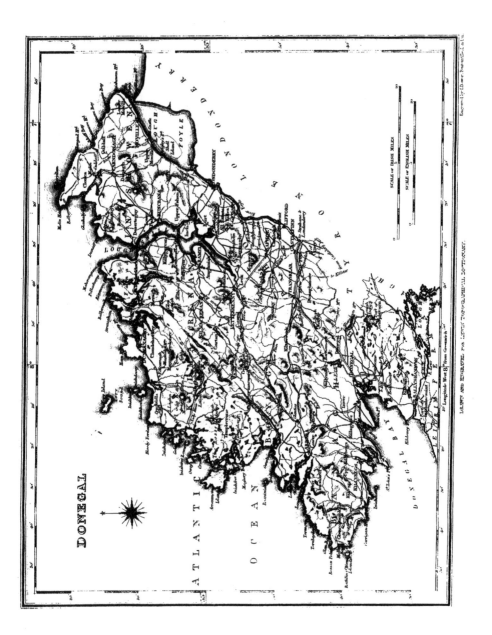

DONEGAL

ATLANTIC OCEAN

12

working on the Ordnance Survey, judged 'the mass of the people' to be 'farming for existence only'.[31]

As the balance between population and resources grew increasingly precarious, landowners became preoccupied with 'improvement', insisting on the cash-payment of rent and asserting their legal rights over occupiers' customary claims. In particular, they identified rundale as an impediment to 'progress': its 'tight villages' were blamed for underpinning custom with a strong communal identity, while its scattered plots and the concept of use rights in land were held to discourage individual enterprise. In the early 1830s Charles Norman of Fahan, the owner of a small estate centred on Rosnakill, demolished the 'gaggle of dirty houses' in which his tenants had 'congregated' and provided financial assistance to help them build new houses on neatly fenced squared-holdings.[32] Nathaniel Clements (1768–1854), the second Earl of Leitrim, was landlord of the largest estate in Fánaid, of 12,176 acres—just under half the parish—most of it leased from Trinity College, Dublin. He also held an additional 42,669 acres elsewhere in north Donegal—most of it around Milford—and over 40,655 acres in Galway, Leitrim and Kildare.[33] By the late 1830s he had decreed that his tenants (and their subtenants) were to surrender their rundale plots as leases expired and move to single strips or 'cuts' allocated by his agent. 'Improvement', however, met opposition and change was at best fitful.[34] When Leitrim's head bailiff and surveyor were laying out new cuts in Doaghbeg in 1840, James Martin openly threatened to kill them and demanded to see 'the man in Doaghbeg that would put a spade in any of the ground he had occupied'. He had, he warned the bailiff, 'been in St. John's before and had a loose foot still and could go there again'. Hearing Martin's wife, Hon-

---

31. Lancey, 'Condavaddog, 1835', pp. 3, 8–9; Maturin, 'Replies, 1825', p. 10; Montgomery, 'Lough Swilly, 1823', p. 127.

32. Lancey, 'Clondavaddog, 1835', p. 6.

33. Acreage of Leitrim's Donegal estate calculated from R. Griffith, *Union of Dunfanaghy, valuation of the several tenements comprised in the above-named union situate in the county of Donegal* (Dublin, 1857); idem, *Union of Millford, valuation of the several tenements comprised in the above-named union situate in the county of Donegal* (Dublin, 1858). For the acreage in Galway, Leitrim and Kildare, see W. E. Vaughan, *Landlords and tenants in mid-Victorian Ireland* (Oxford, 1994), p. 292. For the management of the Trinity College estates, see W. J. Lowe, 'Landlord and tenant on the estate of Trinity College, Dublin, 1851–1903', *Hermathena*, 120 (1976), 5–24.

34. As late as 1845, an army officer working on the Ordnance Survey reported that the 'great opposition' to the break-up of rundale on the Leitrim estate meant that it might be 'many years before the intended network of fences etc. is unravelled': quoted in J. H. Andrews, *A paper landscape: The Ordnance Survey in nineteenth-century Ireland* (Oxford, 1975), p. 218.

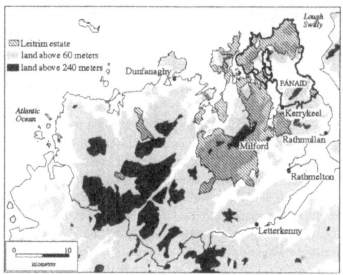

Barony of Kilmacrenan, c. 1858

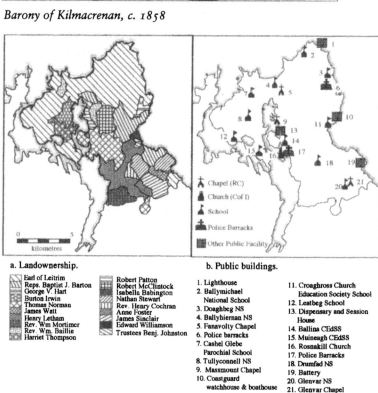

a. Landownership.

Earl of Leitrim	Robert Patton	1. Lighthouse	11. Croaghross Church
Reps. Baptist J. Barton	Robert McClintock	2. Ballymichael	Education Society School
George V. Hart	Isabella Babington	National School	12. Leatbeg School
Burton Irwin	Nathan Stewart		13. Dispensary and Session
Thomas Norman	Rev. Henry Cochran	3. Doaghbeg NS	House
James Watt	Anne Foster	4. Ballyhiernan NS	14. Ballina CEdSS
Henry Letham	James Sinclair	5. Fanavolty Chapel	15. Muineagh CEdSS
Rev. Wm Mortimer	Edward Williamson	6. Police barracks	16. Rosnakill Church
Rev. Wm. Baillie	Trustees Benj. Johnston	7. Cashel Glebe	17. Police Barracks
Harriet Thompson		Parochial School	18. Drumfad NS
		8. Tullyconnell NS	19. Battery
		9. Massmount Chapel	20. Glenvar NS
		10. Coastguard	21. Glenvar Chapel
		watchhouse & boathouse	

b. Public buildings.

District of Fánaid (parish of Clondavaddog), c. 1858

ora, swearing in Irish to their three sons that the surveyor should not get out of the townland with his life, the bailiff and surveyor downed tools and applied to the constabulary for protection.[35]

Paradoxically, as the gentry and tenant-gentry became more assertive in their economic capacity, the expansion of the central state restricted their administrative functions. From the late 1790s, when they first fell back on government, power had ebbed from local notables. Responsibility for law and order passed from part-time justices of the peace and yeomen to a professional officialdom—peace officers and chief magistrates in the 1810s and, by the 1830s, constables and stipendiary magistrates. Recruited outside the district, working from new 'public buildings', and answerable to an increasingly bureaucratic Dublin Castle, these officials represented a higher, more formal and accountable authority than that exercised in the big house or, in a rougher manner, on the back road.[36] Jealous of their autonomy and alert to political criticism, they defined themselves apart from, if not in opposition to, landed interests.

There was occasional friction. In winter 1828 Chief Constable Dominick Persse, whose district included Fánaid, instructed his men not to post notices circulated by John Hart, the High Sheriff of the county. The notices were to convene a meeting of 'the Protestants of Donegal' to petition parliament to 'take measures for the preservation of our Constitution from the encroachments of the Roman Catholics'; Persse judged them to be 'political'.[37] In general, however, the shifting relationship of state and society was a more subtle, long-term development. Constables did not act as bag-men for landowners or their agents on rent days; stipendiary magistrates were government's eyes and ears, not justices of the peace (indeed, the latter grudgingly conceded them the

35. N.A.I., Outrage Papers 1840/7/5729, Letterkenny, 29 March 1840, A. K. Fox to Inspector General; Information of Thomas McAteer, Leatmore, 26 March 1840. Thomas McAteer of Leatmore was the bailiff; Robert Montgomery of Lifford was the surveyor.

36. Fánaid's first constabulary barracks was in Tamney. For proposals and objections to the erection of a second barracks in Doaghbeg, see N.A.I., Outrage Papers 1841/7/11777, Petition of the Inhabitants of Clondavaddock; 1841/7/12055 Tamney, 9 Aug. 1841, J. Boyce to Viscount Morpeth; Declaration of Clergy of the Parish of Clondavaddock, 4 Aug. 1841; Rathmullan, 28 July 1841, C. Rea to J. Boyce; 1841/7/13177, Cumberland Place, 28 Aug. 1841, Leitrim to N. MacDonald; Memorial of the Inhabitants of the Parish of Clondavaddock, 19 Aug. 1841.

37. N.A.I., Chief Secretary's Office Registered Papers Outrage Reports 1829–31 D. 2/1829, Rathmelton., 29 Dec. 1828, D. Persse to T. D'Arcy; Kilderry, 1 Jan. 1829, J. Hart to T. D'Arcy; Belfast, 3 Jan. 1829, T. D'Arcy to J. Hart; Kilderry, 7 Jan. 1829, J. Hart to Lord F. Leveson Gower; Kilderry, 25 Jan. 1829, J. Hart to Lord F. Leveson Gower; M. 9/1829, Birdstown [Burnfoot], n.d. [Jan. 1829], P. B. Maxwell to Lord F. Leveson Gower; C.S.O.R.P., 1829/44 [Carton 1640], Kilderry, 19 Jan. 1829, J. Hart to Lord F. Leveson Gower; Humble Petition of George Weir, late a constable in the Civil Police and stationed at Letterkenny.

title 'resident magistrates'), and if the new agents of authority were officious, they included a significant proportion of Catholics and were less
partisan than the much-resented yeomanry, largely redundant by the
mid-1820s but only required to disarm in 1834–6.[38] In the same quiet
manner, the establishment of a dispensary at Rathmullan (1833) and the
opening of a workhouse at Milford (1846) unpicked the threads of def-
erence and dependence and, with a part-elected board of guardians,
promoted democratization.[39]

An expansion of the administrative capacity of the Catholic Church
created a third force for cultural change. By the early 1800s priests were
aggressively attempting to reform non-canonical 'superstitions' and to
regulate lay behaviour. They had prohibited an annual *turas* in Doaghmore in honour of St Davaddog, the local patron, about 1805, pro-
scribed drinking at wakes in the 1820s, and forbidden drinking at
'stations' and the reading of masses in parishioners' houses in the 1840s.
This 'civilizing offensive' had mixed fortunes: drinking at wakes
decreased among Catholics (but not Presbyterians), yet the *tobar beannaithe* in Doaghmore was still 'much resorted to by the inhabitants' in
1835.[40] Similarly, the priests failed to prevent Catholics from sending
their children to schools established by the rector, an active figure in
evangelical circles, in the late 1810s and early 1820s. Sponsored by the
London Hibernian Society and Kildare Place Society—groups denounced
for proselytism by Catholic clergymen—these schools had a number of
advantages over existing hedge-schools, not least in their having trained
teachers, free books and regular inspections. By the mid-1820s only two
of the seven schools in the parish were not receiving support from an
education society.[41] Various factors reined the 'influence of the priests' in

38. For the abolition of the yeomanry, see S. H. Palmer, *Police and protest in England and Ireland, 1780–1850* (Cambridge, 1988), pp. 327–8.
39. Lancey, 'Clondavaddog, 1835', pp. 6–7. For democratization, see Dickson, 'Derry's backyard', pp. 405–46.
40. Lancey, 'Clondavaddog, 1835', p. 5; Maguire, *Diocese of Raphoe*, pt. I, vol. I, p. 325; Otway, *Sketches*, pp. 111–13. For the notion of the Church's efforts to reform popular culture as a 'civilizing offensive' and a useful discussion of the diocesan context, see L. J. Taylor, *Occasions of faith: An anthropology of Irish Catholics* (Philadelphia, 1995), pp. 102–44, 149.
41. *Second report of the commissioners of Irish education inquiry*, H.C. 1826–7, vol. XII, pp. 332–3, returns schools at Tamney, Glenfannet, Glinsk, Muineagh, Ballyhoorisky, Bally-nalost and Drumfad. The Ballyhoorisky and Ballynalost schools were not receiving support from an education society; the masters in these schools were Patrick Shiels and Neil Dorien (*sic*). Maturin, 'Replies, 1825', p. 11, claims that 'by the influence of the priests, Popish chil-dren have been generally withdrawn from Protestant schools', but Lancey, 'Clondavaddog, 1835', p. 7, lists five schools, all of which were attended by both Protestants (246) and Catholics (200). Maturin was the Donegal county member of the Church Missionary Society's London Committee: see D. Hempton and M. Hill, *Evangelical Protestantism in Ulster society,*

*Interior view of Massmount Church, c. 1975. The building was erected in the
1780s, but much of the fittings and furniture dates from Dorian's childhood. The
classical altarpiece (located on the south wall) and the surrounding fluted columns
are a very fine example of Catholic vernacular architecture. There was often a
striking external resemblance between Catholic and Presbyterian churches erected
in north-west Ulster at this period.*

these years. There were, for instance, complaints about the lax conduct
of individual clergymen. In 1801 sixteen priests opposed the succession
of Fr John McIlroy, Fánaid's parish priest, to the bishopric of Raphoe,
alleging that he was 'a man of scandalous life', 'addicted to drink',
'addicted to women', had criminal knowledge of Margaret Crawford, an
old woman in Rathmullan, and had fathered a child to Elizabeth Braden,
a Milford Protestant, and another to 'a woman of evil repute named
Coyle' who had been his housekeeper in Fánaid.[42]

The Church's greatest problem, however, was limited resources in a
period of rapid demographic expansion. In the first three decades of the
century, there was often only a single priest ministering to Fánaid's seven

1740–1890 (London, 1992), p. 50. For a short memoir, see Dill, *Autobiography*, pp. 12–14.
Rev. Charles Maturin (1780–1824), the Gothic novelist, was a relative; he drew on accounts
of Hamilton's assassination when describing a killing in *Melmoth the wanderer* (Oxford,
1968), pp. 256–7. We are grateful to Jay Walton for this reference.

42. C. Giblin, ed., *The diocese of Raphoe, 1773–1805: Documents illustrating the history
of the diocese from the Congressi volumes in the archives of the Congregation of Propaganda
Fide, Rome* (Dublin, 1980), pp. 47–54, 160–8.

to eight thousand Catholics. Massmount was still the only chapel in the parish and while the priest read additional masses at *scáthláin*, 'wretched sheds' that half-covered rough altars, congregations were small, particularly in poor weather. According to a return made by Dean Peter Gallagher, the parish priest, only 1,000 of Fánaid's 8,157 Catholics attended Sunday mass in 1834; even if this figure excluded attendance at *scáthláin*, it was low and had clearly been lower.[43] By then, however, a more efficient and assertive church administration was taking shape. There were normally two curates in the parish from 1830 and, with the appointment of Fr Daniel O'Donnell as parish priest in 1835, the church had a firmer hand at the tiller and a clearer sense of direction. Although elderly, O'Donnell was an energetic modernizer. He oversaw the erection of the parish's second chapel at Fanavolty (1835–8); extended, re-roofed and ornamented Massmount with a bell-tower (1843); introduced a 'Register of Births, Marriages and Funerals' (before 1847); and enthusiastically promoted temperance.[44] He also brought state-funded elementary education to the parish, acting as manager of a school at Ballymichael approved by the commissioners of national education in 1842.[45] O'Donnell's plans had been considerably more ambitious—he had applied unsuccessfully for approval of five schools in 1838—yet the opening of this single 'national school' was nonetheless significant, heralding the emergence of a viable alternative to the 'society schools' that had dominated education in Fánaid for a generation (and which were themselves revamped in the early 1840s when Dr William Baillie, the new rector, brought them under the auspices of the Church Education Society).[46] The national system gave the Catholic clergy increased access to the faithful and greater influence and authority—masters were answerable to priests as managers of the schools and Saturdays were set aside for 'religious instruction'—and, in

43. *Reports of commissioners of public instruction, Ireland (first report)*, vol. XXXIII, pp. 48, 270a–1a; one of the curates ministered in Glenvar and the other in Glenfannet. On Gallagher, see Dill, *Autobiography*, pp. 10–11. Dr Edward Maguire, who was appointed parish priest in 1910, comments that 'a very old resident, since deceased, told [me] he was frequently present at Mass in Drumany, when, on Sunday, not more than forty people formed the whole congregation. In the summer, however, close on 1,000 worshippers could be seen scattered around, in prayerful silence, and straining their eyes to get a glimpse of the half-concealed altar and the officiating priest': see Maguire, *Diocese of Raphoe*, pt. I, vol. I, pp. 317–18.

44. Maguire, *Diocese of Raphoe*, p. 325.

45. *Ninth report of the commissioners of national education in Ireland, for the year 1842*, H.C. 1843, vol. XXVIII, 'Appendix XI', p. 45.

46. For O'Donnell's efforts to establish national schools in 1838–9, see N.A.I., Education Department 1/23 Folio 96 (Ballymichael); Folio 102 (Kinnalough); Folio 103 (Fallaneas); Folio 104 (Roughan); Folio 105 (Tully).

the medium term, it helped to orient Catholics towards chapel in the same subtle manner that it transformed notions of time and discipline and accelerated the language shift.[47]

And yet the tea leaves of a later social order are too easily read with hindsight; the prophecy-men who foretold a different future had informed audiences, abreast of wider developments. North Donegal's lower-class Catholics—described in 1834 as 'moping over their misfortunes, real or supposed, and reading the newspapers, looking forward from day to day for some change for the better'—had a realistic expectation, certainly one conjured by Daniel O'Connell, their great magician, that political change (however achieved) would deliver a more equitable social order within their own lifetimes.[48]

The Great Famine, then, was the thimble-rigger. Fánaid's population—10,344 in 1841 and probably close to 11,000 in 1846—had fallen to 8,244 by 1851. A secular decline followed: by 1891 it was 5,778, just over half of what it had been less then fifty years earlier, and between then and 1961 it would halve again to 2,846.[49] The immediate victims were those with little or no land—the families of cottiers and landless labourers, tinkers, tailors and old soldiers—but hunger and disease came to most doors. On the eve of the Famine, the bulk of the population—the four-acres-and-a-cow families—had been dependent on markets for food in the lean weeks between old and new potatoes, and that period, once *mí an ocrais* (the hungry month), had become alarmingly extended in the years before the blight.[50] Furthermore, landowners

47. Dr William Baillie, rector 1842–60, was prominent on the conservative wing of the Church of Ireland, which objected to national schools as an encroachment on the church's national responsibility for education. With the support of the Church Education Society, he maintained a number of society schools in Fánaid; the most successful of these were in Cashel Glebe, Croaghross, Muineagh and Ballina. Rev. Daniel Mooney, rector 1860–72, also opposed national schools at a time when many ministers were adopting a more flexible attitude. For the Church Education Society's activity in Fánaid, see *Sixth annual report of the Church Education Society; with an appendix, and a list of subscribers* (Dublin, 1845), p. 57. For Baillie and Mooney, see Leslie, *Raphoe clergy*, pp. 51–2; W. Baillie, *A brief review of the Church of Ireland, in its early purity and independence; its subjugation and restoration* (Dublin, 1863); N.A.I., E.D. 1/26 Folio 28, Fannet Rectory, 8 March 1864, Rev. D. Mooney to M. Hickey.

48. W. Lancey, 'Parish of Mevagh, county Donegal, statistical report ... 1834', in Day and McWilliams, *North-east Donegal*, pp. 59–60.

49. For population data, see *Census of Ireland, 1841*, H.C. 1843, vol. XXIV, pp. 306–7; Census of Ireland, 1851, H.C. 1852–3, vol. XCII, pp. 124–5; *Census of Ireland, 1861*, H.C. 1863, vol. LV, pp. 124–5; *Census of Ireland, 1891*, H.C. 1892, vol. XCII, pp. 382–4; *Census of population of Ireland 1961. Vol. I: Population, area and valuation of each district, electoral division and of each larger unit of area* (Dublin 1963), pp. 55, 135.

50. N.A.I., Relief Commission 2/441/15 Z18244, Croaghan, 13 Dec. 1845, R. Patton to Sir J. Stewart; Fannet, 15 Dec. 1845, H. Letham to Sir J. Stewart; 3/2 2/441/41 16551, Fannet, 27 March 1847, H. Letham to [R. Routh].

grasped the opportunity provided by dearth, disease, death and general disorder to intensify efforts at 'improvement' and, in particular, the dismantlement of rundale. The old 'villages', the pivot of the rundale system, had been made up of coop-like hovels—*prochógaí* (caves; dens), according to a folklorist who saw the last of them in the 1940s—that could be easily tossed by a bailiff with a crowbar.[51] The landscape, therefore, changed rapidly. The 1841 census classified clusters of twenty or more houses as 'towns'; it records 63 families in 58 houses in 'Doaghbeg Town', and 51 families in 48 houses in 'Ballyhoorisky Town'. By 1851 the number of houses in the Doaghbeg cluster had slipped below twenty and it lost its 'town' status in the census; the Ballyhoorisky cluster had ceased to be a 'town' by 1861.[52] Stricter land-management and smallholders' own uncertainty combined to discourage subdivision, checking the growth of surviving 'villages' and narrowing options for the young. Evicted tenants and cottiers, non-inheriting sons and dowryless daughters left Derry quay for Glasgow, Philadelphia and Boston.[53] Those that remained adjusted to a changed world, marrying later or not at all; in 1961, Donegal's nuptiality rate was the lowest in Europe.[54]

There was therefore a dispiriting cultural dislocation. The footloose people 'removed' by the Famine and its aftermath had included some of the most vital agents of cultural reproduction—fiddlers and pipers, singers and storytellers, hedge-schoolmasters, herbalists, wise women and, ironically, the prophecy-men themselves; and, above all, the Famine had reaped a swathe of the elderly, the great interpreters and adapters of tradition.[55] The transformation of the landscape also had a disheartening effect. The rundale 'villages' had been convivial stages for song, story, music and dance and conducive sites for the formation of hurling teams and harvesting parties. They had also been the organizational unit for the performance of the rites and rituals that surrounded the great seasonal festivals of *Oíche Fhéile Bríde, Bealtaine, Oíche Fhéile Eoin, Lúnasa and Samhain,* and the everyday coping and adapt-

51. R.B.É., 705, 630–68 [hereafter Ó hEochaidh, 'Baile Uí Bhorascaidhe']. Several sizeable house-clusters survived into the late nineteenth century: see *Base-line report, Fanad*, p. 12.

52. *Census of Ireland, 1861*, H.C. 1863, vol. LV, pp. 124–5.

53. Boston was an unusual destination for west Ulster emigrants, Philadelphia and New York being the 'favourite centres': see *Base-line report, Fanad*, p. 12.

54. S. Cotts Watkins, 'Regional patterns of nuptiality in western Europe, 1870–1960', in A. J. Coale and S. Cotts Watkins, eds, *The decline of fertility in Europe: The revised proceedings of a conference on the Princeton European Fertility Project* (Princeton, 1986), pp. 315, 319.

55. For the contribution of *lucht an tsiubhail* (travellers), particularly the Doherty family, to local culture, see Ó hEochaidh, 'Baile Uí Bhorascaidhe', pp. 659–60.

ing customs for birth and death.[56] A maudlin resignation to 'cruel fate'—
the general harshness of life, particularly migration—and a concern for
the county or country rather than the particulars of local events and
experience now seeped through popular culture, and artists' relationship with their audience lost a certain intimacy. There was a coterie of
songsters in Ballymichael for much of the century, but although they
composed in Irish, their best-remembered songs—*Coillte na hÉireann*
(The Woods of Ireland), *Slán le Dún na nGall* (Farewell to Donegal),
Míle Fáilte 'na hÉireann (A Thousand Welcomes to Ireland) and
Moladh Thír Chonaill (Praise of Tyrconnell)—are closer to the come-all-
ye emigrant farewells to 'old Ireland' and 'the county Donegal' in hawkers' broadsheets and nationalist newspapers than to a vernacular
tradition that was genuinely 'racy of the soil'.[57] Irish itself, however, was
now in retreat. Migration chains hastened language shift and dimin-
ished regard for things old and particular to the community; the nine-
year-old 'scholar' reading aloud an 'American letter' written to
form—'Dear father and mother, I hope this letter finds you well ...'—at
'End of Track', a place fixed only in the imagination, would take the
seat at the fire once reserved for an old man to recast tales of *na trí
Sheán*.[58]

In this context, the Catholic Church with its narrative of endurance
offered a false sense of continuity and order. Attendance at mass and
other chapel-centred devotions, such as confession and the Stations of

56. Writing in 1898, Edward McCarron (b. 1842), a native of Carryblagh, traced the decline
of fairy stories and the new 'dullness' of rural life to the time when the landlords 'began to
scatter the villages': see E. McCarron, *Life in Donegal, 1850–1900* (Cork, 1981), p. 19. On
hurling in Fánaid, see Traynor, *English dialect of Donegal*, p. 294; Ó hEochaidh, 'Baile Uí Bhorascaidhe', pp. 657–8. For seasonal festivals in Fánaid, see J. Forbes, 'Folklore and tradition in
Glenvar, County Donegal', in *Ulster Folklife*, vol. III (1957), 37–41.

57. R.B.É., Bailiúchán na Scol, 1091, 312–13. *Filí Bhaile Uí Mhíchil* (The Ballymichael
Poets) were Tomás Beag (1806–99); Seán Buí (1801–85); Séamas Bán; Mícheál Mac Giolla
Cearr (1799–1883); Domhnall Ó Baoill (1796–1846) and Mícheál Dubh (1793–1848). The
informant comments that all the songs they 'wrote' were in Irish and notes another songster,
remembered only as Diarmuid (1820–1910), who composed in both Irish and English.

58. In 1940 Tomás Ó Siadhail of Ballyhoorisky, who was born about 1885, recalled that
every time the master heard him speak a word of English at school, he would draw a stroke
on a slate; at mid-day he would receive three slaps for every stroke; the same again before he
went home at three o'clock and the same the following morning when he arrived at school. In
part due to the use of proselytizing texts in Irish in 'society schools', the clergy also encouraged the speaking of English. According to Seán Ó hEochaidh, who collected folklore in
Fánaid in the 1940s, 'shiubhail siad thart eadar na scoltacha agus eadar na daoine agus dub-
hairt siad leis na páisdí go gcaithfeadh siad Béarla a fhóghluim agus a labhairt' ([The priests]
went around the schools and amongst the people and they told the children that they would
have to learn and speak English): see Ó hEochaidh, 'Baile Uí Bhorascaidhe', pp. 662–5.

the Cross, increased while older practices were abandoned, reformed or repressed.[59] Saints that had occupied a central place in the older religious system were now sidelined and stripped of their warm and sinful humanity. None changed more than Colm Cille: the boisterous, irreverent, endearingly imperfect character of oral tradition became the cold and lonely icon Saint Columba. With lasting implications for gender roles, the Mary figure also changed, the flesh and blood 'wailing woman' giving way to a blue-sashed, serene virgin.[60] A mission conducted by the fire-and-brimstone Redemptorist Fathers at Massmount in 1866, the first of its kind in the parish, consolidated ground gained since the Famine and confirmed the trajectory of change; Dr Edward Maguire, who became parish priest in 1910, believed that 'an impression was made on the flock (by the mission) that manifested its abundant fruits for a generation'.[61]

Bitterness defined the Famine's political legacy. Inadequate relief and imperial ambivalence towards excess mortality and migration accentuated animosity toward the landed élite and, more particularly, the British state. As early as September 1847 the *Ballyshannon Herald,* usually the shrill voice of small-town Toryism in Donegal, had acknowledged as much in a candid assessment of the effects of 'distress':

59. In an interview with Seán Ó hEochaidh of the Irish Folklore Commission in 1940, Tomás Ó Canainn, a 68-year-old smallholder from Toome, comments: *'nuair a bhí mise ag éirighe aníos bhí na seandaoine a bhí ann ins an am sin, bhí siad fíor-dhiadhganta agus siúd agus go raibh siad fíor-dhiadhganta, cha dtabharfadh an eaglais isteach do chuid mhór dá raibh siad a dhéanamh. Sin í gcúrsaí léigheastaí daoine agus eallaigh agus fiabhras croí ...'* (When I was growing up the old people were very devout, yet, even though they were so devout, the Church did not approve of a lot of the things they were doing. That's as regards cures for people and animals and heart-fever ...). Ó Canainn then recalls the clerical condemnation of Bríd Nic Suibhne of Arryheernabin, a wise-woman who cured sick animals, and his own father's hostility to *pisreogaí* (superstitions): see R.B.É., 705, 669–79 (Tomás Ó Canainn, 68, Tuaim, 17 Meán Fómhair 1940).

60. *Dán na hAoine* (The Fasting Poem), transcribed in the early 1900s from Nuala Nic Ghiolla Bhríde, 'a pious old woman near Mulroy Bay', illustrates traditional representations of Mary: see É. Ó Muirgheasa, eag., *Céad de cheoltaibh Uladh* [One hundred Ulster songs] (Iúr Chinn Trá, 1983), pp. 174–8. For a discussion of the poem, see ibid., pp. 287–8, and A. Partridge, *Caoineadh na dtrí Muire: Téama na páise i bhfilíocht bhéil na Gaeilge* [The keening of the three Marys: The theme of the passion in Irish oral poetry] (Baile Átha Cliath, 1983), pp. 215–16.

61. Maguire, *Diocese of Raphoe,* pt. I, vol. I, p. 326. McCarron, *Life in Donegal,* p. 52, recalls how 'anxious' he was to attend the mission and the difficulties he experienced, on account of the large crowds, in having his confession heard by one of the 'holy fathers'. For an analysis of the early Redemptorist missions in Donegal, see L. J. Taylor, 'The languages of belief: Nineteenth-century religious discourse in southwest Donegal', in P. H. Gulliver and M. Silverman, eds, *Approaching the past: Historical anthropology through Irish case studies* (New York, 1992), pp. 142–75. The first Redemptorist mission in the diocese of Raphoe was held at Letterkenny in 1851; the atmosphere of the mission is evoked in E. Hosp, 'First Redemptorist missions in Ireland according to Father Joseph Prost's diaries', in *Spicilegium historicum Congregationis SSmi Redemptoris,* vol. VII, no. 2 (1960), 453–85.

Social disorganization is nearly complete. The mass of the people are steeped to the lips in poverty ... Class is divided against class. The proprietors of the soil are generally regarded as oppressors of the cultivators of the soil. Dreadful hatred of England, of her institutions—is widely diffused among the humbler orders in Ireland.[62]

Filling the vacuum left by O'Connell and feeding on socio-economic uncertainty and moral outrage, Ribbon societies—largely moribund in north Donegal from the mid-1810s—revived in the late 1840s to promote a decidedly Catholic nationalist agenda. By the 1860s the Irish Republican Brotherhood, popularly called Fenians, had a smaller and more discreet presence, articulating an analysis that was at once more secular and more anglophobic; both groups organized in Fánaid.[63] Critically, the Famine and the flood tide of emigration also accentuated animosities within the Catholic community: some had hoarded food when neighbours starved; others had grabbed land to which custom gave them no title, and many felt they had lost out in the allocation of new holdings, receiving rock and bog while the bailiffs' favourites took the meadows. Bailiffs unable to meet obligations to their connections were now reduced to the level of landlord flunkies and as such resented. Violence lost something of its communal rationale and became a more spasmodic, individual reaction. Hugh Blaney was among the casualties. In 1857 Blaney refused to grant land formerly occupied by William McSwine to William 'Luggy' Blaney of Rosnakill, a cousin, who duly threatened revenge. On the evening of Sunday 13 December 1857, Hugh and his son Michael went drinking in the Widow Doherty's in Rosnakill. As they returned home, Hugh saw the shape of man behind a hedge and shouted 'Thief Luggy, don't murder me!'; a stone struck him on the back of the head and he died roaring over Christmas.[64]

Change was most traumatic on the Leitrim estate. On the death of the second earl of Leitrim in 1854 his son, William Sydney Clements (1806–1878), succeeded to his lands and title. A complex figure who

62. *Ballyshannon Herald*, 17 Sept. 1847.

63. For Ribbonism in post-Famine Fánaid, see N.A.I., C.S.O.R.P. 1857–8/6317; 1857–8/6709; 1859–60/16149. For the controversial case of Michael Gallagher, alias O'Callaghan, an alleged Fenian organizer in Rathmelton, see *Londonderry Standard*, 10 March 1866; C.S.O.R.P. 1866/4851; 1866/8057; 1866/14323.

64. N.A.I., C.S.O.R.P. 1857–8/11765, Buncrana, 3 Jan. 1858, J. Considine to T. Larcom; Information of Hugh Blaney, Ballykinard, 17 Dec. 1857; Information of Sheila Dorrian, 28 Dec. 1857; Deposition of Michael Blaney, Ballykinard, 21 Dec. 1857; Information of Const. John O'Connor, Rosnakill Station, 24 Dec. 1857; Buncrana, 14 Jan. 1858, J. Considine to T. Larcom; Information of Isabella (Sheila) Dorrian, 11 Jan. 1858; Information of Widow Mary Doherty, 5 Feb. 1858.

displayed signs of mental instability—paranoia, low self-esteem and megalomania—Leitrim immediately instructed Robert Wray, his agent, to collect all arrears on the estate and to evict those tenants who failed to pay.[65] With a blizzard of notices-to-quit and ejectment orders, Leitrim redoubled his father's drive against custom. Tenants who still held land in rundale had to abandon their scattered plots and bid for newly squared holdings; charges were introduced for gathering seaweed and flotsam on the shore, cutting turf in the bog and grazing stock on what had recently been common pastures. To enforce these regulations, he oversaw a bizarre routinization of the bailiff system; a veritable army of bailiffs, bum-bailiffs, bog-bailiffs and shore-bailiffs—some occupying 'protection stations' which overlooked large areas of the estate—filed daily reports on the doings and dealings of their neighbours and on each other. Tenants who incurred Leitrim's displeasure were evicted, as were those who sheltered or supported the evicted; to smooth the legal process of eviction, all his tenants were served notices-to-quit every April (in some instances printed on the back of rent receipts), enabling Leitrim to evict them if he so chose when the notices expired six months later.[66] This approach to estate management perturbed even conservative opinion; as early as 1857, the *Londonderry Sentinel*, the north-west's main Tory newspaper, was warning that Leitrim's 'bearing towards his tenants' would inflame 'evil passions' and reduce many families to destitution.[67] These passions were already evident: that March, three men disguised as sailors stopped Wray's car on the road between Fortstewart and Rathmelton, but finding that he was not travelling in it they let the driver proceed; the resident magistrate warned Wray that he knew 'beyond doubt' that his life was in danger.[68] The late 1850s and early 1860s witnessed violent confrontations over the right to gather seaweed and wreck timber, and bitter controversy about the allocation of new holdings.[69] Protracted litigation followed in the late 1860s and 1870s

65. N.A.I., C.S.O.R.P. 1856/13212, Buncrana, 17 March 1856, J. Considine to T. Larcom; L. Dolan, *The third earl of Leitrim* (Letterkenny, 1978); S. Mac Philib, 'Profile of a landlord in oral tradition and contemporary accounts — the third earl of Leitrim', *Ulster Folklife*, vol. XXXIV (1988), 26–40.

66. N.L.I., Larcom Papers MS 7633 No. 94, Rathmelton, 17 June 1861, J. M. Studdart to County Inspector; McCarron, *Life in Donegal*, p. 43; Vaughan, *Landlords and tenants*, pp. 103–4.

67. *Londonderry Sentinel*, quoted in L. Dolan, *Third earl*, p. 29. Also see D. Holland, *The landlord in Donegal: Pictures from the wilds* (Belfast, n.d. [1858]), pp. 14–18.

68. N.A.I., C.S.O.R.P. 1855–6/13212, Buncrana, 17 March 1856, J. Considine to T. Larcom.

69. For an inventory of 'outrages' in north Donegal, see *A return 'of the outrages specially reported by the constabulary as committed within the barony of Kilmacrenan, county Done-*

when occupiers began to go to court as 'tenants' to compel Leitrim to fulfil his legal responsibilities; the insistence on 'legal rights', which owners had used to obliterate the sub-tenant strata, was becoming the whip that would scourge them.[70]

Fánaid finally dealt with Leitrim the old way. On the morning of Tuesday 2 April 1878, Michael Heraghty of Tullyconnell, Neil Shiels of Doaghmore and Michael McIlwee of Ballyhoorisky ambushed and assassinated him at Cratlagh Wood, as he travelled from his residence at Manorvaughan towards Milford. Charles Buchanan, his driver, and John Makim, his clerk, also died in the attack. Heraghty and Shiels were Fenians; McIlwee was a Ribbonman. None of them was ever convicted of murder. Heraghty, the only one of the three arrested and charged, died of typhus while awaiting trial in Lifford Gaol. Although Heraghty was a journeyman tailor, one of the most lowly occupations in rural society, some 3,000 mourners wearing green rosettes, led by 20 cars and followed by 200 horsemen, met his cortège as it entered Fánaid. McIlwee apparently died of fever a few years later, but Shiels, another journeyman tailor, lived out his life in the peninsula, dying in 1924; he rarely spoke about the assassination.[71]

Besides Michael Heraghty, six other men were charged with murder: Patrick Heraghty of Tullyconnell, a brother of Michael; Anthony, Bernard and Young Thomas McGrenaghan, all sons of Thomas Sarah McGrenaghan of Gortnatraw North; and Anthony and Michael McGrenaghan, first cousins of the other three and from the same townland. The Heraghty brothers had been arrested when the constabulary

---

gal, during the last ten years; specifying the nature of each offence, the number of parties arrested on suspicion, and whether conviction had or not', H.C. 1861, vol. LII, p. 585. For an attack led by Francis Sweeney and Michael McGlinchey on the house of James Friel of Cooladerry, a shore-bailiff, in May 1857, see N.A.I., C.S.O.R.P. 1857/6317, Rathmelton, 24 May 1857, J. McNeys to Inspector General; Buncrana, 12 July 1857, J. Considine to T. Larcom; n.p. 20 Apr. 1857, T. FitzGerald to Chief Secretary; 1857–8/6709, Information of Michael Sweeney, Ballyhiernan, 27 May 1857; Information of Patrick Connor, Ballyhiernan, 28 May 1857; Information of Ellen McCay, Fanavolty, 28 May 1857. On the beating of Edward Shiels of Rinaboorey, another shore-bailiff, by Patrick Coyle of [?Aghadreenan], see 1857–8/12045, Rathmullan, 18 Feb. 1858, J. Considine to T. Larcom. For disputes over the right to gather timber and seaweed on Ballyhoorisky and Rinboy strands, see 1859–60/3321, Buncrana, 12 March 1860, J. Considine to T. Larcom; 1859–60/16410, Milford, 1 June 1860, J. Considine to T. Larcom.

70. Londonderry Standard, 6 Apr. 1878.

71. Ibid., 19 Oct. 1878. Dolan, Third earl, provides the most detailed account of the events surrounding the assassination, drawing heavily on a long letter relating local accounts of the assassination: Carryblagh, 27 July 1951, P. Shiels to Rev. E. J. O'Doherty, copy in possession of editors. Also see Anon., The Fanad patriots (Letterkenny, 1960).

traced a gun butt recovered at Cratlagh Wood to John Doak, a carpenter from Ballymagaghey; Doak swore an information acknowledging that he had made the butt for Michael Heraghty. A piece of paper recovered at the scene resulted in the arrest of the first three McGrenaghans. The paper—which had been used to wrap lead—had been torn from a school copybook, and writing on the paper led the constabulary to their sister Mary McGrenaghan, a pupil in Cashel Glebe National School. Bloodstained clothing uncovered in a follow-up search of their uncle's house led to the arrest of their cousins. Michael Heraghty was likely to have been convicted had he survived to the spring assizes, but the evidence against the others was largely circumstantial and none of them was brought to trial; the last prisoners were released in February 1879.[72]

The Crown's failure to secure a conviction in such a high-profile case became yet another proof that Fánaid was a place apart. At the turn of the century, visitors to the wild north-west were being told that that 'the chief man in the affair [was] living there yet' and that 'every Irish-speaking person within five miles of Milford, and many others, could, and would not, tell you exactly who it was that killed Lord Leitrim'.[73] Certainly, long after the event, people still spoke in hushed tones about 'the accident': 'the place of the accident' was Cratlagh Wood and 'the year of the accident' was 1878.[74] But the silence that shielded Leitrim's assassins was not the same web of class, culture and connection that had screened the killers of Betty Thompson over fifty years earlier. Nor was it as complete: Heraghty had been arrested within two weeks of the attack and by the summer of 1880 £17-10-0 of government money had been paid to persons who could be relied on 'with the most perfect confidence' for 'private information', that not only identified McElwee and Shiels but also confirmed that the meetings to plan the assassination had taken place in Thomas Sarah McGrenaghan's house in Gortnatraw North, and that McIlwee and Shiels had stopped at Anthony McGrenaghan's house to change their clothes on their return to Fánaid; the McGrenaghans were related 'by marriage and also by blood' to McIlwee and Shiels.[75]

72. Dolan, *Third earl*, pp. 103–13.
73. S. Gwynn, *Highways and byways in Donegal and Antrim* (London, 1899), p. 175.
74. Traynor, *English dialect of Donegal*, p. 2.
75. N.A.I., Fenian 'A' Files, A625 (Carton 5), Milford, 1 July 1880, W. Murphy to Under Secretary.

II

Hugh Dorian was born into a smallholding Catholic family in 1834, probably in Cashel Glebe at the western end of Kindrum Lake where he was living in the 1850s. Little is known about his family background but his father or a close relation may have been a hedge-schoolmaster: Neal Dorien (*sic*) had taught a hedge-school in Ballynalost in the early 1820s and Dorian was not a common surname in Fánaid.[76] Hugh, his parents, one sister and one brother are known to have survived the Famine; the fate of other family-members, if any, is unknown.[77] Bilingual and literate in English with a probable family involvement in teaching, he was well placed to accommodate himself to the emerging social order. In 1851 he was appointed master of Fanavolty National School, at the age of only seventeen. Fr Daniel O'Donnell died on 2 January 1854 and three weeks later Fr James Gallagher, as administrator of the parish, appointed Dorian to a new national school in Tullyconnell; Thomas Dorian, probably a relation, was appointed to Fanavolty in his place. Gallagher closed the school four years later due to low attendance.[78]

Tullyconnell School, where Dorian was to teach for the next decade, was a single-roomed, slate-roofed building, 22 feet long and 16 feet wide, with four large windows. The average attendance in 1854 was 67 children (45 boys, 22 girls). Most 'scholars' squeezed eleven abreast into five desks eight foot long; the others squatted on the damp clay floor, while the master sat at a desk on a small rostrum. The school hours were nine to three in summer and ten to three in winter, six days a week. Parents regularly kept children at home to assist with farm work, particularly herding; Dorian told one inspector that 'the parents say "the children have too much to do at home to be engaged at books"'. Dorian

---

76. *Second report of the commissioners of Irish education*, pp. 332–3. There were only nine Dor[r]ian households in the parish in the late 1850s, viz. Edward Dorian, Ellen Dorian, and Neal Dorian in Magheradrumman; Michael Dorian and Hugh Dorian in Cashel Glebe; Mary Dorian in Toome; and Edward Dorrian, James Dorrian and Catherine Dorrian in Rosnakill: see Griffith, *Union of Millford*, pp. 126–7, 132, 148. It is not known if all of these families were related. However, there had been Dor[r]ians in Fánaid since the 1600s; Neile O'Dorian is listed as an Inquisitor in a visitation book of 1679: see Leslie, *Raphoe clergy*, p. 53.

77. N.L.I., Leitrim Papers MS 5178, (Cashel), 22 March 1866, H. Dorian to Leitrim.

78. N.A.I., E.D., 1/25 Folio 49 (Fanavolty); 1/25 Folio 109 (Tullyconnell); 2/13 Folio 46 (Fanavolty); 2/14 Folio 44 (Fanavolty); 2/50 Folio 74 (Fanavolty). Maguire, *Diocese of Raphoe*, pt. I, vol. I, p. 328, claims Fanavolty was 'forcibly closed and unroofed' on Leitrim's instructions, but official files indicate that Gallagher requested the school be closed.

also had difficulties procuring slates and other basic equipment and had to teach monolingual Irish-speaking children through the medium of English. Still, he proved a capable teacher; attendance at Tullyconnell improved after his appointment and Patrick Keenan, an advanced educationalist who inspected the school in 1857, noted that he had a 'very good' manner and a 'good idea of order'. Teaching, in turn, brought financial security: his starting salary in Tullyconnell was £15; the children paid a shilling fee, making up a further £8 or so; he received small premiums from time to time and, in the early 1860s, an extra pound per annum for training James Dorian, a fourteen-year-old whom he appointed 'junior monitor' in 1861.[79] In 1856 he had married Catherine Gallagher and brought her to live with his parents in Cashel; he was then twenty-two. By 1872, when they left Fánaid, they had at least six children—Mina (1859), John (1861), Ellen (1864), Thomas (1866), Maria (1868) and Hugh (1870).[80]

Although the young Dorian family had a firmer foothold than most in a rapidly changing world, their future gradually clouded. Dorian's appointment to Tullyconnell in 1854 had come shortly before the succession of the third earl of Leitrim to his father's estates. By the early 1860s, Leitrim's concern to exercise total control over his property had extended to the education of his tenants' children. In summer 1863 he established a new school at Ballyhoorisky and applied successfully for its recognition as a national school; Dorian, his pupils and monitor transferred to this school—of which Leitrim was patron and F.S. Murray, his agent, was manager—in August of that year.[81] Leitrim's establishment of this school was part of a wider strategy to wrest control of education on his estate from the Catholic clergy. When the lease on Ballymichael School had expired in 1861, he had sought the surrender of the premises and, in return for keeping the school open, he had himself and his agent named as patron and manager.[82] Similarly, Leitrim and his agent would

---

79. N.A.I., E.D. 1/25 Folio 109 (Tullyconnell); 2/14 Folio 88 (Tullyconnell); 2/50 Folio 92 (Tullyconnell); *Twenty-fourth report of the commissioners of national education in Ireland (for the year 1857)*, H.C. 1859, vol. VII, p. 144.

80. The baptisms of the first three children are listed in N.L.I., Mic. 4600, Clondavaddog Parish Register; the other children's dates of birth are calculated from General Register Office, Index of Deaths 1886/March quarter/2/179 (Thomas Dorian) and N.A.I., Census of Ireland 1901, Londonderry 48/3/20 (Maria Dorian; Hugh Dorian). Burial records for Catherine Dorian give Ardara as her place of birth and name her parents as John and Mary Gallagher; Ardara is in south-west Donegal and it is possible that this is an error: see Derry City Council Cemeteries Department, Register of Burials: City Cemetery Plot DA136.

81. N.A.I., E.D. 1/26 Folio 28 (Ballyhoorisky).

82. N.A.I., E.D. 2/50 Folio 13 (Ballymichael).

William, third earl of Leitrim (1806–1878). He inherited the title and huge properties in 1854 after an army career. A bachelor, he built a new residence for himself, Mulroy House, c. 1865. His eccentric style of estate managment made him a notorious figure in his lifetime, and his violent end perpetuated the memory.

become patron and manager of Doaghbeg School in summer 1866.[83] Leitrim took a keen interest in these schools, requiring weekly reports from the masters and making unannounced inspections.[84] And, significantly given the continued operation of society schools in Fánaid, there was no evidence of any proselytizing intent on his behalf. Rather, an obsessive desire to control his tenants' lives was his motivation; Denis Holland, a nationalist newspaperman and land-campaigner, observed in 1858 that Leitrim did not care if his tenants worshipped 'Mummo-Jummo' provided he could get the rents out of them.[85]

Notwithstanding Leitrim's indifference to his tenants' souls, Dorian's move to Ballyhoorisky set him on a collision course with the Catholic

83. N.A.I., E.D. 2/50 Folio 83 (Doaghbeg).
84. McCarron, *Life in Donegal*, pp. 55, 60. For an annual report filed by Dorian, see N.L.I., Leitrim Papers MS 5178, H. Dorian, 'Report on the state of Ballyhooriskey National School for the year ended December 1865'.
85. Holland, *Landlord in Donegal*, p. 86.

clergy. The parish priest in 1864 was Dr Dan McGettigan, a nephew of Dr Patrick McGettigan, bishop of Raphoe. More theologian than pastor—'his brains were his chief asset in life' is the backhanded compliment in the diocesan history—McGettigan left the day-to-day running of the parish to Fr John O'Boyle (1833–1910), who had been appointed curate in 1859. When McGettigan accepted a professorial post in 1866, O'Boyle became administrator of the parish and four years later he was officially made parish priest, a position he retained until his death in 1910.[86] Formally, O'Boyle had supported the establishment of Ballyhoorisky School; the district inspector of national schools interviewed him and reported that he was 'most anxious to have the school established'.[87] In practice, O'Boyle was more circumspect and ambivalent if not actively hostile towards the school: he does not appear to have taken an active part in its management and he endeavoured to keep Tullyconnell open through 1863–5. Ultimately, in summer 1865 O'Boyle applied to the commissioners of national education for Tullyconnell to be formally struck off as he proposed to establish a new school at Ballyhork.[88]

The storm that had been threatening since Dorian transferred to Ballyhoorisky finally broke in January 1866. On Sunday 7 January O'Boyle gave Dorian 'all manner of abuse' from the altar, telling the congregation 'that there was none more wicked in the place' and ordering him from the chapel. Surprisingly, he did not condemn him for his association with Leitrim. Instead, O'Boyle claimed to be in possession of a letter that 'went to show' that a 'number of people' had met in the chapel on 17 December to plot to commit murder; this letter was allegedly in Dorian's hand and his name was signed on it. The exact content of the letter is unknown—it could conceivably be an informer's report of the meeting in the chapel—but as O'Boyle intended to forward

---

86. Maguire, *Diocese of Raphoe*, pt. I, vol. I, pp. 326–7. McGettigan did not make a deep impression on *seanchas* (oral history); *'cha raibh aon chuid mhór mhaith ann'* (he wasn't any great addition) was the blunt appraisal by one man interviewed for the Irish Folklore Commission in 1940: see R.B.É., 718, 5–14 (Padaí Ó Canainn, c. 68, Tuaim, Baile Láir, 25 Meán Fómhair 1940).

87. N.A.I., E.D. 1/26 Folio 28 (Ballyhoorisky). In his memoir written in 1898, Edward McCarron recalled that his neighbours felt that Leitrim had acted in a 'very arbitrary' manner by taking over the management of the national schools and that 'it was feared he would replace the Catholic teachers by Protestants'. However, McCarron, a Catholic, accepted the post of master in Ballymichael; according to his account, he first consulted O'Boyle and the priest was 'very glad' that he had been offered the post: see McCarron, *Life in Donegal*, pp. 48–9.

88. N.A.I., E.D. 2/50 Folio 92 (Tullyconnell).

it to Leitrim (and he subsequently met with the landlord), it is more reasonable to assume that the letter exposed Dorian as a participant in this plot and that Leitrim or someone associated with him was its intended victim.[89]

O'Boyle's denunciation of Dorian occurred at a tense time in Fánaid; evictions were pending on Leitrim's estate and there was a 'very bad feeling' towards Murray, his agent, who had received several threatening notices over the previous six months.[90] This situation arose from an assassination attempt on Robert Wilson, one of Leitrim's bailiffs, on 12 October 1864. Wilson had left Ballyhiernan Cottage in his 'tax-cart' at about 10 a.m. to carry out a routine weekly inspection of land in Leatbeg. Passing Dorian's abandoned schoolhouse in Tullyconnell, he had noticed an unusually shaped stack of corn-sheaves. As he drove towards the stack, shots were fired from it, riddling the car and hitting him in the arm, leg and chest. He had survived but resigned his position and left Fánaid. Leitrim's bailiffs had spent considerable time and energy in 1865 collating information about those involved in the planning of the attack; several were served with ejectment notices and were among those to be evicted in the New Year.[91] January 1866 was also a moment of high political drama at national level. Fenians who had fought in the American Civil War were returning to Ireland in large numbers and there was considerable speculation that there would be an insurrection in the spring, St Patrick's Day being mentioned as a likely date. Adding to the sense of crisis, James Stephens, the Fenian Head Centre or national leader, had escaped from custody in November 1865. Since then the press had been reporting 'sightings' from around the country, creating a false impression of official ineptitude and republican cunning.[92] In this general context, O'Boyle's allegation against Dorian was a very serious matter indeed. O'Boyle, however, went further. On 9 January he opened a new school in Ballyhork a short distance from Ballyhoorisky, but on the estate of Burton Irwin not Leitrim; O'Boyle had

89. N.L.I., Leitrim Papers MS 5178, Ballyhoorisky National School, 10 Jan. 1866, H. Dorian to Leitrim; n.p., 21 March 1866, H. Dorian to Leitrim.

90. N.A.I., C.S.O.R.P. 1866/1919, Letterkenny, 1 Feb. 1866, E. Peel to Chief Secretary.

91. *Dublin Evening Mail*, 13, 15 Oct. 1864. For Leitrim's efforts to gather information on those involved in this attack, see N.L.I., Leitrim Papers MS 13339 (5–10), Donegal estate reports. These reports also convey the agent's impression of increased Fenian activity in Fánaid in the winter of 1865–6.

92. Fánaid's reputation as one of the most troublesome districts in the north-west resurfaced at this time; there were rumours in Derry that 'the renowned Head Centre had been patronising the Lough Swilly Railway Company and that Stephens was to be seen on the route towards Rathmullan': see *Londonderry Journal*, 10 March 1866.

employed Neil McBride, an eighteen-year-old, as teacher, and shortly afterwards he applied for recognition from the commissioners of national education. The school was clearly intended as a rival establishment to Ballyhoorisky.[93]

Dorian's response was immediate and emphatic. Believing that O'Boyle was about to forward the incriminatory letter to Leitrim, he wrote to the landlord on 10 January. He acknowledged that it was 'the common talk among the people of this district that I was the occasion of getting all the people who are now to be dispossessed put out of their holdings' and recounted how O'Boyle had 'read' him from the altar. Denying that he had written the letter attributed to him, he pointed out that he had been teaching for fourteen years and many children had learned to write by copying his hand. His explanation of the affair was a conspiracy theory: 'my enemies ... my wicked enemies ... a class of idlers who mind nothing but how to upset the one they take spite at ... wicked and unmerciful people who care for neither soul or body' had been striving to do him harm for over a year; 'they think any man connected in any way with the Earl of Leitrim is a wicked man and a man for doing harm and they wish to banish if not kill all such out of the country and then that they might live as they pleased'. Now, they had 'poisoned' the priest against him. Knowing these people to be 'against' him, O'Boyle had treated him unjustly. Dorian had already written to the bishop asking to have his case investigated. He did not belong to any 'connexion', had 'very few friends' and was now 'at the mercy of all the wicked people of the place'; if they took his life, the priest would be responsible.[94]

Leitrim accepted Dorian's account. In another letter dated 21 March 1866, Dorian thanked him for a visit and conversation—'your presence and the few words ... consoled me very much and revived my drooping spirits'—and alluded to information—'some documents'—that he had given Leitrim for 'my own defence and self-preservation', which would help to 'point out the ill-disposed from the good that all might not be

93. O'Boyle made the initial application for recognition on 19 January 1866; the application was rejected in March due to the irregularity of the school's records. In May O'Boyle re-applied for recognition; the district inspector of national schools supported the application, reporting that there were 'very few places in which a national school [was] more required than Ballyhuirke'; the commissioners again rejected the application for irregular record-keeping but the school was approved shortly afterwards: see N.A.I., E.D. 1/26 Folio 4 (Ballyhork); Folio 67 (Ballyhork).

94. N.L.I., Leitrim Papers MS 5178, Ballyhoorisky National School, 10 Jan. 1866, H. Dorian to Leitrim.

blamed and that the innocent might not be accused'. He then proceeded to denounce 'party-men and combinations', alleging that O'Boyle was the only clergyman he had ever heard not to condemn such groups and insisting that the abuse he received in the chapel would 'be the means of sending my name where my feet will never go'. Until quite recently, 'many people here thought that they could rule the country as they wished, that the English law was dead [and] that they could do with landlords as they pleased', but times had changed. Now 'party spirit' was dying away; many party-men were quietly going off to America and the suspension of habeas corpus would deter others from 'crime'; Leitrim, meanwhile, was preventing further 'crime and strife' by assisting those he had 'dispossessed' to emigrate. Dorian hoped Leitrim would visit his estate more often, as 'when you are for a long time absent they begin to forget and then the idle and the mischief makers get time to go about making rules of their own just as of late many became so infatuated at the suggestion of a few as to think that they could upset the government and all combinations are the same in that respect but that some aim at higher objects and some begin at home'.

There is another item of interest in this letter. In commending Leitrim as a landlord, Dorian singled out his treatment of Hugh Friel of Doaghmore. Friel was a tenant of Leitrim's who had fallen into arrears; he had been ejected but then reinstated. Dorian presented him as an individualistic figure whom an 'illegal combination' had repeatedly sought to enlist: 'he would not in his ways and conversation be like one of themselves ... they would sooner have him than half a dozen of others but they never could get him as far as I understand to join any illegal combination'. By his lenience, Dorian argued, Leitrim had denied Friel's neighbours the satisfaction of seeing 'the innocent' suffer.[95] Dorian and Friel were friends. A letter from Friel to Leitrim, dated 20 March, is apparently in Dorian's hand and on the same type of paper as his letter of 21 March and another of 22 March. The tenor of the letter is also similar to Dorian's: Friel thanks Leitrim for his indulgent treatment, commenting that eviction would have given satisfaction to 'my enemies and perhaps yours' as 'they could never get me to do anything contrary to your Lordship's regulations and this same gave me enemies enough in the country'. He then expresses satisfaction that 'one of my worst enemies McElroy is put out of the way'; he blames McElroy for telling 'lying

95. N.L.I., Leitrim Papers MS 5178, n.p., 21 March 1866, H. Dorian to Leitrim.

stories' about him to Capt. Bacon, a former agent, and suggests that Bacon had cheated him by not issuing a rent receipt. Finally, he concludes with a postscript in which he—like Dorian—appears willing to pass information to Leitrim: 'if it would please your lordship to put any questions to me, I do not wish any to be present while I am with you'.[96]

*

O'Boyle's denunciation of Dorian may have resulted, at least in part, from his remaining in a landlord-managed school in Ballyhoorisky when a new clerically managed establishment was opening in Ballyhork; by staying on in Ballyhoorisky, Dorian was overtly challenging O'Boyle's authority. But was Dorian involved in a conspiracy as O'Boyle alleged? Even opponents of Leitrim acknowledged that 'those who could humour him in his eccentricities could otherwise live comfortably at cheap rents under him', and Dorian's letters—which clearly played on Leitrim's own insecurities—can be read as attempts at smoke and mirrors.[97] Certainly, his Narrative displays a deep antipathy towards landlords in general, and Leitrim in particular; the author did not have a high regard for 'English law' or authority in any of its manifestations. Yet the Narrative also exhibits an acute hostility to 'party-men' and the leaders of connections.[98] And Dorian's counter-allegation—that O'Boyle was in league with 'party-men'—muddies the waters still further.

O'Boyle was a caricature of the post-Famine parish priest. He vigorously promoted chapel-centred devotion; furnished Fanavolty with 'handsome pews, Stations of the Cross, and a chaste, devotional high altar'; and provided 'still more costly seats for floor and galleries in St. Columba's'. A man of great hubris, he abandoned the converted revenue barrack in Rosnakill where McGettigan, his predecessor, had lived and bought 'rich lands' and a 'lordly mansion' in Tamney. Some of his parishioners were inclined to locate the move in a sectarian context—the inhabitants of Tamney had been predominantly Protestant and O'Boyle's house was a marker of Catholic advancement—yet it betrayed an ecumenical arrogance.[99] O'Boyle's political views, however, are unclear. He

---

96. N.L.I., Leitrim Papers MS 5178, Doaghmore, 20 March 1860, H. Friel to Leitrim.
97. *Londonderry Standard*, 10 Apr. 1878.
98. See pp. 164–73, 223.
99. For the conviction that O'Boyle had managed to acquire the house and farm despite local Protestants' determination '*gan aon Ghael a ligean isteach go Tamhnaigh ar leabhar an*

developed a reputation as 'one of the few people to openly oppose Lord Leitrim' and in 1878 he appeared sympathetic to the earl's assassins. He established an appeal fund to cover the prisoners' legal costs, visited Heraghty when he was awaiting trial in Lifford, and presided at his highly politicized funeral. Indeed, there was whispered speculation in Fánaid that O'Boyle and Fr George O'Flaherty, his curate, had been informed of the plan to assassinate Leitrim and approved it.[100] Still, the priest's political opinions in the mid-1860s remain a matter of conjecture and there was little in his background that would have inclined him to Fenianism. Born in Leitir Mhic an Bhaird in west Donegal, O'Boyle belonged to a tight network of Catholic families that had enjoyed quiet prosperity through the eighteenth century. Like others from this milieu, his political instincts were probably conservative and he was unlikely to find the secular and anti-clerical elements in Fenianism attractive. Furthermore, O'Boyle had been part of the last batch of Raphoe seminarians to study at the Irish College in Paris. His years (1850–3) in Paris had been characterized by a conservative retrenchment after the *événements* of 1848 and any radical ideas he may have picked up were unlikely to have made it out of St Patrick's College, Maynooth, where he had completed his studies in 1853–7.[101]

Dorian's hostility to 'party-men', on the other hand, was not incompatible with an involvement with the Fenians. Although Fenian and Ribbon organizations would collaborate and in some instances merge in the 1870s, there was considerable rivalry between the two groups in the 1860s, and many Fenians scorned the Ribbon lodges as corrupt cabals.

Agent' (not to let any Catholic into Tamney on the Agent's book), see R.B.É., 718, 5–14 (Padaí Ó Canainn, c. 68, Tuaim, Baile Láir, 25 Meán Fómhair 1940). 'To his ever-lasting regret', Dr Edward Maguire, who succeeded him as parish priest, purchased the house and farm in Tamney—which had been O'Boyle's private property—for the parish: see Maguire, *Diocese of Raphoe*, pt. I, vol. I, p. 329. O'Boyle's management of the parish was notoriously high-handed. For instance, in 1898 Anthony Sweeney of Ballincrick was the occupier of a holding to which O'Boyle believed he had 'not the shadow of title'. When Sweeney rejected instructions from O'Boyle and Dr Patrick O'Donnell, his bishop, to send the disputed occupancy to arbitration, O'Boyle instructed Francis Friel, master of Doaghbeg School, to expel Sweeney's four children for 'insubordination'. Although Charles, the eldest of the children, had a 'hostile attitude' and had been heard to say that O'Boyle could 'go to the lower country', a euphemism for hell, there was no evidence that the other children had done anything wrong. An inspector who investigated the matter thought it 'incredible' that Mary, the youngest of the children, aged seven, could be so insubordinate as to warrant expulsion. For correspondence on this affair, see N.A.I., E.D. 9/6535.

100. Dolan, *Third earl*, pp. 108–13; Carryblagh, 27 July 1951, P. Shiels to Rev. E. J. O'Doherty, copy in possession of editors; Maguire, *Diocese of Raphoe*, pt. I, vol. I, pp. 327–8.

101. Maguire, *Diocese of Raphoe*, pt. I, vol. I, pp. 328–9.

Certainly, north Donegal lodges invited such criticism, not least due to their involvement in the shady *poitín* trade. In Fánaid, for instance, the dominant figures in the Ribbon Society in the mid-1850s were Long Owen Begley of Shannaghdoo and Big Thomas McAteer of Ballyhiernan. They organized a 'corps' or 'lodge' in the 'bottom half' of Fánaid in 1854 in which 'every man from Kindrum to the Lighthouse was embodied'; this 'corps' intimidated revenue-men and coordinated resistance to Leitrim's 'improvements' in 1857, even though McAteer, its leader, was then Leitrim's head bailiff.[102] Later in the 1870s, Micí Bacach McIlwaine, the owner of a public house in Ballyhiernan, was a prominent Ribbonman; he was reputed to have been a heavy drinker.[103]

The 'documents' Dorian passed on to Leitrim raise another issue: was Hugh Dorian an informer? Circumstantial evidence casts him in this role. On 28 January—a little over two weeks after Dorian's letter to Leitrim complaining about O'Boyle—over 150 constables conducted a 'strict search for arms' in Fánaid. The *Londonderry Standard* noted that 'such a large party of men ... caused great excitement as it was thought they were sent to prevent some movement on the part of the Fenians'. In justifying such a large search—which 'has not resulted in the finding of many arms'—the resident magistrate pointed to the 'several threatening letters' that Leitrim's agent had received and 'more especially ... private informations'.[104] These 'private informations' possibly originated with Dorian but they may also have come from O'Boyle—who met with Leitrim to discuss his allegation against Dorian—or a third party. Critically, however, Dorian did not scruple to pass on tittle-tattle to Leitrim in the hope of favours. In early 1866 land adjoining Dorian's holding became vacant in Cashel Glebe, the occupier having left his wife and gone to America. On 22 March Hugh wrote to Leitrim to ask for a £24 loan to acquire the tenant right from the Rev. Daniel Mooney, the rector. He was, he wrote, most anxious to prevent Michael Dorian of Cashel Glebe from getting the holding; Michael, he continued, was a 'distant relation of my own but ... one of my greatest enemies as he is

102. N.A.I., C.S.O.R.P. 1857–8/6709, Buncrana, 7 Aug. 1857, J. Considine to T. Larcom; Tamney, 6 Aug. 1857, Sworn Information of Lieut. Henry Ware; Knockbrack, 25 May 1857, Sworn Information of Michael Sweeney, Ballyhiernan; Knockbrack, 28 May 1857, Sworn Information of Patrick Connor, Ballyhiernan; Knockbrack, 28 May 1857, Sworn Information of Ellen McCay, Fanavolty.

103. Carryblagh, 27 July 1951, P. Shiels to Rev. E. J. O'Doherty, copy in possession of editors.

104. *Londonderry Standard*, 31 Jan. 1866; N.A.I., C.S.O.R.P. 1866/1919, Letterkenny, 1 Feb. 1866, E. Peel to Chief Secretary.

connected by marriage with the others who are so his wife being a Shiel'; Michael was also 'a man who has been busy circulating bad language against landlords and the authorities', and he had done his best 'this long time for to drive myself and father out of our little holding'. Michael knew that if he got the land, Hugh and his father might abandon their holding, 'for we could not live with him as he could not pass to or from it but through ours'.[105] Leitrim's response to Dorian's request is unknown.[106]

Although this letter tends to show Dorian as willing to inform, his claim to be estranged from the Shiels complicates matters. Donnchadh Dhiarmada Shiels and Neidí Mhícheáil Óig Shiels were reputed to have been the gunmen who ambushed Wilson at Tullyconnell in October 1864, and *seanchas* (oral history) identifies several members of the extended family as Fenians, most notably Neil Shiels of Doaghmore who would participate in the assassination of Leitrim at Cratlagh Wood.[107] Dorian may have been out of favour with the Shiels—as he told Leitrim in March 1866—but, if he was, it was a recent development, occurring after November 1864 when he and Catherine had witnessed the marriage of Darby Shiels and Susannah Shiels.[108] And the fact that he himself told Leitrim that he was unpopular with the Shiels—whom Leitrim almost certainly considered 'trouble-makers'—left a question mark over the schoolmaster's actual agenda.

*

105. N.L.I., Leitrim Papers MS 5178, (Cashel), 22 March 1866, H. Dorian to Leitrim.

106. Nor can Leitrim's response be deduced from land valuation records; these records do not show any tenant to have left the townland in the 1860s and indicate that both Dorians increased their acreages in a redistribution of holdings at an unspecified date in the 1860s. Seven tenants held 118a. 3r. 4p. in Cashel Glebe in 'common' in 1858; these tenants and the percentage of the total valuation (£23) accounted for by their shares of land were Hugh Dorian (4.3%), Charles Carr (2.1%), Michael Dorian (23.9%), James Sweeney (32.6%), Hugh Friel (6.5%), Michael McGinley (6.5%) and George Shiels (23.9%). The shares of land were redistributed in the early or mid-1860s (the total valuation remained the same)—Hugh Dorian (5.4%), Charles Carr (2.1%), Michael Dorian (27.1%), James Sweeney (30.4%), Hugh Friel (7.1%), Michael McGinley (6.9%) and George Shiels (20.6%). For the valuation of holdings, see Valuation Office, Revision Book, 1858–1932, Fanad West Electoral Division, Milford District, Cashel Glebe.

107. Dolan, *Third earl,* pp. 50–5; Carryblagh, 27 July 1951, P. Shiels to Rev. E. J. O'Doherty, copy in possession of editors.

108. N.L.I., Mic. 4600, Clondavaddog Parish Register. If Dorian had fallen out with the Shiels, it may have resulted from the redistribution of holdings in Cashel Glebe in the early 1860s when George Shiels lost land of a higher valuation than any of his neighbours: see above, n. 106.

Spring 1866 found Dorian and his family in an invidious position: he was teaching in a school managed by an erratic and unpopular landlord; he had been condemned by his priest (whose authority was soon inflated by the first Redemptorist mission in the parish) and, finally, he had penned several letters which—if revealed—could expose him as an informer. School registers record comments and complaints about the personal and professional failings of masters, mistresses and monitors. From 1866 inspectors' entries in the Ballyhoorisky register show Dorian to have steadily lost interest in both teaching and the condition of his school. In May 1866 an inspector instructed him to devote increased attention to 'writing and explanation'; two months later he was 'admonished' for the low proficiency of the pupils and the schoolhouse's 'want of cleanliness'; and in December he was told to improve his pupils' dictation and arithmetic. In May 1867 the scale of the problem became apparent when an inspector formally reprimanded him for the state of the school and threatened to cancel the grant—effectively strike off the school—if he did not improve it.

Over the next few years, Dorian appeared to be drinking heavily: in May 1868 he was 'reprimanded very severely' for 'unbecoming conduct on the night of the 6th Jan. at Shovelin's public house', and the inspector warned that if he was again 'guilty of brawling or associating with drunken people' he would be dismissed. In January 1871 an inspector drew the manager's attention to the falling number of pupils attending the school; and the master may also have been playing truant—an inspector had reprimanded him for late attendance in August 1870. Matters came to a head in late 1871 when one James Kerr informed the commissioners that magistrates had found Dorian to have been 'drunk and disorderly'; Dorian only escaped dismissal when Leitrim lobbied the board on his behalf, claiming that Kerr's letter was 'malicious'. Although his job had been saved, Dorian applied for a retirement gratuity in July 1872 at the age of thirty-eight; when the commissioners rejected the application he resigned and left Fánaid. No replacement teacher could be found and the school was formally struck off in 1873.[109]

Positively identifying James Kerr, the man who reported Dorian to the commissioners of national education—and establishing his motive—might help to explain Dorian's decision to leave Fánaid and, more importantly, help to locate him in Fánaid's underworld. However, this is

109. N.A.I., E.D. 2/51 Folio 32 (Ballyhoorisky).

problematic: only his name appears in the commissioners' files and his surname, often spelled 'Carr', was the most common surname in Fánaid in the mid-nineteenth century. Thirteen James Carrs are listed as house-holders in the parish in a return of tenements compiled in 1858. He may have been any one of those men or a son of another householder named Carr; the alternative spelling was not used in the return.[110] It is *possible* that the man who wrote to the commissioners was James Kerr/Carr, a son of Shane Kerr/Carr of Doaghmore; this man had been implicated in the attack on Wilson in October 1864 and annotations in Leitrim's rental indicate that he was to be evicted if he did not emigrate.[111] Members of the Shiels family were the gunmen who fired at Wilson. *If* the man who tipped off the commissioners was James Kerr/Carr of Doagh-more, then Dorian might appear—as he presents himself to Leitrim—an opponent of party-men, falsely accused by O'Boyle of conspiracy to murder, and his intimation to Leitrim that he was estranged from the Shiels (though it is certain that he was friendly with them as late as 1864) would be creditable. That scenario has a certain symmetry, but the man who tipped off the commissioners of education may have been another James Kerr/Carr; indeed, this appears to be a strong possibility as Shane Kerr was not evicted, suggesting that his son may have already emigrated.[112]

The failure to positively identify James Kerr highlights the difficulty of constructing biographies for 'ordinary people' in the past.[113] That difficulty is further highlighted by an additional circumstance in the spring of 1872. At the Donegal assizes in March, a man named Hugh Friel won a landmark case against Leitrim for violating the Ulster custom; again, however, none of the consulted reports on the case identify the townland where this man lived or, for that matter, indicate that he was from

---

110. Griffith, *Union of Millford*, pp. 110–52.

111. Another man, James Kerr of Ballynalost, had been an informer in 1863. He told Leitrim's agent that Owen Martin of Pollet and Myles Sweeney of Ballynalost had proposed to kill anybody who occupied a holding from which John Martin had been evicted in Pollet. Martin had suggested burning the house and occupants; Sweeney said that fourteen pounds of gunpowder should be put under the hearthstone to 'blow up the house and the man that would put on the first fire in it to the elements'. For information supplied by Kerr of Ballynalost, see N.L.I., Leitrim Papers MS 13339 (9), Ballyhiernan, 30 March 1863, R. Wilson to Leitrim. For the proposed eviction of Shane Kerr of Doaghmore, see ibid., *Donegal rental*.

112. For Shane Kerr's holding in Doaghmore, see V.O., Revision Book, 1858–1932, Milford Poor Law Union, Fanad West Electoral Division, Doaghmore (Lot 9a; Lot 16 from 1861).

113. For a discussion of changing approaches to lower-class biography, see C. Ginzburg, *The judge and the historian: Marginal notes on a late twentieth-century miscarriage of justice* (New York, 1999).

Fánaid.[114] If this was Hugh Friel of Doaghmore, this might plausibly lead to the conclusion that Dorian's representation of himself as a friend of Leitrim's in 1866 had been quite disingenuous. It is unlikely, however, that it was the Doaghmore man, as land records show that he and his brother John were evicted in 1875.[115] According to a twentieth-century account, they were evicted after a gun-attack on Leitrim's head bailiff; the head bailiff's wife insisted that a scarf found at the scene belonged to John Friel, who was himself employed as a bailiff. Although John Friel produced his scarf, he and Hugh were evicted nonetheless. And still there is another twist. After the assassination, Leitrim's heir agreed to reinstate evicted tenants provided they had a reference from O'Boyle. Hugh and John Friel were the only tenants who did not receive a reference from him; the priest 'would give no reference to a bailiff'.[116]

Must we accept Dorian's denial of O'Boyle's allegations against him and his insistence that he was an opponent of party-men, particularly the Shiels (even though he was friendly with them as recently as 1864)? Perhaps not. When Dorian left Fánaid in 1872, Thomas Sarah McGrenaghan of the neighbouring townland of Gortnatraw North took over his holding in Cashel Glebe; there is no evidence that he went to live there.[117] Presumably, Dorian had sold his 'tenant right' to McGrenaghan, raising the possibility that they were friends; certainly, there is no evidence that Dorian was financially embarrassed in 1872 or that he would have been inclined to sell to somebody he disliked. McGrenaghan was a *poitín*-maker. More importantly, he was the man in whose house the assassination of Leitrim would be planned in 1878 and whose three sons and two nephews would be arrested and charged with the murders of Leitrim, Buchanan and Makim. And, as noted above, the McGrenaghans of Gortnatraw North were related by 'marriage and also by blood' to two of the assassins—Michael McIlwee and Neil Shiels.[118]

114. *Londonderry Standard*, 6 March 1872. For Friel v. the Earl of Leitrim, see W. C. Stubbs, *The Irish Law Times digest of cases decided by the superior and other courts in Ireland, 1867–1893* (Dublin, 1895), p. 333.

115. V.O., Revision Book, 1858–1932, Milford Poor Law Union, Fanad West Electoral Division, Doaghmore (Lot 2b; Lot 3 from 1861).

116. Carryblagh, 27 July 1951, P. Shiels to Rev. E. J. O'Doherty, copy in possession of editors.

117. V.O., Revision Book, 1858–1932, Milford Poor Law Union, Fanad West Electoral Division, Cashel Glebe (Lot 1a), Gortnatraw North (Lot 2b).

118. N.A.I., Fenian 'A' Files, A625 (Carton 5), Milford, 1 July 1880, W. Murphy to Under Secretary.

*

After Hugh quit Ballyhoorisky in 1872, he and Catherine moved to Derry where he found work as a writing clerk. By now they had six children and Catherine was pregnant with their seventh; this child, Annie (1873), and another two children, Ellen (1875) and James (1877), were born in the city.[119] By 1874 they were living at Alexandra Place, off Foyle Road.[120] Alexandra Place was a 'respectable' working-class street of well-kept two-up-two-down houses. Many of the men were tradesmen and others had the coveted positions of fitter, guard and ganger on the railway; moreover, while Catholics constituted a slight majority on the street by the turn of the century, it remained 'mixed'.[121] For the Dorians, however, it was something of a downward shift, and none of their children still living at home in 1901—as listed by their father in the census return in his distinctive handwriting—had attained the lower-middle-class status of schoolmaster. Hugh, the eldest son then at home, was a labourer; James, the youngest, a printer (a 'good trade' but working-class), and Maria, the eldest girl, a shirt-factory worker. Ellen, who had married James Kyle in 1898, was also living at 9 Alexandra Place in 1901 with her husband and their eighteen-month-old son, John James; Ellen was the housekeeper and Kyle a labourer.[122]

The Dorians had their share of trouble in Derry. Ellen died in 1874 aged ten (the girl born the following year was given the same name), Annie in 1876 aged three and a half, and Thomas, a writing clerk, in 1885 aged nineteen. The causes of death were smallpox, whooping cough and 'the decline', a term for wasting diseases, especially pul-

119. G.R.O., Index of Births 1877/7/237 (James Dorian). The dates of birth of Annie and Ellen Dorian are calculated from death records and the 1901 census return: see ibid., Index of Deaths 1876/7/163 (Annie Dorian); N.A.I., Census of Ireland 1901, Londonderry 48/3/20 (Ellen Dorian).
120. Burial records for members of the family who died between 1874 and 1899 give their address as 'Alexandra Place' (1874, 1876); '3 Alexandra Place' (1885) and '9 Alexandra Place' (1899): see Derry City Council Cemeteries Department, Register of Burials: City Cemetery Plot DA136. The *Londonderry Sentinel* published an almanac from 1864; editions consulted do not include house numbers for Alexandra Place until 1900: see *Derry almanac, north-west directory and general advertiser for 1901* (Londonderry, 1900). The family may have moved house or the street may have been renumbered.
121. N.A.I., Census of Ireland 1901 Londonderry 48/3/Form B1 (Alexandra Place). On Derry in the late nineteenth century, see B. Lacy, *Siege city: The story of Derry and Londonderry* (Belfast, 1990), pp. 187–219.
122. N.A.I., Census of Ireland 1901, Londonderry 48/3/20. Hugh Dorian Jr was listed as 'married' (not a 'widower') in the census; his wife, however, was not listed in the return.

monary tuberculosis.[123] And, as in Fánaid, alcohol compounded their troubles. At 6:45 on the evening of Saturday 23 December 1899 Sergeant Thomas Barbour found Catherine Dorian standing in a gateway in Waterloo Place; she appeared to be 'dazed from the effects of drink and rather unwell'. Barbour brought her to the constabulary barracks on the Strand Road where he took her into the police office and sat her down in front of the fire. She seemed 'weak and famished' and asked for a glass of water, which he gave her, and she then lay down on a stretcher in a corner. At about 10 p.m. she appeared 'quite sensible' and asked that she be let home to get someone to release one of her daughters who had also been arrested for drunkenness and brought into the barracks; she was then discharged. This was the last time she was seen alive. Early on the morning of Wednesday 27 December Thomas Maguire, the mate of the *Margaret Elizabeth,* a schooner in the Graving Dock, saw her body lying against the wharf; he notified the harbour constable and brought the body ashore in his boat. The constable who searched her skirt pockets found a handkerchief and five pence in coppers. Press reports described Hugh as 'a respectable, hard-working man' and related his deposition at a coroner's inquest on Catherine's body held later that day in Kitson's public house on Sackville Street:

> He stated that he last saw his wife alive between two and three o'clock on Saturday. At that time he was home for dinner. He gave her some money to make the necessary purchases for the household. He returned home again from work after six o'clock, but his wife was then absent, and did not come back. He waited for her return up to eleven o'clock. After that hour his daughter came in and inquired about her mother. Witness then left the house and walked around the city, searching everywhere for the deceased, but in vain. He walked through almost every street in the city, and also along the quay, but could find no trace of her or of any person who had seen her.

Dr James Craig, who made a superficial examination of the body, noted a flesh wound on the right side of the forehead and a slight contusion on the lip; these wounds had been caused before death and did not contribute to it. From the appearance of the body he believed the cause of death was drowning. Sergeant Barbour deposed that there had been no wound on the 'old woman's' face when she was discharged from the barracks. The coroner's jury, chaired by Mr. W.J. Watt—iron-

---

123. G.R.O., Index of Deaths 1874/7/147; 1876/7/163; 1886/March quarter/2/179.

ically, he was probably a manager of Watt's distillery—returned a verdict 'in accordance with the medical evidence': 'by drowning/accidental/instantaneous'. After the inquest Catherine's body was brought back to Alexandra Place and the following morning she was buried in the city cemetery in the same plot where she had buried three of her children.[124]

III

Dorian began the Narrative in 1889; he was then fifty-five and he had been out of Fánaid for seventeen years. He appears to have completed it the following year.[125] In the opening passages he acknowledges that a political event provided the immediate motivation to write; specifically, he presents the Narrative as an attempt to penetrate the controversy surrounding the killing of District Inspector William Martin of the Royal Irish Constabulary.[126] In Feburay 1889 Martin took a large force of constabulary to Gaoth Dobhair in west Donegal to arrest Fr James MacFadden, the local parish priest. A charismatic land activist, MacFadden had ignored a summons to appear in court on Monday 28 January to answer a charge of incitement to discourage the payment of rent, and a warrant had been issued for his arrest. The warrant did not allow forcible entry and he now refused to surrender himself to the constabulary. On Sunday 3 February, Martin detained him as he left Derrybeg chapel after reading mass and unsheathed his sword as he led him away

124. G.R.O., Index of Deaths 1899/Dec./2/129; *Londonderry Sentinel*, 28 Dec. 1899; *Derry Journal*, 29 Dec. 1899; *Londonderry Standard*, 29 Dec. 1899; Derry City Council Cemeteries Department, Register of Burials, City Cemetery Plot DA136.

125. Dating the completion of the Narrative is problematic. In the first chapter Dorian clearly indicates that he began it in 1889, but the date of his introductory remarks could be read as either 1890 or 1896. His reference to the 'Gweedore terror' as 'recent events' in some 'explanations and additions' to the text—reproduced below as footnotes—led us to favour the earlier date. The title on Dorian's manuscript is 'Donegal Sixty Years Ago'; this echoes J. E. Walsh's *Sketches of Ireland sixty years ago* (1847), which concentrated on the lost world of pre-Union Dublin. A popular work, it was re-issued in 1877 as *Ireland ninety years ago*, and in 1911 as *Ireland one hundred and twenty years ago*.

126. The publication of two collections of memoir by Rev. James Reid Dill in 1889 may also have encouraged Dorian to reflect on the transformation of his home community. A high-profile Presbyterian minister, Dill belonged to a tenant-gentry family in Fánaid and presented an idealized picture of Protestant society in the 1820s and 1830s which Dorian would have found jarring: see Dill, *Autobiography*, and idem, *Dill worthies*. Dill's memoirs are reputed to have caused a dissident member of the family to publish a rejoinder entitled *The Mad Dills*; the author, however, supposedly recanted and burned all the copies that he could find; we have not been able to locate a copy: see 19 Dawson St., Dublin, 16 Feb. 1951, S. Ó Domhnaill to J. C. MacDonagh, letter in possession of editors.

*Monument erected in the early 1890s to District Inspector William Martin in St
Anne's church, Kilbarron parish, Ballyshannon (Church of Ireland)*

by the collar of his soutane. A woman shouted that the policeman was killing the priest. Within minutes the dispersing congregation had bludgeoned Martin to death with paling posts and stones. The state responded in a ham-fisted manner, stationing frigates off the coast and flooding the district with police and soldiers who arrested forty-eight men and three women and conveyed them to Derry Gaol. Ten people, including MacFadden, were charged with murder and thirteen others with conspiracy and brought to trial at Maryborough (Port Laoise) in October. Fearful that a glaringly packed jury would find at least one prisoner guilty of murder, the defence counsel reached an agreement with the attorney general: MacFadden pleaded guilty to obstruction and was immediately released. Seven of his co-accused—six of whom pleaded guilty—were convicted of manslaughter and received sentences ranging from six months' hard labour to ten years' penal servitude. Nine others received short sentences for obstruction. When the Liberals returned to power in 1892, they released those still in gaol.[127]

The entire episode—from killing to court case—became part of the contemporary debate about land and home rule. For Unionists and Conservatives the 'barbarous murder' by mass-goers was evidence of the 'savagery' of Irish Catholics and established that they were incapable of self-government. In a striking variation on an old theme, Rev. R.R. Kane, a prominent Orangeman, told a massive 'indignation meeting' in the Ulster Hall, Belfast—'one of the finest meetings ever held in the city', according to the *Belfast Newsletter*—that the people of Gaoth Dobhair were 'as innocent and credulous as the painted children of the prairie' but manipulated by their parish priest for his own sinister ends. The implication, however, was the same: Home Rule would be Rome Rule and destructive of life and liberty.[128] Nationalists and Liberals, on the other hand, presented the inhabitants of west Donegal as a monolithic group of innocent 'peasants' persecuted by avaricious landlords and an alien state; the excessive state reaction became the 'Gweedore Terror' and was cited as evidence of the need for further land reform and speedy political devolution.[129]

127. For an account of the episode, see B. Mac Suibhne, 'Soggarth aroon or gombeen-priest: Canon James MacFadden (1842–1917)', in G. Moran, ed., *Radical Irish priests* (Dublin, 1998), pp. 167–70. For nationalist propaganda photographs taken after the killing, see Ulster Folk and Transport Museum, Glass Collection (1889).

128. *Belfast Newsletter*, 15 Feb. 1889. For Conservative and Unionist reactions to another controversial incident in 1895, see A. Bourke, *The burning of Bridget Cleary: A true story* (London, 1998), pp. 114–29.

129. For a pamphlet by an influential Liberal, see H. W. Massingham, *The Gweedore hunt: A story of English justice in Ireland* (London, 1889).

The indignation at the smallholders' treatment (in print as much as in prison) that forms the starting point for the Narrative both explains one of its most striking features—Dorian never identifies Fánaid by name (it is sufficient that it is in Donegal)—and, paradoxically, raises it above polemic. To the extent that the Narrative has a central purpose it is to illuminate the alienation and violence of 'Donegal' smallholders by reference to living memory rather than distant history and, in so doing, to assert the ordinariness of a people represented as savage. Dorian makes no claims for the uniqueness of Fánaid; he abbreviates discussion of sensational events, including Leitrim's assassination; and, most importantly, he insists that 'what happened in a part must have happened elsewhere'. This approach—that of 'the native as anthropologist', albeit one preoccupied with supra-local politics—sets the Narrative in a different category from the classic insider accounts of life in rural Ireland, not least the heroic biographies produced in the Blaskets and in various parts of Donegal in the mid-twentieth century.[130] In short, while there is a pervasive sense of 'the world we have lost', there is no hint of *ní bheidh ár leithéidí arís ann* (our likes will not be seen again).

Insofar as there is a literary context for Dorian's Narrative, it is in the nineteenth-century writings of a very small number of educated Catholic Ulstermen who found a voice in fiction, in local history, or in folklore composition. Drawn from the west and south of the province, these were writers who had been reared on small farms and remained strongly influenced by their family and parish backgrounds and who, whatever their personal fortunes, were committed to exposing the injustices of that religiously mixed but highly unequal world where the Catholic 'peasant' segment was the unvalued repository of tradition, victimized, oppressed and little noticed. Some may have been destined for ordination but, perhaps surprisingly, few priests contributed to this literature; the most notable exception was Dr James MacDevitt (1832–79), whose *The Donegal Highlands* appeared five years before he became bishop of Raphoe in 1871. Presented as a guide-book for English tourists, it avoids the recent past and all political controversy, concentrating

---

130. H. L. Gates, Jr, 'Introduction', in *Narrative of the life of Frederick Douglass, an American slave, written by himself; 150th anniversary edition* (New York, 1997), xiv. For a discussion of rural memoirs in Irish, see M. Nic Eoin, *An litríocht réigiúnach* (The regional literature) (Baile Átha Cliath, 1982). For writing from Donegal, see N. Mac Congáil, eag., *Scríbhneoireacht na gConallach* [Donegal people's writing] (Baile Átha Cliath, 1990), passim, especially the chapter by P. Ó Conluain on memoir.

instead on descriptions of scenery, mythological tales and romantic accounts of the O'Donnells, the county's pre-conquest élite.[131]

Other voices were openly political. The earliest of these from Donegal was Fr John Boyce (1810–64), whose novel *Shandy M'Guire or tricks upon travellers being a story of the north of Ireland* (1848) vividly recreates the socio-economic and sectarian tensions in Donegal town in the 1820s. The novel, which was interspersed with sharp attacks on landlordism, the Union and the Orange Order, went through three editions by 1853 and a dramatized version was staged in 1851. Boyce was a curate in Fánaid from 1839 to about 1845, when he emigrated to the United States, and his third novel—*Mary Lee, or the Yankee in Ireland*—is set in the north of the county in the aftermath of the Great Famine; it presents a satirical portrait of an American in Ireland to refute Yankee 'national prejudice' against Irish immigrants.[132] Thomas Ainge Devyr (c.1810–c.1890)—like Boyce a native of Donegal town who emigrated to the United States—published *The odd book of the nineteenth century* (New York, 1882); a scrap-book of political writings and memoir, it details his political formation in Ireland and his later involvement in Chartist actvity in England and land, labour and emigrant politics in America. At home, William Harkin (1855–1906), Creeslough hotelier, Land Leaguer and author of *Scenery and antiquities of north-west Donegal* (1st ed., Londonderry, 1893; 2nd ed., 1898), was another activist turned author. Despite its obvious function as a guide-book for Donegal tourists including Harkin's many guests, his

131. Anon. [Dr J. MacDevitt], *The Donegal Highlands* (1st ed., Dublin, 1866; 2nd ed., Dublin, 1895). The bishop was himself the subject of a substantial memoir by his brother, Dr John MacDevitt: see Rev. J. MacDevitt, *The most reverend, James MacDevitt, D.D., bishop of Raphoe, a memoir* (Dublin, 1880).

132. 'Paul Peppergrass' [J. Boyce], *Shandy M'Guire or tricks upon travellers being a story of the north of Ireland* (New York, 1848); idem, *Mary Lee, or the Yankee in Ireland* (Baltimore and Boston, 1860). He also published *The spaewife; or the queen's secret: A story of the reign of Elizabeth* (Boston, 1852), an historical novel, and *The satisfying influence of Catholicity on the intellect and senses* (New York, 1851), a lecture on the nature of Catholics' religious experience. For an insightful discussion of his work, see G.M. McNamara, 'Rev. Dr. John Boyce ... 1810–64', *Donegal Annual*, vol. VI, 2 (1965), 141–9; C. Fanning, *The Irish voice in America: Irish-American fiction from the 1760s to the 1980s* (Kentucky, 1990), pp. 96–113. For Boyce's opposition to the erection of a barracks in Doaghbeg, see above n. 36. It is also worth noting Patrick Sarsfield Cassidy's *Glenveigh, or the victims of vengeance: A tale of Irish present life in the present* (Boston, 1870), a novel based on the clearance of 244 persons from the north Donegal estate of John George Adair in 1861. Although born in Dunkineely in the south of the county in 1852, Cassidy had lived for period with an uncle at Churchill near the townlands cleared by Adair. He emigrated to the United States about 1869 and published the novel the following year when he was about eighteen. For details of Cassidy's life and work, see Fanning, *Irish voice*, pp. 81, 139, 173, 363; W. E. Vaughan, *Sin, sheep and Scotchmen: John George Adair and the Derryveagh evictions, 1861* (Belfast, 1983), pp. 12, 40–4.

study was informed by an active antiquarian curiosity and a commitment to social improvement. William Harkin was as conspicuously successful in adapting to the new order as the older Dorian was a marginalized failure, yet politically they were not at all unlike in their sympathies.[133] A Donegal contemporary who was better known nationally than either was W.J. Doherty: he published his magnum opus, *Inis-Owen and Tirconnell* ... (1st ser., Dublin, 1891; 2nd ser., Dublin, 1895) shortly before his death. One of Victorian Ireland's leading civil engineers and High Sheriff of Dublin, Doherty was the son of a modest Inishowen land surveyor. In search of Donegal's 'literary remains' and of the great heritage that he felt Protestant Ulster ignored, Doherty 'nationalized the Donegal landscape and peopled it with ... heroes and Catholic saints'.[134]

There was little of the recent past or of *seanchas* in the work of William Harkin or W.J. Doherty. In contrast, another Catholic author from east Donegal, Michael Harkin (1830–98), had produced in *Inishowen: Its history, traditions and antiquities* (Londonderry, 1867) a remarkably successful blend of topography and parish history, book-learning and folklore, punctuated by anecdote and verse. Though not polemical in tone it was nationalist and Catholic in sentiment, anticipating 'a good time coming' when a future generation would complete Daniel O'Connell's work. A fuller knowledge of the past, Michael Harkin believed, would energize the people, allow them to appreciate their own dignity, and give rise to a new 'spirit of manly, generous independence' in place of all the 'cringing, hollow sycophancy', for 'the peasantry are not inferior to their would-be masters'.[135]

The Famine makes little impact in Micheal Harkin's account of Inishowen; Dorian's chapter on the subject pulls no punches. And where Harkin's blackguards were the magistracy who long ago had exploited the penal laws and more recently had tyrannized the community during the era of illicit distilling in the early nineteenth century, Dorian's blackguards were in living memory, men he had witnessed: proselytizing min-

133. P. J. McGill, 'Five Donegal historians of last century', in *Donegal Annual*, 11, i (1974), 57–60. Harkin referred (2nd ed., p. 11) to the 'late lamented earl of Leitrim', assassinated in 1878; some of his readers may have felt such a sentiment sounded strange coming from a Land Leaguer.
134. J. McLaughlin, 'The politics of nation-building in post-Famine Donegal', in Nolan et al., *Donegal*, p. 596 (McLoughlin is however incorrect in attributing this work to Father William Doherty, then a county Derry curate). See also McGill, op. cit., 60–3.
135. McGill, op. cit., 63–5; McLaughlin, op. cit., p. 596; D. Dickson, 'Preface' in 'Maghtochair' [M. Harkin], *Inishowen: Its history, traditions and antiquities* (3rd ed., Dublin, 1985).

isters, corrupt public functionaries, and of course the third earl of Leitrim. But Dorian had seen deliverance—in the form of William Gladstone. He was after all writing about Donegal in the aftermath of the Land War and in the wake of the electoral transformation of the county's politics: in 1880 the old dominance of the Tories had finally been broken by Liberal candidates; and even more sensationally, Parnell's Irish Party candidates in Donegal had out-polled both Liberals and Tories in the 1885 election—when the electoral register had quadrupled and the Catholic vote had triumphed in each of the four new county constituencies.[136]

Dorian's Narrative is indeed a tableau of a downtrodden but resilient community, well-stocked with the selfish and vain, the superstitious and the God-fearing, most of them lovers of drink, long nights and company. In this he invites comparison with William Carleton, the great spokesman for another corner of west Ulster through his fiction of the 1830s and 1840s, much of it strongly autobiographical. Carleton's writing was crafted and polished and layered with meaning in ways that Dorian's prose could never aspire to be.[137] But the rural worlds they remembered and wrote about were not dissimilar, and a number of the character types in Carleton may be found in Dorian's chapters. Similarly, Carleton's ambiguous relationship with the reader finds an echo in Dorian: self-deprecating in their self-assessment, at times identifying with the suffering people about whom they wrote and at times the disengaged critics of a gullible, naïve and unlettered peasantry who had so often been led into trouble and disaster by wily outsiders. Carleton's personal rejection of the Catholic Church and his antipathy towards Repeal found of course no echo in Dorian; whatever the latter's private feelings towards particular local priests, his respect for the traditional pieties and an uncomprehending contempt for Protestantism run throughout the Narrative.

Michael Harkin, William Carleton and Hugh Dorian have one common feature in their biographies that is of great importance: they started out their adult lives as tutors, itinerant teachers or schoolmasters. In that respect they represent a critical group within nineteenth-century rural Ireland—respected by the less educated, undervalued if not spurned by their social superiors, and sensitive to a wider world and a deeper past than those with whom they socialized. The characterization by an

---

136. J. Tunney, 'The marquis, the reverend, the grand master and the major: Protestant politics in Donegal 1868–1933', in Nolan et al., *Donegal*, pp. 676–9.
137. A good starting point is W. Carleton, *The Autobiography*, ed. B. Kiely (Belfast, 1996).

anonymous writer in 1820 has obvious resonances: 'the country school-master is independent of all system and control; he is himself one of the people, imbued with the same prejudices, influenced by the same feel-ings, subject to the same habits; to his little store of learning he gener-ally adds some of the traditionary tales of the country, of a character to keep alive discontent. He is the scribe, as well as the chronicler and the pedagogue of his little circle ...'.[138] The attribution of subversive intent to the race of schoolmasters had become a well-worn theme since the 1790s and one, though much exaggerated, with a grain of truth.[139] The more important point, however, is that the role of the teacher as cultural agent, collector, transmitter and re-shaper of the collective past was a growing one in an age of expanding popular literacy, and it not only sur-vived but flourished in the post-1831 era of national schooling and gov-ernment financial control. Men such as Patrick Kennedy (1801–73), the great folklorist of north Wexford, Peter Magennis (1817–1910), whose poetry and novels sought to evoke his Fermanagh childhood and his memories of Ribbonism, and Bernard Magennis (1833–1911), Mon-aghan poet and Dublin newspaperman, may have been unsuccessful teachers, but their writings reveal their Janus-like position between the oral world of their clients and the printed world of national discourse.[140]

A roll-call of Donegal teachers or quondam teachers who sought to create a narrative out of the corpus of local 'tradition', lore and history, or to represent it in fictionalized form, confirms this pattern. Peter McLaughlin (1811–33) was an Inishowen classical teacher, antiquarian and contributor to the *Dublin Penny Journal*. T.C. McGinley ('Kinn-faela', 1830–87) was a native of Glencolumbkille and an exact contem-porary of Michael Harkin who unlike Harkin remained a teacher all his life; his *Cliff scenery of south-west Donegal* (1867) belied its title and was a mix of folklore, natural history and local anecdote, tinged with sharp social comment, notably on the Famine and on recent land clearances.[141]

138. *Thoughts and suggestions on the education of the peasantry of Ireland* (Dublin, 1820), quoted in P. J. Dowling, *The hedge schools of Ireland* (2nd ed., Cork, 1968), p. 90.

139. L. M. Cullen, 'The cultural basis of modern Irish nationalism', in R. Mitchison, ed., *The roots of nationalism: Studies in northern Europe* (Edinburgh, 1980), pp. 102–3; idem, 'Patrons, teachers and literacy in Irish', in M. Daly and D. Dickson, eds, *The origins of popu-lar literacy in Ireland* (Dublin, 1990), p. 36.

140. See entry in A. Brady and B. Cleeve, *Biographical dictionary of Irish writers* (Dublin, 1985). Bernard Magennis's publications are listed in his *War between our Irish political and literary gladiators or patriots* (Dublin, 1895).

141. 'Kinnfaela' [T. C. MacGinley], *The cliff scenery of south-west Donegal* (Londonderry, 1867), pp. 14–15, 33, 79–80; Doherty, *Inis-Owen and Tirconnell* (2nd ser., Dublin, 1895), pp. 246–7, 276–7; McGill, 'Donegal historians', 53–5; B. O'Hanrahan, *Donegal authors: A bibli-*

Seumas MacManus (1869–1960) was a teacher for more than a decade before the international success of his London-published collections of stories in the late 1890s led him to a literary career abroad. But however far his mature writing took him from his Mountcharles origins, the enduring strength of his early folklore compilations lay in the directness of their local inspiration. Not for nothing was he a founder member of the Gaelic League, an organization whose extraordinary diffusion through rural Ireland after 1900 would have been impossible without the commitment of hundreds of its school-teacher members.[142]

There is finally the case of Edward McCarron, a native of Carryblagh on the eastern side of Fánaid and a few years Dorian's junior. McCarron's early career shadowed Dorian's quite remarkably, even to the extent of his becoming a young teacher in one of Leitrim's schools—before he escaped to become a lighthouse-keeper. He also committed his early days to paper in an account that was published in 1981. His reminiscences of the post-Famine parish offer an intriguing counterpoint to those of Dorian: they are more personal and low-key, more precise on material culture and more specific on farming routines. However, McCarron is far less reflective, and far more comfortable with the ways of the world and the status quo.[143]

*

The complex role of the 'master' as cultural agent of 'his' community continued to have many variants in twentieth-century Donegal—for example, Thomas Kearney, the Church of Ireland teacher at Ballintra,

ography (Dublin, 1984), pp. 161–2. For contemporary comments on the character of early national teachers in north-west Donegal, see M. Daly, 'Literacy and language change', in Daly and Dickson, Popular literacy, pp. 155–6.

142. O'Hanrahan, op. cit., pp. 170–7; N. Mac Congáil, 'Seumas Mac Manus', in Mac Congáil, Scríbhneoireacht, pp. 211–28. MacManus was also the convenor of the first meeting of the county board of the Gaelic Athletic Association in Donegal. For an early recognition of the importance of MacManus's work, see McCarron, Life in Donegal, p. 13. On the wider issue of teachers and political mobilization, see T. Garvin, Nationalist revolutionaries in Ireland, 1858–1928 (Oxford, 1987), pp. 24–9.

143. McCarron's Life in Donegal and Dorian's Narrative were not the only nineteenth-century memoirs that did not appear in print during their authors' lifetime; Wall, Glenswilly, pp. 10–11, comments: 'I have only recently come across a manuscript written by Neallie Browne, a man from Drimenaght, who left this country in 1870 because of a difference of opinion with a gamekeeper; and it is certainly a tribute to the educational standards in the glen at the time. He kept a log of the day-to-day happenings on a ship on which he sailed from Liverpool to Sydney, and from there to San Francisco, and back to Queenstown in Cork. Apart from the interest of the account of life on a sailing ship, the manuscript has many nostalgic references to Glenswilly, with poems about Ireland and about Drimenaght.'

producing a parish history in 1903—but Catholics from the partially Irish-speaking west of the county were the most conspicuous. The list of teachers or quondam teachers who produced substantial works of local history now includes Seán Mac Fhionnlaoich and Cáit Nic Ghiolla Bhríde of Gaoth Dobhair; Séamus Ó Grianna, Seosamh Mac Grianna and Eoghan Ó Dónaill of Rann na Feirste; Niall Ó Dónaill of Loch an Iúir; Peadar O'Donnell and Pádraig Ó Cnáimhsí of An Mhín Mhór; Seán Bán Mac Meanman of An Cionn Garbh and Patrick McGill of Ardara. Such people were perhaps exceptional, but one suspects that the labours of many other teachers have been underestimated in the world outside.[144]

The classic Donegal autobiographical memoirs of the twentieth century have not come from the pen of teachers, but in one respect the work of Patrick MacGill, Hiúdaí Sheáinín Ó Domhnaill, Micí Mac Gabhann, Paddy the Cope and Eoghan Ó Colm share a common feature with Dorian's Narrative (and McCarron's memoir): they composed their stories—or dictated their memories—after spending a formative part of their life outside their home community.[145] Only the Inishowen memoir of Charles McGlinchey, *The last of the name,* came from an insider, but in a sense he too was a man apart, a craftsman in a world of farmers.[146]

The thread that links the diffuse literary productions of these twentieth-century authors with Boyce, Harkin, McGinley, Devyr and Dorian is their uncondescending identification, explicit or implied, with the society they were describing, a posture unlike that adopted in most of

144. In spring 2000 Raidió na Gaeltachta broadcast a series of lectures on the history of Irish-speaking communities in Donegal; of fourteen lecturers, five were local schoolmasters and four were involved in third-level education: see L. Ó Laoire et al., eag., *Pobal na Gaeltachta: A scéal agus a dhán* [The Gaeltacht community: Its tale and fate] (Indreabhán, 2000).

145. P. MacGill, *Children of the dead end: The auto-biography of a navvy* (London, 1914); idem, *The rat-pit* (London, 1915); idem, *Glenmornan* (London, 1918); H. S. Ó Domhnaill, *Scéal Hiúdaí Sheáinín* (Baile Átha Cliath, 1940); M. Mac Gabhann, *Rotha mór an tsaoil* (Baile Átha Cliath, 1959); P. Gallagher [Paddy the Cope], *My story* (Dungloe, n.d.); E. Ó Colm, *Toraigh na dTonn* (Cathair na Mart, 1971). MacGill's influence is evident on subsequent memoirs in Irish and English. O. Dudley Edwards, 'Patrick MacGill and the making of a historical source with a handlist of his works', in *The Innes Review,* 37, 2 (1986), 73–99; S. Mac Giolla Uain, 'Patrick MacGill', in Mac Congáil, *Scríbhneoireacht,* pp. 229–240, and S. Ó Catháin, 'Patrick MacGill agus an Lagán', in Mac Congáil, op. cit., pp. 241–51. For biographical details, see P. O'Sullivan, 'Patrick MacGill: The making of a writer', in S. Hutton and P. Stewart, eds, *Ireland's histories: Aspects of state, society and ideology* (London, 1991), pp. 203–22, and Mac Suibhne, 'Soggarth aroon', pp. 148–51, 170–84.

146. A. O'Dowd, 'Seasonal migration to the Lagan and Scotland', in Nolan et al., *Donegal,* pp. 625–48; C. McGlinchey, *The last of the name* (Belfast, 1986).

the antiquarian and folklorist literature emanating from Dublin and the south. In general they did not 'de-historicize and de-politicize the image of the Irish peasantry', as other (mainly Protestant) writers in the field have been accused of doing—not least William Allingham in his idealized memories of Ballyshannon and 'the rushy glen'.[147] This northern Catholic literature, of which Dorian's memoir now forms a fascinating part, deserves to be seen as distinct genre, explicable only in terms of the singularity of Ulster's history.

IV

In 1903 Hugh Dorian moved from 9 Alexandra Place, the street on which he had lived for thirty years; he was sixty-nine and it is probable that he had recently retired. Maria Dorian, Ellen and James Kyle and their children moved with him. After a spell on Bridge Street, they moved to 55 Nelson Street in the heart of the city's Bogside. 'The Bog' was a web of narrow terraces spun out beneath the city's western walls. Its inhabitants were predominantly Catholic. The men were mostly labourers, many of them carters and dockers, and, confronted with the double jeopardy of male employment that was at once seasonal and casual, their families depended on the pawnshop and women's earnings as seamstresses, laundresses and shirt-factory workers. The houses were poor and chronically overcrowded: on Nelson Street, for instance, there were 79 families (non-kin) packed into 57 houses in 1911; 12 houses lay empty. By that stage, Ellen and James Kyle had three children—John James (1899), Kate (1902) and Hugh (1910); another child, Margery, had died at three months in November 1903. They shared three rooms of the house with Hugh and Maria; Anne McLaughlin, a widow in her fifties, and her two grown children—Dan, a labourer, and Maggie, who took in laundry with her mother—occupied the fourth room.[148]

147. J. Leerssen, *Remembrance and imagination: Patterns in the historical and literary representation of Ireland in the nineteenth century* (Cork, 1996), pp. 162–70.

148. The last listing for Dorian at 9 Alexandra Place is in *The Derry almanac, north-west directory and general advertiser for 1903* (Londonderry, 1902), p. 154. Subsequent editions of the almanac do not return him as a householder. For the census return Dorian completed at 55 Nelson Street in 1911, see N.A.I., 1911 Census of Ireland, Londonderry 52/37/55. Margery Kyle died at 55 Bridge Street in November 1903: see Council Cemeteries Department, Register of Burials, City Cemetery Plot DA136.

Dorian died in that overcrowded house on 25 April 1914.[149] The city had experienced an economic slow-down in the early 1900s and his last years had probably not been easy. The political landscape had changed too. In late 1890—the year Dorian had apparently completed the Narrative—the Home Rule party had split and, as the prospect of political progress receded, nationalism had taken a cultural turn: nationalists formed clubs to play the 'Gaelic' games of hurling and football; arranged classes and competitions for 'traditional' music and dance; set up Irish-language classes for young men and women who had grown up speaking English; and campaigned for the language to be taught in schools. The enthusiasm for Irish language and culture extended to the Bogside; on Nelson Street the children of monolingual English-speaking and, in some cases, illiterate labourers and carters learned to speak and read Irish.[150] Protestant politics had also changed: the 1890s and early 1900s had witnessed the emergence of partitionist unionism and the elaboration of political and, from 1910, paramilitary networks through much of Ulster. Indeed, given Dorian's satisfaction at the breakdown of Protestant hegemony when he wrote the 'true historical narrative', there was a certain irony in the date he died: on the night of 24–5 April unionists illegally landed massive consignments of arms and ammunition at Larne, Bangor and Donaghadee and distributed them to the Ulster Volunteer Force. The navy, coast guard, constabulary and military stood idly by, exposing the state's unwillingness to enforce the law. The process of democratization that had progressed, however fitfully, through Dorian's lifetime had stalled.

149. G.R.O., Index of Deaths 1914/Apr./2/126.

150. N.A.I., 1911 Census of Ireland, Londonderry 52/37/52; 52/37/62. On Alexandra Place, Uilliam Mac an Bhaird, a thirty-nine-year-old *saor-amaid* (carpenter) from county Derry, completed his census form in Irish apparently as part of a campaign by the Gaelic League. Mac an Bhaird's wife and children, who were born in *Cathair Dhoire* (Derry City), all spoke Irish and English: see ibid., 48/3/1. In the census forms he completed in 1901 and 1911, Dorian returned himself as bilingual and his children and grandchildren as monolingual English-speakers. For the rural poor who were the majority of 'native speakers', the 'revival' of urban and particularly middle-class interest in a language that had become an embarrassing badge of poverty was an unexpected and somewhat disconcerting development: in Fánaid *'Gaeilge cheannaiste'* (bought Irish) became the dismissive and vaguely resentful term for the stilted speech of Irish students: see Evans, 'Vocabulary of Fanad and Glenvar', 190, 218.

V

In the summer of 1940 Seán Ó hEochaidh of the Irish Folklore Commission arrived in the impoverished townlands of *íochtar Fhánada* (the bottom of Fánaid) to record and transcribe song and story. *Cré ghorm* (blue-clay) and flag floors were giving way to cement and oil-cloth; blue-striped tea-cups were replacing bowls and the hiss of Marconi radios was hushing weaker voices. Ó hEochaidh had a clear sense of a community that had experienced massive and sustained change over several generations and a sense too that this movement of change was nearly complete. The last vestiges of the rundale system had largely passed away and the ruins of the old house clusters were crumbling; most houses now had slate roofs and it would not be long, he thought, until there were no thatched houses left. Kelp-burning and fishing had ceased to be economic and the bogs were almost completely exhausted: '*níl rud ar bith níos cruaidhe a chuireas ar na daoine ins an pháirt seo dó 'n tír, nó 'n tine. Tá an mhóin iontach gann agus mar go bhfuil na daoine an-bhocht níl siad ábalta gual a cheannacht*' (the greatest hardship endured by the people in this district is the cold. Turf is very scarce and as the people are very poor they aren't able to buy coal). Home-spun clothes were becoming rare, the young in particular preferring shop-clothes brought home by seasonal migrants. Long favoured, English was now the most widely spoken language among the young and Ó hEochaidh worried that he might be a generation too late to collect *seanchas*:[151]

> *Níl duine ar bith le fághail anois atá ábalta sean-scéal a innse nó sean-abhran a cheol. Tá an bunadh a rabh na sean-scéalta acú uilig marbh le fiche bliadhain ar a laghad, do réir na seandhaoine, agus an brioscar atá acú anois fhéin, níl ann ach conablach an rud a bhí ann ins an tsean-am. Níl ann anois ach go n-aithneochtha gur chualaidh siad scéalta i n-am ínteacht. Tá siad mura gcéadna leis an tsean-cheól, tá na h-abhráin uilig measctha suas acú agus tá ceathair nó cúig a cheannaibh acú i n-aman-naí astoigh ann aon cheann amháin.*

(There is no one here now who is able to tell an old story or sing an old song. Those who had the old stories are all dead for twenty years or more, according to the old people, and the bits that are left are only the scraps of what they had in the old times. You could just about tell that they had once heard stories. They are the same with the old songs. They have the songs all mixed up—four or five of them at times all in the one song.)

151. R.B.É., 705, 630–68.

The note of despair was not new. When John O'Donovan had come to Fánaid to collect the 'rhymes and rags of history' for the Ordnance Survey a century earlier, he had complained that many minor place-names—'the names of the rocks, clefts, holes, waves, heads or points of the coast'—were 'so arbitrary and of such recent imposition' that it was difficult to find 'any eight persons able to pronounce with certainty what they ought to be'.[152] And yet, Ó hEochaidh thought the people were convivial and helpful and he hoped he would be able to collect whatever *mion-seanchas* (minor oral history) that they had left.[153] He would not be disappointed. Smallholders and fishermen talked vividly and at length about *am na caorthaíochta* and *na trí Sheán*; they pointed out *Carraig Fhiabhair*, a rock half a mile from Ballyhoorisky which had a mysterious attraction for people who 'wandered'; and they recalled too that the old people had been very devout but that the Church had disapproved of their customs, particularly their cures. Many of those interviewed raked over topics in Dorian's Narrative—sectarian contention, *am an Ghorta* (the time of the Famine), landlords and evictions—and, time and again, they echoed one of his central themes: that they were living in better times than their fathers and grandfathers and that the political and demographic decline of the local Protestant community was a marvel the old people could never have imagined.[154] And at least one respondent told a tale about two cottiers who tried to rob '*an máistir* Dorrian'; however, given the family's long involvement in education, it is unclear which *máistir* it concerns.[155] Still, it is possible that other stories told in the dimly lit kitchens of the 1940s—stories only sampled in the preparation of this edition—will answer the nagging questions about the life of Hugh Dorian. Or perhaps a constabulary file, a newspaper report or additional correspondence between Dorian and Leitrim will come to light. Or perhaps the questions can not be answered and the man that lies in an unmarked grave in Derry's city cemetery will remain an enigma.

---

152. Ramullan (Rathmullan), 30 Aug. 1835, J. O'Donovan to T. Larcom, in O'Flanagan, *Letters*, pp. 19–21; Ros na Cille (Rosnakill), 3 Sept. 1835, J. O'Donovan to T. Larcom, in ibid., pp. 24–6.

153. R.B.É., 705, 668.

154. For examples, see R.B.É., 705, 427–31 (Tomás Ó Siadhail, 55, iascaire, Sean-Bhaile, Baile Uí Bhorascaidhe, 8–9 Iúil 1940); 705, 432–48 (Liam Ó Siadhail, c. 62, iascaire, Baile Uí Bhorascaidhe, 8 Iúil 1940); 705, 461–89 (Briney Mac Giolla Cearra, 87, feirmeoir, Baile an Chonic, 11–15 Iúil 1940); 718, 5–14, 100–8 (Padaí Ó Canainn, c. 68, Tuaim, 25 Meán Fómhair, 1 Deireadh Fómhair 1940); 740, 23–43 (Brian Mac Giolla Cearra, 85, feirmeoir, An Tóin Bhán, 13 Nollaig 1940).

155. R.B.É., 234, 417–21 (Mícheál Mac Fhionnghaile, 82, feirmeoir, Baile Mhíchil, 17 Iúil 1936); this story was transcribed by Liam Mac Meanman.

Note on the Text

Confronted with a manuscript of Dorian's Narrative that is of uncertain status, we have chosen to incorporate a number of minor abridgements in the text. Our intention has been to produce an edition that respects the voice of the author and reproduces the 'unvarnished' character of his prose, while at the same time giving the reader a lucid text which we hope can be read with ease.

The following editorial protocols have been as far as possible applied: apparent mis-transcriptions and word repetitions have been corrected; capitalization and spelling have been standardized; and syntax and grammar have been modernized—without, it is hoped, sacrificing vernacular idiom. The author's intermittent use of the historic-present tense and of various techniques of reporting direct speech have largely been respected, but we have made some attempt to standardize his conventions. Paragraph divisions have been altered, but chapter and section divisions are as in the manuscript version. In some places words, phrases or whole sentences have been cut; elsewhere words, phrases or sentences have been transposed within paragraphs. Such editorial interventions have been made in the interests of clarity and have been done silently. Where whole paragraphs have been cut, ellipses (. . .) have been used; large excisions on this scale have been done to remove repetition or to maintain the coherence of the narrative. In all, less than 5 per cent of the original text has been cut. Finally (and perhaps contentiously) we have in many instances added one or more words to sentences where it seems likely on balance that words were accidentally omitted in the manuscript, or where the addition of such words loosens an otherwise awkward literary construction. Only where we regard our interpolations as in any way open to variant reading, or where we feel that the additional word or words might have stylistic implications, have square brackets been used; otherwise our additions are invisible.

We recognize that there is a price to be paid for producing a 'reader's edition' in this way, but we hope that our editorial interventions do not compromise the integrity of Dorian's 'plain tale'.

D. D.
B. Mac S.

Introductory Remarks

The following narrative is a brief historical sketch of the manners, the doings, and the sufferings of the peasantry in a particular section of the County of Donegal, and commencing with about the year of 1830, and continued down to the present time, the year 1890.

The stories under different headings are not very long in themselves, and it is by a perusal of the same that the reader may judge for himself, but the writer satisfies himself that there is no attempt at exaggeration, that he has written nothing but facts, most of which came under his own knowledge and observations, and if sometimes facts are added in substances, more or less touching on matters bordering upon the ludicrous, still they are no less facts, and may be interesting as they are intended to show the difference in various ways between the people at the present day and those who lived a little more than half a century ago.

Chapter XII is opened with a few words, or rather the explanation of a few words taken from History, but the remainder is original and all equally applicable.

H. D.

Londonderry 1890.

The county Donegal,[1] sometimes called Tirconnell,[2] as is well known, holds its place famous in Irish history. It is therefore intended in what I am going to relate to quote but as little as possible outside the limits of the prescribed time. At the present time, 1889,[3] all eyes of feeling Christians of the United Kingdom and of many parts elsewhere are directed towards Donegal, owing to the occurrence of recent events,[4] although it might be rather said the recurrence of sufferings experienced too often by its people. Heretofore many cruel acts were done throughout the length and breadth of this large county of which the nations had an imperfect knowledge, but at the present day nothing is hidden and different men, differing in opinions, judge for themselves, as inclinations lead them, of the justice or injustice of such acts.

1. [Dorian's note:] Donegal: Dun-na-Gael: The Fort; the Stronghold of the Gaels.

2. [Dorian's note:] Tirconnell: the share, the division, the patrimony of Connell. Teer may be of large or small extent, for instance a county or part of, as Tirconnell, Tir-Owen (Tyrone), Tir-Hugh, &c.

3. [Dorian's note:] For 'the present time' substitute 'not long ago, 1889'.

4. [Dorian's note:] Referring to the Gweedore evictions. The resistance of the people with no other weapons than old spades and hot water—England's strength brought to bear upon them. Irish Constabulary, long swords and knapsacks not able to cope with them. A regiment of English soldiers from Derry invaded—Short police as they were called by the peasantry. The men were short and small and their dress in colour similar to the police—hence the term. Balfour's maiden—the Battering Ram—Martial Law—and all laws put in force, for demolishing the castles of the inhabitants. Priest and peasant, the old man, the sturdy youth and the blooming maid, taken prisoners, marched between two file of soldiers from Gweedore to Derry gaol. Anyone who had seen witnessed the procession from Pennyburn to Bishop Street Queen's Hotel, can never forget it. England's strength, cavalry, infantry with swords drawn, guarding

Writers have exhausted their knowledge in giving descriptions of the sceneries of Donegal, and of the manners and different ways of living of its people, very often penned as fancy suggested, which could not be otherwise in hasty excursions by non-residents through the Wilds. When sad events such as famine or wholesale extermination occurred, the voice and the pen of one might be raised in pity, while the hand and the feeling of another was exercising continued cruelty, thus showing the extremes in human nature. It may therefore be interesting to hear a true and more minute description of the people and their ways of living within the period and, without naming the place in particular, give a sketch of the scenery of the locality in which our story originates.

I will therefore suppose the reader transported with me to a place [which is] the rising ground at the end of a ravine, or as it is commonly called a "glen": we commence to take our survey—first in a northerly and easterly direction as far as the eye can reach: take a hasty glance at the horizontal boundary, firstly of the ocean looking over our left shoulder, then trace on till we strike land on the east, and soon we perceive a ridge of mountains sloping from a view of the water but gradually rising till, as we shorten the view, they become lofty, bold, and in parts precipitous, and this range at length is abruptly terminated towards the west by an inroad of the sea. A deep gap is therefore formed separating this [range] from its kindred and rather more precipitous mountain facing it on the west side, and each one looking frowningly or rather mournfully at its neighbour opposite as much as to give to understand, "we were once united."

This separation, this deep chasm was formed at the period of the great convulsions of nature, a period antecedent to the Creation of man when land and water each in turn claimed mastery, and it was then that the water from the outside ocean found time and space after a very circuitous route to flow in by stealth as if it were, and filled up the chasm to ocean level. It would appear too that the water made strong efforts to join mother ocean in its triumph in this direction but failed; otherwise a very large irregular shaped island would have been formed. Baffled in this attempt, the water wreaked its vengeance and obtained its ascendancy curtailing the land to such an extent that, on the western

---

barefooted girls with a piece of a shawl about their shoulders. Pity they had not a few field pieces to make the victory more complete. It could not be compared to Roman victory or procession in days of Paganism. It was more like hell opened until the iron gates closed upon their prey, a few defenceless young men and young women handed over to the cruelty of unmerciful gaol keepers.

side, the foundation to the mountain was left so bare of soft or clayey material that no attempt was ever made for the formation of a wider pathway than that beaten out by the feet of flocks of sheep, going of necessity single file.

On top of this mountain the Danes in after ages thought fit to build one of their strongholds, the ruins of which remain to the present day. So strongly did nature supply a foundation that it was almost impregnable from its elevation and the difficulty of approaching it. It commanded the greatest view that could be obtained of the whole country for miles around. It is called *Cashel More* (or the Great Castle) to distinguish it from the many minor forts in the surrounding district.[5]

When people began to multiply in the adjoining low parts of the country, necessity caused men to cut a space through the solid rock on the opposite mountain side and form a path, so that an outlet might be formed of nearly sufficient width for a broadway, or as it is called high road, and when the time arrived for making such [it was done] without consulting any method, even the simplest of engineering, but up hill and down hill, or as the saying is "guided by the stars", and so the public road still runs through this gap or cutting

On a bright day the proximity of the facing mountains, the contrast of their dark sides hanging over the clean water, the rays of the sun concentrated, dancing and sparkling from off the surface of the green calm sea water, are a sight most beautiful to behold. We then shorten our view from ocean sea and mountain to the diversified scenery of hill and dale, lake and river, fertile and cultivated ground, the beautiful green pastures interspersed with bogs and patches of heatherland covering ...

Still nearer our attention is attracted by the beauties of rural scenery as painted above. This is no novel painting or exaggerated story. Italy has its charms and has a right to claim a place among picturesque countries, but we need not leave our own Old Erin to find those charms of nature which are to be met with in very few countries. Our fields are the most verdant in the world and with us grow trees and bushes which will flourish in scarcely any other country. What more beautiful sight than our common whitethorn, our holly, our arbutus, and these are rare in most countries? Vines may grow [elsewhere]; birds beautiful to the eye may sit in the branches of tall shady trees. But when passing through Old Hibernia, travellers from other shores must admire our healthy elms, our sturdy old oaks, our songsters of the grove unrivalled. There

---

5. *Caiseal*, (ancient) stone fort; *Caiseal Mór*, great stone fort. Cashel Glebe, where Dorian lived, took its name from one of these forts.

are places in Ireland celebrated and sung of throughout the world—"By Killarney's Lakes and Fells", "The Green Banks of Shannon"[6]—but there are districts "in song unsung" which are as charming, as beautiful and as rare as any of our frequented scenery.

How strange it is that man will admire the beauties of nature in a strange country and never think of equal or superior beauties at home. What can be more beautiful than the hillocks and hillsides covered with daisies, the primrose banks, the brown heath? For the sportsman, what a variety of pleasing pursuits at short distance. Along the lakes and marshes, he finds the snipe plentiful; within gunshot distance he may turn to the rabbits. A short distance and he finds the partridge in its own locality. Perhaps after discharging his fowling piece he looks around and sees the timid hare climbing the mountain side. The angler can satisfy himself on the lakes where trout are abundant. All these advantages, added to the beauties of nature, are never spoken of, never—by those whose lives are nearly all spent there ...

The fresh water lakes are the next objects on which the eye would naturally rest. In the neighbourhood there are no less than eight of considerable extent, "reposing in still repose" at the foot of the mountains. The largest, the most singularly beautiful of these, stretches out immediately before us, being more than one mile in length, breaking off at either side into two arms, thus forming a kind of cruciform shape, the longest part in our direction and the arms to the right and left. At the head of this lake and nearly touching the water's edge a beautiful plain white building, erected in the memory of the present generation, cannot escape our view.[7] This may be reckoned the only permanent structure, the surrounding ones being liable to change as they become tenantless.

In this, our simple and first survey, we accidentally cast our eyes at the foot of the Glen and here perceive the ruins of four stone walls, now cold and solitary, but we recall that the same was once the habitation of human beings, the spot around which many footprints were stamped in days gone by and to which, as the story proceeds, special attention will revert ...

After satisfying the eyes, the mind takes an ungovernable flight and carries the imagination backwards half a century; a cloud of events and of rapid changes rushes upon the memory which for a little bewilders

6. Late nineteenth–century popular songs.

7. Fanavolty Chapel, erected 1835–8; this chapel served *íochtar Fhánada* [the bottom of Fánaid], the north-west of the peninsula: see W. Lancey, 'Parish of Clondavaddog, county Donegal, statistical report ... April 1835', in A. Day and P. McWilliams, eds, *Ordnance Survey memoirs of Ireland, vol. 38: Parishes of county Donegal I, 1833–5: north-east Donegal* (Belfast, 1997), p. 4.

one's ideas until they are calmed down by reflection. Banishing for a short time from memory the countless number of human beings who once and for a little while cast their shadow on the spot of earth just spread out before the eye, one cannot forget how vain, how short, how insignificant are the works of man; even the works which men in their ungrounded pride, or simplicity of thought, might call grand and lasting have disappeared almost as soon as themselves. On other hand the works of the Great Author of nature remain still as grand, still as magnificent—unchangeable as at the Beginning. Study and contemplate the works of nature, and it is impossible but that the thoughts turn to the Supreme. Again, what a thrill of horror is felt at the thought of the departed, each with his span in this life, some shortest, some shorter, but all short. Gone, the span of life ended. Eternity opened—entered upon—never to have an end.

... Looking further northward and eastward the first thing that naturally strikes the eye is a large expanse of the Atlantic ocean, which view is bounded by the apparent meeting of the sea and sky, a view so extensive as to satisfy the eye of the most curious.

The view of the ocean is bounded on the sides by two large headlands; one to the east is jutting northwards, the other to the west of us pointing eastward. Each of these is topped by a Martello tower.[8] These Martello towers are square blocks of strong masonry, built in the most precipitous parts overhanging the deep waters of the ocean; the entrance doorways were halfway up and admission was effected by means of a ladder which was drawn up when not in use. The walls were so strong that they are still in good preservation. They were built at the time of the French wars for the purpose of giving signals, and so remain as standing memorials to the memory of Old Bony at the time he was striking terror to *all* Europe.[9] They were garrisoned by a few soldiers who kept a constant look out, and if anything suspicious appeared on the

8. Various types of defensive military structure were erected around the Irish coast during the Napoleonic wars in expectation of a further French attempt on Ireland, the most famous such buildings being the circular 'martello' towers. Lough Swilly was heavily fortified with new forts and batteries, notably the martello tower at Muckamish. But what the author here refers to as 'martello towers' were the two rectilinear signal towers at Fánaid and Melmore, built between 1804 and 1806. These were designed to communicate by flag and ball with some 80 other signal towers around the west and south coast, and with shipping at sea. The system only seems to have operated fully for a brief period, but the signal towers at Fánaid and across the Swilly at Malin Head were strategically located and thus were kept open throughout the wars. Manned by locally recruited 'sea fencibles', they were intended to give advance warning to forces within Lough Swilly as to the movements of French and American shipping.

9. Napoléon Bonaparte (1769–1821), French general, first consul (1799–1804), and Emperor of the French (1804–1814/15).

waters, immediately the signals were hoisted [and communicated] from one to another, and lastly to the man-of-war ships wherever they lay stationed in the different harbours ready for action. No wonder the English took good care of the wonderful hero after he surrendered for by that act he relieved them of many a restless day and sleepless night. Such was their dread whilst Bony conquered that if an extraordinary large seagull's wing appeared on the horizon, it was in the hurry of the moment taken for French canvas, and the telescope was adjusted.

Behind us are hills and mountains of different elevations—bare, rough, and in some parts very precipitous, but as we propose confining ourselves to the space before us, the area radiating out from where we are placed, we will proceed no farther at present with any description of the bulwark behind us.

Shortening the range of our survey, we behold smaller headlands, creeks and bays, some of the latter sandy beds, some whose surfaces are smooth and level, others rough, rocky and in parts impassable, the dark colour of the rocks contrasting with the beautiful silvery white sand. At ebb tide too many parts of the coast are studded with immense black rocks but it is when these are hidden at high water, especially in calm weather, that they are dangerous to navigation; not so in stormy weather, for their position is then well known and they are seen for miles around from the white froth receding from them and from the immense height the waves rise over them. You see from a distance the mountain-blue wave coming on smoothly until reaching the island rock; it is at once turned into dazzling white, and the report arising from the contact is like thunder. What is singular is that those immense waves are not always caused by storms or the force of the wind; on the contrary such convulsions can be seen in the calmest weather, and it is well known by the seaboard men that when such a rock "speaks", a great fall of rain is approaching; another [rock] is the index for high wind; another for dry weather, and one for frost or frosty weather. So acquainted were the observing among the people with the workings of these rocks and the manner in which the waves broke, the particular roar for different states of the weather, that each rock was a weather guide in itself. Nor did they require to see them, for they could tell at the fireside by the sound which each one gave ...

The beds of some of the bays and creeks are covered over with smooth rounded stones and pebbles, converted into this shape by the continued action of the water and with the rolling and rubbing of one against another for years and ages, which causes the hardest granite to be ground down to beautiful pebbles and afterwards into sand, the smaller of the particles being always nearer the land so that at length they are blown onto dry ground, being shifted farther and farther by the action of the wind, turning other substances into the same dry nature— thus large tracts of sand have been formed; even land that had been once good and cultivated has been rendered useless by the action of the blowing sand.[10]

... Stones detached from rocks of different formation are of every conceivable form, and some are curiously bored or holed through as if by the action of worms. At the time that country looms were in use and operation, the weaver was the only one who cared much about such stones, being used by him as weights and suspended in a particular part of his machinery; this he could easily do by putting a strong cord through the hole.

... Tracing the more extended view before us and circling a little southward, the eye soon rests on an extensive flat of ground running nearly parallel to the ocean shore and separated from it by a narrow ridge of beautiful rounded hills of sand, all covered with long bent, a species of coarse grass.[11] Bent is the only kind of vegetation which first takes root in clear white sand and is the only preventative against blowing sand. It is also the only safeguard on such soils for other plants, moss and grass so that after some time the whole surface is coated over, and then the bent itself begins to decay. It can never be overtopped by the sand; no matter what shape or height the sandy hills may assume, the bent will always try and overtop it, and where the greatest shifting of sand is going on, there is to be found the longest of the bent. This species of grass is used for thatching houses and for making ropes, and is far superior to the best straw for such purposes. I have also seen it made into nice hats. It is among these hillocks of sand that beautiful clean rabbits are plentiful and where they have no difficulty forming safe retreats for themselves—but for the ingenuity of man who by his invention steps in and treacherously traps and snares the poor creatures for table use, to satisfy the appetites of those living in Liverpool or distant London.

10. From the mid-1780s, the erosion of dunes on the north coast of Donegal had caused extensive areas of arable to be covered by sand; by the 1820s Rosapenna House, a mansion built by Lord Boyne about 1700, was almost completely covered: see C. Otway, *Sketches in Ireland, descriptive of interesting portions of the counties of Donegal, Cork and Kerry* (2nd ed., Dublin, 1839), pp 13–15; W. Lancey, 'Parish of Mevagh, county Donegal, statistical report ... 1834', in Day and McWilliams, *North-east Donegal*, pp. 58, 61–2.

11. Bent, strictly *psamma arenaria*, used to refer to several unrelated types of bogland and sand grass.

Such is poor Ireland—England's pantry—so that not only the egg laid by the hen must be sent there but also the wild animals, which by the gift of nature and without any cost of production save that of setting traps and snares must go to the body already daintily stuffed. The egg the Irish-born peasant must deny himself to meet taxation, and the rabbit though within his view and reach is a trespass on law to meddle with. The rulers hold control to add to their income, and for this end appoint keepers and others to punish traversers.

This level plain is called *"Traigh-a-logh"*, the strand of the lough, for here are two strands one facing the lough, one adjoining the sea; the latter is called the *"Traigh-wain"*, the white strand.[12] The plain has been the scene of many exploits prevalent among the sturdy peasantry in the "good old times", principally horse racing, mule racing, donkey racing, and as a wind-up on such occasions came man, foolish man, for no other gain but to show—to gain applause for—the power of his breath, his lungs, the strength of his limbs, his sinews; the trial was running double the distance against another, and that other carried a man supposed to be equal in weight to the man who ran double the course ...

What encouraged [people] to keep such sports going was that in those days there were not a few who imagined that their kith and kin were superior to the generality of people and who in fact assumed themselves [to be] the "gentility." It appears that this false pride is what man cannot get rid of, [this sense of having] a seemingly higher blood than his neighbour, for we find it from the savage in the bush to the man of the present day who accumulates wealth by fraud and robbery, all the time forgetful of his ancestors. In addition to these there were others placed in a position so near approaching royalty as that important station in life an Under-agent, a Bailiff, or a Bum-bailiff.[13] In fact one belonging to the connexion of a bailiff claimed a superiority. A bailiff in those days was *somebody* and not so detestable as they are now. All these classes and their subordinates possessed power and they exercised it, forcing anyone and everyone dependent upon them, to attend them and serve them at call or bidding. Not only those who might seem to be immediately under such slavery or submission but many others [attended them]. Those who were, so to speak, independent of such authority might from other selfish motives pave the way to gaining favour with the bailiff, or even with his subordinates, [by showing

12. *Trá an Locha*, strand of the lake, stretches from Kindrum to Shannagh; *An Trá Bhán*, the white or fair strand, lies opposite it.

13. Bum-bailiff, colloquial for under-bailiff, specifically a writ-server.

themselves] on such occasions and by giving a helping hand and a good deal of cajolery; such persons would console themselves with the thought "not knowing what day it might be in the power of *such-a-one* to do *harm*." With some there were other unpleasant objects in view to gain favour: the bailiff was the medium for obtaining some paltry object detrimental to a neighbour ...

Thus the *Turf*, the only fuel used there, was cut and dried for such people by unemployed and unpaid and strange hands; the work was done at a distant place chosen solely on account of [it being a] better quality than what could be obtained nearer home, and because it was at no pecuniary loss to the owner. These "duty days" were given by many on the supposition that such and such a thing might or might not happen. At the same time the thoughts of many were anything but charitable to the governor; yet they considered [it] wisest to have the bailiff—then the highest lay functionary—as a friend for the reason that he can exercise friendship and can bestow a gift at no loss to himself but at the expense of some other. So when the day approached for drawing home the turf, scouts went around a day or two previously to warn people, so that they might be in readiness and for no one to have an excuse next morning every animal capable of carrying any burden was on its way to the bog, no matter what the distance. Word was passed round by the overseers and idlers that as soon as the turf would be all gathered in and the stack completed, the sports, that is to say the *races*, would commence. This induced all who were fond of sport to work and make all others work and drive harder, and so by united exertions long before the time of the setting sun, men and horses were encamped on the "strand", not indeed before the surrounding hillocks were already crowded with spectators, young and old from all directions far and near, to witness the sports.

One corner of the ground resembled a market place: here were the fruit sellers, the cake and candy sellers; there was a tent erected by someone who had the privilege of having his name printed on a board, stuck over his door when at home, in addition to the words, common on such signs, "Licence for selling spirits"; in the present situation of things, as it was impossible for him to carry the house, it appeared that the transfer of the "board" was a sufficient guarantee to protect the tent. At this time the officers of the Revenue seemed satisfied wherever the board was exhibited. In other words, the signboard was a protection, but if the officers of the law came the rounds, how in the absence of the board would the house look wanting its security? Luckily the Constabulary men had no power to interfere at this time, else the scale might soon turn. The man under the shelter of the shadow of the board acted with boldness and authority in distributing his liquids; nevertheless he did not have it all to himself: at a short distance in some secluded corner out of sight of the police—for the Revenue and peace preservers attended such places—hovered about the "shebeen woman" with her jar and bottle and pocket horn, depending on her own customers for a call.[14] She was not unknown to her friends and was also sure to get her share of patronage, and why not—"her stuff was just as good as whiskey that licence was paid for" and, what was better, if a friend ran "short of change" a whisper to her opened the way.

The promoters of the races would meet, certain rules laid down, distances set up, and starting points scored out; then came the betting, the picking out of horses supposed to be well matched, or if there was any on whom money had been laid "to run at the races" such always got first chance on the course. The other animals, those belonging to insignificant parties, got leave to go out afterwards in threes and fours at a time, and often a man's horse was taken contrary to his wishes and set on the course to keep the sports going. The owner of the winning horse got as a first prize, a bridle, value about eighteen pence or two shillings, the second a piece of iron, "real *Swedish*" which was supposed to make a full set of horse shoes; sometimes this piece of iron could be turned into three shoes, but seldom if ever the "set" [of four]. The third and fourth horses came in neglected and unseen—and got nothing. Such was the paltry reward given, but the name was enough for the sports.

At this horse racing, disputes very often arose as to foul play after a few hasty words, a free fight would very likely be the result, with much noise and confusion for some time; or else an agreement was struck and as a method of final settlement, the same horses went over the same ground again to settle the prize.

As darkness is setting in, a donkey race is proclaimed, and everyone who is not afraid of getting himself trampled upon by twenty others joins in pursuit of this race, and so half the crowd is in commotion. But it often times happened that the one supposed to be the swiftest or best runner disappointed its friends not through the fault of the poor brute, but should the donkey miss its footing and stumble, or be crushed to

14. *Síbín*, unlicensed dram-shop, speakeasy. The Irish Constabulary was a highly centralized paramilitary police force established in 1822 and reformed in 1836. The Revenue Police was established as a disciplined institution with a centralized command structure in 1836. At its peak it had 1,100 men and a steamer to patrol western coasts and islands. By the time the force was dissolved in 1857 the prevalence of illicit distillation had greatly declined.

earth by force, a crowd is soon on the top of it and all hopes of winning are lost, for during the time this struggle is going on the other animal is forced or almost carried forward to the winning post. By the time darkness precludes any further racing, other sports are set on foot such as dancing to the music of the fiddle or the bagpipe, and by the time all are on their way home the uprising of the lark shows the sign of morn, and the following day is lost in sleep, or the time is taken up in telling stories of how the feats of the previous day passed. Such is a sketch of the races on the "strand" when reckoned satisfactory or good.

This same ground is also memorable for its *camman* play, now called by the name of "hurly-game."[15] The best of the men picked from the opposite parts of the parish met here and an equal number of men were set to face each other for the start; then each side commenced in earnest to take away the ball or "bool." This ball, made of hard wood, was sunk in the ground and two men, one on each side, began to unearth it, pick it up, and try to have the first blow sent in his own direction. A good deal of sparring went on at this interval, during which time their abettors had their eyes strained, waiting for their turn. The ball at length got over ground and the game started with at first fair play and regularity; soon discipline was forgotten as the players got heated, order was broken up, and each side strove by every means, foul or fair, to win mastery. For years all these sports have been at an end and the green grass has got leave to grow over the greater part of the plain; only the breadth of a road in the middle is still beaten up by travellers.

We now withdraw our extended view and the eye soon settles on two or three beautiful green hills, one of which is close to the head of the large lake already spoken of. The sight of this green hill recalls to memory a subject of a more pathetic nature: maybe from its natural position wonderfully secluded from the invasion of enemies, it was chosen as one of the spots where the Divine Worship was performed, that is the Holy Sacrifice offered up under the open canopy of Heaven. Or in other words where in those days a *scallan,* a rude shed, was the only means of shelter for the persecuted celebrant and his faithful followers.[16] The pious worshippers came from afar and with faith enough to guide them, in fact forced on by that inherent gift, the spark of Divine Faith. Though trembling in body [but with] the faith of their fathers and the love of

---

15. *Camán,* hurley-stick, hurl, hence 'common', a name for a form of hurling. For common, see L. P. Ó Caithnia, *Scéal na hiomána: Ó thosach ama go 1884* [Hurling's story: From the beginning to 1884] (Baile Átha Cliath, 1980); K. Whelan, 'The geography of hurling', in *History Ireland* vol. I, no. I (Spring 1993), 27–31.

16. *Scáthlán,* open-ended shelter.

God predominating, they made their way to the *scallan*, knelt around it, having nothing to cover them in all and every vicissitude of weather; underneath was the green sod, or a flagstone to protect the knees from the effects of the mud in wet weather. Here then was well enough exemplified the words of the Great Master of the Universe: "The foxes have holes and the birds of the air have nests &c."[17] And worse than this: the foxes and wolves have taken possession of the shelter. For their former sanctified and saintly shelter, once their house, their forefather's house of worship a few miles distant, is now in the hands of the stranger.[18] I say house of worship for the reason that the word "church" was then and there understood by all the people as being that of a Protestant place of worship, and "chapel" alone that of the Roman Catholics. In the same way the two religions were distinguished and were designated "Clan-na-gael"—Catholic—and "Clan-na-gal"—Protestant, or shortened "Gael" and "Gal", and "Galtagh" meaning a Protestant of any denomination or description.[19]

In this house of which I make mention, the forefathers of the now persecuted met years long before, when religion was undisturbed. But they were dispossessed and forced to abandon it at the time that the strong arm oppressed the weak. This edifice of four walls stood in its place as when built by the saints, and somehow or other had escaped the demolition which befell many of its kindred structures in many other places. But as I say, it had passed into other hands, the hands of the stranger, and a sight of the old walls thereof was now more shunned, and the old structure now more hated, by the descendants of the old inhabitants than it was once venerated by their forefathers. Whether from a real or imaginary odour arising from the persons of the late appropriators or from whatever cause, whether the house was opened or not opened, the descendants of the ancients could and would pass it with a side look or no look at all.

Preachers may say with an air of piety "I love", or "Love your enemies", but I say it is the last rule, if ever, put in practice, and I would like to see the best preacher do it himself for an example. In my own lifetime of over half a century I could enumerate just two and only *two*

---

17. Luke 9:58.

18. The parish church at Rosnakill became a Church of Ireland place of worship in the 1600s; it was rebuilt by subscription in 1785: see Lancey, 'Clondavaddog, 1835', p. 4; E. Maguire, *A history of the diocese of Raphoe* (Dublin, 1920), pt. I, vol. I, pp 316–17; J. B. Leslie, *Raphoe clergy and parishes* (Enniskillen, 1940), p. 53.

19. *Clan na nGael, Clanna Gael*, Gaels, Catholics; *Clan na nGall, Clanna Gall*, foreigners, Protestants; *Gallda*, foreign, Protestant.

men in their lifetimes who showed that they loved their neighbours as themselves, that is they would not be revenged when they could have been. If we consider this, it is not to be wondered at that the poor down-trodden and persecuted race could [?not] so easily conform to Scripture injunctions when their betters and better educated in worldly affairs would not do so. Even at the present day in ease and freedom [the point] is still good—[we see] not forgiveness and forgetfulness, but revenge and spite in all grades of society. Why do men go to law for the least tri-fling cause—to be revenged? Why do men foam with rage at the least insult—surely this is not the charity they seem to profess?

The very walls of the old building had become dismal and repulsive looking, stripped of any attractive ornament, inside and outside, on which the eye might look or learn. Even the very emblem on which the Christian loves to look—that emblem of hope, the Cross—was pulled down, nowhere to be seen.

The only thought or concern which at that time carried men's minds towards this place lay in the necessity of using the church-yard, for as yet persons of all creeds had to be interred in the old burial place. And when the rightful owners, now the dispossessed, oppressed, weather-beaten community, had to perform the mournful duty of burying their dead, the same was carried out in dread silence and, if not really beg-ging to get permission, it was the same in form at least, for leave had to be got from a gate-keeper to open it, and there was a dread of liberty of entrance being refused in having first to intercede with a man who had no sympathy with the friends of the deceased, differing from them in religion, and if law would allow the dead to be overground, he would in his feeling hardly give leave to bury their dead [sic].

The "Minister", for want of a better name, the Government officer on whom this confiscated property was bestowed for the time being, attended there once a week in company with his own large family. [He would] drive to and from in coach and car, attended by butler and dri-ver in brass buttons and uniform, as great a sight in those days, as big an eye opener, as a railway train in after years. Following the Minister and his attendants were a couple of squire landlords, each with a simi-lar vehicle, and carrying half a dozen or so more decrepit, humped and crippled old women or dry maids—ladies as they were called—a Miss Hannah or a Miss Bessy, muffled in furs and cushions. So rapidly were they going at horse-flesh speed that if a poor man differing from them in his manner of praying, or—what was proof enough—carrying a frieze coat to his back, happened to be on the road, his only refuge was knee-deep in the mud of the ditch along the roadside, so as to save himself from being run over or trampled upon by spirited horses.

This was the compassion, the charitable feeling, of those Gospel readers, returning from what they call a message of prayer. If we consider that this would be the hasty return time, to the enjoyment of a hot dinner when the stomach is as much thought of as the soul, we may make a certain allowance for such break-neck speed, but then there is very little sign or appearance of charity in the act of driving a human being, the same perhaps hungry too, into the mud. In addition to those spoken of, there were forty or more corpulent farmers, men of extraordinary size in every limb, blue-faced, sulky looking and very easily distinguished even by any stranger. For although in some the fat beef showed in the cheek, yet the blue pattern, inverted rainbow-like under the eyes, was never wanting in all. Close to the skirts of the parents came members of their families, clownish looking young sprouts, splay-footed and big headed, carrying large books under their arms; whether arising from innate nature or from whatever cause, so shy were they, and so much afraid of the appearance of a stranger, that on the approach of such their retreat was immediately to the leeward of their protectors, taking hold of his or their skirts, and keeping watching the passer-by until a safe distance was gained.

Whether such traits arose from their late importation, or from the fact of their being nestled on the fattest soil, or probably both—the churchmen were in fact easily known by their appearance alone, differing from the true rosy-cheeked, the small frame and the light of foot—his neighbours on the hillsides, the descendants of the Celts.

Let us contrast here the different ways of going to [worship], see the ease, the luxury of one compared with the poor persecuted race in which we may instance the grey-haired old man with his staff in one hand, his hat in the other to ease perspiration, hurrying along; the old woman also is in sight, accompanied by her stout, healthy, rosy-cheeked, simply but cleanly clad daughter, at a convenient distance to render assistance to the old one if necessary. Not far off heading in the same direction is the light-of-foot young man trotting on, each and every one having before them the task of surmounting the hills, the rugged paths, the bogs, the byways and nearways, and all watching the sun as their guide for the time of day, hoping not to be too late to fulfil the object of that never-dying faith, the love of God, for which and for whom they knew they were created, to whose presence as they knew they were then hurrying, to their hidden and lonely place of worship,

Lag-na-haltara, no house, no temple, no shelter, simply the "Valley of the Altar."[20] So many long years had passed with this state of things that the people became accustomed to it, losing all hope of their condition being ever improved, such worldly outcasts as they seemed to be. But at the thought of one man, all other considerations were expelled, the house, the temple, the shelter were forgotten—enough for them that there was their consoler, the *Soggart-a-roon.*[21]

Time makes many changes in every state, and so in this: in the course of years as if by a special gift, as if by a coincidence with the will of the Great Giver of all things, or as if in reward for their patience and sufferings, their faith and piety, a good landlord rose up, who felt so generous as to listen to their petition and grant the site for a suitable house of worship, at and within a few feet of the place—the very place sanctified by them—where the people and their faithful pastor together prayed so often before.[22] Thus had they the pleasure when they came into possession of the new house of constantly beholding their old place of prayer, and like the one who clings to the homestead they felt naturally satisfied in being near to it.

So overjoyed had these poor people been in hearing the glad news of getting a chance for erecting a house in honour of their Redeemer that the men of each household within a certain distance rushed to the nearest quarry, competing as to who would be the first man to come on the ground for the intended site with a stone on his back, or carried in his arms, whose name would therefore be held in honour and remembrance as the first assisting at the building. Until the chapel was built men carried stones on their backs and shoulders of their own free will so that the work might speedily proceed, and those having horses gave their assistance and every possible spare time in drawing stones, lime and sand, early and late. All these united exertions, in money as in labour, being so willingly put together their work soon came to an end: in the year of grace 1838 a neat house of worship was completed sufficient for their accommodation. This edifice stands at the head of the great lake close to the water's edge, and its whitewashed walls look more beautiful from the effects of the reflection of the sun's rays off the surface of the water.

20. *Lag na hAltóra,* hollow of the altar, 'mass-rock' in Ballyhoorisky; after the erection of Fanavolty chapel, people from the immediate locality who were too old or infirm to attend Sunday mass went to *Lag na hAltóra* to pray: see Roinn Bhéaloideas Éireann, 705, 427–31.

21. *A shagairt a rúin,* oh, dearest priest; the use of this expression to denote a priest regarded with great affection by his parishioners was well established in English by the mid-nineteenth century.

22. Nathaniel, 2nd earl of Leitrim (1768–1854), was the landlord of Fanavolty when the chapel was erected.

... Pursuing our ocular survey southwards as if completing the circle we are suddenly cut short by the long ridge of mountains, yet nearer to hand and partly detached from them rising almost perpendicular from the water's edge is a hill of a very uncomely shape; it is somewhat like a huge dromedary reared on its hind legs. Two sides as well as the hind part of this hill are rising nearly perpendicular and the top, or back, is nearly as dangerous to tread upon as the sides, for it is shaped so that if an object is put in motion upon it it would undoubtedly be precipitated into the dark waters of the lake below, the waters rendered dark by the shadows cast by the unsightly hill. From the shape and situation of this hill may be understood its usefulness and the security it afforded to the worshippers at the *scallan* in the age of persecution, when a certain class of men called by the name of Yeomen thought it a service to their king to hunt down, take prisoner or kill a priest or papist, and banish and frighten his flock.[23] It was therefore for safety's sake that such out-of-the-way places were chosen, and they were protected here on one side by the lake, fully a mile long, on the other side by the mountain. The only route by which the enemy could arrive, and that with some difficulty too, was [along here;] therefore when the enemy was seen at the distance, sufficient time was at the disposal of the little congregation to disperse and to hide.

The thought may occur to the reader that the rehearsal of this is going too far back into unpleasant history. But he will be convinced otherwise if he takes into consideration that close upon the era of Emancipation itself in backward parts of this country, where there was no law, no protection but what was in the hands of the ascendancy party, there they and those in alliance with them kept the wheels of terror, the dregs of penal laws, going on long after the real persecution ceased in many other places, and this so long as their acts were hidden from the knowledge of the outside world.[24] In fact, the first relief was not from Government, but were the result of contentions among themselves.

The foot of the unsightly hill is also memorable for witnessing the rash act of one of the inhabitants in the neighbourhood: he had been reprimanded by his priest for some bad deeds, the mention of which would be disagreeable to the ear. At all events [the man] being incorri-

23. The term 'yeomen' is used not in the specific sense of members of the counter-revolutionary yeomanry corps raised by the Government in 1796, but in the looser sense of armed and mounted Protestants, operating as members of (earlier) local militia corps, or as informal paramilitaries.

24. Referring to 1829 and the concession to Catholics of the right to sit in Westminster and hold most high offices.

gible sought to vent his wrathful feelings and temporarily satisfy himself, and to show contempt of the religion which he then forsook; his first open act of apostasy was to throw his *beads* into this deep and dark hole at the foot of the hill. It is said, and on no way doubtful authority, that this same man not many years after died miserably mad in his barn, being tied up there to prevent him doing harm to others, and that when found dead, his body was fastened upon and in the act of being devoured by rats. Be that as it may, he died, and his descendants of the first generation hated the religion renounced by him with more bitterness than did those who were longer removed from the old stock. His descendants however enjoyed the world's substance and had the rich and the powerful to associate with, which is in great measure a remedy for stifling the remorse of conscience, and some of that race, to the writer's own knowledge, possessed worldly substance much beyond many of their deserving neighbours; in fact, work or no work, sleeping or waking, wealth was flowing to them. But so niggardly were the young and old of them that the possession thereof was to them no enjoyment. They were the only Protestant family in the locality and were surrounded by Roman Catholics who never showed any ill feeling towards them on account of what happened or whence they sprung, and they and their neighbours were always on friendly terms.

In after years there lived in the neighbourhood one by the name Stephen Macaroon,[25] who was now old, and through age and rheumatism he greatly deviated from his original upright shape; he could do no work, but for all that he could not be kept at home, and he went about with a bit of a short stick sufficient in length, when added to the stretch of his arm, to support his side, and he used to call often at this dwelling to get newspaper news of which he was very fond. One day being tired on the road, conversing with whomsoever he met, he walked in, his object being on this day as much to relieve his limbs as anything else. But to his disappointment it was a Friday, and a female descendant of the above—a toothless old hag—was sitting at the fireside eating, or rather trying to rake beef off an old bone with such a machine as she had, and her visitor coming unawares upon her; trying to get out of her dilemma, to give a cloak to her act and to exhibit her scriptural abilities, she at once addressed Stephen, "What goeth into the mouth defileth not the soul, Stephen." Stephen was taken rather suddenly, being unprepared for any controversy, was hardly seated, and did not get time to ease his aching limbs. He was not in temper just then for

25. Pseudonym. Dorian uses pseudonyms for many characters sketched in the Narrative.

convincing proofs, but he gave his reply as short and as rough as possible: "Pray madam, did you ever read that Eve ate the Apple in the opposite direction." Exit Stephen. He immediately threw his left arm under the flap of his coat, disappeared, paddled off muttering.

... Perhaps in no other locality in Ireland can so many "*cashels*" or, as they were supposed to be, Danish *raths* be seen.[26] *Cashel-More* has already been alluded to. It stands at an elevation commanding a view of the country for many miles in all directions inland, and for more than forty miles of ocean coast. The traces of no less than six minor castles can also be pointed out, not to mention many mounds, foundations, and other formations ...

What is most singular about each and every one of the *cashels* is that the foundations on which they stood were destined by nature to be remarkably strong. The natural foundation and formation [are similar] from the greater to the smaller with the same quality of solid rock of a hard bluish colour or of the nature approaching flint stone. These wonderfully natural foundations for strongholds moulded alike at the Creation would from their shape and situation convey the idea that in the earth's revolution from west to east, while the crust was in formation and before the dry land had assumed its solid form, one immense wave swept away the soft material or clayey substance of all such places on the western side, leaving them bare, almost isolated, for all easily moveable substance has been shifted away from their bases, thereby leaving the rock bare, and [in a westerly] direction almost perpendicular. The east side of each of these isolated rocks is connected with the adjoining land by a narrow stripe of earth, and on the tops of such rocks were built the "*cashels*" or castles in circular *raths*. Before the introduction of gunpowder in warfare, these strongholds would be most difficult to capture. On the western side access was nearly impossible, and on the eastern side only one narrow entrance had to be defended. This entrance was rendered narrower and made more difficult of approach by a trench and the removal of earth; therefore one or two men could oppose and defeat their number twenty times over ...

... Opinions are divided as to the use of these strongholds; some men say that they belong to the time of the pagans of old, and that such places were residences for their princes and for religious observances. Others give as their opinion, and with some degree of proof too, that they were strongholds of the Danes. Assuming that they were constructed and held by the Danes, their enemies must have been in the sur-

26. *Ráth*, fort, especially earthen ring-fort.

rounding neighbourhood, and the original inhabitants must still have been numerous to need such forts for the invader's preservation.

A more likely opinion is that the Danes in after years found their strength decreasing and that their few numbers were in perfect security within these walls, so that when their brethren from Scandinavia made descents on these coasts for the purpose of plunder, such places were to them refuge fortresses; from their commanding height signals could be given from one to another while engaged in collecting the spoils or while making a retreat. It is said that those Northmen would arrive yearly in their long boats and, assisted by the men of such garrisons, carry away everything they could take hold of back to their own country.

Many places from the sea to the mountain will ever retain the name of the scene of a deadly conflict between natives and marauders. But as the natives designated every stranger of that description by the term *Albanagh,* or Scotchman, naturally supposing them to come from the land nearest, that suffix is generally added to the names of particular places—such as *"Ard-a-nalb-ny"*, meaning the hillock where the foreigner was killed. *Albnagh* strictly means Scotchman, but it came to be applied to "Protestant", and in this part of the country is so used in the Irish language. But for the three nationalities they use the words:— *Erinagh—Albnagh—Sassanagh.*[27]

... There are many artificial underground caverns in this district. Of one or two of them tradition gives fabulous accounts: their size is immense, they are to be used for the safety of the elect, those who are to be saved from the wars when the time comes for the downfall of England but before that final overthrow—when Ireland is to be almost cleared of human beings. The location of one of these in particular is known, but the entrance is long ago lost (owing to the fact that only one man in a particular tribe and family had the gift to find it out). This is the belief among the peasantry, and the writer was personally acquainted with one man who prided himself as being the then custodian of the secret. Unfortunately now all of that tribe have disappeared, the last having emigrated along with his friends to America and carried the secret with him; many attempts have been made by the next of kin, as yet fruitless, so the entrance is still in obscurity.

The *"Caluraghs"*, or as they are called "Calvaries" or ancient burial places, are also memorials of the past, and are generally marked by one

---

27. *Éireannach,* Irish person; *Albanach,* Scots person, Protestant, especially Presbyterian; *Ard an Albanaigh,* the Scotsman's hillock; *Sasanach,* English person, Protestant, especially member of the Church of Ireland.

or two upright granite stones uncommonly long, standing in a nearly perpendicular position to the present day the like of which cannot be got in the neighbourhood so that it is certain the stones were brought from afar.[28] The people in their traditional simplicity called them "giant finger stones", and say that they were flung from incredible distances and fixed by giants. The people are careful not to remove or meddle with such stones or to cultivate the ground within a reasonable distance of the supposed plot of ground. Indeed wherever such places are to be met, they are remarkable for the extreme softness and greenness of grass. On some few occasions, strong-headed men had the audacity to till such ground, but the result showed labour lost as no crop was reaped for, if it grew, it ran uncommonly high to the top and never came to ripeness or maturity and, what was still worse, in the language of the people, "the world did not go well with the man who thus trespassed ever after." Worldly losses or sudden deaths were always noted by the neighbours as the punishment or, as they would say, reward for such foolhardiness, never thinking that such misfortunes also happened to those who never dug such *rich* soils. It had the effect of preventing others from meddling with them.

In such places, the *unconsecrated* graves of the unbaptised are to be met with, over which no animal will graze, and if a human being accidentally walked over so as to come in contact with one of the graves, he was sure to get a crust of ugly warts on his feet or hands or perhaps both, so that such spots are carefully avoided. Perhaps intentionally and with good reason, it is instilled into the minds of the young the danger, and danger was exaggerated to make them keep at a distance.

Next come the "Beds of Dermod and Graina", one of which on nearly every hillside is to be found, the simple formation of which, so far as can be seen at the present, consists of a nearly circular form made up of flat stones, set upright or in a slanting position, and such enclosures are supposed to be the resting places of those famous runaways.[29] Certainly the strength of the two even when combined was more than ordinary, for some of the stones are of a very large size and they must

28. *Cealdrach,* pre-Christian burial ground.

29. *Leapacha Dhiarmada agus Ghráinne,* the beds of Diarmuid and Gráinne, popular name for neolithic portal graves or dolmens. *Tóraíocht Dhiarmada agus Ghráinne* (the pursuit of Diarmuid and Gráinne) was a well-known story in *An Fhiannaíocht,* the 'Fenian' or Ossianic cycle in which the central characters are Fionn Mac Cumhaill, his son Oisín, and the members of their warrior band *Na Fianna.* The tales can be found be in manuscripts dating from the eighth century and are well represented in oral tradition: see D. Ó hÓgáin, *Myth, legend and romance: An encyclopædia of the Irish folk tradition* (New York, 1991), pp. 168, 203–8, 213–23, 350–3.

have had a very busy time of it planning and constructing so many and at the same time removing from place to place. If an opinion was allowable, I would rather say that such places were constructed by the inhabitants to give shelter to their herdsmen. In remote days each townland had one, and this would be their look-out while watching their flocks, but such opinions would not be listened to by the natives at present. In proof of the latter supposition, it is known that in olden times every townland had its herd who followed no other occupation, only taking care of all the sheep and some of the cattle, and special privileges were allotted to each, such as a free dwelling [and] plots of ground free of rent, and such lands are to the present day called "Herd's Park" &c. It is said that the father of Graina, a warlike and powerful man, pursued Dermod for years until his wrath cooled down with a feeling of the greatest animosity, but that he never could get him in view, and in his anxiety the only information he could get regarding him was obtained by biting his thumb, from which he derived only the knowledge whether Dermod at that particular time slept on sand or on heather, meaning coast or hill. Dermod found means to evade the pursuit of his enemy, having such knowledge of course by the advice of his wife Graina, and for this end he carried with him both sand and heather, and while he slept on the hill he spread the sand under himself, and made his bed on heather while sleeping on the sand. [It is] something in substance like the story told of the fool George when he stood before the king in England and on Irish soil at the same time, the Irish clay being in his shoes or boots.[30]

The ancient stone altars are still in their original simple shape and preservation, except the marks of time—the moss, the briar, or the ivy— are encroaching. In some places, they may be partially covered for the reason that most of them were built under the shelter of a projecting rock. The natives still look with veneration on such places and disturb them they would not, as they very well know that these simple constructions are momentoes of the dreadful persecutions suffered by their forefathers for their religion and of the dangers their clergy underwent for the sake of the people. The respect for such places is such that I have seen old men take off their head-dress when passing them, and old people of a Sunday when not able to go farther go there to say their prayers and find relief in doing so. Curiously enough too, explorers and visitors of other religions at the present day feel a certain regard for visiting such spots. This I can vouch for having seen it myself. What is curious but

30. Fool George: not identified.

not to be wondered at, with respect to such simple monuments and their construction, is that the greatest care was taken in selecting the most hidden places [but where] from their commanding position there was still a view of the farthest off distance possible so that worshippers could hardly be taken by surprise.

It is true that this part of the country is described as not much wooded, but about the neat cottages, many of which are in sight, are clumps of trees of different varieties affording shelter and ornament, but nowhere can we lose sight of the sturdy old hawthorn with its branches drooping invariably to the east. The explanation given for this peculiarity is that in ancient times a certain king reigned in Ireland and so wicked was he, and in detestation of his wickedness, the Great Ruler of the Universe caused the wind during this wicked king's reign to blow from only one direction, that is from the west, or as the people say "from the *Ard-garve*"—*Ard* means high and *Garve* meaning coarse or stormy.[31] *Ard-garve* is always understood by the peasantry to signify the western direction, and a storm arising from which is the only one they are in dread of. The westerly winds are always the most destructive here, and therefore the wise people make preparations at the right time to secure their cottages to meet and overcome the effects of the high winds, which generally come at regular times. Skill is also considered when cottages are being built to keep them close to a hill or rock and to have the same between them and the storm. Very often a storm comes on while their crop is growing and at such a time they see their property lost without being able to render assistance.

Our description comes to a conclusion, and we are still supposed to be where we began at the head of the Glen from where we commenced our survey. Once more we take a hasty and final glance in a general way over smooth and rounded green hills, bogs and lakes, ending at the entrance to the Glen, [a spot to which] we must return in another phase of our story.

---

31. *An aird gharbh*, the direction from which a storm comes.

CHAPTER 2
Method and Source of Literary Instruction

The Irish have always been remarkable for two things: they have ever been a religious and a knowledge-seeking people. The history of the world bears testimony—the fact is too plain to need proof. At home virtue solid and true is practised, and abroad that virtue which forms part of their very being is proclaimed to the world by their purity of morals and their unimpeachable character.

It is sad then to think that even so late as the year 1838 the people of a certain district, as well off I suppose as many others and a large and populous one in Christian Ireland too, had no house of worship in which they might meet and adore that God whom they loved so much—Him who made heaven and earth, the Lord of prince and peasant. This being so, we can conclude at once what state education was for a certain class. A short inquiry will not be out of place. The subject is an unpleasant one, but the reader may find interest in recalling to mind the hardships his fathers endured for him, and learn not to blame their ignorance but to glory in their virtue.

The contrast between our own times and half a century ago is wonderful. Nothing can better describe it than a sketch of the old schools and schoolmasters—now teachers—and the many disadvantages both they and the people laboured under. Little do we know of the scanty means and straightened opportunities that were then afforded for the accomplishment of reading and writing in the backward parts of the country. The fact is we should marvel that anything worthy of the name of learning existed at all and that everything of the kind was not entirely forgotten. Thus was lost the material for many a gem in literature—yes, many a bright and giant genius was born and did not even "blush unseen", who with opportunities would have been famous in the annals of history. The lives of many poor Irishmen who left their old homes and travelled to distant lands prove what I say.

Few of our modern scholars can realize the position of those in the past. Schools are now at easy distances, books and other requisites are fairly cheap and, what is of greater importance, there is not only no hindrance to their attending school, but rather an inducement. The case was not so in olden times. True, many had good places of education, but they were those who belonged to the church of the minority, or in other words to the church propped upon bayonets. But alas, this was useless to the vast numbers who belonged to them not. These had an intention of attending such schools much the same as if they did not exist. The poor inhabitants kept aloof from them, from such places, as much as they shunned the new church—their own old chapel—both were alike to them; and admission into one was as detestable as admission into the other. In other words the tomb was welcome when compared with either. There were indeed some few of the upper class to be found who sent their children to the "respectable schools", but I can testify from experience that for the most part, after growing up weak in their own faith and wanting proper religious training, their career was sad and their end miserable.

Such examples did much good, for thus was strengthened and stereotyped the belief that the parish schools were best to be avoided.[32] There is implanted in the heart of man a craving for knowledge. In some this passion is stronger than in others, but it is true of all. How many good fathers and mothers do we see—yes fathers and mothers who suffered in youth—how many of them I say, be they ever so illiterate, anxious to give that opportunity to their children that was denied to themselves! Poor parents may be seen who are struggling and working out their life's blood to give their little family all they can give—some education. This their fortune, this their bequest.

One is inclined when recalling to memory scenes of the past to have mingled feelings of sorrow and joy, glory and shame; sorrow for the hardships of his poor fellow countrymen, joy at their perseverance; glory at their acquirements, such as they were, and shame not for them,

---

32. The Church of Ireland rector maintained a parish school at Cashel Glebe.

but to think that human nature could be so cruel towards them. How extremely ignorant, how wilfully blind, must the bigot be of the present day who accuses the Irish of ignorance. The Irish, especially those living on the mountain sides and on the sea coast, deprived of every means for the acquisition of knowledge. Why did they go to the shelter of the hedges or the shady side of the hill to meet the old schoolmaster? Simply because no roof [existed], as not a few perches of ground could they get on any account from the rulers of the soil whereon to build a cabin for a school house. We ask then how they could be skilled in letters when every means were shut out from them. Is it because they kept alive their native language that they are called ignorant? The German, the Frenchman is not reputed ignorant for using his native language in Ireland, but the Irishman is mocked at, is in fact something from another world, in short is ignorant, if he uses his native language on Irish soil.

At the time they were thus suffering under such unequal laws, when a letter was to be written a despatch was sent forthwith four or five miles to someone who could write it as it should be written, or address it as it should be addressed. For this a fee of course was exacted. Sometimes the *scrivener* was invited to the house, and here in addition to the usual sum he was entertained with a hospitality far beyond the employer's means, and all this to ensure complete satisfaction as the work was then done in the presence and hearing of the whole family ...[33]

Again on rent day, learning and wit were often put to the test to find out the last receipt. Perhaps the cleanest piece of paper was a guide, or it might be that the edge was turned up, but in most cases the agent had some ransacking through a bundle. This is now a thing of the past, and we are happy to be able to say that there are few families which all cannot read and write, and perform their family transactions without an interpreter.

The American letter was then a thing as anxiously awaited and as joyously received as an estate out of chancery. Crowds of people might be seen loitering about the village post office on days longingly looked forward to casting eager glances for the letter carrier.[34] At length he arrives, enters, and immediately a rush is made towards the door. The post-master was always obliging enough, even though he put himself to a disadvantage to let as many of the hopeful inquirers into the room as it could conveniently hold. They often delayed both him and themselves, but human nature is ever curious. The fatal moment has come—

33. *Scríbhneoir*, writer.
34. The post-office was in Tamney.

the bag is opened—the letters fall out, and one may see if there are any American envelopes in the lot from the bright beaming countenances. But how do they know yet? They know it well, for at that time there were yellow envelopes peculiar to the "Americans". Sometimes the old postmaster would come out himself to see if the mails were coming. He had a sundial outside the door and this he should read every time Phoebus illumined the land to satisfy the people as to the hour.

The letter carriers however little heeded the unerring sundial. The duty of carrying the mail was equally divided between two—Tammey and George. The distance was about ten miles. They went up and down, each on alternate days, and Tammey had the reputation of being a better pedestrian than George. Poor George was nearly always blamed for the delay: he never fell out with the "barley-bree", indeed was a little too fond of it and, wonderful to say, even when he took it in moderation it had an effect on him different from what it had on most men.[35] Instead of making him increase his velocity it only stupefied him and caused him to slacken. His shortcomings though many were not grave, and they were often and easily forgiven. One day after having struggled well and kept the "top of the road" till he was near the end of his homeward journey, he unfortunately lost his centre of gravity just at the door of the police barracks and fell at his full length, bag and baggage. The vigilant sergeant soon collared him, deprived him of his bag, took to himself the honour of conveying it the rest of the journey, summoned him to petty sessions and had him fined. Poor George! Other misdemeanours of a similar kind cropped up and he was finally dismissed.

A postman in the backward districts often presented a curious appearance; now he was bespattered with mud, and again covered with dust; but he always carried the sealed bag strapped on his back, the most conspicuous part of which, the centre, was ornamented with a brass plate and stamped with the insignia H.M. Mails—it might mean His or Her Majesty's.

The distribution of the letters was rather a difficult thing. There were always first admitted into the post office a privileged few, such as the village doctor, the minister's butler, a policeman &c. The directions were all read aloud as the letters were sorted. Greater respect was always given to the "Americans", smaller ones and those made up in the old fashion of folding the sheet in two being laid aside for the present. This being done, the bulk of the crowd began to disperse. Dick and Tom were constant attendants at every arrival, and they were assailed by the

35. Barley bree, whiskey.

crowd standing outside to tell for whom and for what localities letters had arrived. This being done, speedy feet were soon on the way and when they came to a house too much out of the way but for which a letter was lying at the post office, they shouted to the parties in the fields about the good news for so and so, and the story passed through the neighbours like wild fire, everyone conjecturing what the news might be.

The postmaster had his own difficulties in delivering the letters. He was not much acquainted with the people; he held no intercourse with them; he had the disadvantage of not being a native, and the number of those who had the same Christian name and surname was legion. Thus was he often perplexed to know whether or not he was giving a letter to the right owner. What aggravated matters was the responsibility attached to the delivery of American letters. It was the same as if they were cheques.

There was a curious way and I believe it still exists of distinguishing between so many families who had the same name occurring in them. Among those who called frequently at the post office—a strange fact the postmaster thought—there were no Abels, no Adams, no Noahs, no Samuels, no Isaacs, but of Johns, Pats there was no end, also James and Michaels. How ever were these to be distinguished, the surnames being the same? In this way—John the son of James (John Hemus); John the son of Pat (John Paddy); John the son of young Pat, John John Ogue; John Bawn (White); John Roe (Red). As yet John senior or John junior had too much of the Latin attached to be understood. Many had their occupation or trade affixed, such as Cahir Cooper, that is Charles the cooper; John Tailor, James Carpenter; Sheumas na-brogue, meaning James the shoemaker, and these appendices were hereditary in the family, whether such members followed the trade or not. Often the mother's name was introduced as Hugh Kitty Thomas, that is Hugh the son of Kitty, the daughter of Thomas.

The above-named Dick was often called into the office to give some assistance at interpretation. This he did willingly whenever called on. Dick knew every townland and every one in it, the genealogy of every family, and he had the advantage, though a Protestant, of being able to speak the Irish language fairly, for he mixed among the people and was on very intimate terms with them. He had little or nothing to do and lived chiefly on an income which descended from the time of the Ulster settlement. This income consisted of the rents and other appurtenances arising from a couple of townlands tenanted by Roman Catholics, and at this time nearly all speaking the Irish language. Dick from his infancy had occasion to visit them regularly. Not only that, but he took a notion that he would go and live for weeks among them. To this can be attributed his knowledge of the Irish language. This circumstance shows the free, the forgiving nature of the descendants of the old Irish, for though still suffering in the dregs of persecution, now mitigated, yet would they hold no ill feeling towards those, individually, who differed from them. Not only that, but should a single Protestant happen to be in a locality surrounded by no one but Roman Catholics he had the quietude of life [sic], he above all others was the only person unmolested just because he was such and lest he might think that any evil was thought towards him.

Dick was truly a wonderful character. In dress and general appearance he was like a common day-labourer—there being no great difference between them, the latter often did some work, the former never did any. If idleness is one of the qualifications for a gentleman he was surely one. He was to be seen at every hour of the day: no matter how early you might start, or how late you might return, Dick was sure to be the first and last you saw, and no two could meet in conversation on the village street without Dick making a trio of it. His religious life was something mysterious: it might lead you to be believe that Dick was a bad Protestant and also a bad Papist; in other words, that he cared for no creed or church. The truth is on Sundays he went nowhere: Dick had no love for dressing himself in a suit of finery conformable to those of his co-religionists, and as regards the chapel he knew his presence was not expected, much less exacted, or he might have gone. For these reasons the Roman Catholics entertained hopes of his conversion, and [showed] the greatest forbearance towards him should he give insults. This indeed he never did, at least knowingly.

Dick was willing to converse with everybody or anybody, but his chief and indeed only real companion was the parish priest, a man of extraordinary stature, good natured, and very fond of innocent jokes and of receiving the current news of the day with which our hero always supplied him.[36] It was very strange but somehow or other it always hap-

36. Fr Daniel O'Donnell, a native of Templedouglas near Letterkenny, acted as administrator of Fánaid from 1835 to 1837 and parish priest from then until his death in 1854. O'Donnell erected Fanavolty chapel, oversaw the establishment of the first national school in the parish, promoted temperance and introduced a register of births, deaths and marriages. His early career is unclear but he was an 'old man' when he was appointed to Fánaid. Writing in the late 1910s, Dr Edward Maguire described him as an 'ideal priest in every respect' who had been the 'idol of his flock' and whose name was still 'breathed in reverence'. Curiously, Maguire noted that Fr Brian O'Donnell, his brother and curate from 1838 until 1847, had

pened that the big man could never take his walk late or early unknown to Dick. They lived in the same village and Dick was always on the alert, and when the big man unfurled his great cloak, Dick was not far off. When he thought it a fit time to read some of the Divine Office, his faithful lingered behind, occasionally pulling up a flower here and there to while away the time, anxiously awaiting to resume the conversation. Whether this intimacy was owing to the humorous and entertaining way of telling a story or tended to other or more important ends was never known, for poor Dick was rather suddenly carried off without manifesting his convictions. One day he went on a short excursion trip by sea, and the old boat allowed water to enter more quickly than Dick and his companion could bale out; it was engulphed [*sic*] and Dick was drowned. Thus did he meet a sudden death, and he went to that land from which he cannot return or communicate. His companion managed to gain the shore alive and the lifeless body of the much lamented Dick was dragged up on the beach.

It must occur to the reader how came it that the parish priest and Dick met so often and were on such close intimacy. A little explanation is necessary: in a part of the district a little farther south but still in the same parish the people were favoured with the good luck of obtaining a plot of ground on which to build a small chapel. This gift was bestowed on them through the influence of the bishop with one of the landlords possessing a small fee-simple estate.[37] The situation was clean and neat, but far removed from the convenience of those willing to worship there. Nevertheless the act was considered a great boon and through this act of generosity the donor established for himself and heirs a degree of honour among the people never to be forgotten. It was in order to be as close to the chapel as possible that the P.P. took up quarters in the village in which Dick lived.[38] This village was remarkable in the character of its inhabitants. There were nearly as many creeds as householders: the Roman Catholics consisted of the P.P. and one or two servants; the Church of England man who followed the minister's carriage; the Presbyterian of one or two forms; the Covenanter and others who when they thought fit met in some private house and had public

---

'delighted in playing practical jokes on his superior': see Maguire, *Diocese of Raphoe*, pt. I, vol. I, p. 325.

37. St Columba's chapel was erected at Croaghan, popularly Massmount, in 1785 on a site provided by William Patton: see Lancey, 'Clondavaddog, 1835', p. 4; Maguire, *Diocese of Raphoe*, pt. I, vol. I, pp 317–18.

38. The village described here is Tamney; technically, however, O'Donnell probably lived in the adjacent townland of Croaghan (Massmount). O'Donnell may have lived for a period in Kindrum: see Maguire, *Diocese of Raphoe*, pt. I, vol. I, pp. 325–6.

prayer; one or two families who were too poor to dress for church and remained at home on Sundays, but whose creed was to hate the Roman Catholics all the same. The village itself was so situated that four public roads branched from it, and therefore people from different markets passed and repassed going to fair and market. Here then the post office was situated, a police barrack, the Petty Sessions court house, the dispensary and medical doctor, a public house for beer and spirits, a bakery, and the cake and the fruit seller's shop, also a manufactory for making besoms and disposing of the same through the country.[39] The village had no house of worship of any description—but in it was placed the parish school, and many signs of modern civilization. When we combine all these advantages, we must admit that this was the place agreeable to the tastes of the man of no work—Dick.

Dick's means of support as already said were neither that of the farmer, labourer or artisan, and therefore he might have aspired to a certain grade of aristocracy, but he had no such aspirations: he lived according to his means and appeared in garb less imposing than that of the common day-labourer. He wore a pair of corduroy trousers, a large sleeved moleskin vest, and except [i.e. only] in very cold weather would he wear a coat. His headwear was a cap with a leather peak, but he had the peculiarity of wearing the peak over his ear instead of his forehead. Poor Dick even before his death met with some misfortunes. He had the luck one night to meet with a neighbour and a friend a few miles from home and got the chance of a ride home in a cart, but a public house on the way was the primary cause in leading to a serious accident. Whether it was from a misunderstanding between driver and horse, or too much perfume arising from imbibed alcohol, it so happened that at the first precipitous place on the roadside, horse, cart and occupants tumbled down an incline and the result was the cart was broken, the horse and owner somehow escaped, but unfortunate Dick got his leg broken ...

The P.P. was therefore deprived of his companionship for some time as Dick was confined to the house, and when the leg got spliced and made stout [sic] it appeared to be shorter than the other, yet withal Dick was disgusted at the idea of carrying a stick and when he was again able to accompany the parish priest, he propelled himself in such a manner that one would think the longer leg was always front. He carried his left arm stuck in his trousers' pocket, and the right hand beating the air at the greatest possible speed

The P.P. was a powerful, tall, strong and stout man, few in the parish

---

39. Besoms, brooms or brushes.

to equal him for bone and rough strength and, when outside, he always wore a loose overflowing cloak, so that going side by side, Dick appeared as a mere boy. If a sick call came to the priest, Dick knew it before him for the reason that he was always on the street, and if ever he saw a pony with its rider coming at a trot, he walked forward to meet them and got all the information at once. Dick being always ready, no change of uniform wanted, and while the priest was getting ready he stood in the kitchen or at the door getting talk out of the messenger. The priest steps out and before mounting examines bits of leather holding the stirrups, pieces of cords &c., takes hold of saddle and mane and with Dick's assistance mounts. The great cloak is adjusted and there is so much of it to spare as to completely cover the pony with the exception of the neck and ears, reminding one of the story of Shane O'Morgan riding on a goat.[40] To prevent the toes of his boots striking the ground the stirrup was instinctively held back so that the knee and heel were at equal distances from the ground. In this attitude he and Dick jogged along and if the direction of the journey was pleasing, the latter went the whole way, but if not he halted at some roadside house till the return of his reverence. Or he threw himself in the corner of a field as long as the old farmer remained to give him chat. But if the sun was on the decline and the man in the field resumed work, then Dick dodged along up and down the field, adding to the old story or inventing a new one, till at last the big man seated on the pony was seen drawing near.

To resume our subject. Owing to the number of messengers going through the country, no letters lay long at the post office. Should word come to any house at a late hour, and the distance be considerable, it made no matter. Peace was at an end in the family, work was suspended. Every one was restless until the precious document was brought home. The old woman could not go to bed—there was no use in attempting it—for now her dreams which she told nobody were fulfilled; for certain it was—she saw in her sleep last night, a yellow horse coming up to the door, and then she awoke—at all events, something was troubling her the whole day as everybody might know: "Jamey *agra*, are you sure the letter is there?", and Jamey replies, "I am of course" and swears by hedges and ditches, that he saw it with his own eyes, but he thought there was no use in asking for it, and he was sure from the stiffness of it that there was something in it.[41] Honest Jamey though telling the truth did not tell the whole truth, for before leaving the post office, he had

40. Shane O'Morgan: not identified.
41. *A ghrá,* love (term of endearment).

exhausted his language as to honesty [sic] for the sake of getting the letter to take home but in vain. The old woman gives vent to her grief and cries out, "Oh! who knows but it is about the death of my Pat" (or Biddy or poor Kate). Hope claims a share and she adds, "Or it may be that some of them is coming home to see us". The letter she well knew was weeks on the way, yet now she believes it would not be prudent to let it lie for one night at the post office. A trusty messenger as well as a good horse is searched for. The rider mounts on bareback. If he dreads fairies or ghosts, he has no difficulty in procuring a volunteer to sit behind him, and away they go as fast as the pony can gallop—one would think it was for life or death. Having arrived at the village, [they find] their difficulties are not yet over ...

Perhaps they are ashamed at calling at so late an hour, or they may have their own doubts whether they would succeed in getting the object of their mission. To make surety sure, away they march to the famous Dick, and after making known to him their errand, they wind up the explanation with, "Dick, what will you take"—that is drink. Dick takes a dram of the best and goes willingly with them to the post office where he explains all the connexions with the rightful owner and, should the postmaster still seem doubtful, Dick settles the matter by declaring that he will go second-hand security that there is no attempt at fraud [sic].

The letter after much fumbling is at length delivered. The recipient as it leaves the hand of the postmaster begs to be excused for his irregularity in calling, explains the nature of the case, and adds that if it were not for their friend Dick (no blame to himself) they should go home as they came, without it. The governor well used to such things listens attentively and in a few words qualifies still further the good services of Dick, "Oh! yes, nothing is so useful sometimes as a friend". This is intended to remind the strangers, if they have not already adverted to the fact, what they are supposed to do. They speedily reply. "Indeed we know that he was always kind to our people, we say it not merely before his face—but as I was going to say—perhaps you could take something yourself master." "Well it is seldom I take anything from anybody, but as it is now a late hour, and business is over, and on account of Dick being your friend, I have no objection this time". The consequence was a return call to the house but lately left with Dick, the very house bearing a sign "Licence to sell" on it. Here again the best is tapped for. The end of the whipstick comes against the table and "half-a-pint of your best". The postmaster is first served out of a jug, and there is only one glass vessel to accommodate the lot, but his is filled to the "spilling capacity" and he swallows his dram as quickly as possible—to hurry home for fear of Margaret, or as I should say Peggy ...

Dick is in no such haste, he fears nobody, a second supply is not far away, and a few squeezes of the hand are given over the glass, with ejaculations of many wishes of good luck and happy news to the old couple. The answer invariably being "hope so", and soon the homeward journey is commenced. All speed is made and the pony at last arrives panting at the end of his journey. They are met at the door by the old woman who scarcely left it since they departed for she could not think of sitting, and since she should stand, of course it was at the door—imagining every moment that she heard the trampling and drawing the attention of others to the fact At last she is rewarded for her vigilance as she first receives the anxiously awaited message from beyond the seas. All members of the family and some friends gather round. Each one gives his opinion as to the best way of opening the letter without damaging the contents. "The Scholar" is sent for. He perhaps is not at home just then, or he may be rather long in coming, but as everyone could distinguish an "American ticket" by the picture of the Eagle from another part of the document, anxiety overcomes patience, and a breach is made in the cover with a scissors or knife. Not a breath escapes while this operation is being performed. Soon fold after fold of the enclosed manuscript is opened. The last one is being turned up and alas!, between hope and despair, the "ticket" appears. Then a whisper steals around, a nod here and a nod there. There is something in it whatever it is. This part of the letter—the pearl as it may be called—is taken in charge by the old woman who opens her long cloth purse, or a bag containing several purses or pouches sewed to one common back similar in shape to a segment of a waterwheel, and in the inmost-bucket or cavity the American Eagle finds a safe retreat.

In every family letter there is always something which strangers have no right to know. This is one. The value of the piece of paper is kept secret and the reader knowing this from experience passes over the mention of it. The old woman herself, though, knows it well, for the man of letters always takes a long glance before reading aloud to see what is to be read and what is not. After doing this he notifies certain things to the old landlady and proceeds with his business.

Notwithstanding his preparation and caution he has great difficulty in steering safely through. Often he nearly "sells the pass". Here he meets with a difficult word, there with something illegible, and again he begins to tread on dangerous ground: "Dear mother I send you this letter"—stammer—cough—he resumes—"Dear mother I send you this letter to tell you &c". Thus there is a lot of blundering in getting over it. Moreover all difficult passages—nearly the whole contents—to be interpreted as he goes along. Every American letter of the sort invariably commences with—"I take this favourable opportunity of writing these few lines to let you know that I am well and doing well". Few lines, even though they extend to the length of two columns of the "Times" reading matter. This was considered as necessary as the heading of a law document. Then work and wages, a minute description of the markets, flour, beef, sugar and tea, and rates thereof in cents and dollars, the kindness of friends and their well-being, the great heat, and the long frosts and snow—all followed. There were also heartfelt blessings poured out on father and mother, brothers and sisters, friends to the fourth generation and all those who were at the "convoy" the day they left home (the convoy was when any persons emigrated, it was an act as binding upon friends and upon neighbours to see him or her a part of the way, and as much grief shown as if it was a funeral—a living funeral in fact, and the nearer the relative, the farther he went).

After a day or two, when the letter is fully understood, an answer is sent running much in the same strain, for everyone must return the compliment, so that the writer has the same names to inscribe as he read before and if he forgets any it is at his peril. Nay, more are added, for an odd one steps in and wonders how he could have been forgotten in the general enumeration, and to remind them on the Other Side, now sends his blessing and best wishes. All is wound up with many blessings from father & mother. The ideas of all present are exhausted, and the wearied penman longs to see the end, but he is still held back in expectation of the appearance of some distant thought which can never come out. Unfortunately the sheet of paper is of the largest size and not easily dirtied. "Send out for Jamey Tam, maybe he has something to say." Jamey appears. "Oh! what have I to say? Send him my blessing and the blessing of all the neighbours and tell him to send my passage." The old dame says, "*Machree*, if it were to be done tomorrow, would not I have far more to say? It is when I am in bed to-night that things will be going through my head."[42] Finally he is told that "there is no more at present, but as there is plenty of paper put in another blessing" from the father and mother, "and if you have anything to say yourself that will make

42. *Mo chroí*, my heart (term of endearment).

them think of home you can fill a corner with it. Something funny, if it is only to make them laugh, they will know who wrote it: also put your name to the letter. Write anything, there is no use in sending white paper. I see a white corner there that would hold a little." A man must needs have a good memory if he made an attempt to cheat, for he has to begin and read aloud all that he has been told, everyone remembering well what he or she contributed. Seldom indeed was there any attempt to hoodwink, but after long practice the thing was not at all impossible, as every letter bore a great similarity.

There is no such ceremony now. The mere children of the house can unfold a letter and explore its contents, thus keeping the whole a complete family secret. Strange as it may seem, it is no less true that education was in this backward state, here as well as in other districts, at or about the year 1849. National School Education was known only by the name [i.e. reputation] till after 1850 in this part.[43] There was no one to take advantage of the Government grant which could then be obtained for the good of the people. It was difficult besides for any one who had such good intentions to get a grant of a fitting site for a school-house. All the knowledge then and the amount of "book learning" imparted was given by old men unfit for anything else, and the extent of the scholar's proficiency seldom exceeded spelling and reading, very few being taught to write.

Just at this period, there appeared on the scene an old soldier who had seen the Sierras, the placid rivers and sunny land of Spain during the sojourn of Wellington on the continent. Like many of his class he had seen many and strange things and could "a round and varnished tale deliver" of the "wondrous fortunes and sieges he had passed". It was shocking to hear of the bloody battles in which he had taken part or, if it be all the same, in which he said he took part. He tried to force upon the poor people's credulity that he was at almost every engagement in the Peninsular War, but for fear of mistakes he wisely admitted that he was not at Waterloo, although he often took pride in telling that he was within one day's march of that ever memorable scene.[44]

His usual epithet was "We were". Fortune smiled on him. He was permitted to return home, no one knew why. It might be owing to a reduction in the army at the restoration of peace or to some other cause, most probably a defect in his visual organs, for his sight was failed very

---

43. Fanavolty National School, established 1850: see National Archives of Ireland, Education Department 1/25, Folio 49. 'This part' refers to *íochtar Fhánada*, not the parish as a whole.
44. Peninsular War in Portugal and Spain, 1807–14; Battle of Waterloo, 1815.

much. In any case he was liberated and rewarded with a pension for life.

Naturally enough he loved to revisit his native hills and the scenes of his childhood, and lived for many years among his friends and relatives. His history in the latter part of his life is much the same as that of many old pensioners. Bills were drawn on the Great day and creditors looked forward to this as the day of retribution. Indeed to do him justice, the pension between one thing and another was distributed in less than three days, and bills were opened on the same conditions as before, the sheeban [sic] dealer receiving and returning the greater share.

Years were gliding past in this way when a friend suggested to him the happy thought of changing his life and bettering his condition. So he took a wife and became the father of a family. His expenditure necessarily increased and he was forced to look about for some way of supplementing his rather limited means. A happy thought struck him. He found a trade requiring little apprenticeship and for which there was little or no competition—he set up as a school-master.

We have made some remarks before about the difficulties of procuring proper school-houses, even when an improved school system came into operation. Up to the time of the old veteran of Mars, the disciples of Cadmus used to instruct in barns or other such out offices which the generosity of some neighbour, perhaps to his own advantage, left at their disposal for two or three months in the year, or perhaps a few weeks, for such simple grants were no way binding.[45] Itinerant preceptors occasionally put in an appearance. These old dupes would suddenly present themselves, and as to their past career and place of birth, all was a mystery. They generally got their qualifications made known through what they considered the leading men of the place. On these they imposed themselves and by them were installed into office, thus becoming additional dispensers of literary lore. These wandering satellites had no interest of course in the place nor indeed in any place, their only object being to rest a while and get what would carry them further on their journey. Many a one suffered sorely at their hands, for as a rule they proved to be hypocrites and swindlers. All of a sudden one would hear that they had absconded at a loss to their benefactors of money and clothes lent.

It was amusing in the highest degree to see how these vagrants introduced themselves. They would come with the most solemn faces, apparently religious and well-disposed, and were half clerical in dress and in

---

45. Mars, the Roman God of War; Cadmus, the hero in ancient Greek mythology credited with introducing the alphabet to Greece.

their behaviour. They would recite to the old men and women prayers of undoubted efficacy to all hours of the night—prayers composed by St. Patrick and St. Columb which very few knew—and as for hymns they could sing them *ad infinitum*. They were a sensitive class of persons. Oh! yes, very sensitive, they would grumblingly find fault with this thing or that, consider this or that an abuse, in a word nobody was faultless in their eyes. This way of palavering succeeded very well in country places. It was in fact a cloak and one which very often carries with the world generally, but at the same time it is an unmistakable sign of the impostor. One would marvel that persons should over and over again be such dupes; but such was the cause and such was the case.

In their simplicity these good-hearted people were easily blinded. Yet they were not altogether to blame. On the arrival of one of these characters, some simpleton, privileged with the appelation of respectable among his neighbours, would first allow the old knave to make a fool of himself, and then he welcomed the advent of the Newcomer, and expatiated on his qualifications. A first rate teacher—ex-fellow of a college somewhere; in fact a cousin of some church dignitary, who acknowledged [he has] committed a trifling fault, but nothing else against him and deserves to be pitied. These and as many more qualifications were set forth, and after a few days spent in encircling the neighbourhood, the neighbours were prepared and he commenced his work. Whatever school requisites—books or other things used by the scholars—had of course to be supplied by themselves and carried away by them at night and nothing left but the bare walls, except what remained of the turf not consumed during the day.

Through such channels as above mentioned and by such means as described, some few after all managed to imbibe a share, an incredible share, of learning. On the other hand many others who got the same chances always remained in the background—the backward state—and could never advance; as years went on they merely kept the simple remembrance of days misspent in youth, and could in after life only relate their tricks while thus congregated, their many challenges fought and the pugilistic encounters with other boys; the many sound thrashings got from the master, their recollections of his severity—what a great rascal he was—the tricks they played on him—the day they heated the wrong end of the tongs and how he burned his hand and fingers when he went to light his pipe, and how in spite of all the old master could do, they never could get beyond spelling "words of one sylable" [sic].

Some boys indeed put in a winter season idly lost with no farther advance than a turning of leaves between the large and small alphabet and the "a b, a b c".

These were the unwise among the rest of the crowd who had no one to counsel them, no reasoning, no explanation to give them, but still liked to be in the crowd, and therefore spent the time idly, and while here they were dispensed with doing anything at home [*sic*], yet could never know the difference in shape between the letters d and q, b or p. These were hard puzzlers. In after years when better facilities set in, many of these who were by then grown to manhood, when they saw the progress the young were making, bitterly lamented the time they themselves had lost, had misspent, and would not even then be ashamed to take up the "Primer" and commence anew at the "a b, a b c"; they would be willing to pay anything they could afford if they got any one to teach them.

At this stage of life, however, no matter how willing, age and a duller intellect combined with other cares were against them, and finally they would necessarily be forced to relinquish the hope.

Woodcuts were used to illustrate the fearsome moral tales that enlived a Dublin edition (c. 1845) of Daniel Fenning's Universal spelling book. *For many hedge-school pupils, these were among the first printed images they would have seen.*

Chapter 3
The School and Schoolmaster

Our would-be "Waterloo hero" was the first of the instructors of youth who became permanently fixed in the place and who devoted all his time to teaching—which act in itself was reckoned by the people a great boon. He soon gained the reputation for subduing incorrigibles, as no species of cruel punishment of offenders was too severe in his eyes, and towards him in a short time were centred the hopes of many parents; from henceforth any "wandering schoolmaster" had no chance of showing his face, much less of approval among the people. The term "hedge schoolmaster" is often used when speaking of the olden times but in this particular case, if any term be applied at all, the more appropriate one would be "cave schoolmaster", from the very miserable looking habitation of which he was man, master and owner. The house, if I may term it so, was situated at the entrance of a deep glen, the very same from we commenced to trace our story and from which we gave a sketch of the surrounding country. The Glen opened towards the east, and at the entrance was this dwelling, solitary and remote from any other habitation; it was situated between the confluence of two streams, which in the winter season and other rainy times swelled almost to rivers, the waters of which rolled down in torrents, sweeping the stones and pebbles along their banks, and along the foundation wall of the dwelling. It was to this lonely habitation in the Glen—which by the bye was called by the name "Red Jacket Glen", not from the present inhabitant being a soldier, but from the fact of another who wore a red jacket having died there, and as no other would wear the relic, it was deposited in a cave, where it lay for years in a state of preservation and an object for frightening children—it was to this habitation as I say, that the youth or in other words the scholars, all the young persons residing within a circuit of five miles, might be seen on a cold winter's morning each one with two or three or sometimes more than that of turf under the arms, according to their strength, a book of some description stuck in the breast or in the pocket—but no satchel as there was no thought or no knowledge of a mid-day piece; in fact the material used now for the manufacture of the lunch, that is to say meal and flour, was seldom in use then, and whatever simple fare including potatoes was taken at early morning served till evening.

Accoutred in the manner above, each one made his way over bogs, rough roads and craggy hills with all possible speed, competing as to who could or would be the first to enter; this hurry was not without good reason, for each one got his choice of a seat according to the time he put in an appearance, except in the cases of such, and they were the few, as carried no turf, and who thus by not complying with the general rule, lost their title, and therefore at the complaint of any one else could be removed and expelled from the fire as well. As there was no fixed hour, no fixed rule for the time of assembling, any one was at liberty to put in appearance at day-break if he thought fit, or if he got up with the light of the stars.

The scenery of the surrounding district is wild and picturesque, bare rugged low hills, intermixed with lower smooth green hills and flats of bogs, marshes and many lakes in the lower lands, pretty large fields as well as many patches of cultivated ground, clusters of villages scattered everywhere. An artist taking his observations from the top of the Glen could depict to himself a scene the most naturally grand, the most varied and perhaps for its extent really unequalled for variety on the whole surface of our island. The house itself—I cannot leave off the term however inapplicable—was not, as is considered now when building, made to face the sun to gain light; even this simple idea was then lost sight of, perhaps not thought of. On the contrary it was built in a direction parallel to the hills on both sides, that is up and down, and rather close to the southern side; from its peculiar situation even when the sun was on the meridian this unskilfully constructed domicile was in the shade and so deprived of natural light, which therefore was denied to the inmates. Art afterwards made very little additional [light] by way of improvement. There was only one small window and that consisting of only four small square panes of glass, not always in complete repair either, for sometimes a piece of rough board, supplied the place of the fourth pane.

This and the door, which was always left open except when a hail or snow storm set in, was all that admitted light, and the latter gave ventilation as well. An additional opening may be mentioned, the aperture for the escape of the smoke through the roof, wide enough to see a fair extent of the sky thereby. The area or dimensions within the four walls of this building for the reception and the accommodation of perhaps 40 or more pupils of different ages may be easily calculated by supposing the length to be 16 feet, and breadth 14 ft., certainly not more. Even this space was not altogether at their disposal: a bed was in one corner, the side of which occasionally served as a sitting place for a chosen few. Luckily there was no cradle wanted at this time, and the tubs and pots were left outside the walls during school-hours. It was the best well-wishers of the madam who were permitted sit on the bedside; during this unavoidable and temporary occupation of it the mistress and younger members of the little family had recourse to sitting inside the bed.

Here then were compressed boys varying in age from 7 years to that of 21, many of whom could lay their hands to the roof when standing upright, and each and every one repeating to himself, at the highest pitch of the voice, lessons from "A, B, C", to the making of many unsuccessful attempts at spelling and pronouncing the words "antiquarianism" and "ante-diluvian", so that a passerby or any person unaccustomed to such would be forced to halt and listen a while, and would certainly imagine that no human brains listening to and forced to do such could bear such noise.

Sometimes this unsonorous noise or coarse music went on by permission of the master, as often at his command and that command was so understood by all—to bawl out as loud as they could. The master's own meaning and end for this was to enjoy a little relaxation to himself and consequently freedom of thought, as during this time there was less disturbance, and he would then sit on his chair, the only one in the apartment, with his elbow resting upon his knee, and neck bent, the palm of his hand supporting his chin, and having in his mouth about three inches at least of pigtail tobacco, doubled and twisted and a small thread tying the ends, the same undergoing a hurried process of mastication. But to further the end of economising the wear and tear thereof, he had a very peculiar method, not often seen nowadays, of making the ends meet evenly when twisted and then tying the double of it with a thread. If to show respect to, or comply with, the wishes of a neighbour, visitor, or to satisfy the suggestion of his own thought, he went to the task of passing some of the same kind of ingredient into vapour, the mouth plug was abstracted for the time being and safely deposited in the waistcoat pocket, until the cravings of the appetite demanded a change which same was suddenly and surely satisfied and again the moistened plug was reinstalled in its former position between the jaws.

While [the master was] in this meditative mood, an attentive observer would at first think that he was enjoying the inharmonious voice of his pupils, but on reflection one could easily understand that his mind was totally engaged on something else, for every now and then could be heard escaping from his lips, unawares to himself and in a loud enough voice, from amidst his thoughts, a mention of "Waterloo, Badajoz, Gibraltar, Elsinore, Nile", or the name of some regiment—the 98th, Connaught Rangers &c.—while at the same time, the actions of those around him were unheeded.[46] At last when sufficiently recovered from his reverie, he would suddenly start, bounce up to his feet, and [stand] holding a bunch of rods in one hand, and running up his left hand under the tail of his regimental swallow-tail-coat perhaps intuitively thinking as in former days of his search for the bayonet—for even now in this his last profession, he still loved to wear the uniform of his earlier years, less the arms of course, and it is no way wonderful or unnatural to suppose that in his mental wanderings he would thus forget the loss of the steel appendages, and in imagination be ready for a charge.

Standing upright in the manner described and wielding the bundle of rods, the sign of real authority and terror, he would utter in a tremendous voice the words, "Silence, Silence", gradually lowering his voice on the third or fourth repetition; suddenly the great noise ceased, except for an odd giggle or half-suppressed laugh from two or three who had been all the time enjoying themselves at the twitchings of his lips and watching his other manoeuvres. Silence being thus partially restored, he again commenced his routine of giving each one his lesson in turn. Who is first? Here again was the opportunity for mischief and idleness, because those who were in the rear banished from their minds the idea of having to prepare for lessons at all, and so made their escape outside in hopes of missing altogether, or else they spent their time unprofitably inside and were only too glad to get off unnoticed which was not hard to do.

46. British military and naval victories in the Napoleonic Wars; celebrated regiments in the British army.

The seats were arranged in all possible manner in every part of the floor, but firstly there was a regular solid seat ranged all round along the wall, commencing at the fireplace or, as that hallowed spot was commonly called, the "Backstone", that is a projecting piece of stonework to keep the fire farther into the floor. This seat or rather the elevated part of the floor was constructed of flagstones of a smooth surface (easily procurable from the hillside near at hand) and to prevent the cold arising therefrom a thin scraw—a grass surface—was placed thereon cushion-like, and by means of this preventative, those seated thereon were saved from the disagreeable effect which might be felt on coming in close contact with the cold stones. The moveable seats were of smooth rough or round timber, a plank or part of a tree as best could be procured, and as they required to be removed at evening there were large fixed stones at the regular distances as guides to mark the replacement of the wooden network in the morning, which act was done by a few boys daily who knew how.

... The fire was at all times good, a great comfort in itself; this arose from the supply brought by the scholars and the addition given by the master who never wanted turf of his own, and so a blazing fire was always kept up. The united action of the heat arising from the large fire, the nearness of the roof of the building, the close atmosphere of smoke overhead, and the compressed state of the boys at their seats [meant that] few, if any, had much reason to complain of the cold. In fact those who were near the fire were always too hot, and after undergoing and unreasonably suffering a degree of insupportable heat and perspiration, they would gladly exchange with a well-wisher—but only for a time though without in the least forfeiting their claim for that day to the re-occupation of the same seat when they thought fit. As I said, those who came in first sat in a similar rotation, and thus it was not unusual to meet some of the boys at daybreak on their way to the Glen vying with each other as to who should be first. Many boys would be up before the fading light of the moon disappeared, preparing their breakfast and ready to be off as soon as day cleared, and so tight would the race be from opposite directions that very often it happened that three or four would come shoulder to shoulder in the doorway, and a tumble-over or bustle would occur.

The master followed a similar plan in giving the lessons, beginning at the right hand side of the fireplace, and as each one got through the performance singly and separately, as soon as, or before the last word the usual announcement is made by the master, "Who is next?". There was no class lesson except one spelling class which came near the time for dispersing—no fixed hour either, it varied as the darkness set in—for those who were competent, all who could spell and give the "meanings", commencing first at "Abel", "a man's name", and so on, a column for each night, and all the competitors were arranged around the walls (the juniors by this time being allowed to depart).

During the day while there was sufficient light the master sat in the middle of the floor on the chair, and each one approached him in turn with book in one hand, a rounded piece of wood or some sharp instrument in the other for pointing out the letters and words, and after placing himself in position, shoulder to shoulder, [each one would] lay the pointer to the first part of the lesson, whether in spelling or reading, as much as to say though not expressly in words "there is where I am". The pointer is carried by some, while on the march, between the teeth, and if so, it is immediately placed between the fingers and ready for action, leaving a wet spot at first bounce. The master gets hold of the book with one hand, lays his other forefinger to the heading as well— "now go on"—and then master and scholar pursue and capture every word as they go along to the end. If the darkness increased quickly, as often happened on short winter days, the master was forced to bring the book nearer his eyes and, as he always sat in stooping position and always wore a large Highland woollen cap with an overhanging broad rim, the lesson and the book were nearly altogether shut out from view of the learner, who was therefore beyond rehearsing after the master the words unseen. And if he tried to gain or to learn anything he would be under the necessity of bending the knee and turning the neck sideways, so as to get a sight at least of the page under the jaw of the master, or in the [case of a] careless boy, just repeating monotonously the words after him without seeing them at all, and in this way the lesson is brought to a close and back he goes to the seat with as much advancement as at starting. It was not uncommon to see those who were encumbered with rather elongated vertebrae being obliged while in this act to go on two knees to perform the ordeal.

From the example set by the master in always wearing the large woollen cap himself, it may be said that the scholars had the same privilege and were at liberty to keep on or take off headwear as they pleased. The boy who could read tolerably without much stumbling had the advantage of standing upright at the master's shoulder, and the latter from his acquaintance with the lesson, or from his knowledge of the English language, knew when a word was read or pronounced wrong, or as he used to say "miscalled", and then he commanded a halt, "Stop, stop", and the boy was set to spell over again and again and correct for himself. If when a mistake occurred as it often did and the master's ear caught it, his method for recalling the scholar to a sense of his mistake was novel, and that was to utter some inarticulate sound; frequently he made use of "blub, blub, blub", or else he would command him to "stop", stare him in the face, and command him in language not very complimentary to "clean your mouth", and he used other expressions of his own stamp—"take out the *sloak*", "take out the wilks", "your tongue is thick enough already", "it is in the breed of ye"—and a string of epithets, nicknames and so forth, were pronounced upon the learner who all this time stood trembling, sweating through shame and dread, attempting to correct but as often wrong, again making every speedy effort to recover the lost word; at last the difficulty would in some way be made smooth and so to proceed again.[47]

The books in use at that time were the "Primer" in red paper cover, the "Reddy-may-daisy" (Reading-made-easy), the Dublin "Universal Spelling Book"—numbers of which were sold by pedlars and hawkers at fairs and markets.[48] Everyone who could safely say that he went through the "Universal" from cover to cover was in those days reckoned a good scholar, as this was supposed the highest pitch they could arrive at, that is to say a "country scholar", and parents who could neither spell nor read of themselves made it their business if for no other errand to go to the market for the purpose of selecting this book, though all the time having to depend to the word of the vendor, who is turn showed his "wee bit of learning" by his exhibiting the type, spoking the leaves in rapid succession with his thumb in a peculiar way, a bit of manual exercise which no countryman could do. He would then as if angry, when not agreeing about the price, lay it down out of the way for a little while, just as carefully as if he never intended to lift it again, but no sooner thus fixed than he would as suddenly take it up again, present to view the picture in some one page: "Do you see that?", "The boy amidst the boughs of the tree stealing apples and do you see here the old man pelting stones at him? Eh! and do you see this one?" The bookseller while exhibiting such gave himself vent in such words as, "My good man, if you want a book for your son as I know you do"; "Here is one, the one that will just answer you"; "Your son will find in this book—

47. *Sleabhac*, edible seaweed.
48. Daniel Fenning's *Universal spelling book* was first published in London in 1756, and went through many abridgements and more than ninety editions in Britain and Ireland over the following hundred years.

the very book I am showing you, lessons from the A.B.C., to the story of Tommy and Harry, and farther on here the Principles of Politeness". And what will he not find in it? "See, man alive, there at the very end are the pictures of all the reigning sovereigns of England since the world began". "Look at Henry the Eighth there, or do you see there Queen Elizabeth dressed in all her flowers. And here is No-bow-cod-o-noser, the King of the Jews (Nebuchadenezer). It was him built Jerusalem". This child knows something. "Eh! man, you don't know anything, and dear look to the best of us, it is little we know, and what you want to know this book will tell you. Good for them that has the grip of the learning, they will not be led by the nose by everybody and it is not hard to carry."

Such oratorical utterances being intended to prevent the intended purchaser from asking questions, interfering with or demanding any reduction in the price, and his words have the desired effect: out of the leather purse or tobacco spag comes the silver two-and-sixpence or three shillings piece for a leather bound [copy], and no matter how reluctantly the precious coins were parted with, their loss is soon forgotten and the father seems consoled and proud to be able to tell a neighbour that his son wanted and got a "Universal Spelling Book", that the master said he was too long without it.[49] The book was tied up in a handkerchief, brought home, and hardly used for more than one day till it went through another operation for its safety and preservation, much to the disappointment of the scholar in being deprived of looking at the beauty of the nice cover; that operation was a second covering and binding, and the material used being sometimes strong canvas or a lamb skin dried, woolly side out. To preserve the leaves from the effects of the thumb, a triangular piece of cloth called a "marker", suspended by a thread, hung at one end. Without this protector, as cleanliness was not enforced, the first limb [sic] of the left hand if it did not wear through to the cover left an indelible trace behind on a considerable surface of the leaves—a black thumb stamp—which could not be effaced.

The method of [learning] spelling at that time was very different from what it now is, little regard being paid to the loss of time: there was a constant repetition in the formation of link after link, syllable after syllable of a word until its completion, and then came out the full pronunciation. For instance, if the word "antitrinitarian" was to be encountered, the scholar went on as rapidly possible: "an" (an)—"ti" (ti) = "anti"—"trin" (trin) = (antitrin)—"i" (i) = (antitrini)—"ta" (te) =

---

49. Spaga (Eng.), pouch, purse.

(antitrinita)—"ri" (ri) = (antitrinitari)—"an" (an) = antitrinitarian, and then of course the meaning followed: "a mere barbarian".[50] Such drudgery as this would now certainly be laughed at, nor do those who at a much later period thought themselves wise to condemn it deserve much credit for their invention, seeing how plain it is to any one the time lost. Not only that, but how it was that the learner could keep within sight of his own ideas without wandering was something extraordinary.

... There was only one door to the building, and when it had to be kept shut to prevent the snow or rain from dashing in, those who sat in that region (who were always the late comers) were left in total darkness and had to sit there idly watching. If they were attending to anything [it was to] the appearance and reappearance of the glimmering light through the small window; that aperture was also often marred in its duty, for the simple reason that the master was under the necessity in case of a disputed or difficult word first to lay his finger to it, next to vacate the chair and proceed to the light where he stuffed himself into the little window—head and neck up to the shoulders—so that the whole floor would be in a state of total eclipse and the only visible sign of day was to be discovered by looking at that part of the roof from which the smoke escaped, that is the chimney, and the same was pretty wide—so wide indeed that after a heavy hail shower, much of the substance would be deposited on the hearth, so that the extremes of heat and cold could be easily experienced at the same time and place without changing position ...

It was generally at such times that the idlers, the mischief makers, found an opportunity for executing their tricks a shout of pain or distress was repeatedly heard coming from some dark corner, followed by a form of complaint such as "master for this fellow", "stabbing with a pin"; though the complaint was thus made, "this fellow" was on inquiry unknown. But the sufferer had to make known his pain in some shape, nor could the real offender in many cases be discovered, as no one would tell, and the patience of the master was tired out to limits unendurable—no one brought to justice—the same offence repeated in rapid succession—grievous complaints anew. His routine of business was often interrupted—threats proving of no avail—and the cup of wrath now full he would at long last have recourse to sudden and severe acts of coercion, and a general scourging punishment of the innocent in

50. The challenge of spelling antitrinitarian is also noted in E. McCarron, *Life in Donegal, 1850–1900* (Cork, 1981), p. 4.

expectation of catching the guilty quickly followed. Taking up the bunch of rods, consisting of perhaps half a dozen or more hazel twigs, he began an indiscriminate switching performance from one end of the seat to the other, or at any rate laid his attention more to that quarter from which most of the complaints issued so that the innocent suffered equally with the guilty, the offended as well as offender, and as there were no desks or forms, nothing but the low seats, the bare feet therefore had no shelter, no protection, and were always exposed to danger, and it was at the bare feet that he aimed on the supposition that he would overtake the guilty somewhere. Attempts were made by as many as possibly could to evade the blows and to hide as much as possible, which was not an easy matter, the action coming so sudden, for in his rage hand and foot kept time, and as fast as the one could give a blow and the other move, he lost no time. When this terrible visitation was to him satisfactorily performed, at the cost of some perspiration, he sat down half exhausted, muttering and threatening what he would do next.

This visitation over, many would be left agonizing, some left bleeding, others faintly laughing and congratulating themselves on their lucky and comparatively easy escape, for withal it was only chance work—blind man's bluff—for the blows were not intended for any one in particular at that time, and anything which came in contact, whether shoulders, arms, knees, feet, sticks, stones or perchance the wall, suffered and got their proportion of the passing rod of vengeance. A mournful silence then followed, peace was restored for a time except an odd complaint from some lad or lads who still kept sobbing and weeping as their pains were not yet sufficiently abated, and the nature of their complaint was to the effect that "such a one" "put out his tongue at me", or some such trifling offence, but always liable to punishment according to the statutes made and adhered to, and therefore the "such a one" was summoned, was called to Justice—on which occasion the master again suddenly vacated the chair, called for the culprit, made him sit thereon the better to get at his feet while he underwent the punishment of the birch, that is so many strokes as due to the crime, according to the law made and provided. In cases of this description there were no pleadings; the guilty party saw his condemnation at once and so walked to punishment as there was no chance for denial.

His mode of punishment for offences committed varied according to the class of crime and were in some instances very severe. This severity may be overlooked if we consider the number of boys packed so closely together, many of whom were idle and unruly and by their actions raised his temper to red-hot anger. In justice to the master it may be mentioned that although he was no way scrupulous in the many expressions out of his own mouth and could easily let fall an avalanche of fearful oaths still he strictly forbade swearing in any degree from any of the boys while under his care or elsewhere, nor did any one of them ever try to imitate him in that particular failing. He was also extremely severe against any one who would dare to attempt a falsehood in the least degree, and punished very severely any infringement on the rules of honesty.

When cases for trial came on by civil action, that is when the accuser brought forward the name or names of the accused, everything was done calmly according to law, no one suffered without a patient hearing and at the testimony of witnesses on both sides, if the case were thought difficult or serious, a jury was empanelled to hear and to determine. These proceedings taking up some time in which all were anxious spectators to hear the decision, business was suspended: if found guilty the condemned got the punishment laid down in the unwritten code; if however the accuser failed to substantiate his charge, then in imitation of some forgotten law of early ages the punishment due to the crime in question devolved upon himself. This was a preventative against false charges.

In some instances the condemned was tied to the bed post, his back laid bare in imitation of military flogging, and some one was ballotted to give a certain number of strokes; if the appointed one—the executioner—refused the task, he ran the risk of being substituted instead. Some would take it having their minds made up to give it easy. The methods of punishment generally were executed by the master himself; he placed the trembling culprit on the chair and gave him so many strokes with the rods on the bare feet. There were instances in which the offender was put on the back of a stronger lad, who held him by the arms over his shoulders; scenes occurred in which the culprit undergoing the process of flagellation crept up the other's back, caught his ear between his teeth and made him leap about. Thus justice and revenge were satisfied at the same time. The supporter held out as long as he could suffer pain, but in a short while had recourse to the only remedy for relieving himself, that was by falling or rather throwing himself to the ground with his burden under him and so getting rid of his tormentor.

It may appear strange to the reader why parents should pass unheeded such treatment as this towards their offspring. There were various reasons for their non-interference. At that time there was no choice, not as is the case now when a very disobedient boy can go from one school to another to please his fancy. Again, in most cases the rough treatment was unknown to the parents until a considerable time after, because the sufferer himself would be the last to tell. If the story did escape it might be long after the occurrence that through some other source it came to the ear of the parent, and thus many considerations arose—the lapse of time, the respect in which the master was held in the meantime, the unwillingness of the parent to fall out with him after their late intimacy. Time then faded on and his authority in such matters was not interfered with, and therefore he was suffered to go unheeded.

Human nature is not equally forbearing and there was one instance indeed in which a father was so provoked at the unmerciful abuse given to his son that he made up his mind to go and chastise the master. He made his way to the Glen, entered the school about noon one day not in any appearance in a friendly mood to be sure, but quite the contrary carrying in his hand a blackthorn stick of terrifying dimensions the sweat oozing at his brow. On his appearance he was bid the time of day and the master got up to give him the chair. Soon he explained that his mission was not friendship, and a few short and angry words between the two immediately followed when up goes the blackthorn. It happened as well for the master that he was on his feet and still had his hand to the back of the chair, which he at once raised up as a shield, and as quickly put round his other hand and grasped an iron crook which hung on the fire.

A bit of sword drill now began. The weapons were now pretty well matched and a blow from either might be deadly, and in this attitude the two kept daring and threatening. All the boys fled to the hills except a few of the strongest who remained at the cries and solicitations of the mistress; they did their best to keep the combatants separate until they became exhausted in making attempts, and each of them showed good skill in defending himself in the art of sparring. There was not much damage done on either side, in fact no damage at all, but oh! the breaking of the laws, "entering a man's house with the intention of—me knows not what". Oh! what an act of madness, and what appeared in the eyes of the people still worse, an act so foolish—to come in contact with the only man who knew the law, the whole law, every nook and corner in it, and what attorney would go against him, he who could and would bring out his case in its truest colours, for he had the tongue and the head to do it. "And where was the use of a countryman to stand before him?"

It appeared to the eyes of everybody considering the circumstances that nothing short of transportation would result from the affair if it was proceeded with; therefore in a few days when matters had slightly cooled down, arbitrators and pacificators went to work imploring and with all manner of promises, but to no avail; at length the Quarter Sessions approached, and all the able-bodied persons who were present at the scene of the encounter were reluctantly invited to the court of justice.

The old veteran, knowing well that he had the advantage in law, was immoveable to all the solicitations from relatives and friends, and as many as could venture to speak to him of reconciliation did their best. It was at the court house and twenty miles from home that he began to soften and was prevailed upon to come to terms by the friends who followed, so proceedings were stayed, a new treaty of friendship was concluded, the defendant gladly paying all costs, and needless to say also the expense of a good drink for all parties—at which some through rejoicement [sic] took more than enough, and all having fortified themselves with food and drink returned home together on the best of terms. News having reached home of the unexpected settlement, a party mounted on old nags went to meet them, and found them in a public house on the way, and all arrived in the small hours of the night guided by the instinct of the horses. Some walking, some riding, the air resounding with the attempts at singing *"Tierna-we-augh"* and *"Coleen-dhas-bleggin-na-mho"*.[51]

As regards learning it was the unchangeable opinion of the master, and through him of the parents as well, that no person could read until he could spell words of all syllables, and for this end the boys would be kept drudging at spelling words in columns, from book to book, year after year—of course the winter season of each year is meant. From the method pursued, many who could spell without any difficulty the word "antediluvian" or words equally lengthy, if handed a paragraph in monosyllables [to read] could not make any attempt without allowing themselves to burst out into spelling ...

The time came with many that they would have to withdraw altogether, and they possessed no more book-knowledge than that of spelling and no other certificate than that of "the numbskull". "Sure the archbishop of Canterbury could make no scholar of him"—insinuating a good deal or everything on the side of the master, but very little for the poor "numbskull". This saying of the master's was by him applied to

---

51. *Tiarna Mhuigh Eo*, Lord Mayo; *Cailín deas bleán na mbó*, the fair milk-maid. Both were well-known songs.

every supposed blockhead and partly satisfied the curiosity of his guardians, for they were convinced that the fault lay in the head, that the head was thick, and that he was one of the same born with the frailty. However if this abandoned individual, who showed so much proof against learning, could manage to put together the letters on a signboard on entering a town so as to form a name and find out where he was going to, he thought himself happy in his own estimation, and if he could find out a house without making many inquiries, he thought himself repaid for his time lost at school.

Ingenuity early arises in youth: some who were unable to make much progress and who hated the task of returning to the doubly hated columns, adopted the plan of tearing out the leaves as they proceeded and destroying them, and by this simple act proving that if the "learning" was not in the "head", it was sure not to be in the "book". To recompense in their own mind for the loss of the leaves torn out, such ingenious boys held out to themselves the hopeful idea that they could not be turned back, that some one would be at the expense of getting or buying for them a new book and that therefore there was a chance of a step in advance. On the other hand there were among the rest many boys intelligent enough, in spite of all difficulties, to be able to read and write, and some few to cypher a little, the latter though at an advanced age.

The master was not proficient in his knowledge of "arithmetic" but he held out the promise that any one who could master the "Five Common Rules" and know them well, and "The Rule of Three", had as many figures in his head as were wanted for any man.[52] To make up for the master's deficiency in arithmetical knowledge he had recourse to the assistance of a substitute, which was perhaps as old as himself judging from its colour and from its appearance—a bundle of old leaves in manuscript which he termed a Fair Book—and in all difficult questions, the Fair Book led the way, being copied from a Key.

As was the case with the "Spellers" and "Readers", so also with the "Writers": each grade spent the greater part of the day at that particular exercise alone. The master's duty to the writers was very light. He managed, or got others, to give them headlines and they daubed and scored away. The writers were set as much as possible apart from the rest to give them "elbow room". The materials which everyone who was fortunate enough to be so far advanced as to commence writing had to supply himself with were as follow:— (i) a piece of board something

52. Referring to sections of Gough's *Practical arithmetic*. See p. 115, n.54.

larger than the copy book for placing on the knee; (ii) an ink-bottle either of glass or earthenware material, having a leather strap attached to its neck by means of a slit or hole cut in one end of the leather, and the other end similarly cut so as to hang by the thumb or from a button on some part of the garments, generally at the left shoulder; (iii) a ruler was another indispensable requisite, as the paper was of an inferior quality and not ruled, and as a supplement to the ruler each one had to provide himself with some sharp pointed instrument or else made use of the finger nail for drawing along the ruler to form straight lines; (iv) a pen, made from a quill taken from a gander's wing only, as that from the goose was considered too weak; and to be able to make a quill pen required some practice. The master had a small black-handle knife similar to those bought now for three pence, but he had it as careful as a surgeon's instrument, and he lent it to some elder boy to make and mend pens.

Those who had any idea of the use of lead pencils but found it not possible to get any, tried to supply the want by running molten lead in a quill or in a piece of stiff straw or reed, called by them a "quill-rod" and if successfully made, the possession was much coveted. But as lead was not always and everywhere to be found, recourse was had to many expedients and any one who could produce a piece of lead got in barter some other article of greater value, and a promise of friendship along with assistance at lessons.

In those days, sash windows in their full meaning were not so numerous as now, and if a dwelling had the advantage of a middle sized glass window it was reckoned a step in advance of the times or rather a sign of being wealthier than many of his neighbours, because most of the windows among the poorer classes were merely small holes in the wall into which the frame was stuck and immoveable, the small panes of which were set trapezoidal in frames made of lead—unfortunately for the windows. Hence from the usefulness of the much coveted lead-pencil arose the idea of making "sorties" and invasions at late hours against the leaden windows, and from the effects of repeated havocs, such windows disappeared and have never since recovered in that locality.

Very often the hoary headed old grandfather on awakening in the morning, would utter his first prayer against the intruding ruffians who broke his window—the very same window his grandfather before him had put in, and which on that account he valued so much, so much so, that for his grandfather's sake he would as soon lose a piece of the ear as lose a part of the window that was there for so many years and no one ever thought of meddling with it before. The old fellow hurriedly tumbles out of bed to meditate over his irretrievable loss, but to add sufferings to his sorrow, and already in half frenzied temper he now finds that he is attacked with the toothache, caused surely by the very act of the ruffians who made way for the cold wind to whistle about his ears and nostrils all night while he was asleep. He went to bed with a "touch of a headache", but now he did not know if the head was on him, he felt so dizzy and his nostrils so stopped. Dear oh dear, not fit to stand it.

While dressing himself a short colloquoy [sic] passes between him and the old woman: "Norah will you light the pipe? or the head will get away from me"; "Make haste!". Norah is obedient to the request and at once puts her hand to a hole in the wall at the fireside, gets the "old stumpy" already half full and as quickly gets three or four bits of straw from under the bed, lights them at the fire and sets to the pipe. Takes a puff or two. "Here take this quickly it is now going." He pulls and puffs and during this temporary relief, he feels his jaw, Oh! it is so swelled, anybody could see that. May as well go the bed again for the day.

"But Norah, who would have the heart in his body to come and destroy our window, I wish I could know him, I would make him leap where there is no mire". "Now Micky take hold of your wits. Now Micky you need not ask me such a question—You know right well, as well as the soul is in your body, you know it was your own flesh and bones, your own grandson Micky Hemus and no other. Did I not see him spying about the whole day yesterday?" "O yes true for ye, it was the ruffian and no other, for he did not darken our door the whole day. I might know he had some bad brewing on his brains, and by the blessed white sun that shines this day, if I get a hold of him, if I get a hold of him I will break his four bones and that may be before the sun sinks in the sea, I will, I will make an example of him the villain. But he will deny it, the rascal I know, and, Norah, it is better you tell him to keep out of my way while the anger is on me. Light the pipe again it is out. Oh! this jaw will take my like, my oh! my". In the way as above, ere long the glass windows, the heirloom of generations, disappeared, and in its place remained a hole, stopped with a bundle of straw or a piece of board. Sometimes a neater material was nailed on—a parchment—may be a sheep skin well stretched the wool having been carefully plucked off. This latter material would answer much better than wood as by its partly transparent quality a small degree of light penetrated, at least as much as to show day from night. But the latter invention was liable to the danger, that if the old patriarch did not keep a closed mouth, or if he made use of threats towards his supposed former assailants, a knife would very soon render his last artificial invention useless, so that unless specially privileged, the latter expedient would be of short duration.

The ink used was made from materials found at home a mixture say of the juice of boiled briar roots or at a certain season the juice of blackberry itself, and if indigo and coppers could be got, so much the better for the writer.

All these requisites being provided, not forgetting the long goose quill, the student began his first exercise in writing, that is to say, "straight lines" or as they were called "polsticks".[53] The master set a "headline", in the tracing of which he was more guided by the hand than by the eye, for it was not unusual for him to finish part of the drawings on the board after the pen escaping from the paper, and either the roughness of the surface or the unusual squeaking of the pen would first recall to his mind the idea that he had proceeded far enough, indeed a little too far.

The writer after some time was thought qualified to leave "polsticks" and take to "large-hand"—very large hand—about two inches between the rulings no less, then "round-hand", reasonable in size by comparison, and lastly "small-hand". What was curious enough at this time was that the smallest of the small-hand writing was reckoned the best, even if illegible by the writer himself.

The writer of small-hand after a considerable time arrived at that important stage, the introduction to the ever memorable "John Gough", the only treatise on arithmetic allowable in those days, and in which were questions from the simplest to the "never-to-be-learned" to my astonishment it is not many years ago since that an old man where I happened to be present was making anxious inquiries to be directed to where he could get a "John Gough" to purchase.[54] The bare mention of "Gough" recalled to my memory what had almost disappeared from it, and which I thought was forgotten by everyone else. The affectionate old man was led to understand that his son was an adept at learning and

53. Polsticks, possibly a variant of palstaff or palstave, a hoe.

54. John Gough (1721–91), a Dublin Quaker. His *Treatise of arithmetic in theory and practice* was first published (in Dublin) in 1757, and was soon re-issued in a simplified edition as *Practical arithmetick*. In a variety of formats, this became the standard primer in Irish schools for almost a century, and was widely used elsewhere. An edition published in Bruges in 1805 claimed to be the 49th edition, but there were many later Dublin and Belfast editions circulating in rural Ireland before national school textbooks finally displaced them. For the high opinion of 'the Goff' [*sic*] in Fánaid, see McCarron, *Life in Donegal*, p. 4.

therefore, to crown him with knowledge, wanted John Gough to complete him as a scholar, for so he had been credibly informed by a knowledgeable friend and neighbour that it was the "only book". This little incident goes to prove that traces of the teachings of the system of the Old School are not entirely forgotten.

Whether the master in the Glen had a thorough knowledge of this author's "Arithmetic" in his youth is more than can be said with certainty, but at the time he endeavoured to give the benefit of it to others he forgot most of it himself. He had the luck to possess what he termed the "Fair Book" alluded to above, the "Key": in this old manuscript-book questions and answers were written out on very old and dirty paper which had suffered from the effects of soot and smoke for many years. Probably this was copied by someone who thought that he had a treasure. When questions of any difficulty were met with, and there were many, recourse was had to this valuable production, and by its aid, though difficult enough to decypher at the corners, the learner was waded through what he had no more knowledge of when it was done than a man asleep in a ship had known of its navigation. Arriving thus far he met the stunner, the real full stop, the turning point:

"In the midst of a meadow well stored with grass,
I must take two acres to tether my ass;
How long must the cord be that feeding all round;
He may not graze more nor less than the two acres of ground?"[55]

… [the learner had no] idea of a circle, a diameter or a circumference but had to return to where he first began, and if gifted with a good memory he had a little more knowledge and found it somewhat easier to proceed the second course than the first time.

The learner in arithmetic had also to provide his stock of working materials, but not so many of these as when he was at writing: a slate—of the same quality and description as those for roofing houses and made smooth on one side only by the process of wetting and rubbing; a round smooth stone brought for the purpose from the seashore when polished served very well [for this purpose]; with some of the more tasty lads the slate was so valuable as to get it framed at the carpenter's. One "John Gough" served for three or four or more, as it was handed round and they took it in turns, for once the sum or question was put down it took a good while to work it out. The slate pencils were made from

55. Verse also quoted in McCarron, *Life in Donegal*, p. 4.

lengthened pieces of broken slate, first cut, then filed and made somewhat round, but as this process was tedious another material was found
to answer: a flat white crumbly stone, a species of flagstone, dug out of
a hole on the hill side not far off, and from this the surroundings derived
the name of "pencil hole". Unwarranted expeditions of five or six or
more of the boys often started to go to the "pencil hole", more for recreation of their own and to pass the time than for the great need of pencils, but the fact of being there was a sufficient excuse in the view of the
master to withhold punishment which otherwise would be dealt out for
desertion or absence.

The only class lesson given by him was "Spellings & meanings", and
that for the seniors alone or those competent and just immediately
before they were dismissed. This test commenced at the head or the first
in the row, and as a word was "hit or missed", there was heard a constant repetition of "all right"—"turn up"—"turn down"—"down with
him, ha, hah!", and if he intended to add pain to degradation "down
with the sloth".

These "turns" or promotions and depressions were also irregular as
well as unjust, because the boy who first failed had such a downfall as
to exchange place with the correct speller should it be at the end of the
class. The law was very foolish as it gave the opportunity of cheating to
some who could if they wished spell the word correctly but would wilfully make a wrong attempt, and by signs entice others to do the same
for the purpose of laughing at the first unlucky boy brought so very low
and thus be revenged for some grudge during the day.

This lesson or examination over, the master turns round, as hitherto
his back was to them, and gives "titles" to many in the class before parting. The first and consequently supposed best, though his position
might be only accidental, got the title of King, the second Prince, the
third Paul and so on to the nearly last, and the last of all got bestowed
upon him some infamous name, something unmentionable, or worse
than ridiculous, and with this appellation he skirted out, fled from the
rest, downcast and hooted as if he had committed a crime, and which
name he could not possibly disengage himself of till the evening of the
next day and then he got a chance.

Another very foolish idea on the part of the boys in preparing this
lesson was to make sure of the words only, which by their places in class
should fall to their turn by rotation, and so escape or pass over the other
words as if coming to others in the class. This showed well enough as

long as no one missed, but if the memory of one boy failed, the charm was broken, lost, the chain broken, and then all were worse than ever. If it happened that all or nearly all the attempts were bad, the class was dismissed to prepare and to repeat the same next evening.

During school the scholars had sufficient time for a recreation or open-air amusement, not that their limbs required it for many of them had long walks, nor was it thought necessary for the accumulated vapour to escape from the house, but for another reason: at the approach of the time for the master to get his mid-day meal—the only one which he took at home in the twenty-four hours—all present got liberty to go outside, rush to the hills, climb the steep rocks, play and fight as they thought fit, and when wanted inside again a crier gave the call at which they all rushed back again.

At a fitting season of the year, and on particular days, all would accompany the master to the bog to assist in raising his stock of turf, removing it to high ground and so on. Neither did he let their toil go unrewarded, for when the turf were all dried and placed in safety ground [sic], he would then give them foot-racing on the nearest green or field of a sufficient length. He started the boys in batches of fours and sixes according to age and size, and the first coming in after a double race got a prize. What? a large brass military button, showing the picture of two or three cannons on the back of it, and called by them "Artillaries". Only one or two of the brass buttons were given away at a time as they were reckoned first prizes, and the supply lasted him a good many years as the great coat and jack-coat [sic] were plentifully stocked with them. Lesser prizes consisted of "hornys", a description of button made of bone. If the prize was disputed, the parties claiming had to run it over again, and when all were tired the sports came to an end.

Another great disadvantage in the way of a learner in that district at that time was nearly the total want of knowledge of the English language. While at home the language spoken was Irish; on the way to and from school, and still worse while there itself, every word spoken, except what was taken out of a book, was Irish. Therefore the use or understanding of what they were repeating and learning was to them as Greek or Latin, but after all they gradually crept into a foreign language. On Saturdays and some other days, catechism and prayers were given, and these totally in Irish. It is not difficult to understand what a great hindrance this in itself was, in addition to all others.

The days teaching being over, it was the custom for the master for "to go round" with the scholars in their turn, in other words to go with someone to his home for the night, and these welcome lodgings were freely given in addition to any other remuneration he received as school fees. The fees were very trifling indeed, hardly ever exceeded one shilling per quarter payable at any time, and if three or four came from the same family the third and fourth got free. His stay at a family however was in proportion to the number of scholars, and it was always announced by him at the close of evening where and with whom he was to take up quarters for that night. This announcement was considered a mark of honour or distinction by the boys on whom it was bestowed, for though it was a general rule, yet there were many he did not go to at all, and on the other hand some to be on the roll of honour gave him invitations.

It was the most respectable householders that he condescended to visit most, but on every occasion the boy so honoured remained behind all the rest until the master was ready to start, buttoned on his great coat, got his staff, and off they would start; the youth went on a little distance before, the master prodding his way after him to his home, the boy acting in the capacity of a guide, pointing out the best path and avoiding the dangerous one, and he was a protector in keeping the dog in subjection when approaching the dwelling.

As word always preceded them, the lad's father was on the look-out, and when he saw their appearance, he watched their approach and made haste himself to meet them, took the guiding of the master upon himself, much to the joy of the young fellow thus relieved, who soon got disentangled from his charge and speedily escaped home to fasten on any eatables he could get. By the time such journeys were completed, it was in most cases nearly dark, or it might be sometimes after night if the distance was considerable and the ground uneven. But on arrival the master was made welcome under the roof, to the best of accommodation, board and lodging that they could bestow upon him till the next morning.

£10 REWARD.

I HEREBY Offer a REWARD of

TEN POUNDS

To any Person who shall, within Six Months from the date hereof, give to me or to the Head Constable at *Ramelton*, such information as may enable me to discover and bring to Justice the Person or Persons who, on the night of the 4th instant, broke 5 panes of Glass in the *Hibernian Society* School-house at *Tamney*, in the County *Donegal*.

R. F. MACDONNELL,
County Inspector.

Letterkenny, 16th November, 1839.

12,963—G.

The glass referred to in this notice was broken on the night of Monday 4 November 1839. The schoolmaster who lived in another part of the house heard the glass breaking but when interviewed by the constabulary said he could neither accuse any person nor assign any motive for the attack. Nobody ever claimed the £10 reward.

CHAPTER 4
Local Celebrities

We have said that our veteran hero, our schoolmaster of the time, was unique in many ways, but among the rest of his oddities he formed to himself the idea, and complied with the same, to go circuit with his scholars to their homes, stop and sleep at their parents' residences for the nights. This was certainly of some gain to him as he got supper and breakfast at his lodgings, the best they could afford, and also relieved his own family of his presence. But it was not so much for the luxury of eating or drinking that his mind was so riveted on, it was for another—a different but in his view a more important end—to mix with the celebrities. It would appear that his tongue could not be at ease either by day or night except when asleep, and we must now dispense with him in his capabilities [*sic*] as a teacher and introduce him in another sphere of society, that is as foremost in the rank of the men of knowledge—the wise men, or those who presumed to be such; no meeting was complete without his presence, was in fact at wandering without his guidance [*sic*], so we may style him as president whenever or wherever they met.

What is to be understood of the meetings was the gatherings of the wiseheads in one house for the purpose of discoursing upon anything or everything this house, this place of meeting, depended entirely on where the master was located for the night.

In our last chapter we find him safely landed at his destination. Here a more important scene was enacted, that is to say the introduction and

discussion of politics, and as it was always so well known to the neighbours from information got through the scholars, when and where the
master should be billeted for that night, so it happened long before
darkness set in that some of these men who had a considerable distance
to go were to be seen making headway to the place of rendezvous.

This early start was a wise thought on their part and very necessary
too, as well to avoid the inconvenience arising from the darkness as to
have a chance of a sitting place secured in the house of meeting, or what
may be called a parliament house on a small scale; in the event of, or
expectation of a throng, more speed was put on so that the house was
invaded and seats taken up long before the arrival of the master and his
guide. The members who arrived early did not indulge in much language, kept rather silent, for just then their chief outlook [sic] was to get
themselves comfortably seated.

At last the head of the assembly, the expected visitor, arrives, and
partakes of some refreshments which were awaiting him (in this respect
he was always easily satisfied, no one ever heard him complain of his
diet or what he got in this house or that). His wants being hurriedly satisfied, his long staff safely laid aside in a corner, the most comfortable
place in the house was prepared for him close to the fire which was blazing from extra fuel, and the apartment as well lighted as possibly could
be. The man of the house, not forgetting his duty, or rather a mark of
decency binding on him, produces the pipe and the tobacco; a good supply of the latter is laid up for the occasion and the master of course is
the first invited; after him all present are asked to produce their consuming machines and all are quickly supplied with a "round", as many
as could indulge in the luxury and very few were the exceptions.

Then a few short introductory discourses follow as to the state of the
weather, the appearance of the setting sun (portending good or bad
weather), the appearance of the crops and so forth, a few words about
births, deaths, marriages, or accidents happening in the neighbourhood,
the narrow escape some neighbour's cow had by falling into a drain and
the great exertions used by some man instrumental in her safety, or
again some other passing everyday news.

In this way the time was passed for a little, and this was purposely
intended to give the late-comers a chance of listening to and joining in
the more serious discourses—the deep subjects. So while nothing valuable was lost, fresh arrivals put in appearances—the real politicians—
those who took upon themselves to discuss, to ask and to answer
questions, and because of this distinction, this supposed pre-eminence,

they had always the best and most conspicuous places assigned to them at every meeting, no matter where.

As to these men who were so very willing to make use of the power of their tongues and who assumed such importance to themselves, it may not be out of place to give a short description of a few of them and to commence with one Patrick Wiseman; singular as it may be thought to rank him in this class when he did not know the letter A from B.[56] But he had other qualifications: he had in the first place leisure hours and made it his daily avocation to start from home every day early in the morning, circle as much by actual measurement of the rational horizon as he possibly could, have a "call in" wherever he expected "any news", make haste for the next station, and so end the circuit close upon the time of sunset in an opposite direction from that which he headed in the morning. Pat on his return had a short call at his own dwelling with a little more authority and freedom than at his neighbour's, for here he got something to eat and was not ashamed to ask for it and, while partaking of which, heard the progress of work at home, saw if his morning directions had been attended to, gave some fresh instructions as to certain things best to be done in household matters, and then immediately started anew to the school-master's lodgings to meet his friends and associates for the night's discussion.

Very often Pat dispensed with his first return homeward if owing to distance or unfavourable weather, or he had relatives on his circuit, and he would be at no loss taking up quarantine in some comfortable corner during a storm or on the approach of a shower; when thus weatherbound the kindest of hospitality would be shown him, and from this safety place, he would emerge at dusk and proceed to the real seat of news; when thus necessitated, his return to his own home would be only to sleep. Pat had a certain dread of seeing images in the dark; he therefore did not wish to be far from his place of security unless a neighbour promised to attend the meeting also, and on these conditions he felt at ease in delaying for some time until his companion was ready. Pat always had a great liking for the good heat of the fire for the good reason that he was never "out of a cold"—a short dry cough—and therefore he laid claim to the fireside corner which was always reserved for him. This predilection became so ingrafted in him that in every house he went to, he claimed the corner nearest the fire as his right which in a short time was understood by nearly all and they therefore made way at

56. The celebrities' names, or some at least, are more likely to be the invention of the author than actual local nicknames.

his approach. Comfortably seated, he would sit during a long winter's night, the chair leaning backwards, his one leg resting on the other knee time about, his foot kept dangling all the time, one hand stuck on his bosom; in this attitude he had all the advantages of breathing freely, keeping a sharp look out for every word uttered by any one, and when opportunity offered intermingling in the discourse.

His knowledge as far as reasoning and proof were concerned was indeed very limited, nothing beyond hearsay, but withal his "gather ups" were many, and if not able to carry a point in argument he was well qualified to give a good deal of interruption and when plainly defeated he would still adhere to his own opinion—in fact might be termed a real obstructionist.[57] Persisting and refusing proof in argument he would be brought by some means to desist, but he signalled the same by a giggling laugh peculiar to himself, not at all understanding his own defeat nor how far he was defeated. Though Pat was incapable of entering into deep subjects he was very useful in collecting stories of current news, and whenever he got a chance he was ready to put in his odds and ends for the benefit of his hearers.

Stephen Swanson was much superior in point of knowledge compared with Pat; Stephen had the advantage of being able to read and at this time of life his only ambition was the possession of a newspaper to while away the day. Though he also travelled for news, he differed from Pat's method of collecting; he had only one place mapped out for himself for the very reason that no one except the clergy or an odd squire in this part of the country were then subscribers to newspapers it was to the priest's residence he often winded his way, and his step and his shadow was as well known as if he had been an inmate of the dwelling—to the watch dog who never barked at him, and to the maidservant who was always ready to admit him with a smile and with the salutation, "There comes Stephen", and as ready to supply him with the needful, that is to say, "last week's paper".

When Stephen went in pursuit of a newspaper, he did not look around or stop with everybody he met his business was more important, he had an air of speed about him and always went at a clap-trap, half-trot gait, dragging his staff which was a piece of the best hickory, ornamented with two brass eyes, through which a leather thong or whang passed and a twist of this round the wrist gave him an easy method in sword-like fashion of towing the hickory stick, sometimes by his side or

---

57. In the late 1870s, Irish nationalists who adopted filibustering and disruptive tactics at Westminster to raise the issue of Home Rule were known as 'obstructionists'.

trailing after. He always wore a low pair of strong leather shoes, well bottomed with coarse nails, paviors as they were called, and the shoes were purposely made too large and of the fashion and shape called at that time "straight shoes", so that one served for either foot. This shape was adopted to give more wear and supposed ease, and no toil or time lost in tying on, as there were only two holes, one in each ear of the shoe, which any piece of cord could tie, or a grain of tow twisted roughly between the fingers in the case of hurried necessity, and when twisted and tied the balance, if not too long to get under the sole to trip him, was slung about for want of a knife to cut.

From the continual friction going on between the heel and the strong leather, no stocking made of wool could last the wear and tear for any length of time, so that the hind part of the foot was exposed and bare at every rise of the step, and from the same cause—friction—arising between the leather and the skin, the latter was as black and as hard in substance as horn.

Our gladsome Stephen being put in possession of his temporary treasure, the fulfilment of the object of his visit, he would choose for himself an out-of-the-way seat in all humility, and his next operation was to abstract from a pocket in one of the skirts of his swallow-tailed coat, a rough wooden case containing a pair of spectacles to which was attached a strong cord. The hat, a thick felt one, being laid aside, the glasses carefully fixed on the nose in their proper position, and the cord brought down on the back of the head, thus serving a double purpose, first as stays to the specs, and secondly as a band keeping the grey hair tightly to the head behind, so that even with the hat off the cranium felt no cold in that direction. The forepart of the head was rather destitute of its natural covering, but as a substitute for that deficiency it always carried a goodly share of mother earth in the shape of cemented dust, dried and firmly fixed, and this served as a protection against cold in front. All arrangements being satisfactorily completed, he was then in the right mood for reading, and took up the paper from which he would not desist—blow high or blow low—until he felt satisfied, or until the daylight was withdrawing, by which time a stock of general news, his own interpretation of course, was then collected by him, suitable to his own knowledge and his own version, and as carefully stored up for the night's proceedings, his ambition being satisfied if he was able to carry to the board something new, strange or wonderful, and to be able to enlarge on what he had read.

... Should he be disappointed in neither seeing a paper nor getting one, he made back for home in such haste as if he was fleeing before his enemy, or as if he had committed a crime, so that on nearing his own dwelling his speed was such that his iron heels knocked fire sparks out of the very grey granite rocks on which he walked, and woe the unsuspicious cat or dog which should happen to be at the fireside on his arrival; the hickory stick came down without warning upon it, and the poor brute was as likely to leap into the fire scattering coals and ashes in all directions and, heedless of the danger of setting anything on fire, he would prepare to get himself drawn in and stretched in a box bed at the fireside corner. Not even the good wife, who at all other times [when he was] in his worst of temper would break words with him, at this time darest not ask him if anything was wrong or bid him the time of day, for every one knew without making any inquiries what was wrong and so kept silent; neither did his own faculty of speech recover him until refreshed by a good round of tobacco smoking in the boarded enclosure of a hammock, and then his first expression was in sorrow for not seeing the paper.

In his choice of a newspaper, Stephen was not hard to please, no way particular about dates, nor yet [as to] the establishment from which it was issued. Anything bearing name and shape and size was good enough, but if large so much the better; nor did he easily part with it, once he got it in his grasp—no, the precious article was read and re-read, and at every perusal he found out something new and in this way one paper served for many days; at the end of the week after so many perusals, it was still thought of value, and the woman must be a very near relative or a particular friend who after much application and solicitation got the dirty old worn copy for the purpose of converting it into a "pattern" for mantle-making, the final use for which newspapers were valued by the women in those days. They placed great value on the old newspapers so that the giver of one was fairly rewarded as far as language and a full flow of benedictions could go.

Dominick Carson: we now bring forward as the third of the selected celebrities one of the wisest, the most serious, and also not the least informed of the members. He was much inclined to be present at the assemblies but was very slow in making himself in anyway conspicuous or in proposing much which might attract the attention of the house towards him or get himself entrapped in any way. But when he did advance an opinion, he did it in a quiet modest way and with some sense, and carried with it the force of argument and good judgement. He was not much given to reading at this time of life, but he had read a good deal and whatever he read, good or bad, when young was not forgotten by him. His repetition of fables, of rhymes and such like was to a degree of perfection incredible. The Arabian Knights, Gulliver's Travels, and especially Burns' Poems were to him as easy as the alphabet. Stories about Scotland, of Scotch witches; or, turning to Ireland, the History of Finn Macool, Ossin, or the extraordinary doings of one-eyed Giants whose strength and stature were everything great.[58] It made no difference which of these he took up, all were to him at his finger ends. Fabled as many of these stories were, still the language was impressive and interesting as he could deliver them in Irish as well as in English; not only that but the mind must be looked upon with admiration that could so secure cavities in it which could compress and retain within its precincts through the vicissitudes of youth and of manhood till nearly old age, such lengthened and unprofitable harangues. Neither was he destitute of some useful knowledge. He could repeat in verse means by which he could tell the age of the current moon, the date on which Easter would fall, and many other things which seemed mysterious to nearly all the people at the time.

Hugh French comes next; like Pat Wiseman he had no book-learning whatever but had to depend to his memory for everything, and this faculty was extremely acute and retentive to an extraordinary degree. Anything ever heard by him worth retaining was never forgotten and was always near to him when wanted or when occasion arose—whether passages from the authors of great works, say Caesar for instance in his Gallic Wars, or into the religious subjects, Dr. Gallagher's Sermons, or quotations from sermons heard by him years before, or verses from the Scriptures, especially in support of his own religion.[59] He knew the geographical situation of the states of Europe, their capital cities, and their populations in round numbers and, in particular, their strength in "fighting men" and other armaments, their religions, and their manner of government. And what was most extraordinary for a man unlettered,

---

58. Fionn Mac Cumhaill and Oisín, the central characters in *An Fhiannaíocht*.

59. J. Gallagher, *Sixteen Irish sermons in an easy and familiar stile* (Dublin, 1736). Dr James Gallagher (d. 1751) was bishop of Raphoe (1725–37) and Kildare (1737–51). Written in Irish, Gallagher's *Sermons* was intended as a handbook for priests and became 'the principal guide to Irish-language preaching during the eighteenth century'; it went through fourteen editions by 1820: see N. Ó Cíosáin, *Print and popular culture in Ireland, 1750–1850* (London, 1997), pp. 120, 126, 159–60, 167. Nineteenth- and twentieth-century memoirs attest to its distribution among the laity: see C. McGlinchey, *The last of the name* (Belfast, 1986), p. 12. Other memoirs corroborate Dorian's recollection that sermons were committed to memory and recited by laymen; for example, see E. J. Mullin, *Mount Silver looks down: Supplement to 'History of Raphoe'* (Glenties, 1952), pp. 25, 36.

he could trace a map of Europe satisfactorily, and better than many a one who could read. This he learned by getting some of the younger generation to teach him, to point out to him as he himself first dictated and questioned; he was so readily taught that he at once could lay his finger to countries, cities, rivers, seas, mountains and battle scenes after a lesson or two ...

Although Hugh could hardly give exact dates for certain events he arrived very close to them, and he could lecture on the Great Revolutions in the History of the World, the names of generals, admirals, battles and sieges, where fought and by whom the victory was gained. He was very much on the side of "Bonaparte the Great", loved to hear of and to rehearse his victories, of how he progressed, and of the bravery of the French soldiers.

He had an inveterate hatred towards English rule, a never-ending hatred which was equally divided between the Red-coats of England and the men of the "Black-gowns", the former meaning the soldiers and the latter the preachers or ministers, and his belief was that one was as much in the service of their Maker as the other. He could enlarge upon the life and doings of Henry the Eighth, Elizabeth, Cromwell, and down to the men in "Black gowns", viz. the Protestant ministers who were in his opinion the offspring of Harry, and who were there by the strong arm and were protected by steel bayonets, supporting wives and families, driving in cars and carriages on the proceeds of unlawful possessions which by right belonged to the widow and the poor in each parish.

I often thought how cruel death was in that it separated this man from the world before the reigning days of liberty-loving Gladstone, for it never occurred to him otherwise than that the Black-gowns would hold the sway and be supreme as long as there was a crown in England. He was firmly convinced, though, that they would "come down" but not till the overthrow of heresy, and that was sure to happen in the future. No one knew then, no one thought of the changes which were soon to follow. Had Hugh got the least glimmer of them, his last days would be happy. But the unexpected changes would disarrange his prophecy, and it would require all his talents to reconstruct his former inculcations and bring them to bear proof [sic].

Above all, he had by memory nearly all the prophecies attributed to St. Columbkille, and in this he most delighted and felt the greatest of pleasure pouring his knowledge into the ears of his audience.[60] He tried

60. Prophecies ascribed to Colm Cille (c.521–97) were widely circulated from the late eighteenth century. For prophecies ascribed to Colm Cille in pre-Famine Fánaid, see Rathmullan,

to impress upon his hearers the belief that the end of the world was even then much nearer at hand than what the people of the present day would be willing to think or inclined to believe, though after adding half a century to the history of the world they still go on and banish that thought farther and farther away. He aimed at giving an explanation of the time that this earth would come to an end, basing his knowledge upon the fact that great events occurred at the end of every period of 2000 years, but that the last period was to be shortened so that the vengeance of the Almighty might be satisfied against heretics and especially England. Mahomet and all others He could easily forgive for the reason that they "never had the faith", but to forgive England He could never do, for they had the faith but forsook the faith, and their end was to be terrible. Ireland was to be relieved, but Ireland was to suffer to "the extremity of the rod" at the hands of England—by the sword.

After the downfall of England there would be a reign of peace, and only one fold, the true religion, up to the coming of Antichrist. Antichrist, an offspring of Mahomet, is to be a great scourge and is to make war against Christians. Anyone not submitting to him will at once be put to death, and anyone whose faith is dead and surrenders to him will be converted by putting on the "sign of the beast", with a cut made in the forehead and signing one's name with one's own blood and by then following the army. In this way he will gather an immense strength and at last his pride will become unbearable, so much so that he will lift up his sword and blasphemously make a declaration of war against the Almighty, but like all enemies of the true faith he is to be overcome and his end is to happen in a tremendous way, for the earth is to open and swallow him up, and after his defeat and destruction there shall be peace till the Last Day, but the term not known.

He would give the signs and the wonders which would appear in the sky, on land and sea, many of which he would enumerate, being the forerunners of certain events already come to pass, and when such were verified beyond contradiction, "who would or could have the face to say against the rest" which were to follow. The truth of it was that his mind was so much occupied with the thoughts of prophecy and the future that he got careless about the things of this world, and put up his days in rather a simple innocent way so that unscrupulous neighbours with whom he had dealings, like all men of the world caring less for the

---

31 Aug. 1835, J. O'Donovan to T. Larcom, in M. O'Flanagan, ed., *Letters containing information relative to the antiquities of the county of Donegal collected during the progress of the Ordnance Survey in 1835* (Bray, 1927), pp. 21–3.

future than the present, acted as knaves towards him in his dealings with them, taking advantage of his credulity and using flattery to their own gain.

Had his span of life on earth been extended a little farther he would have seen a great change come upon the black-gowns he so much dreaded, for by one bold stroke of the Great Liberal he would soon see the varnished coach, the proud family, the hunting and watchdogs, the guns and canoes and fishing tackle disappearing very suddenly, the circular gravel walks before the hall-door neglected, and the green grass growing over them—places on which in his day he would be afraid to tread.[61] If these changes did not altogether conform to Hugh's prophecy, they would have convinced him still further that the minister's preaching and religion lay in his wealth and his love of self, not love of God or the salvation of his fellow man, for when his wealth was taken away he and his religion disappeared.

One thing which we may learn from a knowledge of the people is this, whether openly expressed by the unguarded such as Hugh, or the same thoughts subdued by the wiser, and that is that hatred towards England is, if the word could be used, justly instilled in the Irish heart. We may talk of charity, of forgiveness towards enemies, of this Bible or that, but without entering much into theology, how can one forgive who never gets the chance of doing so, who does not get time to forgive, what with the rod always to his back? It takes parties on both sides to come to a reconciliation before there can exist real forgiveness, but this state of things is yet to come to pass between the oppressor and the oppressed: no lenity ever came from English rule towards Ireland but when they could not help it. Why then upbraid the "men in the mountains" with disloyalty, where no loyalty is due, how can a slave love his unmerciful master, surely loyalty is not expected when persecution can go no farther, [and when one] is forced to yield? The Donegal peasant has got all the historical learning he requires; he has his ancestors' history open before him every day he rises; it is exhibited in the large characters—the ocean, the mountain, and his own state of poverty—and if he reads anything he must read how is it that he is there and why.

Hugh was held in great estimation by most if not all of his neighbours, no matter whether they gave credence to his lectures or not, and many were willing to be counselled by him, and in disputed cases as often happened among the best of friends his arbitration was adhered

---

61. Referring to the disestablishment of the Church of Ireland in 1869 by the Liberal administration of William Gladstone (1809–98).

to; the disputants would be guided by his advice, as they always found him the peacemaker; in addition he always discountenanced all sorts of vice by word and example. He did not try to give the colour of soft language to what he meant, for he came out rather glaring [sic]. The public houses he styled "the hot-beds of hell" and a drunk person was already lost in his opinion, for that person by his wilful act "threw off the garments of heaven", denied Peter and Paul, St. Patrick and the rest, and put on the "livery of Lucifer", and what could save him or her? If an injury was done to him, he was ready to bear it rather than attempt to obtain what other people called justice but he called revenge that is going to law. To prevent such he always advised all who would listen to him to bear with insults and even injury rather than go before what he called heretical judges, that is the justices of the peace at petty sessions. He was thought by most people to be a great scholar and passed off with many as such, and from the amount of languages at his command, he was always reckoned a worthy member at the meetings; as this was not unknown to himself, he lost no opportunity in all weathers of being present at such gatherings.

John Nicholson: among all the worthies who claimed superiority and aspired to knowledge John Nicholson deserves pre-eminence, not only that he was thought so by all the people as being the best speaker and the best scholar, but he had qualifications superior to most of the others, and this not unknown to himself. Knowing that the people fancied him as such, he never lost the opportunity of putting his knowledge to the best advantage whenever opportunity offered.

With the single exception of the old soldier, he had the "best hold" of the English language, and as the people used to say "could speak the two tongues" to perfection. He was most polite in his discourse, able and ready to talk to and address any man from the peer to the beggar, not in the least miserly himself in giving information or asking for the same, and always ready to pick up and seemingly to understand anything new at once. He had another advantage not possessed by his colleagues, and that consisted of inheriting some books by good authors and of ancient date, and he could the spare time and was fond of reading. His one favourite work was that of Pastorini, and from this he could quote at all hours.[62] There was hardly any subject that John was

---

62. 'Signor Pastorini' [Charles Walmesley], *The general history of the Christian church from her birth to her final triumphant state in heaven, chiefly deduced from the Apocalypse of St. John the apostle* (1771). Charles Walmesley (1722–97) was an English Catholic bishop. His *General History of the Christian Church* was a commentary on the Book of Revelation that predicted the overthrow of 'heretics' in 1825. Six or seven editions were published in Ireland

not ready to launch into, whether theology, astronomy, geography, geometry, mineralogy; he was acquainted with mensuration, as well as being a good arithmetician and was remarkably accurate in history and historical dates. As for agriculture, he was the model, theoretically and practically, for the whole neighbourhood, besides being a good mechanic, and so conceited was he that he kept tools belonging to trades some of which he could use and some he could not. He did not boast much of navigation, but could "box the compass".

In historical matters, there was no era or memorable event from the Creation that he could not repeat during a night's sitting. As for the history of the Carthaginians, Egyptians, Persians, Grecians and Romans, all were his own as not more than one in the assembly could either contradict, oppose or assist him. In his dissertations on the above, he gave the names of eminent men, the great conquerors and rulers of old, their rise and fall; and his hearers would listen with amazement until he became breathless with exhaustion. In his lectures on the United Kingdom, he gave the names of all the kings and queens of England, the length of their reigns and manner of succession, whether as lawful inheritors or usurpers, and these things as well as other events in the history of the three kingdoms were to him like a song. He would give long explanations on what led to the cause of the expulsion of the Fallen Angels, the Creation, and the Fall of Man, and why it was that man got free will—to give no excuse to the angels on the last day that an injustice was done to them, for if man was created incapable of sinning, then they could say "man was favoured". In describing the patriarchs of old, he entered into Bible history, and for biblical knowledge no one then or there could equal or cope with him. The book, the chapter and the verse were at his command—no scratch of the cranium had he to undergo for to think or quote what he wanted.

His hearers would in turn be favoured with a very elaborate description of the sun's course, his size and distance from the earth, and also the matter of which that luminary is composed, his size and distance from the other planets relatively; the names and sizes of some of the planets in themselves, as many as he knew, and also their course, not forgetting the comets, and how it was remarked at all times that some

---

between 1790 and 1820 and extracts in pamphlet and broadsheet form were widely circulated among lower-class Catholics after 1815, contributing to a popular expectation of 'deliverance' in the early 1820s: see J. S. Donnelly, Jr, 'Pastorini and Captain Rock: Millenarianism and sectarianism in the Rockite Movement of 1821–4', in S. Clark and J. S. Donnelly, Jr, eds, *Irish peasants: Violence and political unrest, 1780–1914* (Dublin, 1983), pp. 102–39; Ó Cíosáin, *Print and popular culture*, pp. 192–7.

memorable event happened at the time of the appearance of one. The "tail star" was always an object of dread as the forerunner of war or famine, and the young and old trembled at the sight. The cause of the tides he would also explain, the revolutions of the earth, and its more than probable departure from its original course, and how the same may effect [sic] or be the real cause for the well-known change in the seasons as differing entirely from what old men now knew and experienced when young. For instance, the heavy snows, which they remembered filling up the valleys, the longs frosts in the proper seasons, followed by fine weather. And there were the herring fishing seasons, and the boats that went out in the evening and remained at sea out of sight of land till day-break next day without any dread. These opportunities were at times of the past, as now there was nothing but changeable and fickle weather, giving no chance to the fishermen to venture to sea as they were accustomed to do. The nets, as many as were preserved, were hung up, but most of them were rotten or useless and the boats were mouldering on dry ground, as the industry which was once very profitable dwindled to forgetfulness.

How John obtained all his knowledge was problematical to many, and though he would not clearly admit it himself, it was known and understood by many that most of the learning he was now so willing to expound was derived from one of those extraordinary personages, by name Pat Garey, one of the old house-to-house school-masters. Pat Garey had been rather a private tutor, that is he stopped with only the few, and must have been a very clever character in his day as no branch of knowledge was hidden from him. No one knew whence he came, but in any case he remained for a long time in the locality when education was a hidden mystery; he wandered about and spent his time with the better-to-live-among [sic], the people by whom he was invited, and they remunerated him on the understanding that he would impart some of the knowledge he possessed to their sons. Of many who had the advantage of experiencing the abilities of Pat Garey, John Nicholson was the most brilliant pupil. Garey's oddities were well-remembered by many of the people and often rehearsed by them. His manner of living was extremely curious, for he would eat nothing in the presence of anyone, and what was the most extraordinary and in the eyes of the people the most nauseous of all his oddities was that he cooked and made use of frogs, which he termed "bog-fish".

He was never known while in the locality to sleep on a bed, never was seen to stretch himself to rest for sleep, but when that natural time arrived for people to go to rest he got into a sack and by means of a rope tied to a part of its mouth and the end of the rope held by himself, he got into the sack and swung himself to a peg in the wall and thus rested till morning.

Whatever may have been his station, his course or career previously in life, he was wise enough to keep it to himself many were the conjectures but nothing could be found out. At this time any man, let him be good or bad, could live in these backward parts of the country unknown ever so long; but one thing was certain, whatever his hidden life may have been, his learning was extraordinary at that time. He was a real proficient in the art of dialling and some of his handiwork at such remains and is preserved in a few places to the present day. Without the advantage of tables to assist him, he could calculate when full tide would happen at a particular place at a particular time and how long it would be till at the same hour and minute the same would happen again, that is to say an exact coincidence.

But to return to John, all the rhetorical orations and explanations given by him would of course be listened to with admiration, and seldom would he be obstructed or contradicted as no one could except by weak argument. If on the subject of the earth's revolution, someone who could not be made to understand would get up the frivolous objection, "that on every morning he rose, his house was facing the same rock, and the same hill was always opposite the door". Another would throw in his bit of knowledge by saying, "It is an old saying that the wheels of the world go round", that he heard from a good authority that "the earth was supported by four wheels but that he never could get anyone to tell what was supporting the wheels".

Another man wishing his voice to be heard would attempt to show part of his knowledge by setting forth that he had it from good authority long ago that a burning hill or mountain in Italy called Vesuvius was the entrance to that hot region or other world below, to which no one is willing to claim any inheritance, but the name of which is often in the mouths and on the lips of many people who "wish to others what they would not wish to themselves", and for that reason such a place must be under the earth and the earth could not be round, for if so how could such a hot region be under it?

These objections were troublesome enough to overcome, yet John would answer in the shortest and easiest explanatory manner he could produce, but failing withal to make an impression on the minds of some; for in the middle of his discourse when he would begin to think that he had some convinced, someone would shout out, "Now where is the use in talking, for do we not see the sun in the summer season rising out of the sea in the morning and dipping down into the sea in the evening, just before our eyes and who can say against that? And it is well known that sea captains going to America always in the evenings turn their ships' heads to the setting sun". These little differences of opinion did not however lessen John's knowledge in the views of many, and they were therefore impressed with the belief that he had "a head above many", and that these opinions were firmly grounded; in lawsuits he was looked to and consulted for opinions as much as an attorney would. In fact he was their only attorney and often went before the bench to explain and to interpret to the magistrates, who in those days gave permission for this in certain cases. If John succeeded in lessening the charge, his standard of estimation was thereby increased; in cases of arbitration, which were then very common (such as trespass or damage done to growing crops, or the loss of an animal through the fault of another), the side which had or could first secure the services of John were sure that no injustice would be done to them, for "he was the boy left no stone unturned so far as reasoning went". John was always chosen to be umpire by the others sitting on such matters; they gave their views but his decision was agreed to by all.

All situations, however trivial, were at this time obtained by means of petitions and signatures from influential men—ministers, magistrates, and petty landlords—and for such, John was looked to as "being able" to draw out, dictate, construct and address memorials to men in all stations having authority—to the magistrate, "His worship at petty sessions"; to the highest landlord, "The Honorable and Right Honorable"; to the Lord Lieutenant if required, "His Excellency"; and not even all these but he was supposed "to be able" to write and send a letter to the king. Such was the importance of the petitions that a young man if he wanted to get into, say, the Revenue police went for many days in succession from one "big house" to another presenting his paper and soliciting signatures, and if successful thought it the highest honour.

John had the advantage over all the other members of being able to cope to a certain extent with every subject and, when tired of one, he would branch off into another very easily; being naturally gifted with a fluency of speech and ready wit, a retentive and accurate memory, and no dryness in his throat, he was always ready to lecture, to discourse, and to discuss; it was his delight if he could pick up an opponent. It may therefore be understood that his presence at every gathering was sure to attract, was much esteemed and was eagerly looked for.

John opened up, "Well, I remember reading", "I forget the name of the book now but it makes no matter", or by quoting from some book which no one knew but himself no one could oppose him, and such being the case no ground could he lose, nor any the least twist could be taken out of him, for why—because he had read it. Not even the man of all knowledge—the old school-master—had any desire to enter into controversy with him, even though the subject be hurtful to his feelings, as often it was, and stung to the very quick the old soldier. John was no way backward nor delicate in meddling with English history, and exposed and condemned the faults of kings in all their most glaring colours; neither was he afraid but rather prided himself in exposing the blunders of the English general or army on many occasions which he would enumerate, no matter who listened to him; when he entered upon such, it was like picking a quarrel out of the veteran, for a contentious argument was certain to arise between them. But after much heat and talk, they would have to leave off just as they began, each one upholding his own opinion and none among the audience being able to decide but with this difference that, judging from their few words and gestures, John felt satisfied that he had the majority of votes on his side, that his language and argument was the most favourable with them, as in fact it was, whether true or false. The old soldier [i.e. the school-master] knew this right well, but he would not be silent and could not be kept from talking or interfering, once the name of England's army was disadvantageously interfered with. Talk in his hearing about religion, talk about anyone or anything or everything, all is smooth, but say nothing hurtful to the army.

There were a few more chiefs, or minor satellites as they might be called, such as Edward Granard, Tom Strait, Jeremiah Long, Peter Scabbard, Henry Spratt, who could never feel happy in being absent, and into whose abilities and qualifications we need not enter, a few of whom had as much to say upon matters they knew nothing about as that it gave "them the headache", but if "they had as much or near as much in the head as John Nicholson had, they would be sure to go mad, as their heads would not hold it". When speaking of heads and their contents, it may be said that John's as far as dimensions were concerned was the smallest of the lot, yet he never thought of going mad. These lesser celebrities had second-class accommodation reserved for them and they were always expected to be present, and needless to say they were seldom absent. When all these met with the object of ventilating their various degrees of knowledge, it might be easily guessed how the night would pass, as will be treated in the next chapter.

On these occasions the house of meeting was also filled with anxious listeners, many of whom had neither chair nor stool to rest upon, but were glad enough to get inside the door in any shape, so glad were they to be within hearing distance. And in addition to these nightly meetings there were meetings on a smaller scale held on the afternoons of Sundays. These Sunday meetings took place generally in the house nearest to the place of worship. The old soldier was watched on his move towards it, and if he and John met, and if he drew out his pipe on nearing the door, it was a sure signal of entering, so his admirers shook shoulders and made haste after him. No sooner did he enter than those wishing to hear the discussions hurried in, and without meat nor drink forgot themselves so far and sat there during the afternoon of long summer days till near the time of setting sun, slowly dragging themselves home in the evening, hungry and almost weak as the reward for their enthusiasm.

CHAPTER 5
The Nightly Meetings

Those named in the last chapter were the acknowledged chief speakers [at nightly meetings], and they were assumed to have more knowledge than the generality. On the appearance of any one of them there was a sort of intuitive respect shown by the majority, for everyone was at once on the move to make way for them to the front, come at what hour they might, as it was the opinion that no decision could be arrived at, no subject fully discussed, if some of them were absent, so that the night's proceedings were not considered good if all were not present. Of course there were many more members, less informed, who were present on all occasions and who might be termed ground keepers or camp followers; these felt the greatest satisfaction in listening but only interfered in a crisis when opposition got rather hot, and then declared and voted for the side or subject they favoured best, but without knowing why. Many of those outsiders or camp followers could if they wished have good seats themselves but would not do so; in their modesty they rather preferred to remain nearer the door than give any cause to deprive the worthies of the benefit of the front places. The result of such acts of humility on their part was cold and unpleasantness, but they would cheerfully put up with that.

At last the gathering was completed, the house overcrowded so much that many in the rear had to stand and lean one against the other. It was the self-imposed duty of the owner of the dwelling to see that a good supply of dry turf and firewood was near at hand, and a good fire constantly kept up; as seats could not be provided for all, at least the best possible supply was borrowed from the neighbours, and every attempt made to please, to welcome, and to make everyone as comfortable as they could under the circumstances. On this night alone, the owner of the house had consequently little or no chance of joining in the debates to any satisfaction, neither was it expected of him in his own house; elsewhere he had ample time and opportunity for joining in the topics and if qualified could show his abilities at his neighbour's.

The first ceremony, as soon as a goodly number were gathered, would be an attack on the tobacco pouches, the filling of old clay pipes, the setting fire to and smoking of tobacco; after a good smoke and a fair and honest consumption of the weed (the same performance, unknown to them, as the well-known practices of the Red Indians who use the same produce as the harbinger of friendship) and the luxury partaken of by nearly all, some would use it to excess, which could be easily known by the hiccup and requests here and there for "hand me a drink of cold water". The man of the house was always the first to hand out a bowl or ofttimes a wooden vessel called a "noggin", full of the pure spring water, and he supplemented with the wish "if it was better, you would get it".

While the smoking was going on, everyone who showed an inclination to enjoy the weed was handed a piece of turf burning at one end, and it was handed from one to another as long as they could blow sparks of fire out of it; when not in use it was deposited on the floor in a state of burning and smoking till wanted by some other. Those who had a little more patience waited their turn of the tongs, and this iron instrument, if the prongs did not cross and let the coal drop to the floor, was handed round in the same manner, but for expedition's sake two or three would be puffing and drawing fire from the same coal, the same source at the same time. A sudden "start up" occasionally occurred from sparks on the clothes, but what about that "shake them off", "not all silk" and "no harm done".

Men engaged on important transactions are liable to forget on the spur of the moment if the mind is too much engrossed; therefore we must make certain allowances for some of our members in the hurry on leaving home; not everyone had the presence of mind to carry with him his necessary article, the invaluable "duhdeen"—some unfortunately forgot it for the reason that "Molly or Biddy was making use of it, just taking a draw as I was coming out of the house and I never thought of it till I was a good piece away".[63] It is questionable whether the excuse

---

63. *Dúidín*, short-stemmed clay pipe.

was real or intentional as a little gain might be studied in the business, but no matter, no one could be very long at a disadvantage, they were all neighbours and well wishers, and any man's pipe was good enough so long as the tobacco was got for nothing—some had plenty of the stuff and filled the pipes. There was not much delay in doing so, just "stop a grain" in the mouth of one, hand it round and in this way one "duhdeen" served for many. One man lit it, first satisfied himself, handed it to another who in his turn to make the best of the bargain speedily jerked away a multiplicity of "puffs", passed it to a third and so on. Someone along the line always added to the combustible part as the charges were brought low until at last the real owner lost sight of the machine altogether and the last man in whose custody it was would be at a loss to know to whom it belonged. Ultimately it was traced to the rightful owner, and when it was returned to him, he felt some doubts and had some difficulty in recognizing the same portable machine he had so lately parted with, so discoloured had it become from the effects of the sudden change it had undergone in passing through so many hands and performing so excessive an amount of evaporated caloric. Nor could the owner then at once safely consign it to the pocket, until it was sufficiently cooled down by the application of moisture instinctively got, that is to say the spittle, putting finger and thumb to tongue and rubbing [hard].

By the time all these preparations and introductions were going on inside, daylight had entirely disappeared, and outside all was dark wind, sleet or rain as the case may be, but inside the four walls were as many men as it could hold, and every little vacant spot on the floor being covered with cinders, ashes, or the remains of burning pieces of turf. The large fire on the hearth is kept constantly in good trim, and in contact with the roof is a dense atmosphere of smoke already emitted and proceeding from the many apertures of the consumers of that famous luxurious produce of Virginia. We at last come to the hour when most if not all the members are in their places, the night is advancing, the important time for discussion is near at hand: someone would open up by simply asking in an easy-going way, "Well master, what about the war now?"; "Any sign of a break out among the Crown heads?"; "What are they doing in parliament now?"; "Had you any word yourself of late?". All these interrogations are hurriedly put forth, but the latter intended for a good "wash down" of course and it had the desired effect, for it put him at once in the attitude of throwing his one leg over the other, putting the tobacco quid into his waistcoat pocket, and moistening his lips. During this slight interval and before time to speak, another one asks "Are we going to have Repeal?".

In this way subject after subject was promiscuously broached upon—started by someone and followed up by another or others. The answers from him would at first be, "No nation in the world is fit to cope with England"; "Look at her fleet"—and this reference spoken to men who never saw a man-of-war except they might guess it by the size of a sail on the horizon of the ocean. Again, "We would sweep any nation, any power under the sun"; "And that is what you will never see, a parliament in 'College Green' until the very downfall of England, be that long or be it short". These preliminaries of course passed off without much contradiction, no great heat of action yet, and the same headings were re-opened and served the same ends the following nights.

Soon were unearthed and brought to the front for inquest, trial and judgement, Nelson—Wellington—Bonaparte—the Nile—Waterloo—and Copenhagen—Trafalgar—then turning to O'Connell—Lord Derby—Lord John Russell—Brougham—Peel—the Yeomen—the United Men or "Unites"—Smith O'Brien, and other distinguished men and names.[64] From constant repetition their names became quite famil-

64. Viscount Horatio Nelson (1758–1805), British naval commander. Defeated French fleet at the Battle of the Nile, 1798; Danish fleet at the Battle of Copenhagen, 1801; and Franco-Spanish fleet at Trafalgar, 1805.

Arthur, 1st duke of Wellington (1769–1852), politician (Tory) and military commander. Chief secretary of Ireland, 1807–9, military commander at the Battle of Waterloo, 1815, and prime minister, 1828–30.

Daniel O'Connell (1775–1847), attorney and politician. Leader of the campaigns for Catholic Emancipation in the 1820s and the Repeal of the Union in the 1840s. The dominant political figure in Ireland before the Great Famine.

Edward, 14th earl of Derby (1799–1869), British politician (first Whig later Tory). Chief secretary of Ireland (1830–3). Oversaw the introduction of national education and the establishment of the Board of Works. Defected to Tories in 1835. Prime minister (1852, 1858–9, 1866–8).

John, 1st earl Russell (1792–1878), British politician (Whig) and prime minister (1846–52, 1865–6).

Henry, 1st baron Brougham (1778–1868), British politician (radical). Lord chancellor (1830–4) and prominent participant in debate on Reform Act, 1832.

Robert Peel (1788–1850), British politician (Tory). Chief secretary of Ireland, 1812–18, and prime minister, 1841–6; great opponent of Daniel O'Connell.

Yeomanry, part-time local defence corps raised by government in 1796 to repress the United Irishmen. Most corps became almost exclusively Protestant in the early 1800s. Widely resented by Catholics, they were disbanded and disarmed in the mid-1830s.

Society of United Irishmen, radical political society established in Dublin and Belfast in 1791. It developed into a revolutionary republican movement which organized throughout Ireland after 1795 and secured French military assistance for an unsuccessful rising in 1798.

William Smith O'Brien (1803–64), nationalist politician and leader of the 1848 rising. Convicted of high treason, he was transported to Tasmania. Pardoned in 1854, he returned to Ireland in 1856 but avoided further political involvement.

iar with even the little children, who in their turn showing their ready wit bestowed a name on each of our worthies in accordance to what they were accustomed to hear, such as "Brougham" for Stephen Swanson from the very fact of him having that gentleman's name so often introduced. Such like for others—one was Wellington, one was Nelson, another Bonaparte and so on.

The latter name in particular stuck as a cognomination [sic] to the man and his generation for the reason that it happened to be more applicable, he being of a quarrelsome and fighting disposition, and the "Bony Family" became a well-known term. By means of this the names of those great men were transferred to obscure humanity without knowledge, consent or even restitution on either side, and by such names our worthies were properly and personally known in the locality; and as they got no other names except very seldom, they were at last forced to answer to the new, and did so just as well as to their original proper names. No wonder "Lord Brougham" got his present name, for he would forget and forsake gain at home for the time being, even if the harvest was in danger of being lost, and would make his way for a distance of two or three miles if he heard of a newspaper [from which he could] have the pleasure of reading a speech delivered by Brougham.

At that time the Press was not so cheap nor so easily got as nowadays, but sometimes a sixpenny number, dating back fourteen days more or less, might be got by someone who might happen to be selling his oats in the town, or had it sent to him by a friend across the channel. But if any newspaper arrived in the neighbourhood with priest, minister, magistrate or squire, Stephen was sure to hunt it up.

The man who could bring forward a paper of any stamp was sure of having the greatest welcome at the meetings; this act in itself was sufficient to qualify him for having a voice, where before he had none; as someone would unexpectedly announce that he had got a paper about him, immediately he was ushered forward without many questions as to how he came by it, what it was, or what date, but his place of comfort was secure for him for the night. The names of some prints were known to them, but the best in their estimation was "Reynolds": he was the man who told the truth and was not afraid to speak it either, to king, queen, or emperor.[65]

The paper would be opened up before the fire and if it was a good

65. G. W. M. Reynolds (1814–79), English radical, author, and editor of *Reynolds's Miscellany*, and (from 1850) *Reynolds's Weekly Newspaper*. Pioneer of cheap, accessible fiction in the form of the 'penny dreadful'.

size, all seemed satisfied already; the next person sought was the reader, for we must bear in mind that none of the members of themselves wished to read any of it just then as it would prevent them from their share in the discourses. The reader was sought for and got. Pity the reader, for as regards the paper, there was no scruple whatever as to date or editor; he was generally one of the best of the scholars who was captured for to perform. The poor sufferer dared not refuse, but he had the unwelcome and arduous task of reading aloud as best he could for the whole assembly [and received] the correction, explanation and interpretation of the master who as he thought fit gave orders to stop for explanation and to proceed when comment was over. The reader sat with his side to a blazing fire overcome by heat, the sweat oozing out of him, but he dare not complain; his only moments for rest and relief would be when a contention arose among the members on the point at issue.

For these reasons many would procure newspapers for the purpose of introducing themselves. A paper was [not always] available, and then the assembly was at liberty to discuss any subject from Adam and Eve down. Sometimes the past and the present were left behind and they would launch into futurity and according to their knowledge describe the changes which were to happen in the history of the world or tending as far as the day of General Judgement, the proceedings then, and the Final Separation. The Book of Revelations was freely entered into and no hesitation expounding it. The coming of the Antichrist; his career, what manner of man he is to be, and his rigour in the persecution of the Christians; the peace which was to reign, and its duration after the overthrow of Antichrist; the period then till the Last day; the Last Day itself; the Meeting in the Valley of Jehosephat; the mission and the authority of St. Michael; how he is to call to Judgement; the sound of the last trumpet, and so forth and so forth.

Prophecy was recited and expounded. There were to be ships without sails, going against wind and tide. Bridges were to be on every rivulet. Men wearing short green coats serving in the king's name were to be stationed in every parish. And finger posts at all crossroads for showing the way to the stranger. The gaols were to be filled with men without crime. An iron horse was to run through the *Gap of Barnes More*.[66] Men would in the course of time deny their own property. The empty sack was to be worth the contents. The dogs were to be taxed. (Be the rest as it may, the writer of this saw an old book in which men-

66. *Bearnas Mór*, the great gap, a mountain pass in east Donegal; the main Derry–Sligo road runs through it.

tion was made by way of prophecy of the dog-tax years before it was law or came into operation, and the book was so old and worn that the date of its publication and by whom was entirely obliterated.) The iron horse through the Gap of Barnes was a thing they could not understand, though of recent date fulfilled.

In continuation of their recitals, "rooks"—these were explained by them, Ordnance Survey observation marks—were to be on the top of every hill. Special mournful mention was made of the "Valley of the Black Pig" and of the dreadful massacres which were to happen there, but of its precise locality they never could agree. Some would have it near at home, others removed it as far as some part in County Tipperary but no matter, it was in Ireland anyhow and all agreed that the dreadful havoc of human beings was to happen in that valley before the End. There were caves in many places, but known only to a few, and in these retreats some persons of a particular descent were to be saved who afterwards were to propagate the human race after the fearful destruction which was to happen at and during the downfall of England.

In reasoning thus, they would come to the conclusion that so many things as were well known—derived from prophecy—had already come to pass, that there was therefore no room for doubting what was spoken of as to follow, and especially the great wars; accordingly upon the return of the wars, their minds were centred. The greatest interest was felt with the greatest emotion, "Oh! had the prophets told when?", but this was kept a secret. England was surely to go down, but before being humbled all Ireland was to suffer the horrors of fire and sword, and to be "weeded" of human beings.

The first "relief" was to come from the Spaniards, headed by a chief of the tribe of Baldearg O'Donnell who is to make several feint [*sic*] attempts to land in Lough Swilly, thereby harassing the English army on land.[67] By this time the English fleet is annihilated on the coasts of Italy—and on landing without opposition, they see the country so

---

67. Aodh Ball Dearg Ó Dónaill (d. 1704), an Irish officer in the Spanish army. His return to Ireland in 1690 was interpreted by Catholics as fulfilling the first part of a prophecy that an O'Donnell with a *ball dearg* [red spot] on his skin would come from across the sea to deliver them from oppression. His messianic appeal helped him to raise an army of some 10,000 men in Ulster, but he became alienated from other Jacobite leaders and defected to the Williamites, fighting on that side at the battle of Sligo in 1691. He returned to Spain in 1697. The conviction that some Ball Dearg Ó Dónaill would deliver Catholics from oppression made a deep impression on oral tradition in west Ulster. For Ball Dearg and messianism in early modern Ireland, see B. Ó Buachalla, 'An mheisiasacht agus an aisling' [Messianism and vision verse], in P. de Brún et al., eds, *Folia Gadelica: Essays presented to R. A. Breatnach* (Cork, 1983), pp. 72–87; Ó hÓgáin, *Myth*, pp. 337–8.

deserted that they are led to believe that none but heretics are before them; they slay young and old of the few stragglers they meet until marching inland as far as Cruachan Hill near Lifford, where they fall in with a priest saying Mass, and a handful of frightened worshippers about him. The Spaniards then repent of their rashness when too late, and turn to the aid of the inhabitants—the few who are left. The English army is by this time withdrawn for the defence of [missing word], but it is to be swept away and put an end to in England, and that power is never more to set foot in Ireland.

It depended very much upon the disposition of the speakers themselves who among them was to get the lead for the night, that is if the subject to be discussed was pleasing, and the generality were mostly in favour of the doings of the time, and such topics as parliamentary speeches, O'Connell, and other matters concerning Ireland. The importance and interest felt in the subjects could be easily known from the earnest attention given to the chief speakers, the lateness of the hour at the time of separation, and the silent half mournful way on parting. Sometimes old women and children were so frightened that their sleep was restless, and out of their dreams they would cry out for help from the impressions made upon their minds from the dread of war. People of one family connexion would consult what was best to be done from the appearance of events—"they did not know the day or the night, it might be so soon"—and some took the precaution of actually making caves for to hide themselves their terror was so great, believing the time to be so near at hand from the many convincing proofs they got. In fact one man living near to a broad road where there was a bridge was with great difficulty prevented one night by members of his own family, and they had to use force, from setting about throwing it down, as he imagined that by doing so the enemy would have a circuitous route before again reaching his abode.

Many of these poor infatuates lived to see and feel the experience of what was to them worse than what the worthies imagined, that is to say—the years of Famine—in which the thoughts of mostly every one were centred on himself alone for his own preservation, and when war was the last thing spoken of and almost forgotten.

At one of the meetings one night, the owner of the house at which they met went with a neighbour to convey him part of the way after all was over. Three times did they traverse the distance between the two dwellings, about half a mile each way, and with slow and measured steps and occasional halting they would arrive at each other's door, halt, and the conversation not ended, they would return, retrace their steps and the night being beautifully clear, it was close upon daylight before they parted, the subject of discourse being so inexhaustible and their minds so much engrossed with it.

During the greater part of the time at these meetings, the speakers would agree very well, at other times the dispute would run so high as that they would be ready to throttle each other and in the heat of passion would actually rise to their feet, in the attitude of greatest enemies, and by words and insult point their sticks at one another. Without doing any harm this excitement would soon cool down, each one telling the other that he was wrong.

The plans of battles, the positions of armies in the field, of sieges, of camps and of cities would be marked out with the point of a stick in the ashes on the hearth, and the ashes spread out to enlarge the drawing on the floor. Sketches of rivers, seas and countries, with their position and relative sizes, were also drafted on this blank map. If any one through forgetfulness or otherwise had the audacity to speak lightly or was in any way disrespectful of the English or especially the English army, that was just enough for a tumult, for immediately the martial spirit of the old Veteran was roused and, after venting his anger in words not very pleasing, he would then as a conclusion foretell the day, not far distant either, at which time he would die in peace after he had got the chance of "burying his bayonet in the carcass of such a one", and "the only scruple he felt was to dirty his weapon".

Language such as this, if not really successful in striking terror into the bosom of his opponent (and he did actually frighten), would at least have the effect upon himself of relieving his limbs from the fatigue of a long sitting posture by the act of springing to his feet at this juncture and of continuing so while delivering his oration, and in words and gestures forcing his opponent into silence. Peace was again restored through the intervention of several who did not wish the night's proceedings to go to loss, nor did many of them wish to see the master offended, much less so the man of the house who meant to please all. Easy it was then for the old soldier to be bold and to conquer, for he had too many on his side and he knew it well. After a little bombast he would be re-seated, as retreat for him was impossible, seeing that he had to remain where he was for the night, and the man of the house appearing to get angry for his sake, our worthy would cool down and recommence explanation to some one whom he knew was neutral, or to those who seemed to be attentive to him, or who spoke partly in his favour.

Of course there were many who merely listened, who did not at any time interfere, and they fully enjoyed the scene going on among the disputants.

In this manner, night after night during the long winter season, would the meetings be kept up, from house to house and from village to village; at twelve, one, or two o'clock in the mornings such dwellings would get clear of non-residents, and all would be dispersed on their way home, very often in darkness and rain, suffering thus for no other advantage whatever than what they had heard discussed: on the way home some of them musing on the fixed opinion that war was at hand, some under the belief that parliament was coming back to Ireland, and that all good things would follow; others making up their minds for to escape to America, and that by so doing they and their sons would escape from being pressed into the army to fight for England against their own country, as it was prophesied that before the Wars, all young men who were capable of bearing arms were to be drafted into the Black Militia, and that old men were to be turned three times upon their beds to see if they were fit for service.[68] Some who managed to get the money raised got no rest until they made their escape to America, for no other reason but to be out of danger of being pressed into the army as they thought, though nothing of the sort ever happened, and if a story came round that a certain person had fled the country, the soldier to show his contempt and his opinion of who was likely to be a fighting man or not would say, "Well, he might not have left the country, for on the scarcest day that ever Wellington was of men at Waterloo, he would not take him". This might be true or it might not, but certain it was when all others dreaded war, the old soldier made everyone believe that he was wishing for it.

68. The Black Militia figured prominently in prophecies circulated by the United Irishmen in Ulster on the eve of the 1798 Rising. According to a mid-nineteenth-century memoir, in March 1798 'the reports of the fulfilling of the prophecies of St. Columbkille were now revived, with several new and interesting additions. Roman Catholics, in particular, were seriously alarmed by an account of their extirpation by a murderous band called the Black Militia, which was always construed to mean the Orangemen. In the counties of Derry and Donegal, it was reported, and commonly believed, that when the chapel of Convoy should be nailed up by the Black Militia, such persons as repaired to Glenfin would be safe, and on taking a stocking of meal with them for food, it would do them to the end of the wars. Some weak-minded females, however, not waiting for the nailing of the chapel, repaired to Glenfin with their stocking, but its contents soon becoming exhausted, in sober sadness they returned to their homes. About this time a printed hand-bill was sold about the country, headed with an annexed print, "A Zebra Foal", which stated that at a certain place in Ireland ... an animal had been foaled, beautifully striped, which immediately after repeated audibly ... A wet winter, a dry spring, a bloody summer, and no King.' See S. McSkimin, *History of the Irish rebellion in the year 1798; particularly in Antrim, Down, and Derry* (Belfast, 1853), pp. 99–100.

On the other hand, it came to pass in the lapse of years that the history of the war turned contrary, for it was America and not Ireland was the first to experience war, and natives of this very same place skedalled [*sic*] from that country back to the spot from which in earlier life they were first frightened. The latter step was, like the first, hurriedly taken to save themselves from being drafted into the "Union Army". The excuse now was that they would not fight against their brethren in the South, but of course when peace set in they quietly slid back again to America.

Should the nights be without moonlight, the men who had a considerable distance to come and go lessened the inconvenience and difficulty by carrying with them long staves and a pair of tongs, or some other iron made into the required instrument, fitted for the purpose of carrying turf and pieces of fir-wood. They took the trouble of carrying the fir-wood from home and this, added to the burning turf, served as a sort of torchlight while the long staff served as a support and was also used to probe the way through mud and soft ground. A considerable time before the hour of departure a good supply of the best dried turf was set round the fire to season, so that every man or group of men going in the same direction took what they wanted or thought sufficient for the journey. If in the meantime a squall or a heavy shower of rain set in, the time was prolonged, and all would be forced to remain a little longer; some would sit and some would stand, during which time the fire got leave to burn down and would require to be renewed and adding further to the delay, but the man of the house would have plenty fuel, "You are all time enough", "the Clusters are not far round yet", and "that cloud might pass from over the moon".[69] On windy nights these simple inventions showed light enough for the travellers to make headway, every one trying to keep up with the torch-bearer as best he could whilst he was generally the most active man in the crowd and at times, for a trick—for no matter what anxiety, what trouble is abroad, there are always some who carry the light heart and can enjoy a good laugh—he led them into difficult-to-walk-upon and wet ground, where most of them except himself had the opportunity of plunging into mud and water, and the light-bearer now continued at full speed, the sparks of fire flying about him, and through thick and thin the rest trying to keep up with him. One would get entangled, left behind, not able to extricate himself: "Hallo! for the sake of all that is good, are you going to leave me?" "Who is gone?". A halt is then made until all are closely mustered again.

69. The Clusters, the Pleiades constellation.

Some of the neighbours were fretful about the safety of dwellings or other outside goods coming too close to these burning lights; they could not go to rest until satisfying themselves that all danger was past. The wonder of it was that the thatched cottages near to were not set on fire, but they had the luck on their sides that the nights were many of them extremely wet. However to guard against this danger, the torch bearers always kept to leeward and at a safe distance, and those on the way of danger also sat up, the old man having a look around the premises before consigning himself to rest for the night. The precautions thus taken prevented accidents if a turf stack got into grief and ashes in one night, there was little talk about it as it was only a "mishap", nor would the County Court ever be troubled about it; no one formed the idea of compensation, and if a man ran short in that [article] his neighbours divided with him.

It was not forgotten by the man carrying the light that he should make all speed, for if the light burned out or through some mishap fell into a pool of water, he and his followers were then in an unenviable predicament, for they could see nothing at all around them or before them, and all would declare in the strongest language that "it was the darkest night ever they felt", not knowing the effects of the sudden deprivation of light. There they stood and not knowing where to move, their only remedy for extricating themselves lay in shouting and whistling to attract the attention of some friend or neighbour near at hand to their relief, and by means of another set of similar lights he would leave them on the safe road for home again, their deliverer being rewarded with his share of the drenching rain for his kindness. All nights were not equally hazardous, but on such adventurous nights all would at last arrive home wet and dirty from spattering through mud and a downpour of rain, but not in the least relenting for their sufferings; on the contrary their only thought was how to be prepared for the following night.

The family of the household they had left would naturally continue sleeping till aroused by the old dame who would quietly announce that breakfast was ready and that it was near time for the master to be preparing. This was warning enough for everybody to start up, but until this hour had arrived, and while she was in the act of preparing the good things, everything and everyone was as still as if a death had occurred. The child got on his clothes but dare not speak louder than a whisper on pain of being choked. The poultry were banished from the threshold for the time, so perfect quietness reigned. Breakfast over, the

Master then buttons up, and he and his companion, that is the scholar out of the family, start out for the seat of learning to commence the day anew in the old cabin in the Glen ...

CHAPTER 6
The Master's Revenge

The reader would be deceived if he were under the impression that our cultivator of youth was on amicable terms at all times with his neighbours. No, such was not the case, for like most people he had his friends and his foes, real or supposed. To do him justice, however, he was never the offender; he never was the cause of creating enemies to himself. But woe to those who brought themselves under the stroke of his anger; bitterly did they rue it and sorely did they repent what they had done, as he was unrelenting in his revenge. His manner of acting, of demanding what he considered his satisfaction and obtaining justice, was peculiar in the highest degree. It was a creation of his own genius, used by himself alone and never known or heard of before or since in the locality. Strange as this is, the offence generally committed was stranger still. There was only one word and the same is hard to find in a dictionary, which touched the keynote; this one word aroused him to an incredible pitch of anger, excitement, and animosity. Unfortunate word: it was often used by many who knew not its meaning, nor what harm could be in it, but that it just excited him.

There are other circumstances connected with this fatal word. The whole harm lay in shouting it from a distance; then it was enough to set his whole vocabulary in motion. The enormous crime lay in the monosyllable "Twee", meaning "To ye" or "To you" and as far as could be learned having for its full meaning—a shot at random, as much as to say, I'll frighten you. Say this word in conversation with him, the magic was dispelled. The real gravity of the crime seems to have consisted in shouting it from behind a hedge or trying to conceal oneself.

If he really saw the party guilty of the treasonable act or felt certain that he recognised him, he made up his mind at once as to how to act: he hastened home and set to his task "to put the culprit", as he said himself, "in the papers". Seldom or never did he make a mistake with regard to the offender, for so acute were his organs of hearing that he could at once distinguish the very family to which anyone belonged. It appeared to be true what he said of himself, "What I lose in sight I have in hearing".

In case he did not exactly know the offending party, he lost no opportunity of finding him out, not indeed by going directly and making known his object, but by inquiring in the most indifferent and to all appearances heedless manner. The fox is often trapped and however cunning we are, we can find our match and often do. People would sometimes take a hint and use it for an evil purpose. Occasionally he was misinformed. This was done by some neighbours who wanted to see some fun. No matter he believed it, for that was the man. "I cannot put it past him", for he belonged to a family suspected; "Ah! hah! I'll make him dance". This was enough, he was a fit subject for a target. And now the poor fellow's pedigree was traced to the remotest generation, all crimes known and unknown, real or supposed, were imputed to him; in fact everything was noted that thought could brand him with infamy—his lowness of birth, his manner of living, how he was imported into that part of the country, and why he was banished from Connaught. Epithets were also used unsparingly. He called him a Hottentot; a cooley [sic]; his mother a squaw &c.[70] If any one of the family had the misfortune to be afflicted with any deformity or natural impediment it was not forgotten. Words were used alluding to it and these often stuck to the unfortunate sufferers. Dromedary camel, baboon, Gibraltar monkey or some other species, all of which were quite familiar to him, were used as well as terms too delicate to mention. What heightened the evil here was that these were carried on afterwards as nicknames. Some he would characterize with the title of sloth, others with a name implying an extraordinary capacity of belly for gormandizing the most unpalatable food: he would specify the amazing quantity of "poundies" or "*praetee rostae*" (that is roasted potatoes) a person could take at a meal.[71] Language did not always satisfy him. He had recourse also to drawing and would give a rough sketch of his vic-

70. Hottentot, pejorative European name for Khoikhoi people of southern Africa; Cooley, presumably coolie, pejorative European name for a hired labourer in India.

71. *Prátaí rósta*, roast potatoes.

tim, picturing him sitting on a low stool, holding a spoon in his hand with a wooden dish or a pot between his knees, or holding a roasted potato in one hand and picking the crust off with the nails of the other or with his teeth, completing the picture or drawing by placing along his side or on the coals a piece of conger-eel or some such dainty, or a small dish of *sloak*.

A sufficient number of sheets being written with the engraving etc. on the top, his next business was to distribute them. The next fair day he started early with his burden. He knew well that the people were on the road from dawn and travelling for a considerable distance he dropped one here and there, securing it by placing a stone at a corner. He sometimes attached them to fences that might not be passed unheeded and where practicable posted them on gateways and doors. The door of the village blacksmith was sure to receive an early visit from him and its share of the bills. To do the work expeditiously he easily got little rascals to assist him who were only too glad to run about at his direction. The papers were picked up and the news soon spread. Everyone was anxious to know who was the subject and what was the subject matter. Those who could not read preserved it carefully till someone was found that could do so. Crowds often gathered and it was read aloud to them all. It now became the topic in the country about, and every one became familiar with the thrice unhappy offender. Nothing was talked of but the language used in the papers—which if allowed to remain so would pass away in a few days and be forgotten.[72]

72. Constabulary files attest to this type of abuse in north Donegal before the Famine; copies of the following notice were posted along approach roads to Letterkenny in 1839:

Woe be to the Inhabitants of the earth since Antichrist
is born and has set up a shoe shop in Letterkenny
Maxwell Kettle that upstart fop,
in L.Kenny has set up a shoe shop.
He cuts his leather 'pen such a plan,
that it must be stitched by an Orange Man.
He says his boots and shoes must fit quite well,
because he gets his fashions from the craft of hell.
His black painted sole [*sic*] and his Orange ran,
cannot be stitched by a papist man.
Some people say he has lost his sense,
When sold in the materials for eighteen pence.
That the curse of heaven on the man may drop,
Who leaves one penny in the Kettles' shop.
And that's the plan to cut short his strap,
And make his golden fleece with hunger droop.
And man or boy may watch his crown,
That dares attempt to pull this paper down.
For correspondence on this incident, see N.A.I., Outrage Papers 1839(I)/7/1718.

This was not the case with many whose pride was stung and whose family honour was insulted. They took it sorely to heart, fearing that it might lessen their dignity and make them fall in the estimation of society. The reader may now imagine the satisfaction our hero felt when his work had succeeded so well, and as neighbour after neighbour would call in to make known to him as much and more than they knew of the wide circulation of his productions, how well it was done, and how well the parties deserved it: "You first gave them their deserving"; "What right had they to meddle with you or call you Twee?". His heart swelled. If he were told that some man of sense or considered to be "a worthy" commented favourably and enjoyed it, his joy knew no bounds. He paced his room up and down, had a welcome for everybody, and expressed himself now and then as feeling pity for the creatures— devils—but it would teach them not to meddle with him again. They have themselves to blame: let them have it, pooh! hooh!

Now the best of all, or perhaps the worst of all, was that his visitors were the very persons who incited him to operate on the innocent sufferers. These hungry tobacco-seekers took advantage of his then good humour, made it their business to call with him and in flattering terms commented on his cleverness. Thus acting the hypocrite they would spend a few hours in idle cajolery for a mere trifle, as they knew he never wanted the "weed" and that he was in the habit of filling the pipe for all of their sort who came. Those mouths watering all day for want of a "taste" now watered at his expense with the "taste". They were extremely clever. You might see them before they entered preparing themselves for a good job and actually scouring their "duhdeens", scraping out—that they might hold a good charge.

There were two dwellings in the district presenting appearances very dissimilar [at such a time]. We have left one in which nothing but laughing, giggling and feigned merriment was heard, but we can go to another where the scene will be changed. If we visited the published parties as they are now called, we see mourning, grief, and anger unbearable. There they are assembled bewailing their misfortune which was brought on without any cause, or if there was a cause, it was the foolish act—the worst thing that could be said of him now—an unruly son or other relative, who brought on the present disaster and made them the laughing stock of the people: the wife and daughter soft of heart weeping, for now they could never show their heads in public; the father and the son inflamed with anger, grinding their teeth, the one pacing the floor swearing vengeance, the other leaning against the door jamb to be out of the sight of his mother, but both alike foaming and vowing vengeance against the malignant publisher who they believed had disgraced them for ever. "Why did that silly boy—guilty or not guilty—not mind his own business? Why was he guided by advice or what put it in his head at all, to shout that unlucky word 'Twee'?". "Why did he not keep away from Shemus Dhu? It was through him, for he is a *doual deelish*".[73] Such were the ejaculations emitted. There were visitors here too, for a neighbour is not only to be congratulated in success, but consoled and encouraged in adversity. So an odd friend slowly enters, having a sign—real or pretended—of commiseration or anger as would best please. In one case consolation was offered and advice to take the matter quietly, or again an attempt was made to add to the flame of passion that already existed by new suggestions.

This sudden annoyance and vexation soon passed away. The threats were never executed, for the "publisher" was sure to keep out of the way, and the matter was dropped except that some evil-disposed person made a "cast up of it", and so would renew the sores partially. It might also happen that the channel of conversation was turned in another direction sooner than any one expected, and in the course of time one neighbour devised a means to be revenged of another by putting "Twee" in motion. Perhaps while in discourse with "Twee" as he was passing, he had some individual in ambush to give the shout. Twee listens, asks who is "yon". "Well I would not like to say but I would think"—"Tis I know it". Some more exalted personage was made to suffer and was soon made to appear with the same colours; the public attention was changed, for it must be known that no one was spared, it mattered not how exalted his position or how noble his connexions—a former very great friend or a near relative, no matter whom. If occasion were given he suffered his fate, nay, there was more gratification in dealing a stroke at the presumptuous. Oh! yes, that was the bird he wished to get at: he would let them know what they were, what they sprung from. Thrice doleful sorrow: what were their feelings to find themselves associated with, or traced to relatives that they would fain deny?

These attacks had a good effect inasmuch as they were frequent, for in the end anyone was afraid to make allusion to another of his appearance in the "papers", for if he had not yet appeared himself he did not know how soon his time might come. Yes and this when he was least expecting it, for some mischievous individual at that very moment might be confidentially misrepresenting him to "Twee", and his astonishment

73. *Diabhal dílis*, true devil.

might be great at finding himself next morning the common bye-word; and what might vex him most was that it was only two days ago they met and exchanged the greatest friendship. The worst point about our libeller was that he was inflexible once he had made up his mind. If a man went to him on bare knees he would not forgive; if he delayed it was for the purpose of giving additional pain.

This method of retaliation went on for years, till at length he became so bold as to post up his "papers" close to the very house of worship. The old clergyman of the place might be blamed for his non-intervention and never took the courage to speak against him, not even when those with whom he was closely associated were attacked. The very man with whom his reverence lodged, who thought himself and his family the most respectable in the country, were pictured as above, performing the meanest of a servant's work; they considered themselves ruined but could find no redress. The old clergyman, I believe, said that he was afraid for himself, although I am sure he never called out "Twee".

Everything must come to an end. So it was with the publications, and not by the death of the author. A young clergyman who had newly come, on getting his first intimation of such foolish and detestable tricks, determined at once to put a stop to them—a thing which hitherto both clergy and laity were afraid to do. Once and then only was there a recurrence of the scene after his appointment.[74] His proclamation against it was short and severe: he warned the master to stop it and threatened that the next time he attempted any such ridicule against any one in the parish, the punishment would be that he would drive a nail through his ear and fasten him to the first post or door on which a paper would be found. This had the desired effect, for the clergyman was young and strong and, what added still to infuse dread, a little passionate. Old "Twee" was paralyzed with fear, and the people feared him no longer.

---

74. Canon John O'Boyle (1833–1910) was born at Dooey in Leitir Mhic an Bhaird in west Donegal. He entered the Irish College, Paris, in 1850; transferred to St Patrick's College, Maynooth, in 1853; ordained 1857; curate in Killymard, 1857–9; curate in Fánaid, 1859–66; administrator of Fánaid, 1866–70; parish priest of Fánaid, 1870–1910. The diocesan historian describes him as 'a worthy pastor, of lofty ideals and indomitable courage' but also hints at worldliness and neglect of pastoral duties in his last years: see Maguire, *Diocese of Raphoe*, pt. I, vol. I, pp. 327–30.

CHAPTER 7
Villages

A village as every one knows is a cluster of houses or dwellings, but some years ago a village was rather a small town. The country villages then were as many in number as there are townlands, and on one townland there might be two, so they were numerous, each containing many inhabitants who differed from each other in many respects. Some residents prided themselves as being descendants of old stock, and these held land and lived chiefly by its produce. There were tradesmen of different classes—carpenters, masons, weavers, shoemakers, tailors, smiths, coopers; many of such trades were settlers from other parts, but each family possessed a house more or less respectable [*sic*] to their tastes or manner and means of living, and some lived in close and crowded hovels unfit for human beings. Some had free dwellings and free tenements in land from long standing, paying neither rent nor taxes, the gift of some relative who on his death-bed thought fit to do so. As there was no emigration then except with very few, the people had to provide a form of shelter somehow; so many and so closely packed were the dwellings that a stranger on entering a village would have [to make] a scrutinizing survey and withal be under the necessity of the direction of a guide to make his way to the occupier of a certain dwelling whom he wished to visit.

Process servers and summons servers—the only men at this time held in detestation (for the hatred of the bailiff was yet to happen)—were often baffled and in many cases had to leave with as little information as on appearing, for whether their mission was lawful or not their ques-

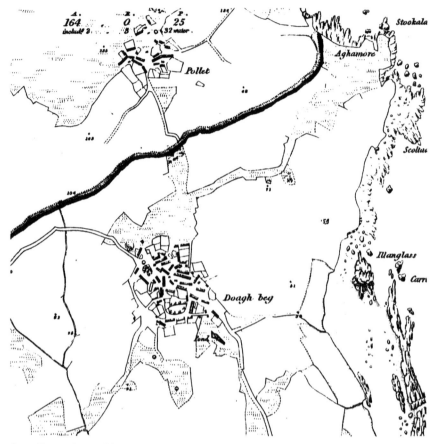

The village of Doaghbeg as represented on the first edition of the Ordnance Survey, Co. Donegal (1836). Large house clusters were not uncommon in the early nineteenth century, and were mainly found in districts of poor soils where recent population growth had been greatest. Doaghbeg, located on the Leitrim estate, was an unusually large agricultural village and was close to its maximum size at the time of the survey. Attempts to re-organize its rundale field systems in the early 1840s were met with resistance.

tions were always and ever answered with the very unsatisfactory reply "I don't know", even by the very children. And such men in their difficulties cunningly made their way to the herdboy or the children behind a wall or fence, but in little or nothing would they be wiser. Nor at the sight of a "bright penny" would they waver.

These were the "happy times" in which if one man in the village had claim to or occupied more land than many of his neighbours, and if he was of an easy-going nature as most of the old stock were, he would

NOTICE.

LET no one of **LEITRIM'S TENANTS** pay **TITHES,** but for the year **1839,** and to get their **Receipts** dated up to that period.

Are you to be robbed by such a **Tyrant** as **LAW**? Look to yourselves Tenantry! What can you expect from the Agent, that will seize **Timber, fine** the People, and cut it up for his own use! Eject good Tenants at Will, for no offence!

If this is to be the Order of the Day, we are blessed as a Tenantry!

DOUGHBEG.

Head Constable James Hay removed this notice from the door of the Presbyterian Meeting House in Letterkenny on the morning of 1 February 1840; other copies were posted throughout the Leitrim estate. 'Tyrant LAW' refers to John Law, appointed agent of the estate—and justice of the peace—in 1839. His approach to estate-management was very high-handed, provoking violent clashes between bailiffs and tenants. The suggestion that the notice came from Doaghbeg plays on Fánaid's reputation for being 'troublesome' and 'lawless'. Sub-Inspector Alexander Fox forwarded the notice to Dublin Castle, where the law-adviser ruled that it was not punishable by statute and that the constabulary should disregard it.

readily and on the easiest terms give the site of a cabin to a friend or a well-wisher. Often such friendship would be gained by invitation to a christening or a few glasses of whiskey at a fair or market—to soften the old fellow before asking the request. The sites of cabins with a dip of ground or a piece of a garden attached were sometimes given free, at other times the conditions were a day's work in the month or so in lieu of rent, if a labourer. Men gifted with any sort of trade had terms of their own making. The creel-maker made a certain number of creels after night or on rainy days on the kitchen floor of his landlord, while the latter supplied the material. This extra work fulfilled his obligations, while it did not prevent him from any other occupation in daytime. Another man thatched houses and corn stacks, and let [*sic*] the twisting of straw ropes mostly after night and was handy in doing many other little extras, and he also got off easy. The weaver had his bargain with the "good wife", and any work done by him over a certain quantity he was to be paid for, the stipulated quantity when performed clearing him of taxation, and so with the shoemaker and the tailor. We may now call these cottiers to the landowner or tenant. The weaver was the only fixed tradesman, for the simple reason that he could not carry his loom. All the other trades went from house to house as they were asked, each tradesman carrying his "kit of tools" and was sometimes accompanied by an apprentice, the attendant being in most cases a son; the two remained in any house as long as the job lasted, which length of time depended very much upon the demand for work. If work was scarce and the hospitality pleasing, there was no hurry in leaving, as every thing had to be done well. A house of good reputation often had the shoemaker and tailor [working there] together.

The tailor on his way to satisfy his customer was indeed not very heavily laden with tools. The only articles visible and emblematical of his trade being the "goose" in one hand; a piece of board which he called the "lapboard" under his arm; and the point of the scissors might be seen protruding from his trousers pocket; all his other instruments, the needle, the thimble, the chalk, the "measure" being concealed about his person. The last named requisite was sometimes carried about his neck, the material of which was dried sheepskin leather; a certain number of lengths were stitched together, the breadth being at first three or four inches but gradually getting narrower. When first used in taking a measure, notches were cut in the side edge of the skin, the reading of which no one but a tailor understood, and as the same might not serve any other person, the notches had to be pared off each time, thus it became narrower and was rendered too fine and useless at last, and a new one had to be procured, leather of his own tanning and his own make.

Arriving at his destination, he was so very welcome that the most comfortable place in the dwelling was allotted him, but his choice was to be as near the fire as possibly could be. The cloth was then brought for the inspection, and he was sure not to be the man to despise it, for it might be his brother or brother-in-law's weaving, and it was "very good cloth", "well put together", "no two sayings about it", "wishing you health to wear it". Yes, it was good cloth, "feel the grip of it", but the old woman had something to do with it, she put the "heart into it", for she herself had spun every thread of it.

The cloth was spread to see what could be taken out of it; the chalk and measure were produced and the old man told to throw off "the old

coat". He was measured round the chest, round the waist, the dimensions applied to the cloth and the chalk leaving its trace; down the
back—"hold up your head man!—stretch out your arm—that'll do",
and each time was heard the clinking music of the scissors taking a bite
out of the sheepskin. "Try if you can spare a piece that will make a
waistcoat for Mikel!"

When evening came on, the tailor always made his own candlestick
and this necessary article he would not be long turning out of the raw
state. He got a sallow rod of proper thickness and, taking his knife in
hand, with two or three strokes he had one end nearly pointed round,
the other end with two cuts he had formed it wedge like. The pointed
end he stuck into a properly seasoned turf, and in the other he cut a
notch and the candlestick was complete. A narrow slip of cloth was put
round the halfpenny tallow candle and the necessary balance slid into
the notch, and afterwards the only trouble was to remove [wax] occasionally as the candle burned low. It happened one time that a tailor had
with him an apprentice, a young lad, and the two of course sat on the
same table with the candle between them, but the old woman thought
that a distinction should be made between man and boy, and though the
light was sufficient for the two, it being a good halfpenny candle—fourteen to the pound—she of her own material manufactured a taper-like
candle called a "sleet" (that is a grain of tow, twisted and dipped in
grease or butter), and placing it near the candle said that it would serve
for the boy.

The coat being finished it was tried on, and every one said it was "a
very good coat", "not too tight at the shoulders", "just the right length"
before and behind. Turn around! It was worth waiting for it. "Not
wishing you a short life, it will last a good many years of your lifetime
by taking care of it. It will last for many a day for it is well put together,
and it fits well, wishing you your health to wear it." The tailor did not
spare thread on it.

When a time came that the financial state of a household afforded
the purchase of some leather, word was sent to the shoemaker, and he
gathered up all his implements in his leather apron and bade "good
morrow" at the house at which he was expected, but first he and "the
man of the house" had to go to the shop to get the leather and both
must have a share in choosing it. The shopkeeper is willing enough, he
shows his stock, the hides are spread out, one is pitched upon, it is
rubbed and felt in all its parts, and at last they are satisfied with its
strength, its grain &c. The shoemaker scores and cuts out, trying to do

justice between seller and buyer, but more inclined to benefit the latter: "uppers"—"sole"—"welts"—"heelrands", and each chosen separately, but all are tied up at last in one roll and weighed and now between pounds and ounces the shopkeeper makes his price. The "whangs" go free. Other extras are charged separately, iron tips—nails—thread—rosin, and not forgetting the required number of half-penny candles.

They then march home, and immediately the shoemaker prepares for work: all his tools are opened out on a "sieve" or other instrument on which he can see them. He places himself on a stool in such a position as to have the small of his back as near the fireplace as possible. He breaks up his rosin, mixes it with butter without salt, melts and boils it in a piece of an old pot—a "cam"—over the fire, turns it while boiling into cold water in a pot or tub; he then rubs and rolls and draws, mixing in every shape, and thus forms his balls of wax with which he covers his threads.

When the work is so far advanced that the soles are to be put on, the shoemaker orders the leather to be steeped in water, and while it is being moistened he then turns round and faces the fire for a chat and a not very short one. At nearly every house then could be found a round smooth stone called a "beating stone", kept purposely for the use of the shoemaker. He calls for this stone, Johnny or Paddy knows where it is, and placing it on both knees, he gets the now softened sole-leather and commences hard and fast pelting at it with his hammer until his eyebrows are bedewed with pearly drops of sweat. The more he beats at it, the more he satisfies the owner who is of the opinion that from this comes the better wear. The shoes are made and well-heeled, the soles well-covered with nails—paviors—and the thicker are the "wearing side"—the toe-points with "bang ups" and a few of the "brogue nails" at the spring of the foot. They are then tried on, and a very "good fit", only a little tight at the "wee toe", no matter—they will stretch, "every leather must stretch". "Cut a 'wee' piece out of the stocking for a day or two."

The red colour of the leather must now be changed and to do so a good handful of straw, a wisp, is burned on the floor, the ashes of which are carefully gathered up and mixed with the melted tallow scraped off a couple of candles, and a very good layer of this compound is rubbed in with the hand as tight as possible, turning the leather black and a proof against water.

At this time there lived in a central part of the district a nailmaker—"a white smith"—who worked late and early, blowing his bellows and hammering at nailrod, making nails and supplying the shopkeepers; he thereby earned a means of living for himself and family. Competition and machinery in other parts in a few years overcame him and he was forced to abandon the trade and seek for a means of living elsewhere, but "Watty's" nails were long remembered as the best.

These professional tradesmen were not always engaged at their particular trades; it was only at certain times of the year that they got work to do, and at other times, when disengaged, they might if so inclined give a helping hand to other members of their families to cultivate potatoes, and as there was no scarcity of food at this time, they had always plenty to eat, working at their trades when employment was to be got, or when willing to work, but the greater part of the year in idleness. These petty tradesmen in general were undoubtedly the laziest of men, very slow in reaching their hands to any other kind of work, for unless they got the work that they were accustomed to they would lounge about, and in anything they had to do depending on the neighbours; the customers were under an obligation to assist, such as ploughing the ground, digging, helping to put in the seed, cutting and drawing their turf, and so forth.

Any man professing any sort of trade always got preference and easier terms [when he sought] to become cottier to the landholder, for the latter, if he had any roughness about him, thought that he could not do well unless some one of these artisans were convenient to him, and they in their turn became so independent of their benefactors that at the least dry word they gathered up and changed abodes, and got other places without much trouble. Though the services of such were considered valuable, yet they were looked down upon in another sense: they were the middle class of people, and one out of a higher or farming class, a young man or young woman, dare not intermarry with one of them under pain of degradation and of disinheritance, so that if a son or a daughter became disobedient in this respect, they were disowned and banished from the family and the union thus formed had no alternative but to have recourse to the cottier tack. In this manner cabin succeeded and was added to cabin, first the father's and next the son's, and if it became impracticable to build or to add to the dwelling already in existence, small though it be, it was divided and a fire set at both ends and, following this, any outside property came also under the rule of subdivision, so that the common receptacle for refuse, perhaps not a yard from the door, had its boundary stones set up in it.

Villages in the course of time became very large, and if it so happened that on the same townland a village became detached, the lately built part was always called by the name "*Balloor*" or "Newton".[75] Strange that no proper name could be got for such additions, and that all the other villages had their proper names. How did their forefathers form names? They were built sometimes in valleys, but mostly on less valuable ground, on hill sides, on the tops of the most uneven rocks, on even and uneven ground, but always so as to have the dwellings as close to each other as possible, the inhabitants there by families and clans united. Each clan was headed by a chieftain, some one who was reputed the best man, the best fighting man of the tribe, who generally did nothing else than fight and pick up quarrels, reckoning upon his followers to be upon his heels; they were called his "backing".

These clans (or what was enough in this respect, to make a distinction—one family name differing from another) often made war against each other on the slightest pretence at first, and this might arise out of some foolish dispute, such as descent or purity of blood, or some high word or fancied insult uttered by some mouth, whose head had been swimming over a heavy ballast of poteen whiskey and, coming home from a fair or a market, lost the bridle of his tongue.[76] In most cases he got a smart rap to waken him or else to silence him there, but in an after-day his blood must be revenged. For his story on arriving home is told in lieing [*sic*] exaggerated words, and so the flame was kindled, and after many lies, treachery, petty fights, challenges in private—resulting in more or less of bloodshed at home—the feeling at last runs high and a challenge for a general day, a day of "banter", is proclaimed for both sides to meet at fair or market-town, and then and there to decide which side, which party, is the strongest. Once such a declaration was made, neither side could think of acting the coward, and so both parties and their clansmen and followers certainly repair to the place mentioned on the appointed day. And in order that no excuse might be taken by any one whether willing or not willing, a herald from each side went round his supporters to see that no good man stayed at home, or if he did under any pretence whatever unless sickness or [otherwise] unable to go, he was sure to bring upon himself the punishment, the degradation of traitor, of being outlawed and disowned by his clan, and ever after called by the appellation "dirty *callagh*", or coward or turncoat ("*callagh*" means old woman).[77]

75. *Baile úr*, new town.
76. *Poitín*, illicitly distilled whiskey, moonshine; see Chapter 13.
77. *Cailleach*, old woman, coward.

The day arrives and all those who meant what they called "a good clean fight" are armed with blackthorns or good hickory sticks, but the worse natured, the less untrained [sic], the brutal among them carries hidden weapons of a more murderous description such as the leaden headed whipstick. Contingent after contingent of forces are mustering and waiting, marching from the different townlands, and on their way they meet and pass portions of the opposing party faction, their very neighbours, perhaps relatives, without a salute or even exchanging the time of day for fear of showing any friendship; thus early in the day they are showing what party they mean for to uphold, what colours they mean to sail under, and all make haste to the "challenge-ground", that is to say the market town.

What has been said might convey the idea that all the inhabitants were of a quarrelsome or fighting disposition; this would lead to a false conclusion such was not the case. Many there were whose names were never known otherwise than as quiet inoffensive people, attending to their own concerns. But unfortunately there were a few, and the few were too many, who kept up the seed of discord and such unnatural acts and uncharitable feelings.

Ignorance had a good deal to do with it; bombast and false pride had a share. It may be said that there were only two tribes who kept up the strife, the one pretending to be of more ancient families, longer residents of course, and more honourable in their descent; the other was looked upon as of later import, partly despised for the meanness of their connexions and for living more or less in poverty. Each of these factions in the course of time increased to have many followers, and they lived in or had their greatest strength close to each other, in separate townlands too, but some of their followers were scattered among every village; a supposed injury done to one was followed up by all the rest, and when the day of retribution came, all hastened to their own standard.

The unlucky day to many, the market-day, comes on, the market is held as usual, the day is well advanced, the fair is gathered, and for the time being, everything is serene. Peaceable men are doing business, the street is thronged and packed with human beings scarcely able to pass or repass, male and female, young and old, showing their gayest attire and parading about. The white canvas shows where the tents of hardware dealers and booksellers are pitched. And a "Jack-at-the-loop" is in some corner surrounded by a crowd, hastily pocketing an odd copper penny which he has fraudulently won or recovered by means of a bit of art or manipulation, performed over the upturned end of an empty herring barrel. Another crowd surrounds a ballad singer who is reciting some verses—not in the print before him or her at all—about love or murder, or what pleases equally as well, a "sea-song"—a shipwreck and rescue. Here and there a crowd surrounds a fiddler, or the music of the bag-pipe, and if the one playing the latter be in the attire of a High-lander, he is sure to attract many. The coppers make way to his feet, and some one in the crowd who is after having a "bucket" is forgetful of cares, throws off his coat, and works himself to perspiration dancing a "hornpipe". Another parts with his coin after two looks at it and calls out for "Play up Royal Charley". At conspicuous places are auctioneers, shouting at the top of their coarse and hoarse voices for the cheapest and best of wares, from the iron, or horny spoon, to the pennyworth of tape or yard of calico. All these musicians—fiddlers, pipers, ballad-singers—and dealers in all sorts are doing all in their power to rise money by fair means or foul, and so by this time the sun is a good piece past the meridian.

The quiet attentive observer if he looks around will soon observe some things different from business, and some busy bodies. He will see groups of men congregated about the door of some favourite public house. Some of these men are serious and savage looking, and careless of the music or of what is passing around them; they are evidently atten-tively engaged in close conversation or whispering to each other, while at the same time some one among them is continually making some object feel the weight of his stick by an occasional blow, or else keeps beating in rapid succession but tamely against a cart shaft or the near-est object, as the effects of the poisonous drink or whiskey is becoming more visible on his face and is making its course through his veins, and he is showing by his movements that he is anxious for the affray.

The hour for action, unawares to many, is drawing nigh and in the midst of gaiety—horror. What! oh! suddenly a satanic yell is heard at a distance from some member of an opposing faction, rushing out from some public house in another direction where mischief was all day brewing also, and he bloated and flushed with the medicine imbibed and brandishing his weapon over his head, shouting at the same time at the top of his voice that he is "master of the street", "Who dare oppose him? Where is the man now to fight him?", "Let the mother's son now face him, who is not willing to follow him? A hurra my bully", and so on, and a crowd of equally evil-disposed persons follow him; the first man supposed [to be an] enemy [that is] met with, often an innocent man, is instantly knocked down and without parley. The opposite party are not hidden or asleep and soon, very soon, the two currents of opposing factions meet and instantly open warfare and slaughter is the order of the day. The sounds of vocular and instrumental music are as suddenly lost—drowned—or have disappeared in the less sonorous but unearthly music of human voices shouting, cursing, moaning, and by their actions, like so many demons let loose, making all possible murderous attempts at each other. What saves life is the very closeness of the combatants so that for want of space, staff coming in contact with staff or staves never reaches where it is intended, and therefore the blow is prevented from having the desired effect.

Instantaneously all is confusion on the street, the gamblers and musicians and the neutrals hasten out of the way, and every wise person gathers himself up and heads homewards, fright pictured on their countenances and spreading the news of the slaughter as they go along. The street thus partly deserted leaves more room for action: now one side is evidently yielding, retreating under the weight of a superior force; soon from another direction a reinforcement arrives and after a struggle the lost ground is regained.

In the advance and retrograding movements, tents, pedlar's traps and other things temporarily fixed are thrown down, are scattered about, and every one regardless of the loss of property is running for life. The poor fruit-dealer, the candy-man, and the tin-woman come in for a share of loss their goods being scattered about and trampled under foot. The free fight continues, the force of Constabulary police after their mustering is not able to separate or subdue them except only a little drawback, an odd prisoner is taken, at a loss to the police of some broken glazed hats or torn jackets. The policeman's hat at that time was easily damaged as it was very broad in the top and shaped in the form of an inverted section of a cone. The fight therefore continues, the wounded are carried off to friends' houses, and meantime a courier runs at speed to the Barracks for all the available force. The Constabulary knows that their whole strength would be of no avail to restore order, and evening coming on, they dispatch a messenger a little farther off to the Revenue Police Force—a party of 12 men and commanded by an officer and a sergeant. They are soon marching at the double quick, and all the King's forces unite. Arriving with all speed at the scene of action, a breathing halt is commanded, their officer surveys the movements of the combatants, finds out the ringleaders and their positions, and sees that it would be a waste of time to attempt to make prisoners just then. But a decisive step must be taken to prevent further slaughter and for this end the street must be cleared. He gives the orders for "Screw bayonets" and "Forward, Charge", and soon the flourishers of His Majesty's naked steel make way, disperse all before them, an odd prod given in the hip or elbow to the slow-of-foot to make them increase speed, and the police have the street to themselves and are trodding in the same mud, the same footmarks, occupied but a very short while before by the wielders of the unmerciful blackthorn and bludgeon. Not however that the latter hid or withdrew themselves without leaving visible signs of savage onslaught in the shape of broken skulls, hanging eyebrows, ugly cuts and bruises, and all manner of wounds.

Evening sets in and the ordinary barracks as well as temporary ones are full of prisoners consisting of the wounded and those comparatively safe mixed together, and all get free lodgings for the night while their friends get leave to supply them with bandages and food. Next day dawns—a day of sorrow to them if the thought would be of any avail, but too late now, they are coupled friend and foe by an iron band called "handcuffs" and marched to the seat of the nearest magistrate if at home, and if not farther on to the residence of some old army general who on retirement got the title of J.P. as a toy in his old age.[78] And here some are liberated, some put under a rule of bail, and some are conveyed thence to the bridewell, and an indefinite time to await the decisions of the doctors on the states and conditions of those at home, who are seriously wounded. As it was impossible for the preservers of the public peace to take as many of the disturbers prisoner as deserved it, many escaped, perhaps the most guilty from the scene of battle, but these were soon looked for, and they did all they could to conceal and escape law and justice. The police did their part in trying to capture them and so for many days and nights, nay weeks for a long time after it, it was nothing new to see the police on the track for executing warrants, making descents upon dwellings in the dead of night, terrifying the children and old women who are suddenly awakened by the officers of the law, searching beds, under beds, boxes, presses and cupboards, and in some instances so close were they to the object of their search that the hidden party had no resource left him but up the chimney in his shirt during the time the door was purposely slowly being opened, stretched himself, destitute of clothing on the roof, and for that time escaped.

78. Justice of the Peace, the local magistrate who presided at petty sessions. Generally JPs were gentry, with Church of Ireland clergymen common in areas with few resident gentlemen. Although they charged fees for some services, they did not receive a salary and were frequently inactive. Eclipsed in the mid-nineteenth century by salaried 'stipendiary' or resident magistrates.

Many instances of narrow escapes might be recorded, sometimes the pursued having no spare time but, mounting on horseback without saddle, bridle or rope, they would drive the old nag as far as it could carry them and then dismount and run to the bogs or hills, or leaping down a precipice, which would appear an impossible act at other times, or sometimes making for the seashore, getting into a curragh and rowing to the opposite shore.[79] The police tried every means for the apprehension of those under warrant, such as at times going about lazily in civilian's clothing on the pretence of being flax buyers; others of the same rank condescended to become rag gatherers with a bag on their shoulder, having a chat with the old women and for the purpose of finding information about someone on whose views they could not get, and the country people who were in dread practised every stratagem to keep out of reach; a strange face and an unknown gait at a distance "like a policeman's" was enough to give one of them the occasion to slide out of sight. While this state of things lasted, magistrates went around in daylight taking depositions, and doctors at their own work poulticing and attending to the wounded.

In many cases, between the doctor's advice and the disabled man's own rascality confinement to the house and feigned weakness were considerably prolonged, but there were more reasons than one for these pretences; the doctor was sure of pocketing money by the transaction, and lengthened his visits as long as he could, and the man who was complaining took it for the sake of vengeance, as he was almost sure of a conviction sometime [and sought] to make it as bitter as possible, as his opponent would have to bear all costs at the end.

The parties on their banishment were in constant anxiety to hear of the state of relief and recovery of the wounded as much as their own friends, for they could not think of surrendering [to the police] until they would hear of their recovery, and so had secret emissaries in the shape of old women, apparently silly, making their way for finding out stories and sending news to them in the other camp; when at last it became satisfactorily known that there was no danger of death resulting, then and then only would they begin to think of reconciling themselves to a surrender. If there was any doubt however, to make sure they would first through their friends get a strange doctor to visit, so as to bring the opinion of doctor against doctor. Those who were the most deeply charged and against whom very strong and clear informations were laid, in other words "heavy oaths", and [who had] no chance for

79. *Curach*, a small boat made of canvas or leather, coracle.

any defence, were still at their banishment; were not to be seen at all; if near at home they were under good cover, or if disappeared it might be across the sea, or away in some distant parish, or concealed night and day under the roof of a trusty relative or well-wisher, and if they showed themselves at the door in the garden to enjoy the light of the sun, it was in women's clothing they so appeared, for the fear the policeman had his "spy-glass" at a distance; in this manner they managed to escape the vigilance of the authorities for a long time, but at considerable toil and uneasiness to themselves in body and mind.

Now they had already experienced the fruits of their inhumanity, the reward of bad advice, and a little of their evil passions. Want of sleep, want of peace, their little cares at home going to loss, they dared not show their faces except like thieves on their own threshold, their wives like widows, their children like orphans; their own state of life was such that they seldom remained two nights in succession in the same house unless on the understanding that it was provided with some secret hidden hole as a sure means for concealment. The man thus on banishment had what may be truly said "the hare's life". If he stopped with a good friend, that friend sat up, keeping watch while the refugee was taking his restless sleep. At other times he tried to sleep with half his clothes on, and at the bark of a dog up he starts and undergoes half an hour's vigilance peeping at the window, to make sure that no feet are approaching.

At length when the wounded parties after a lapse of some months were scrawling out [sic], on foot again, and were pronounced out of danger by the doctor—and this he would grant more readily by getting a considerable fee, a "lump sum"—then the party who was under cover for so long began to show himself in daylight, to consult with his friends, and after a day or two he would get sureties prepared and make way privately to His Worship's mansion, get their "Bail Bonds" secured, and return home publicly and partly defiantly before the very door of the police barrack, as much as to say "I am out of your power now; you dare not make prisoner of me", having that foolish and imaginary satisfaction that the police did their best, but could not catch them. The police too were wise enough to know what errand they had or were after fulfilling; they never interfered and let them pass on.

A few weeks however soon passes away, and all who were thus bound had to surrender at the assizes or sessions as the case might be. Another point considered was always to keep the assizes or sessions as far distant as possible, and therefore at a time when assizes or sessions were going on was the best time to give in bail. At last all had to appear, and the ablest lawyers, attorneys and councillors, the best machinery, were put in motion for the defence, the expenses for such being borrowed and scrambled up in every shape—money which would be more needed in clothing their children or putting seed in the ground. Yet after all pleadings, some got twelve months, some got six months, and others more lucky got off with three months "hard labour" and confinement inside the strong stone walls. Those on long terms of imprisonment, if they behaved well, got into "grace" with the turnkeys after some time, and it would be amusing to hear them after their release tell how they had got to be promoted to boiler attendants and assistants at the making of stirabout and having the distribution of it by means of a long handled ladel [sic], also getting light jobs to do about the governor's house; [they would also tell about] the devices used in getting in pieces of tobacco, while some chewed pieces of leather, the same being taken from inside the heels of their shoes, for the "bacca".

At the time those fights were prevalent, many were the hair-breadth escapes from being killed at such, yet seldom if ever did immediate death result from the beatings; certain it was that many a one "done no good after their beating" till their death. A broken skull could never be the same again, one having the misfortune to get a cracked one had its own affliction, could stand no heat from the sun or immediately the head got light, and dizziness was a frequent complaint with such, and in some cases a slight degree of insanity was noticeable, excitement easily set in, they were unable to do any heavy or even moderate work, so that they were useless to themselves and rather a burden to their families and friends.

The public fights on the public street were bad enough and in daylight, but there were often other encounters in the clouds of the night, equally as bad if not more savage as far as personal injury was concerned, and always happening when coming home from fair or market. On the way home was a public house here and there, and those on one side of a connexion went in gangs together for strength and protection to themselves as well as for bravado. Those houses they could not pass without a lingering call. Oh no, it would be a shame to pass the decent house, and besides it would look as if we were afraid. Indeed there is nothing of the sort in the veins of this mother's son, and sure some of you have not the sign of a taste this day. They might not then immediately have the intention for a quarrel, but if by ill luck they might happen to meet with a lesser gang of their known opponents and few words from some silly misguarded one about a "better man" and the "best man" might set in, and after some angry words, blows soon followed. Noise and confusion at once got up in the house, the tables were hammered with fists, glasses and bottles and jugs were smashed, and other damage done to furniture and the contents of the house.

The weaker party had to decamp just then with some ugly scratches, but on the road again they meet with more and more friends: after making their story and their injury known and adding to it, if they still do not consider themselves strong enough to cope, they await in the darkness for the approach and appearance of their enemies with a volley of stones, blows from weapons they show no mercy and at such encounters, rapid for the time, some got badly and brutally hurt.

The oaths and evidence at the lawsuits following were terribly at variance and contradicted, and mistakes were sure to follow owing to the darkness and waylaying, but in any case the innocent suffered very often and as they were innocent, they did not know their danger until they were apprehended.

Years succeeded years and passed in such hatreds, such acts of inhumanity, something similar to two wild or savage tribes in the lands of the heathen, but the time arrived indeed when such disturbers of the public peace, such evil spirits who incited others to evil and themselves haters of their fellow men and their neighbours, melted away like snow upon the mountains, but strange to say [not so] the remembrance of old feuds; the animosity though greatly abated has not died out, and it is questionable if such will be forgotten by the generations yet to come for this reason: the old stories of the waylayings, the cruelties inflicted upon grandfather, father or uncle, the gaol sufferings endured in years gone by, the false oaths which were the means of confining him though he was as clear as the sun, are all and often fireside talk and stories handed down from father to son and from mother to daughter, and though there is no fighting now, and though the feeling is not openly expressed now-a-days, yet there is a hidden and a well-known hatred slumbering still between opposite bloods.

Were we permitted to moralize we would say that the Almighty in His wise ways has brought about dispersions, emigrations and deaths as a punishment upon the people, as they were too numerous, too unruly, and in their ways of life in this alone, not to speak of hidden crimes, too rebellious; therefore a High Power was needed to curb and to chastise them. Emigration thinned their ranks. Starvation reduced them to weakness, and deaths thinned and decimated their ranks worst of all, but it gave the remainder, though few, a chance of thinking of themselves. Emigration served its own ends in strange lands by the spreading of the people who, being removed from the scene of strife, began to think more of the wholesome teachings of Christianity, got better cultivated and could only laugh in after-life of the folly of those in the old country and their doings in the old times.

Famine led to the dispersion, and Irishmen are to be found spread to all corners of the known world, to the civilized as well as the uncivilized parts, to places which their fathers never heard of and which they themselves never would have seen, had the times not changed, and while this refers to Ireland in general, it can be said of Donegal in particular. The good suffers with the wicked and what is bad for one is good for another. Many of them are now by such changes in positions to do good to themselves and also to those at home, their kinsmen.

There are faults and often heinous faults to be laid at the doors of all classes of society at all times and in all ages and all countries, but of the people we are speaking, many other crimes were unknown, and certain it was that this "party fighting" was their predominant evil at home, which may be reckoned bad enough, but in all other matters appertaining between man and man, honesty, truth and straightforwardness were the prevailing characteristics, purity and modesty with the youth, and honour and submissiveness to parents. Therefore when forced to go to strange lands they had only one evil to forget, and it was no way difficult, no way new to them, to conform with Christian principles inculcated in youth and not yet depraved.

The situation of many of the villages and foundation stones of the cabins in which, years ago, hatred was fomented in the above ways are now solely in the possession of some solitary peaceable head of a family who has no one to dispute with and no one to trespass upon unless he goes far beyond his bounds; but traces of the rough constructed dwellings still remain as miniature monuments of the past, and somehow or other the hand of fate is unable to entirely deface what at one time was the cause of no small puzzle—viz. mapping—to the Ordnance Surveyor.

CHAPTER 8
*The New School**

Time rolled on and time brings on changes, but we find the old master still persevering in his latter day avocation, that is to say "teaching", though [he was] evidently not in such a flourishing state as heretofore. People saw day after day the want of proper education, and were yearning more and more for an opportunity of getting better instruction for their children and they would have been glad to embrace anything in the shape of improvement.

A few years more, a few years longer, and the old man who in his past life had his trial at the sword and the pen would have disappeared from worldly eyes and his system of teaching would have died with him. But the Fates so decreed that he should rather suffer the mortification of seeing himself opposed by a new system and after a little while [he was] left almost solitary, uprooted and silenced, so soon and so sudden was the rush to the new and supposed improved method. Never again did the rocks in the Glen re-echo the shouts or the merry laugh of the children at play and fresh green grass grew up where not long before was to be seen the bare baked clay, caused by the continual tramping of human feet hurrying to and from, and while this state continued, no vegetation dare put up its head along the paths trodden by them.

From whatever cause arising, strange it was too, that the new system was planted and sprung up within less than a quarter of a mile of the

*In the original text, this chapter is sub-titled 'Introduction of the System of Church Education Society School'.

long established seat of learning in the Glen, as if there was some extra-ordinary attraction or attractive influence for learning centred in or somewhere concealed in the Glen. This new change was brought about by the importation of a Church of England clergyman into the parish to replace his deceased predecessor, and to satisfy the wants of the church-men in regard to a spiritual adviser.[80] This man had, in the language of the clerics, the title of "Doctor of Divinity" bestowed on him in Trinity College, and for his services this handsome abode was the gift of the College for the remainder of his life, for to rest and be thankful.[81] He had his mansion situated facing the sun and hidden from the storm, sur-rounded by the fattest of soils, well wooded and commanding a fine scenery. All these inducements, his beautiful house, his splendid garden, his lawns, his gravel walks, his drive to church on Sundays were not enough to satisfy him; he wished to do more and to show what manner of a man he was, and to exhibit his meekness, in very fine weather he left his comfortable and sheltered abode and went on a tour of inspec-tion, visiting in particular three villages, glebe lands, the rents of which went to increase his revenue, and the inhabitants of which he called his tenants; though singular enough, tenants as they were and forced to pay him rent, there was only one single, one only, individual linked to his persuasion in all the glebe lands of the parish.[82]

Whatever may have been his motives in going four or five miles to visit people differing from him in every conceivable form is at this time rather soon to conjecture. The sequel may explain, or perhaps an anxi-ety for the eternal welfare of this individual who was now drawing near his earthly dissolution may incidentally be the cause of the reverend gen-

80. Rev. Henry Maturin (1770–1842), rector 1797–1842; Dr William Baillie (1795–1859), rector 1842–59. Maturin was born into a prominent Huguenot family in Dublin; entered Trin-ity College, Dublin, 1786; awarded B.A. 1790 and M.A. 1793; appointed rector of Clon-davaddog (Fánaid) 1797, in succession to Dr William Hamilton, who had been assassinated by the United Irishmen; married Elizabeth Johnston; had four sons, three of whom became clergymen, and a daughter. Baillie was a Tipperary man; entered Trinity College 1811; awarded B.A. 1816, M.A. 1819, LL.B. and LL.D 1827; ordained 1818; appointed headmaster of Kilkenny College (at the age of 24) in 1820; married Barbara Alcock 1821; had three sons, two of whom became clergymen, and a daughter; appointed rector of Clondavaddog in 1842; died at the glebe-house 1859; his will distributed assets of 'about £4,000'. For both men, see Leslie, *Raphoe Clergy*, p. 51.

81. Clondavaddog (Fánaid) was a 'college living', a parish in the gift of Trinity College, Dublin; the College also owned extensive lands which it leased to the earl of Leitrim. For the management of the College's estates, see W. J. Lowe, 'Landlord and tenant on the estate of Trinity College, Dublin, 1851–1903', *Hermathena*, 120 (1976), 5–24; R. B. MacCarthy, *The Trinity College estates 1800–1923: Corporate management in an age of reform* (Dundalk, 1992).

82. Cashel Glebe, Carrowkeel Glebe and Tonbane Glebe were the property of the rector.

tleman's periodical visits to those distant parts; soon however his days were so fixed that it was generally known when he arrived.

In this he differed from his predecessor, who was an amiable and well-liked man by all creeds and classes, and one who in his day never gave himself the trouble of doing or going beyond what was expected of him to do, that is to go his place of worship on the Sundays and preach according to his learning and ability, and no interference with the so-called tenants beyond that of getting the money collected for him by his agent once a year at November. If he wanted any work done, not only tenants but everyone surrounding were ready to give their assistance.

The Doctor, stranger though he was, soon made his appearance well known, and when he went alone he had a peculiar liking for riding on a pure white-coloured horse, one which was a great peculiarity in the country at the time. This singularity in itself made him remarkable so that he was easily identified at a distance. No sooner did the word circulate that he was seen coming than the men of the village, who were too easily turned into serfs, ran from their work, and a goodly crowd of willing slaves would be waiting along the end of the road to be at his service on arrival, and many more than could lay hold of the stirrups and bridle were rushing to attend him, and a certain degree of jealousy was manifested in who could first have his horse by the bridle and have the honour of leading him to stabling and the best of provender that could be bestowed.

On his dismounting, bald heads were exposed to the sky, be the weather what it may in token of obedience, and tufts of hair overhanging the jaws were nearly pulled from their roots in token of respect, as peasant after peasant, self-made slaves, his tenants of course, one after another presented himself with head bowed down and ejaculating "Your servant sir", "You are welcome your reverence". Many of the would-be slaves, not being heard, not as much as noticed at all, were not even seen by him in thus exhibiting themselves, whilst one or two took the lead in entering into discourse with him while he with his uplifted magnifying glass enjoyed the scenery, and if he took a walk his attendants pointed out the way by calling out "Come this way", "put your foot here", "put your foot there", to be free of and out of mud.

He moved and halted as he thought fit and at intervals blew off an ahem! ahem!, prepared himself for asking a number of questions at random, and would receive true and correct explanations from one or a number assisting each other in a difficulty. From his feigned weakness, his readiness in falling into conversation with any one, he easily gained

the good grace of the people and the impression soon gained ground
that he was a good man for anything and everything, and moreover that
he was bestowing gifts and was for doing so in deserving cases and
many were the explanations, the petitions of real or supposed grievances, put before him which for ever got a deaf ear. Foolish people so
easily led by false impressions.

To the complaints of some he would promise amendment, and in
cases more difficult or seemingly so he ordered the applicant to appear
before him at his own residence on a certain day and hour, a task which
some of them would much sooner not perform or have to undergo, for
the reason that the noise of their footsteps on the gravel walk on
approaching the half-door was a terror which made the frame tremu-
lous, heating the blood in the first instance, but which soon runs chilly
and cold through fear.

These trials partly overcome, a big mastiff, basking on the steps
before the door is to be approached, who fails to show pity, and after
that was to be encountered the trying, the venturesome attempt at
pulling the bell-handle, and another electric shock ran through the
frame as the clinking was heard from the inside, and soon a servant in
livery, "the butler", appears—who between contempt and anger man-
ages to control himself within the bounds of a few questions in an angry
tone, such as "Who are you?", "What do you want?" Between hmms!
and hahs! he finds an unsteady reply. "Well the Master is busy now—
he perhaps might be seen in half an hour or so". "Beware of the doag"
[sic]. Exit.

The dilatory long half hour arrives and the master appears, bringing
only a momentary relief to the poor man patiently waiting all the time
at a respectable distance from the hairy brute, who occasionally shows
his teeth but makes no noise, and if the master as he is termed by the
members of the household considers the party before him worthy of getting into the hall, to be operated upon, he is told to do so, the astonished would-be petitioner by this time slowly moving forward,
attempting to salute, engaged in pulling off his head dress—not all at
once but by stages, firstly pulling it down along the cheek, next for a
short time letting it rest on the shoulder, and finally through excitement
and forgetfulness and making confusion more confounded, the cap or
hat comes to the ground at his heels. He does not feel at ease, he dare
not turn round for he is keeping his eye to the great man before him, but
some ingenuity must be used and, body slanting, he puts down his hand,
gropes and recovers the fallen article.

Now inside the hall, the door closes, but the captive's breathing seems to be faltering, the doctor understands as much and walks instantly on some pretension into another room for a little, leaving the terrified bashful creature to have a view at the weather glass, the papered walls or other curious things surrounding him, and so the sufferer's breathing returns more natural. The "master" returns and his questions are entirely foreign from what was expected and different from the original petition, and the poor tenant is drifted into matter which he had no notion of but, trembling, he tries to give satisfactory answers to everything asked of him.

By such means, by such traps as these, the clergyman—the petty landlord—the wolf in sheep's clothing—in a very short time knows the history of every man and of everything in the place. One frailty in him was like many of high station he took hold of the first plausible story told him—stuck to it—let the same be true or false, and the opinion he then formed, let it be good or bad, from it afterwards he could not be dissuaded, was in fact immovable, and those who by trying to gain his friendship would perhaps in an evil hour forget themselves and give him more knowledge about a neighbour than was compatable with justice and charity. He though wearing the white cravat was not wanting in the spirit of revenge which he never forgot to enforce as soon as opportunity offered, and this he exercised on a few who bitterly came to grief at his hands and who could not relieve themselves from the fetters which made them his sufferers, and for the reason that they would not conform to the rules of degradation and slavery meant by him. His opinion was already formed and a slight difference occurring in words or action on the part of the defendant was enough to incur his wrath.

Thus did he lay up the history of the people about him, how they lived, their means of living, as well as an idea into their religious feelings, and while he pretended to be the friend of many, he was only laying the foundation for his own actions in aftertime to bring him just on a par of cruelty with the other landlords whose properties surrounded him, and at whose hands nothing was expected, nothing experienced but the rack-rent screw.

The people, as I said above, for a long time felt the great want of a school-house in the neighbourhood but had not the courage or rather dared not approach any of the other landlords, as it would be an act bordering upon treason to attempt any such thing as leave from a landlord just then to build a school-house. Men are sometimes led by appearances alone and this man appearing so meek and so good, and so it was with these simple country people, and it occurred to their minds that it was the right time and that it was in his power to remedy their want, and some of the neighbours took it into their heads and consulted with others about obtaining a good house which was then unoccupied on the glebe property and which the tenant could do without, and how very well it would answer for a school-house from its central situation.

The idea was so far so good, but the first difficulty lay with the faint-hearted tenant who would otherwise be willing enough, but for the dread of to know whether his reverence the landlord might not hold views similar to those of his kin, and therefore he must be petitioned first and leave got. After some time they made so bold as to request him, for be it remembered that the dread of landlords was such that the tenants trembled through fear of them, and though this man professed himself to be an expounder of the Gospel, he was also a landlord and therefore the people had some reasons to fear, which proved afterwards to be well founded, for no landlord could be more cruel, could do more to curb, to screw up his few poor tenants when the time of misery set in upon them than what he did by resorting to the method of raised rents and by using severity and extortion in collecting the same.

You may talk of the Bible and preaching. You may talk of Scripture, of chapter and verse, but do not talk of the minister doubling the rent, exacting a payment of shillings to the tune of six for a new impost, bog money, that is to say five for himself and one for the lazy bailiffs, and this for granting permission to the tenant to cut a certain quantity of turf and no more, and for the same a penny never was paid by any man living on this glebe property or never heard of since the days of the Flood. Not only did he do this by limiting the supply and pay for the same to those he overruled, but to add more to his purse he sold out what he reserved to other strange tenants who cut and carried turf away, and by such destruction before the end of his days he had the satisfaction to see the rightful owners, the tenants he left behind him and all who will come after them, in want of that necessity, which if left to their own consumption would last for generations yet to come, but now the living people can look at a flooded marsh where they should get their supply of fuel.

And in further imitation of the real tyrannous landlords, he also fixed two gale days for the payment of his rent instead of one as heretofore, and so strict that in default of payment on the appointed day, the tenant was rewarded with the costs of a distraining warrant. Curiously enough he signed the distraining warrants himself, sent his bailiff to execute and if met by payment even on the very day demanded, nevertheless costs were the first items taken up, and if short, borrow the rest the tenant must do. Some conjectures were afloat that the so-called warrants were not all or altogether legal, but they were printed pieces of paper anyhow, and who knew whether or not. Who dare speak? Who is to bring the landlord or bailiff to question?

All these things of which I speak came to pass in his subsequent career, when he was firmly fixed and in his ruling power, and he so continued to be a ruler and a preacher until the time arrived for the intervention of that famous of English statesmen, Gladstone, thanks to him, or rather double thanks and praise to the Almighty Power who suffers tyranny only for a certain time and to a certain extent and in this used as His instrument, the Good Old Man, to strike in the head the hypocrisy of a Church of England clergyman.[83]

Immediately following the bold stroke of Gladstone were withdrawn from the minister his dogs, his guns, his game, his canoes and pleasure boats or, if not withdrawn, they vanished, all of which were before supported by the sweat and toil of the poor man who himself kept skin and bone together by an occasional application of a mixture of potatoes and salt and the tail of a herring.

But to return to the question of the school-house, the tenant was willing if the landlord would not object, and to bring the subject to a bearing a deputation was formed who went to him straightway and laid their views before him. He with the greatest signs of gravity and without the least hesitation granted their request on the condition and only condition that he himself would supply books, requisites and better still, pay rent for the house, and further and better still to show no signs of deception and to crown to satisfaction more than they expected in this favourable reception, he also promised to them a teacher of their own persuasion.

Much as he was esteemed before, the respect for him now knew no bounds, arising from his willing and immediate concessions. Not long after this interview on one fine day appeared one of his reverence's heavy horses and carts, with less than half a dozen old desks and forms which were out of use elsewhere, and these were immediately and carefully carried to their place of destination on men's shoulders, the house in the meantime having undergone some repairs in the way of cleansing and whitewashing. Next day came a stock of the Church Education Society books, published in a certain street in the City of Dublin for the

83. Referring to the disestablishment of the Church of Ireland, 1869.

instruction and education of the Romans of the North—Romans was the short term used for the Roman Catholics by the Protestants.[84] These were the first gifts sent for the enlightenment of the Romans—and none other here but the Roman Catholics—and now a new aspect from the slumbering state of the cultivation of the mind was opened up and a new and strange cultivator of youth in the shape of a teacher arrived to set the machinery in motion.

The poor easily imposed-upon people were led to believe that this new teacher was possessed of every superior qualification. In his deportment he was ladylike, aimed at refinement, spoke nothing but English of the hardest coin and soundest metal, changed his Irish surname into an English [one] having a similarity of meaning; dressed himself in garb, half cleric, half lay, wore and took great care to expose to the best advantage a large white breast of linen platted into many folds to the style in fashion with only a few of the aristocratic then, and so careful was he of himself and his outfit that his polished boots needed no brush from Sunday to Saturday ...

This method of instruction was entirely different from that to which the boys were accustomed. He introduced classes; "the verse about system" and the "one sentence reading system" that is a boy read from one period to another, let it be long or short. All the attempts to read were commingled, the droning voice, the singing voice, and the half-crying voice, but no one understanding what he read. The juniors might be said to be undergoing hard labour: the poor innocent things were forced to stand all day in a half circle, two or three deep and facing a lettered sheet of paper called a "tablet" hung or stuck to the wall before them, while an elderly one held a pointer and repeated the words to them, forwarding complaints when necessary.

The house was certainly much better than they were accustomed to—it had two large windows, a few desks, slates and pencils and other requisites for inducement ready at hand, and among a few pictures was

---

84. Church Education Society, established in 1839 by Church of Ireland opponents of National Education; for the opposition of the clergy in the diocese of Raphoe to National Education, see *Sixth annual report of the Church Education Society for Ireland; with an appendix, and a list of subscribers* (Dublin, 1845), p. 95. Shortly after his appointment to Fánaid in 1842, Dr William Baillie was responsible for the establishment of Church Education Society schools at Leatmore, Muineagh and Cashel Glebe; in other words, the 'parish school' in Cashel Glebe was connected to the Church Education Society: see ibid., p. 57. In 1858 the society had schools at Muineagh, Croaghross and Ballina and was probably supporting the parish school at Cashel Glebe: see R. Griffith, *Union of Millford, valuation of the several tenements comprised in the above-named union situate in the county of Donegal* (Dublin, 1858), pp. 132, 135, 141–2, 147–8.

one representing the two hemispheres, placed on the wall behind where the master sat as if to adorn that particular part, and the little children in their own ingenuity got as much knowledge somehow of Astronomy as to call it "the two moons", but there it stuck from day to day without any definition or explanation on the part of the teacher.

These simple attractions and supposed advantages caused nearly all the young persons of the surrounding neighbourhood to flock to the new opening, the only drawback being the "penny-a-week"—the school fees—which was equally as new to them and now enforced and in a very short time the house in the Glen—mournful to relate—had become nearly deserted. The books formerly used had to be laid aside, or to be forgotten, and many a one reluctantly had to lay aside the "Universal", the book of books, for to melt in its cover, if he wished to go to the New School and conform to the new system. Many were the unavailing petitions for permission to use the old books for even a part of the day, or one lesson in the day, but all to no purpose, and some boys in order to satisfy, but rather deceiving, their fathers at home, carried the "Universal" from day to day without ever opening it.

There were now for a while used at the school new series of First Books, Second Books, Third and Fourth Books, and endless numbers of the Bible, Genesis, Exodus, Leviticus and Deuteronomy; the Acts of the Apostles, copies of the Four Evangelists—Matthew, Mark, Luke and John. Portions, verses, out of each and everyone of which had to be committed to memory by those who were capable of doing so. Though it was as much as Greek to them.

Not only at home but during the school-hours the greater part of the day was taken up in reciting and committing to memory verses of Scripture, during which time the master employed the lazy habit of sitting, watching any one who lifted his head or looked off his book, and the neglectful one was called up for punishment which he knew was a "slap" in the hand from a flat ruler. At other times for his own convenience "watches" were posted at every desk or division to report on the non-observance of this rule, and well did these constables fulfil their duty arising from an idea of false honour to themselves and to please the master, and while in this position their word was law, against which there was no appeal, but as often did they create enemies to themselves.

Those boys who could repeat the most number of verses on an after-day—the day of inspection—gained praise for themselves but principally for the master who was the entire gainer, and who without any exertion on his part, save that of holding a cruel control and forcing children to learn what they did not understand and what their whole inclination was totally against. Poor children, to make them suffer physically and mentally, make them cry and weep to do that which was against their will. The school being firmly established, and in constant operation, inspection was of course necessary in order to report progress, and for this end a day was fixed and a clergyman of the Protestant church from another and distant part of the country was invited to perform this duty, and this day being in the capacity of inspector he appeared in a garb not in unison with that daily worn by the cleric.

It is true the new master was *something* superior in knowledge to the old man, but he had other advantages in his favour. In the first place he had that of having at his command many more requisites for exercising the children, but he was far short of putting the same to good practice. Enough for him that the child or boy should know as many verses as would satisfy inspection, so that there was a hidden war between teacher and pupil, the latter's feeling being animosity, and the teacher forcing upon the child what he did not like, and the child appearing to learn what he would not get. A column or two of the multiplication table was occasionally added to make a slight variation.

The day of inspection was always made known some sufficient time beforehand so that the teacher had an opportunity of calling in the *absent* whom he knew would be of any credit to him, and knowing this it also gave him a chance of fraudulently keeping names constantly marked *present* on the books who perhaps were absent for months previous.

Many acts intended for politeness were brought out by this teacher, which were before hand unheeded or rather held in the category of ranking as nonsense in the estimation of the old man. Some of these were uncovering the head on entering the School and remaining so bareheaded for the day; the formality of taking hold of the hair on the forehead and of slowly advancing and bowing to the teacher when any request was wanted, such as "Please let me out sir". At evening it was a crime if any one forgot to shout out at the door step on leaving the words, "Good evening sir", on neglecting which the party so forgetting was called back, for the master stood at the door, and detained him to the last.

After all the apparent advantages at the latter school, the state of improvement was not so rapid as might be supposed. In arithmetical knowledge as far as the teacher went, it was given with a little more clearness, a little more animation certainly; he knew the Simple and Compound rules well enough though he met with some difficulties in Reduction, in Weights and Measures, and insurmountable ones in the Rule of Proportion or, as it was commonly called, the Rule of Three, but he had the tact of escaping over these difficulties without acknowledging his inability, and which our old man was honest enough to admit. But as for Fractions, "don't mention", "they were not wanted at all", "they were no use to anybody", "pass them over", "it is only Gaugers uses them".

The day for inspection was made known to the teacher in order that he might have the school and scholars in readiness, the teacher himself appearing in his glittering boots, his large white linen breast and a stiff collar to match, the latter an upright one but slightly a misfit as it was coming in contact with his ears rendering a difficulty in looking sideways, his hair well-dipped in Bear's Grease, a compound not known to many at the time (the simplest ingredient being used by them, that is a taste of water pure and simple to keep the hair smooth).

On this day only did he lay his hat aside, and half a dozen of the elderly boys and girls being invited and in attendance since early morning engaged at sweeping and dusting, cleaning inside and outside the house for yards distance round about. Roll Books, Register and Report Book were left in readiness on a table, a few commands and important instructions issued and repeatedly impressed on the minds of the children and on youth, which tended more towards slavery than civility or politeness. On this day alone the "white horse" was not expected, but equally as great a curiosity was exhibited—a two-wheeled vehicle (and no matter what the shape was, the people always called it a "gig"), and as this could also be seen in the distance, everything was in readiness before the arrival. Everything and every person was hushed, not even the willing slave who was too anxious to render his service to attend to the trap and to take the horse by the head and give him the last stone of oats, if he had no more, not even he while close to the premises dare speak louder than a whisper as there was the doctor and the inspector coming. The doctor and inspector are coming to visit the school, and all the old men in the district are coming breathless to visit the "gig". A railway locomotive coming in from the ocean should not be a greater wonder. The wheels, the shafts, the harness and varnish, to be minutely inspected.

At last the two ministers arrive and there is no want of uncovered heads and willing hands before them, and travelling bags, provision baskets, rugs and such thing as were wanted, the inspector in most cases being accompanied by a tourist or two, and bodily infirmities must not be forgotten. All these articles containing dainties being safely laid aside for a time, the school is handed over to the stranger for the day and he sets to his task. After a short look at the school statistics, during which time a few of the best of the boys are arranged in front rank, and on the first sign the Scripture repetitions commence.

Those who could repeat short chapters or a goodly number of verses got off quite easy, recommended for their attention and rewarded with the title of "Good boys". Others and not a few of them were tremblingly awaiting for their trial, and if their thoughts could be read, there was much more hatred than love for the master stamped in their breasts, and already convinced of their inability, uppermost in their minds was the dread of the interrogations of the stranger and still more the rebukes of the master who was sure at every angry turn afterwards to bring to their recollection their stupidity at inspection.

Their position was sure enough miserable, but no matter for all that some of the boys who had sense enough to know that the "Scripture Verses" did not serve immediate use and who were inclined to learn something else could never be reconciled in mind to learn them, and would prefer to sit idle, huffed and angry the whole day. Nor did it matter much, the difference between idleness and repeating verses, as it was lost time in either case because those who learned and committed to memory the most, either forgot them afterwards or, what was still worse, converted their Scripture knowledge into bad use.

However this was the largest item on the programme for that day; as for Writing or Arithmetic a look at the copy book, or a sum given out by the teacher himself and that one already half a dozen times prepared, was quite sufficient; and as for English Grammar, the "definite article", the proud little thing always in the way, and perhaps for this reason it was the only part of speech attacked, and to make or endeavour to make a distinction between this and the "pronoun" of the same sound gave the whole trouble. The difficulty arose from how to make a distinction between the pronunciation of the words "the" and "they", and after all sorts of twistings and ejaculations, of consultations, approval and disapproval, it was finally recommended by the learned trio, that "the" should be pronounced "the-eh", and "they" [as] "the-ai". This gave exercise to the teacher and pupils for weeks after, lest the important words might be forgotten before the next visit, but he might as well begin to teach German of which he knew nothing.

Next came the turn of the juniors—thrice happy innocent juniors—easily led but hard to conquer and, in their own simple way, they gave more trouble than their elderly brothers, the latter being more docile and could more easily and more readily understand a wink of the eye or a nod of the head and they paid more attention to what was told them, but the younger ones, driven on by some hidden spark, the germ of wholesome animation, would mean to persevere in their own ideas, the ideas probably taken in from their mothers at the fireside, and be the same pleasing now or not pleasing, on they went heedless of correction.

For instance, a rosy cheeked barefooted little fellow not yet in his "teens" was called on to repeat the "Apostles' Creed", and why that form of prayer was the first selected was the mystery, if not to puzzle the little one; anyhow the first word out, the same was got over pretty safely except that towards the end there was "no call", "no necessity" for that word "Roman". Then a command was given to repeat the "Lord's Prayer", and the child in the same words utters "Repeat the Lord's Prayer", not all understanding what was said to him. The interrogation was then put in another form by the teacher himself, with the additional "You stupid", "You booby, say the 'Our Father'". The child looks at the master, his innocent countenance reading, Oh! is that what you mean? and the master appearing sour and shrugging himself.

The child's temper gets a little ruffled, his red cheeks get redder, he is partly ashamed of himself, knowing the "Our Father" so well at home and noticing the master's change of countenance too; he instantly tries to make amends and gets on at the rate of 120 per minute and, without knowing where the "break" lay, he dashes into the "Hail Mary" and then as suddenly the eyes of the inspector open and horror is on his countenance, the danger signal—his hand is up and a hush! hush! stop! stop! The child looks on in astonishment, is a little obstructed but makes efforts to proceed—to persevere.

He is finally brought to a standstill, set to work again, and duly cautioned as to where the danger lay, but in a very few seconds he arrives at and heedlessly leaps over the same bridge as before, into the same depth at the greatest speed, recovers, and is at flying speed again over the old ground. No signal can stop him, and as correction and explanation were useless, and chastisement cruel or next to madness, the teacher was bound to be silent, and the inspector contented himself with a few twitchings of his shirt collar by the fingers, at the same time setting at liberty a few hems! and hahs!, remarking to the teacher, "That would be a smart boy if well trained". The innocent little thing would then be dismissed, sent to his seat, the creature having his smile and impressed with his own ideas that he had answered well.

When all or as many as they wished were examined by them, then there was given a short lecture on what!—on the "Passover", but the lecturer might as well dispossess the loose hmms! and hahs! in him for all the same impression on his hearers, children without a word of English, except what they repeated without understanding. Those having some English at home were a very few.

Lecture over, directions were given to the teacher verbally and written as to how to proceed in the future; the children were then all dismissed for the day, a walk to the nearest hill, luncheon within a good view of the ocean, and a few explorations of the surrounding scenery brought the day to a close.

The important day over, the teacher had a sufficient time to look forward before the day of the next visit, and he then turns his thoughts to other things for benefiting himself and to add to his means of living, and hence his garden had to be attended to, his turf had to be cut and dried and brought home to his very door. Anything he wanted done, he had the choice of strong willing hands ready at his call without pay, and as for thanks there were none. Such are the easily imposed-upon natures of the simple Celts; no matter how they agree or disagree among themselves they are always found to befriend, to think too much of the stranger, and it was after some time that they found out in this man like many another: he might have been of Irish descent, but in youth he lived too near hand the rich lands of the Plantation, and it may have arisen from this that the nature of the Celt of the mountain, the bog, the seashore, must have died out in him, for his was quite the contrary, to say it in the shortest words, a very ungrateful hypocrite who in the course of a very few years was attended to in his wants more through fear than love, and by the few only who courted his supposed influence at the hall of the minister. The best room from one of the nearest neighbours was occupied by him for his lodgings, and here he ate, slept, and spent his unemployed time, in fact a solitary being, living by himself, no way fond of conversation or anyone to converse with, and in this respect differing entirely from our old hero so lately left in the background ...

The parents of the children did not know the difference between what was taught and what was not—how could they, uneducated as they were, or if they or some of them suspected a tendency to, or any evil arising therefrom, were equally as ignorant of where the root of that evil lay. Enough for them that they had now a school-house, and too glad to have one, where there were books and other things for the use of the children and where they could attend summer and winter. Neither did the Roman Catholic clergy of the day interfere who might be supposed to do so, nor did they give themselves much or any trouble as to know how matters stood. One of them, the parish priest, had the ruling power of clergy and people and he alone might be expected to see into the state of affairs, but he was an old man, a rough and ready, simple and easy going old man, one of the skulls of the old school, who knew very well how difficult it was to get an education in his own young days, and no doubt he was deceived in the appearance and the pretended piety of the teacher.[85] Strange too that he was among the first along with one or two other wiseheads who suggested the suitableness of this house for that purpose, and when things had taken a turn which he had no expectations of, it may be that he did not wish now to put a hindrance to what he had a hand in sanctioning.

He lived for many years previously among the people and knew the people had at heart long before the desire of getting some education for the rising generation, but the fulfilment of which was not in his power to give or to assist, and he was therefore like themselves only too glad that their cravings were partly satisfied, that any thing in that shape was in their reach which was considered a service to them, and took it for granted that all was well while others were satisfied, and did not therefore take the trouble of inquiring into the nature of the snares laid. It was then some years after when the contrary seed had taken too deep a root and signs of apostasy appearing that a thought was taken of the danger, and of the safety of souls.

The simple old parish priest lived on friendly terms, as did all his hearers, with the predecessor of our present doctor of the Established Church, and therefore found it difficult to change views with regard to the latter, never suspecting that the late man from Trinity College was wiser in his ways and more crafty than either of them, or that his hidden ambition was to make known, to publish in the south of Ireland, the pretended fruits of his mission in the North. So true was this, that the writer of these pages in the lifetime of the doctor, and while no suspicion of the like was attached to him, was fairly astonished to see in a bookseller's shop in Dublin pamphlets written by him, descriptive of the progress of conversion to Protestantism in a certain part in the North, and knowing the same to be falsehoods and forgeries.[86]

85. Referring to Fr Daniel O'Donnell.
86. Presumably referring to Dr W. Baillie, *A brief view of the Church of Ireland, in its ear-*

Thus smoothly did matters go on in the locality for a long time and the minister's doings were unheeded, the visits of the "man on the white horse" became constant and regular, the objects of these visits being covered with the two-fold cloak of seeing the school and apparently the welfare of his tenants, the grievances of the latter being more for pastime or his amusement than for anything else, for no good ever came to pass but rather the contrary when he had picked up all the knowledge wanted by him.

The wily visitor did not attempt to introduce open prayer in the school-house as that would be rather glaring an act, but he cunningly covered his designs in another way. He first got a crowd assembled as near as he could to the door of the house of the man already alluded to—the one Protestant only—and by this time he was getting infirm and, whether able to rise or not, he preferred the minister to go see him. The minister therefore could not leave without bestowing on him some consolation and he gradually wended his way to his door, and when the people were all attention and in the midst of many questions and answers, he would suddenly step aside, giving all the outward indications to the crowd of—"you may come in".

Inside the walls then, there was a lecture and a form of open prayer under the old roof of the man, the only man he could claim as a co-religionist, and if the same man knew anything, which was indeed very little, very narrow and very shallow, he might be said to know as much of one religion as the other, and that was—nothing. He was only second in descent in the line of Protestant, his grandfather being a pervert and all his relatives were Roman Catholics. His nearest relatives living with him under the same roof were Roman Catholics who after his death succeeded to his property, and at this time his wife still living was reared and always professed to be a Roman Catholic. He went with the majority himself for a while after his marriage until subsequently happening to be disappointed in his worldly views, that is the lack of heirs; he was then a man of considerable wealth, and being so disappointed he got exceedingly sulky and with a revengeful feeling turned back again and in the course of time died as his father died a Protestant. If any one remonstrated with him as to his probable intentions before death, his argument was that "the Church of England must be the best", seeing that they had all the wealth and riches, sway and ease this world can

liest purity and independence; its subjugation and restoration (Dublin: George Herbert, 1853); 'S. Maddock, printer, Letterkenny' appears on the reverse of the title-page, suggesting that there may also have been a local edition.

afford, and when so favoured in this world, they must be so in the next. The line of reasoning speaks for itself. By the bye it happened that Hugh French and he were neighbours and always lived on friendly terms with one another. Hugh did not forget that command to do a little good to his neighbour—he wished everyone to go to heaven, had some notions that that place was large enough to hold all, and harboured some faint but decided hopes that at "the last wind of the hammer" he would turn to the "good path", and to probe him and have a while's chat he occasionally visited him at the time his earthly career was drawing to a close; he tried in his own rough logic to convince him of the great danger of losing his soul but, all in vain, there was nothing to be got out of him but the one answer as above. At last each one was partly tired of the other, and their parting scene came off in this way. French having exhausted all his reasoning powers by solicitations and quotations, the dying man replied that if he knew the lower regions were opened to receive him, he would go the way of his father. The other ejaculated boo, boo, boo, and then without hesitation pronounced judgement— "You not only die, but you die the death—die, die, and at this moment every rib in the house has a devil perched and flittering on it awaiting for the departure of your 'owl sowl'". Exit Hugh and his mission ended. (Ribs mean the small timbers supporting the roof of country dwellings of which there were a good many.)

His friend the minister had the satisfaction to see his body put down in a Protestant grave in the cold month of February, but the grave seemed to rebel against the treasure deposited therein, for as the words were uttered "Earth to earth and dust to dust", up rises the coffin by some philosophical force—in fact hydraulic: the grave was dug the previous evening, very deep and now nearly half full of water, and when the coffin was laid down and a quantity of clay thrown in it, instead of sinking it just upturned, the clay going to the bottom and the coffin uppermost, and some heavy stones had to be thrown in to make it sink.

It was with the well-known intention of getting rich and having companionship with the wealthy and with men in power that he changed coats in his last transformation, yet withal it did not serve him much after his death: his old chest was supposed to contain a welcome treasure of many [?coins] of the "yellow metal", but the heirs on getting possession of the key when his hand was stiff were very much disappointed to find, not what they expected, but just one solitary coin and that one an old tenpenny piece. The surprise was where did the wealth go to. Strange enough too, he would occasionally make mention of a

"Holy Book" he had in the box and given him by a priest who was supposed to work miracles. This book he always kept locked up, and an odd person saw it but no one handled it, and many would be very glad to see it, but he could not use it himself nor let any other persons have the satisfaction of using it, and there it lay till after his death. The "Holy Book" was an explanation of the Commandments and the Sacraments and some very good and pious other reading, but it was soon in leaves and lost like the tenpenny bit.

Arising from his flights of fancy in his creed, he gained for himself the appellation of "*Galsagh*", a word in the Irish language in that part of the country having for its signification—a moth-eaten or mouldering substance, a substance of no good for either seed or bread.[87] Before the death of the "*Galsagh*" and when the minister was giving him special attention by visiting him every day that he came to the place, it was amusing to see the semi-circular retrograding manœuvre before entering the dwelling when he came close thereto, and it was that from his astern motion that he had his face to the crowd and at once saw those who willingly followed him, those who did not but stopped outside, and those who sneaked away.

To their shame be it told some of the neighbours either through flattery or weakness did follow him with heads uncovered, not indeed so much on the score of piety or that they cared for what he said. On the contrary, they had no belief in him or in what he said, but some of them went there for the purpose of paving the way for their own far-seeing wicked designs. There are foxes and foxes, and they went to satisfy him so far—fox though he be in wisdom—to make it appear that they had no conscientious scruples, and that his eye might rest upon them and that they might afterwards have the greater boldness, the greater confidence in approaching him and of gaining his favour when the opportunity arrived for tarnishing, for falsely accusing, and ultimately uprooting their innocent and unsuspecting but more faithful neighbours. The greedy man thinks deeply, his eyes see far, and it takes a length of time to fathom or bring to view his designs.

The landlords are often accused, and justly so, for their oppression, cruelty and tyranny, but unfortunately a man's very neighbour is very often just as pitiless a tyrant as any man. He first covets his fellow neighbour's property, strengthened in his thoughts from some certain signs arising of the latter coming to poverty or unable to meet his demands. The avaricious neighbour sees him going back in the world, he feels glad

---

87. *Gailseach*, a stinking substance.

at this, but the declining man lingers longer in the way than at first supposed, and the man progressing in the world's goods has no claim at
him, has not the law nor the power to grasp at him as he would wish,
but to hasten his downfall he knows the way to do it. He buys up the
bailiff, a thing not too hard to do, as food and drink will do that, next
the agent, and lastly through them the landlord.

The poor man who is unable to meet his demands is at last turned
out and this seemingly industrious man grasps—with apparent reluc-
tance though he had for years previously used every means he could
devise to fall wrongfully into possession. He pretends that he feels for
the "outgoers", and there is a sort of a half promise just to keep matters
cool for the present, that some recompense will be paid, or if in a few
years the outgoing man is able to do the impossible, that is redeem, that
he will be reinstated: "I do not want your land, I have as much as I can
handle of my own, but you see I can't help it, unless I draw the anger of
the landlord against myself and you see one does not like to do that".

The poor man thus undermined is out; he struggles for a little by
some other means of living, hoping for better, but the stranger can turn
his property to advantage where the rightful owner was reduced, and is
still reducing and without thought the rents are increasing on him. In a
few years the price of the land is nearly sunk in rents, as this would be
the first obstacle thrown in his way—the arrears and taxes—if he spoke
of regaining what he had his eye to; no mention, no account of the produce for this time, that he is out of it and he finds to his grief that no
redress is to be got from the landlord who is openly now in favour of
the new tenant who holds on, and if at first he had any remorse of conscience the same is now dead.

In this way and other similar ways, without exactly opening a cry in
the ears of the public, many cruel unmerciful acts have been witnessed,
arising from the joint action of the landlord and his favoured tenant.
And with this landlord of religion—this landlord of prayer and piety—
his share in such acts were in proportion to the most extensive landlords, for he followed them in their footsteps and tightened the screw
when he could.

Years passed on as I have related. The school was open for everyone,
and the minister continuing his visits as usual and no one interfering
with him as yet. There were some improvements among the youth in
reading and writing, and rapid progress in the English language, and as
there was yet no visible sign, there was no dread of any spiritual evil and
therefore the school was well kept up and well attended.

If he meant education alone this ought to satisfy him, yet it was not enough, for in the course of time the Kildare Street Society [sic] took another view, that it was not enough to teach the English language where it was most wanted, that is to the merely Irish-spoken [sic] people.[88] No, that was not enough, and a strange idea occurred to them—Irish must be taught to those who had no other language but Irish, "Not a word of English in their cheeks". It was not enough to distribute Bibles, whole and in numbers, the New Testament, whole and in numbers, scripture lessons, all in countless quantities to all and everyone who took the trouble to put in an appearance at the hall door of the minister, no price, no questions asked beyond the conditional use of your name—and there was the nicely covered book.

Somehow it is in the nature of young people when they begin to know anything of learning to be fond of new books, so there was a craze, a regular rush to get presents of new books, and the boys took every chance of running to the hall. On one occasion a schoolboy, following up the example of his companions and thinking he was as much entitled to get a prize as another, went along and presenting himself got a Bible by giving his name and joyfully made haste home presented it to his father, and showing the name neatly written on the title page.

The father's countenance did not seem to rejoice in the act, he did not even take hold of the book, he gave no word of encouragement nor did he seem pleased, but on the contrary he was in sour temper; and after a little when he gave his opinion, he did not wish to be too severe but he said that he did not care for such a book and to cool the young lad in his disappointment, he gave his excuse that his notion was more for the Historical than that of the Theological learning, and so dispatched the lad back next day with orders to return the Bible and to ask for the History of France.

It would be much better had the boy violated his obedience to his father's command, but this idea could not be thought of by the youth and Oh! Jupiter Oh! horror of horrors, what a sacrilegious act, unwittingly committed, and all for want of a little wisdom; had he kept or hidden or destroyed the book he first got and asked for some other, he

---

88. The Kildare Place Society, the common name for the Society for Promoting the Education of the Poor, was established in Dublin in 1811; for two decades it was the most important state-sponsored agency involved in primary education. The K.P.S. pioneered teacher training and innovative classroom methods, the publication of textbooks and inspection of the many schools under its patronage. Despite its formal dissociation from proselytism, it became suspect in the eyes of the Catholic hierarchy and lost state funding when the national school system was launched in 1831.

might have escaped, but to attempt to exchange the Holy Bible for the History of France—no further reasoning wanted, no questions asked, this was enough, the mere act was condemnatory without any judge or jury, and the Bible was hastily and angrily taken from him, the title page torn out before his eyes and a strict command given him to immediately decamp and never to appear there again.

This incautious act, simple as it may appear and without forethought, was followed by serious results to the man of History, for he was unfortunately for himself a tenant of the minister, and it led to the cause of him being singled out, and to the minister's vengeance falling heavily upon him a few years later, from which a little degree of prudence, and I do not mean any flattery, could have secured him, saved him.

When a time arrived that bitterness began to show face, the minister was stiff and the other was steadfast, but it soon happened that an unprincipled man, a neighbour, one of those as above, an unscrupulous land grabber who was in favour with the minister and taking advantage when opportunity came, that is when the disagreement was going on, helped to aggravate, by fallacious statements, the easily formed opinions of the stronger opponent. Between them they pushed and persecuted the poor man, plundered him first of part of his land and, for fear that he might recover, they threw the entire townland into a new allotment, banished him to the outskirts and to the worst soil for cultivation. They drove him from a state of comparative ease and independence to that of poverty, and in a few years, struggling with hard work, he died of a broken heart.[89]

As I said, the teaching of English by means of English-printed books was not aimed at, as the young only were found to learn it; this was not enough then, and already signs of apostasy were appearing and therefore to strengthen such, the old people must be looked after and Irish must be taught to the "old souls" who knew nothing but Irish. And at this very time how joyfully in the eyes of the philanthropic Doctor of Divinity did that grand opportunity arise, that is to say—the Famine. Oh! the years of the Famine. This was for him the time then to hold out, to exhibit the tempting bait to the starving poor and no time was lost by him; the conditions for obtaining relief were simple and easy. Now he did not any longer hide his true colours nor did he think it necessary any longer to do so.

89. This appears autobiographical. If so, the 'land grabber' may be Michael Dorian, Hugh's cousin, and the reallocation of new holdings complained of most probably occurred between 1842, when Baillie was appointed to Fánaid, and 1858, after which the value of Hugh Dorian's holding increased in another reallocation of land: see above, p. 37 n.106.

Relief was ready and at hand. Here is bread and clothing. First take the Bible and go to church, that is to his place of worship, for the reader is to understand that the word "church" in country places and districts always means the Protestant place of worship, "chapel" being the name for that of the *Roman Catholics*.

CHAPTER 9
The 'Catbrack', or Irish Teaching

At the very first outset of this new and hitherto unthought of method of giving instruction, that is of teaching Irish to the native, to the merely "Irish speaking" people, the cloak that had long been concealing proselytism was by the minister thrown aside, and he now openly set out to make perverts, using as his bait the alluring temptation—money, knowing it to be the surest factor for attaining the ends he had in view, and accordingly remuneration by means of the tempting coin was promised to the "Irish speaking" and to the Roman Catholics who would enrol themselves in learning Irish, and this allowance consisted of something to the scholar and more to the teacher. The idea was laughed at by many at the start who could not of course see any good in it, and their eyes were not yet open to fathom the evil. But owing to the hardships and poverty suddenly setting in, the means for earning money in any shape was as suddenly grasped at, and the sudden enlistment into the *catbrack* caused it to spread like a plague.[90]

Every house, every dwelling, had its scholars, and as many looking up to become teachers as could be admitted. A regular competition went on for teachers' occupations. All sorts of books were printed in that language and distributed gratis day and daily at the hall of the minister,

90. *Cat breac*, speckled cat, (abusive) term for an Irish-language teacher in a society school. An Irish primer distributed in society schools introduced the term. It was widely used in west Ulster and it is unlikely that it was first coined in Fánaid; for Dorian's explanation, see above, pp. 204, 208. Charles Gallagher, a celebrated Irish scholar, was apparently a society school teacher in Fánaid in the 1820s and 1830s: see P. de Brún, 'The Irish Society's Bible Teachers, 1818–27 III', in *Éigse* 21 (1986), 113.

from the primer commencing with the Irish alphabet, the spelling book, and other reading books, and of Bibles there were no end. All the spare time of the doctor was devoted to the giving out of books and to registering the names of teachers, holding private conversations with the more intelligent among them, distributing small sums of money to a few, promising [the same] to others on their arriving at a certain qualification, and thus was he engaged from morn till night whenever he had appointed days.

In the preparatory books each page was divided into two columns, the first being printed in Irish type and alongside, the English translation, so that anyone at all might commence to learn. Learn what? Learn the very language they knew from childhood—learn Irish. Not *Irish* indeed, for it might be perceived by any thoughtful person that this was only a snare from the very first to serve another end; from the very first only one denomination of the people was taken in and that the Roman Catholic.

After the departure of the "*Galsagh*" for the unseen world, there was no one on the property of the minister professing any other religion than that of Roman Catholic, and he thinking perhaps that this state of affairs would appear rather awkward and that the lands from which he derived so much substance were then destitute of someone whom he might call his own. He therefore got transplanted from another part of the country a poverty stricken family of the Protestant religion consisting of only three in number, the mother, the son, and the daughter, and to serve them in the first instance he pretended to be charitable, but he made some others give the charity; he compelled one of his tenants to make way for them and supply them with a tolerably good cabin and a plot of ground without any remuneration whatever, and here came the family of "Boggs" by surname, the first from Adam of that name or sect that ever kindled a fire in that townland, and there they were placed to work out life and to give as much trouble to their neighbours as they possibly could, being protected in wrong and right by the minister.

But though he got these strangers fixed here against the will of his tenants, he made it no part of his business to give them any of the enlightenment which he was so ready and willing to bestow upon others. Enough for him that the glebe property was not without a Protestant. Perhaps the poverty of the Boggs family and their living in an unsightly cabin prevented him from visiting them, and though two of the trio could speak the Irish and English languages yet as to any correctness they were as deficient in one as the other. Still these advantages were of no use to them, they were already Protestant sure enough—for anything not Papist must be Protestant and therefore they would not be supplied with the Irish books and consequently no chance of earning any money from the open fund.

The old dame's name was the very peculiar one of Frank (Frances) and among the young people to whom she was known it was very laughable with them to hear Frank for a woman, as the like they never heard of before. She was also in herself an half idiotic being in her manners and bearing, and her face presented anything but a comely appearance, her two front upper teeth projecting so far as to be in constant contact with the outside of her under lip. She was also in the habit of wearing a man's coat. The children used to amuse themselves by approaching unknown to her and following her unawares, [they would] give a sudden pull to her garments behind and a shout, at which she would give a sudden leap and bound into any place and utter some extemporaneous rhyme of disconnected words. The names of the son and daughter were no way foreign, but stranger still, theirs were the names most common among the Papists—one was Paddy and the other Mary. True they were followers of the minister, but to church or any other place of worship they never went.

Old Frank had serious complaints against the "doakter". She could not understand "av, a" why the "meenister was at a sae guid tee 'the Romans', geeing them money for deeing naething at a", and not "aye penny" would he "gie" them, and that Paddy could "ta'k the Eirish as weel as any o' them". Old Frank's opinion was not without some grounds, being unjustly dealt with in respect to the money when it was to be got so easy. Be the cause of withholding from them what it may, the Boggs were certainly in as much need of a sample to eat as many another and, if not more, certainly not in less need of his gratuitous teachings as any of the Roman Catholics on whom he lost and distributed so much money in ready cash and in books.

It was always known to all who knew her, but time proved that old Frank was miserably ignorant. In her last illness she formed the opinion that a sight of "ae the meenister" would "dee her guid", and when he came he tried to console her by bringing about the happiness of the hereafter, and telling her something about the Saviour, and asking her something about God. She replied in a long excusive evading way of answering, "Meenister dear, me mimry noo is sae very bad, indeed it was nae very guid at any time", "Ye can nae expect ane of mee age noo too answer any money questions", "I din na ken noo whether there were ane or two Gids, I forgot a aboot sich things", and then she branched into, "Meenister dear, will ye gie Paddy the piece of baog he had last year for his turf" ...

Surely then if this Doctor of Divinity was so earnest in his profession, this specimen was a fitting object for operation, as sickly a one as he could select, a body requiring as much light as any other to find out the path to the next world. Instead of doing what lay directly with himself to do he adopted the other method, that of tempting with English coin the poor creatures who differed from him, and he tried to withdraw them from their allegiance to their old faith. With but a very few was he successful in his attempts, for his endeavours proved to be in greatest part a failure, and to him the saddest disappointment [was that] all that ever went over publicly to his side, or showed a willingness to do so, were for the time being only three or four of the very refuse of society.

One of these was a man who differing already in one very hateful respect from all his neighbours and being shunned and hated by everyone on account of his crime, his public scandal, was the first and the last of that particular description, and that was that he kept housed and supported two women at the same time, and as he disputed with one he went and took up lodgings with the other.[91] One, his lawful wife and her family, was living quite convenient. It was tried to make him change his evil life but all good advice was lost upon him, he seemed more inclined and better pleased to aggravate than be convinced, and some years before, he was banned out of the church of his fathers for this crime but still persevered in his wickedness, and when this opportunity offered he slid over to Protestantism.

He knew as much of the history of mankind and the world as those fallen branches of the same type who did the same thing years long before him. The price of parting with faith must be more than is ever thought of when bartering, as when all the ease, luxury and everything this world can give is afforded, still the price is not enough, is not redeemed, man is looking for more. On sliding over, all the privileges his new friends could give were easily given, easily bestowed upon him, lucrative situations for making money, no want of eating and drinking, so that arising from the effects of luxuries his body swelled into unnatural proportions.

91. Hugh Blaney of Ballykinard, head bailiff for Thomas Norman and a number of other landlords. Blaney's wife was Margaret Friel. An 'improper intimacy' existed between Blaney and Sheila Dorrian, who lived with her mother, Catherine, at the Ross Bridge, Rosnakill. The relationship, if any, of Hugh Dorian and Sheila Dorrian is unknown. For official correspondence that refers to Blaney's relationship with Dorrian, see N.A.I., Chief Secretary's Office Registered Papers 1857–8/11765.

This man, or monster that he was, could not be silent in his guilt for all that, for there is something extraordinary, something we cannot understand, in trying to stifle the dictates of conscience, but he tried to stifle such, or at least seemed to satisfy himself so, by at every chance continually giving Scripture quotations about Solomon and his wives, and many other texts wrongly construed but leading to and in his interpretation excusing the sins of the flesh. Nor was this enough, he was constantly provoking his neighbours and relatives by uttering abusive and blasphemous language against the Blessed Virgin, against the Roman Catholic clergy, and everything [to do with] Romanism; much worse would he be, much worse would he try to give scandal to hurt the ears of his hearers, than anything which could come from, or could be imagined by, the already Protestant born. In justice to them, it is but right to say that it would be the odd one among them and that of the lowest class who would in mixed society say anything disrespectful in that way, most of them being very quiet inoffensive people, and whenever and wherever they were in a minority so quiet were they that one would think they had forgotten the method of speech for want of use. Time was indeed in the memory of those living then where there had existed certain tribes of Protestants who were strong-headed, inhuman and very rough human beings, who thought nothing at all of mowing down a Papist, or robbing him of his property. At the time they carried on the strong hand, a party of these would start out mounted on horseback, pistols in front and swords by their sides, parade the country around for plunder, calling themselves Yeomen doing the King's work, and if they met with anything enticing, a fat sheep or a fat goose belonging to a Papist, they would order him to leave the same at a certain place before a certain time, and the command was sure to be obeyed.

Time however made a change with them and suddenly so, for they dwindled away and reduced in numbers, whilst the poverty-persecuted Papists increased. The great disproportion in numbers at this time caused such depredations on their part to cease, hence the quietness and the idea of former quiet on the part of those who were still alive, though some of the greyheads could look back in silence to their deeds of plunder of old.

The conduct, combined with the language, of "the man of two wives" drew upon him the intense hatred of everyone, and none felt it more so than his own relatives. To crown his words and acts, he went in the face of the public an odd time to church, renewing the odium against him, but to please the minister he went, and how he and the minister got enough Scripture to settle the affair about the plurality of wives never came to light, but in any case there was no reform, no change made in that direction. The first thing known was that his going to church brought to him the agencies, the collection of rents, for half a dozen petty landlords, and he therefore had plenty of money at all times at his command, and among the rest, that of the minister's, so that now they were the most confidential friends.

He had now money for to satisfy his appetites, and whether the rich had any liking for him or not, the poor had reason to hate him in greater intensity because, as he advanced in power, so did he in insolence. Yet, horrible to relate, his end while in health and strength and least expected came to a sudden and awful termination [sic]. The shades of night cover many an act.

One night he was on his patrol to the dwelling of his concubine and in close proximity to the public town but near to the church at which he appeared on Sundays; suddenly he was converted into a target and intercepted the velocity of a fair sized whinstone, a hand grenade, moving at a rapid rate from behind a fence. From the effects of the shock, his body in a very few days was hidden in the clay.

He had not been instantly killed, but was able to return to his own dwelling, and next day was raving mad; he never after spoke a word with any sense, and on the third day after his being in health and strength the operations, the actions of the medical doctors and surgeons in sawing up his skull for experiments and for their own information could be distinctly heard outside the walls of the house. Some call this a "post mortem".

The Protestants kept silent and gave no opinion as to his untimely death, though some of them would shake their heads as much as to say we dare not speak, but the Papists made no concealment of their opinions and the drift of their comments was that it was a visitation from the Supreme Ruler, the event confirming them in their grounded belief in Chastity and Holy Faith, much more so than preaching could impress. It was generally supposed that it was one of his own nearest relatives set the small bomb in motion, but there was no proof, and no one ever suffered, and the darkness kept its secret.[92] Such is man—today

92. The attack occurred at about seven o'clock on the evening of Sunday 13 December 1857; the 'hand-grenade' was a stone which struck him on the back of the head. William 'Luggy' Blaney of Rosnakill, a cousin of Hugh Blaney, was the chief suspect; Hugh, as bailiff, had not allotted him a particular farm in Rosnakill. 'Luggy', a son of Neil Blaney, was arrested and charged but not convicted. Dorian's account of the attack differs only slightly from that which can be constructed from official correspondence. First, Blaney was returning from Mary

a proud presumptuous, selfish, unruly mass of moveable matter, tomorrow a motionless putrefying heap, filling a certain space in the granary of worms.

Another of the minister's latest "catch" was a young man of that class "too lazy to work and ashamed to beg", who in spite of every opposition, all counselling, took the Bible under his arm and got his instructions from headquarters to go circuits in the shape of a missionary. Missionary! happy credentials—a raw material taken from the cow's tail, gifted with neither eloquence nor with knowledge, [he] could hardly tell the cardinal points of the horizon, having that impediment of a smothered guttural way of explaining himself and nothing whatever in his accomplishments to attract any one towards him, but on the contrary his manners were disgusting. But with all his impediments it seemed that he had the qualifications necessary to make a "missionary" in those days—he could make a smattering of reading the Irish books. On his commencing circuit, he was for a little while admitted into some houses, but expelled and hunted from many others. This was after the people began to see into the evil and after the general outcry was raised against the encroachments of the "*catbrack* system", that is of kidnapping souls. Expelled though he was, hated though he was, yet he could not be prevented, as it was not very hard for him to make out a false list of his supposed reformers. He watched for the minister going abroad and he then speedily made circuit of a hill and carelessly met him as if coming from doing duty in an opposite direction. His work was applauded, and he could go home then for that day, having visited such and such places! When a time arrived that the opposition became general and that he was received by only a few and even that clandestinely, he boldly turned over to the Protestant church on Sundays and became as true a Protestant that if for six days out of seven he had not had as much of flesh meat as would set the cat a mewing, he was sure to rise a smell on Fridays [*sic*]. In this state of laziness, of deceit and falsehoods, of eating and sleeping, reading the Bible and attempting to preach, did he continue till the death of his patron. He was then forced to emigrate, and it was said with certainty that the Protestant church was no thought

---

Doherty's public house in Rosnakill with his son, Michael, not from a visit to Sheila Dorrian, his concubine; leaving Doherty's, where he drank ale, his rather ironic words were 'I'm on the spree and it will be a long time before I'm on again'. Second, he showed some signs of recovery and was able to walk about a few days after the attack but suffered a relapse on Christmas Eve, became speechless and died a few days later. The inquest took place on 28 December. For official correspondence, see N.A.I., C.S.O.R.P. 1857-8/11765.

to him in the country beyond the seas, that he turned over again in the land of the stars and stripes.

Coming third of the selected, those ensnared by the minister, was, incredible as it may appear, contrary to what any sane man might believe, a rickety old woman, and one of the most abject images of that creation. But any shape in the flesh would please, as the minister it appeared could make his own laws, for contrary to any known law, contrary to his Bible injunction that "woman must not preach nor teach", she was appointed by him to teach. She was a withered old hag, black and blue in the face, one whose days for committing evil had left her, one who had spent her years till grey hairs in wickedness and sin, now good for nothing and already despised and hated by everybody. So the mystery was beyond conception, what manner or means she could appear worthy in the eyes of the minister for dispensing his doctrine rather than to bring disrepute upon himself and his works, for it may be easily understood that the people were not much inclined to receive any spiritual consolations at her hands. Well they might, knowing too well the vessel that the imposition attempted to flow from. But it would appear that shame had left the earth in those days, and according to the minister to save humanity, the Bible, use it or not but take it, was the only life-buoy.

This skeleton in the flesh skirted from place to place like something not earthly and was by some called a fairy, and others who went further in their judgement scrupled not to call her a "She Devil", her withered bones being to her no encumbrance. Pity that no record is kept of any of her species being expelled along with Lucifer, for the people would be sure she was one. One thing she was not amiss at, and that was she could not be kept from talking, her tongue being the only part of the machinery not worn by age. She went around the neighbours' houses at an hour she knew that the men were in the fields, managed to darken a door and get in before being rightly seen, and having effected her entrance, her custom was to sit on a low stool at the fireside, and in this posture, her knees came close to her ears. She then drew out of her bosom a short dark clay pipe, began to smoke, lighting the pipe by setting fire to a few pieces of straw, bent and twisted, and while proceeding with this she prepared and tried the experiment of a lecture "on the world to come", her toes in the ashes and pipe in her jaw. What a pulpit and what a preacher.

Her discourses were not much heeded, not very much welcomed indeed, but the women did not wish to resort to muscular strength to

expel her but would make efforts to get rid of her in other ways by saying, "What you say may be true enough", "I did not hear what you said,
these children are so noisy; would you not better go to the next house,
my children are so cross, and I cannot keep this one from crying whenever he takes fits", and poor Pat gets a slap in the cheek to make him
cry more. If she seems regardless of these hints, she gets cause for a
speedier one, as an excuse is made, "Here is Johnny and Micky coming
home, they will be raging as I have the dinner too late". This was the
stunner, for she knew well that she was extremely detested by all the
men as much as an evil spirit, but she knew the women were backward
in just catching her by the shoulder or telling her to stay out, and in
some instances she imposed by claiming to have a [family] relationship,
thus she blindfolded the weaker sex. Such was the She-teacher.

There were others under the name of teachers who tried for a length
of time—years in fact—in a hidden way to please both sides, that is
attend at the chapel on Sundays, and on other days of the week attend
with the minister, but never went openly to church, and when brought
to understand the evil they were doing, some did give it up. But others
were too far entangled to do so and therefore suffered all acts of abuse
in public and in private. Yet they stuck to the loaf, the leg of mutton,
and the fat goose, until the source of supply dried up and this happened
at the departure of the minister when, willingly or unwillingly, he had
to exchange his mansion house and all its comforts for a narrow home
of clay, and then the "Cats", being shut out from their haunting place,
had to fall back and some of them seemingly repentant beseeched re-
admission into the ranks of their neighbours, the same as upheld by
their forefathers, but whose flag they as renegades had so long and so
shamefully betrayed and dishonoured. The name given to this section of
people, a name by which they were known and by which they were
degraded, and when understood a very appropriate name too, was that
of "*catbrack*", meaning a "speckled cat", a word accidentally put into
their own spelling book, and in the sense in which it was applied meaning exactly what was wanted, that is a person who is of mixed religion,
neither Protestant nor Catholic. Had the compiler of the "Irish Sentences" the least idea what a legacy he was bestowing upon his followers when inserting "*catbrack*": "speckled cat", he would I am sure have
had the charity never to attempt the translation of the word.

Among the reasons for permitting the *catbrack* teachers to roam
about so long at large and thus attempt to inculcate strange doctrine,
one reason was that the Roman Catholic clergyman, the same spoken of

above, was rather simple, rather in a state of stupor to the knowledge of the approaching evil, and he was easily convinced, easily led, to give in to false statements, and through a feeling of charity at the representations of want and distress put before him at the head of every excuse, and it may be for these reasons, he overlooked, or did not object to them earning some money to support life (as they maintained) expecting a turn in the tide of affairs.

The idea of teaching Irish to the Irish, or in other words Gaelic upon Gaelic, was so very childish-looking an undertaking in itself that it was merely laughed at by those who thought they knew something, never just taking into consideration that the same was a snare to entrap, to undermine, the old religion of the people, that those ensnared were playing with and in the clutches of the leopard, that the followers of the same leopard would make it appear by lies and hypocrisy to the priest that there was no harm in what they were doing, that they were only trying to support families, else they would *starve*, and as for renouncing their religion, that there was no fear; and on the very next day, they would be with the minister at private meetings, assisting at where there was nothing but mockery of their religion, and no less than a promise of renouncement of all Popish doctrine, and to listen to and respond to the minister enlarging upon the most scandalous, the most blasphemous language he could utter the most ignorant would be shocked at the idea of an educated man uttering such. When the progress of proselytism had taken rather a deep root, when too many were getting money too easily just by merely going round the neighbours' houses, seeing them at their homes or in the fields, giving the so-called scholars short lessons, enrolling names willing or unwilling, until the reported progress was believed by their employers to be such and such and a list of real names, feigned names, and counterfeit names was made up, it was then thought necessary that the "Irish Inspector" from Dublin should come to see and report on the numbers of persons, young and old, who were on the way of renouncing Pope and Popery in the North of Ireland.

Many a time were the Irish people tried and in many a clime was English gold scattered to injure, to destroy Popery, but never did the giver make so fruitless an attempt or derive less benefit than at this. The gold did not make perverts except the few who could easily be done without and who were rotten branches already—the gold did not make assassins. Tis true the promoters had for a short while under the shade of their banner the lukewarm and a few of the putrefying branches who were leaning towards earth then, who belonged to the earth, and the loss of whom the old stock would never miss, on the contrary could do without.

Exeter Hall mint, once it lost the direction of its flowing, once it was withdrawn from here, the *catbrack*, cats and kittings also disappeared, and beyond the very recollection, very little trace of them is left behind.[93] Not as many as a single soul—a *catbrack*—or the descendant of one is going to church there after all. At the time, the minister thought with gladness and made others think that he and his were dispelling what they called "darkness"; the Inspectors came and stopped for a week or so with the principal among the *catbracks*, during which time he had plenty to drink, and for eating there was no scarcity, and nothing but Scripture and Scripture phrases used in all manner of discourse. These were surely pleasure trips, excursion trips for such men, some of whom were dashing young blades but change coats as they might, they could not change the accent nor the manners of the Clare and Kerry boys, fond of dancing, music and games, and such were the Scripturian Inspectors from Dublin. The people of the district were not amiss in passing remarks in their own way on these jovial fellows, such as "that man never was a Protestant born", "he has the skin and the very appearance of a turn coat", "damn his body! and a fine young man he is, pity that his belly deceived him", "would it not be a nice thing for him to 'list in the so'jers". The so-called Inspector, accompanied by the next in rank and the teachers, made a circuit of a part of the district in the heat of day, and were more like surveyors or cess collectors, being guided by their lists of names [for persons] who were not in existence at all. Excuses were easily got that such persons were from home on that day— unfortunately!—and as that same Inspector might never come the same road again no questions were raised as to truth, falsehood, or forgery.

At this time then and only then did a clear-brained quick-eyed Roman Catholic priest arrive as an assistant to the old man who was parish priest, and this young man being wide awake, his college train- ing fresh in his memory and the doings of the outward world not unknown to him, well understood the danger to which the poor were beguiled into, and to which his superior in rank seemed negligent or at least lent a deaf ear.[94] He therefore immediately opposed the designs of the minister, and the latter increased his exertions in money and mater-

---

93. Exeter Hall in London was a great centre for public lectures, rallies and debates of a strongly evangelical character; it became synonymous with English anti-Catholicism in the 1850s and 1860s.

94. Probably Fr James Gallagher (d. 1859); appointed curate in 1850, Gallagher was responsible for the erection of the national school at Fanavolty.

ial; for years there was no love lost between the two.

In justice to some of the teachers, without much admonition they forsook their positions of their own free will from the very disgust they felt in being present and listening to blasphemy, the most repugnant being on the venerated articles of faith in the religion of their fathers, such as to make the very flesh quiver on any sensitive man, and so vilely put forth by the minister himself at the meetings.

This new Roman Catholic clergyman lost no time and set to work to recall the wandering among his flock, to expose the evil doings, the intentions of the *catbracks*, first by advice and enticement and, when that failed, by public denouncement; numbers at once and for ever turned away from it and renounced their gain and burned the books. Whilst the war of words was going on this clergyman, though his own means were limited, paid for some two or three or more young men to get off to America to be rid of the fetters.

Some few held out disregarding all persuasion and defying all threats, careless of mockery; at last the denouncements became constant but as for shame or disgrace the stiff necked among them suffered all. The word "boycott" was not then in use, but so far as the meaning of it went, the *catbrack* was so "boycotted" that few if any would speak to any of them, either at home or abroad, and they were so clannish that all of them went to the same shop, at a distance, for their goods. There may be other reasons but in this they were no way interfered with. Marked out were they as the lepers among the people, shunned by nearly all and spoken to by only a few; still with all this loneliness some of them held onto the bait and continued to deny their Lord for the sake of satisfying their appetites, and would have ease and money, come from whence it may. They knew very well that many of their neighbours who wrought honestly were nevertheless in hunger, in suffering and in poverty from the effects of bad seasons, while they enjoyed laziness and good dinners, all of which was too good here below to be parted with for the sake of satisfying conscience, and they therefore took the chance of running the risk of displeasing their God and Creator—they grasped at that which satisfies the body and let death, the soul and eternity take their chance—as these were as yet out of view in the distance. As long as the source from which the money came lasted, as long as it was given out to them in spite of priestly denunciations and in spite of coldness and hatred from friends, relatives and neighbours, in spite of brawls and differences in members of the same family household, yet did the few hold on.

In daylight while passing the roads, they were called by their nicknames, "mewed at" in imitation of the "cat", and after dark they were afraid to appear on the public road in the dread that they would be waylaid. This fear however was groundless for no one of them ever got anything worse than the tongue could give and they were often startled at the ever repeated "cat". Yet such was their love for the body that it was only at the disappearance of their patron—the minister—on his being consigned to the clay that their career suddenly came to an end—the money was stopped.

A successor of course was appointed in a short time in place of the man who for years wrought so sedulously, and the rank and file of the "cats" met at their former haunting places to do him homage, profess their faith and their fidelity.[95] But to their great dismay and the disappointment of the pious, very pious *catbracks* and the Bible-readers, they had to withdraw with tears in their eyes, no promise, no word of consolation; the new minister, wiser for himself, was for having peace he would have nothing to do with them, he cared for his own and nothing more: the sight of the "cats" frightened him the first day, and shortly the old state of things and of the people returned to the same standard as they were years before. The appellation "*catbrack*" was first applied to the apostates by the priest as above in the heat of one of his denunciations, and the term was taken up and never forgotten. No, never will.

In other parts of Ireland the same class of people had different names. In the South and West [there were] "jumpers" and "soupers", but a more appropriate name could not be given than that given in the North as it carried its own meaning truly. Strange enough too at the end of all, but the people no way wondered at it, that the greatest of the "cats", the incorrigible chief *catbrack* who held out the stiffest while firmly opposed, when the supply was withdrawn could show no sign of worldly advancement, but [was merely] older in years and worn in garments, the same old coat of home manufacture hanging loosely to his ankles, the very same that he wore seven long years before, in the country term a "slip-on". All his earnings, all the money he got in exchange for bartering his old soul, for denying his Lord, were now eaten and drunk, the shopkeepers were the only gainers, nothing saved, and now he was no way better in worldly affairs than his neighbours. His family

---

95. Baillie died in 1859; his successor was the Rev. Daniel Mooney (1808–77). A Dubliner, Mooney had been a student in Kilkenny Collge when Baillie was headmaster; entered Trinity College in 1823; awarded a B.A. 1829 and an M.A. 1842; curate of Ballymena, Co. Antrim and then of St Mary's, Dublin; married Jane Gray of Longford in 1847; retired from Fánaid in 1872: see Leslie, *Raphoe clergy*, p. 52.

was nothing better, on the contrary despised, and a halo of odium surrounding them, some of them depraved drunken characters, a scandal to the community and to themselves.

Such was the end of the *catbracks*: some of them emigrated in the course of time, but those who remained in the country had to return to their former employment, to the handling of the spade and shovel and the breaking of the clods like other people, with this only difference that they have got a stigma—a name branded indelibly to them which, unless their race, seed and generation become extinct, will remain and will be hereditary in their breed and generation yet unborn, "the *catbrack*".[96]

---

96. In the mid-twentieth century, a Doherty family in *íochtar Fhánada* could still be pointed out as descendants of a society school teacher: see R.B.É., 705, 665–6.

For many, many years previous to the setting in of 1846 and 1847, food was in the greatest abundance and easily obtained. The old people could mention an odd summer in their recollection in which the price of provisions did run high, the same being caused by hurricanes or the inclemency of a preceding harvest, but there was no such thing as starvation heard of at such times. Potatoes, the principal food of the people, grew everywhere and to perfection and on any soil into which a spade could be put; even the white sand in which there was apparently no substance threw up its crop to perfection, and in some places clay would be carried from deep soil to cover seed on the ledge of a rock, and by such contrivances a satisfactory yield would turn out.

The seasons turned out so good and the supply so great that man and beast had plenty to eat, and at the least amount of toil. The sea too seemed to be extravagant in its yield of fish, sometimes the shoals coming close to the dry land, and while one class of men took to labouring the land, another class living nearer the shore took to fishing as a better money-making business (and to make up for the shortness of crops owing to the scarcity of land); there were always two or three in the fishing family who raised as much in crops as possible and who would provide firing, so that a reserve of food and fuel was sure to be laid up for the winter season.

The means of obtaining shelter and gaining a livelihood were so easy that the people, as I have said in speaking of villages, became in a short time very numerous, and everyone who was entitled thereto claimed certain rights, that is their share of what should belong to them; from this arose divisions and subdivisions of land—land then being very valuable—and this went on until tenements were cut up into the smallest patches, and each family was subsisting on whatever means they provided for themselves, very few being in any debt.

It has been some times argued that the Irish could not subsist on what Ireland would or could produce. But between 1840 and 1845 when the population was the largest, they lived within themselves on their own produce, and yet there were thousands of acres which could but never were cultivated at distances not very far off. There was very little imported, and the exports were in proportion—I mean this of the country districts. There may have been luxuries and trade in cities far removed from where we are describing, but there was no Indian meal known then, flour was seldom used, and as for tea or sugar, if such things came under a roof once or twice a year, it was enough. To show how little such luxuries were thought of, there was a shopkeeper in the place, the same being reckoned wealthy; at or before November, when laying in his stock, he brought home a chest of tea, and if he had all sold before that day twelve months, he considered himself at no loss.

It is true tobacco, soap, salt, iron and leather could not be done without, but each of these commodities was used as sparingly as possible. Every beardless brat of a boy did not have a pipe in his pocket or his jaw at this time, and if the old man got an ounce [of tobacco] he always measured it by his finger to see if the ounce was a good or a bad one, and he knew how to use it: a certain allowance was for the day, and when the pipe was "going" the old woman could take a "pull" if she fancied, but she never thought of buying on her own account. Very often the old man was his own messenger as he had less to do and spent the forenoon going certain distances looking out for his ounce of tobacco; being disappointed in too many places, he rattled about from one petty shop to another. The family at home did not mourn much for his absences, as his temper was ruffled in the morning, but if he returned unsuccessful so much the worse.

The people lived on home produce: potatoes, milk, butter and plenty of fish, the latter always with the poorer class. Eggs were consumed at home, and a few who could afford it laid out their accounts to have a fat bullock killed at a certain time. The first man in the neighbourhood who took up the idea of buying and collecting eggs was mocked at, and it was hiddenly [sic] that they were given to him in barter by the women. He went round the neighbours with a large basket on his arm, stealing himself towards the dwellings, being ashamed and partly afraid of being seen by the men; from the nature of his employment, he could not escape a nick-name which stuck to him, *Micky Goo-ga*, Mickey of the egg.[97] When he had collected a sufficient quantity to make up a load for a large, lazy but very quiet donkey, he tackled a pair of "side creels" to the animal and slowly made his way to the town, a distance of over 14 miles. A mail boat now-a-days could not be better watched than were his departures and arrivals then. He did not proclaim his hour of departure, but to go unknown he could not, and he had to oblige the women by bringing home various things. His memory was severely taxed in trying to recollect every person and every thing. To assist himself he would tie up the money and the sample together, and when in town on spreading out the records, he easily knew what he wanted. The people at home soon taught him what articles were needed to open a shop with, and by degrees he was able to supply certain things himself: needles, pins, thimbles, smoothing irons, in short a hardware store on a small scale.

Many had no land, no property beyond the cabin they lived in, and their chief dependence lay on the ocean, that is the seaweed thrown up by it: they [used it for] manuring the land and they turned it into kelp (which will be better explained further on). Such people got land to crop here and there from those who had it to spare, and they paid for it in money, in goods or in labour. Nor was it enough. [In addition to] the residents occupying the already over-crowded houses, huts, and hovels, every one stuffed with inhabitants, there was regularly each year an influx of supplemental population, who arrived about the time the crops were nearly gathered in, that is November; they were induced hither from former experience of the friendly hospitality and plentiness of potatoes and fresh fish. Fresh herrings were so plentiful some winters that the salt which could be got was too scarce for curing them, and a friend or a stranger got as many at the shore as he had means of carrying and the man who brought a bag of salt could please himself in his bargain.

The newcomers or yearly visitants consisted of tinkers, pedlars, pipers, fiddlers, show-men and beggars, and many otherwise idle with no profession. The tinkers carried at that time the idea of their being an honourable people; they arrived in crowds or caravans, women and children and their beasts of burden, the donkeys, forming the advanced guard, and these arrived perhaps a day before the men. Each head of a tinker family owned a donkey or two, and he was reckoned a poor man unless he had one of the best class of animals of that species. This ani-

97. *Gogaí*, (child's name for) egg.

mal was very useful to them, for when properly equipped, strapped and harnessed as a tinker knew how to, on it were placed the children, the youngest of the family, two or three on each side, as also the bedclothes and other baggage (such as the bellows and other articles), and the animals were driven by youths capable of doing so, and they were surrounded by the women. The men kept at a respectable distance from the advance party and formed another procession with long stout sticks over their shoulders; with these they supported boxes made half of leather and half of wood called "budgets" on their backs; marching leisurely they knew from experience where to billet, and for this place they headed.

When encamping in a village or villages, they tried to keep as close to each other as possible, but every tribe, half tribe or family [of tinkers] knew where to set up, and without asking liberty they took possession of some man's fireside and then and there laid aside their traps; a foraging party was told to provide provender for the donkeys, and clean straw for "shake downs"—that is heaps of straw for themselves to sleep upon. Any one in the surrounding neighbourhood having straw or hay shared it with the tinkers, whether willing or unwilling, in fact they almost dared not refuse. These visitants were likened to welcome friends or guests who had been absent for some time; to refresh themselves, they spent a day or two lounging in straw, rehearsing stories about their travels, their adventures and encounters, and the many performances with the blackthorn they had participated in at fairs and markets.

When fully rested, the male portion of the tinkers went to work, that is to mend old umbrellas or broken pots, but as for pans or kettles, they were as rare as a Jubilee coin; there was no talk about them, as the consumption of tea and of the "cake on the pan" was only in infancy years after.[98]

To make up for kettles and pans were tins of all descriptions and sizes, tin pandies, tin plates, tin lanterns, the latter being thought a great and useful invention, as it served a person to carry a lighted candle from the dwelling to the stable. All these things were made by the men; the women sold them for cash or bartered them for goods, the wife starting each morning along with another member of the family, and instructions were given to a third to meet them at a certain time and place with the beast of burden, the donkey, to carry home the provisions and other things collected by them. In this way they put up the winter half year without rent and without taxes.

98. Cake in the sense of griddle bread.

Beggars became so saucy that they refused things offered except those of the best quality, and if their burden became too heavy they would empty their bag into a corn field or other hiding place and leave the contents to rot, and proceed anew.

As for the fixed inhabitants, a few weeks labour in spring and summer served to raise as much food as was sufficient for them and some to spare, and as for winter work, with most of them there was none. That part of the year was gone through in attending soirees, dances, balls, wakes, markets, the public house and the shebeen house. In every second or third village there was a butcher who kept buying and killing sheep, and getting the same mostly by card-playing: he got the money down and more than the price, and if one of these sheep-killers managed at November to make up the price of one to start with, his trade was opened and it was as useful to him as a bank; moreover he often had his own stake in, and he was not, to be sure, the worst of players. So he was kept going for the season; no sooner [was one] sold than another was bought, and very often the animal was played for and the money received while it was yet in the hill with the wool on its back and the purchase to be made.

... Not all were of this turn of mind; the weaver was busy in the [winter] season and other tradesmen got something to do, not forgetting the hackler who was second to the spinner in preparing the flax. But generally speaking this was the state of people when the potato failure came on the greater part of them—just living from hand to mouth, with no thought of a provision made for the future.

As is always the case, men are differently circumstanced in worldly affairs, so when the potato failure came on some were living comfortably, some more so than others, some having more or less livestock, cattle and sheep, some a little money, so all were not reduced to the same level in the scale of poverty at once. But in general, after a couple of years of hunger and starvation, nakedness, coldness and poverty got a hold and over-ruled all classes. It came to this that even the few who had some worldly substance about them were afraid to own it and were afraid to use it except under pressing necessity, and not only that but the persons who had sufficient nourishment in food showed signs as if it did them no good. This in a sense was not to be wondered at, as it could not be otherwise to a man of feeling, knowing that his neighbour, his friend, or a near relative, perhaps his grandchild, was without food and was hungry. And besides this sympathetic feeling there was an uneasiness, a dread of the future preying upon their minds so that what they partook of served not what nature allowed, and along with this, the sleep was restless thereby disturbing the body, leaving it pale and sickly looking though nourishment was sufficient for the time.

In a very short time there was nothing but stillness, a mournful silence, in the villages; in the cottages, grim poverty and emaciated faces, showing all the signs of hardships. The tinkers disappeared—fled to the cities; the musicians of all and every description disappeared, and these classes of visitor have never since returned. Many of the residents also made their escape at once, finding employment or early graves elsewhere. But in general the people were drifting from bad to worse, no one having sufficient food for the family for the year within himself; the best off could only muster from the produce of the land a partial supply for three-fourths of the twelve months at the outside; then they had to fall back upon anything they had for sale—a cow, a heifer or a few sheep—and take it to market being bound to sell at whatever price offered, and with this they would buy Indian meal. Small indeed was the bulk of the Indian meal brought home in lieu of the pet animal which had to be parted with, but the love of offspring was dearer to the parent, and before seeing his children hungry he would sacrifice anything however valuable. [Actions of this kind] served immediate necessity with some, but what were they to do who had nothing to sell and nothing to eat? Their state can be better imagined than described. A mournful silence, no more friendly meetings at the neighbours' houses in the afternoons, no gatherings on the hillsides on Sundays, no song, no merry laugh of the maiden, not only were the human beings silent and lonely, but brute creation also: not even the bark of a dog nor the crowing of a cock was to be heard—and why? These animals had nearly all disappeared.

The women and children were within doors; the able bodied male portion of the families were out in every known direction looking and applying for employment or for relief. A father or son who managed to make his way to Scotland thought himself lucky though absent—out of sight of his dear ones—so long as he could send home as soon as it was earned a few shillings to save his wife, his mother, his brother or perhaps his own little ones from starving, and how readily they would submit to the loss of his presence so long as the expected relief arrived.

After a good deal of unsuccessful petitioning on the part of the starving people, and after many delays and unfulfilled promises on the part of the upper class, the Government at last was moved to extend relief by giving employment in the shape of making "broad roads", as they were called. Government engineers were sent out at a good salary to mark out "new lines" of road through rock and bog and every other impediment. The greatest engineering ingenuity used in laying out these roads was to find the most difficult routes, impossible to make and impossible to tread. Then pay-clerks, check-clerks, overseers, and gangs-men or gaffers were appointed according to whether they had real or supposed knowledge or, better still, through intercession, and at long last the hungry and the naked were set to work in the cold depth of winter, and a selection of those was made—those and those only who were known to be in extreme necessity—and their daily wages were fixed and not even at that valuable coin—one shilling—oh! no, but at exactly *nine pennies per day*.

Of any work that ever was attempted, this was the most useless—for the reason that the roads were never completed; at this day they would remind the historian of like traces left by the hands of the Romans in the ages of invasion. In after ages they will be traced in most places from the partly constructed pieces left here and there: following the course of the lines can be seen the gravel-hole, the quarry, or the sheltered rock from which more than one poor man had to crawl to his home, such as it was, overpowered with hunger, fainting through weakness, and make for his bed, such as it was, lie down, and die.

... These efforts to construct the "new lines" of road served but one end: the sending of many a poor honest man to the untimely grave through hunger and cold, for if he did not put in an appearance on the ground in all kinds of weather, no matter what the distance might be, or if he was not present at every roll call, his pay, small as it was, was reduced one-half or one-fourth. Every man therefore fortunate enough to get his name on the list did his utmost to appear, but some were not able to work, nor yet were much inclined. While on the ground and apparently working, a man in every gang, or as they were called "squad", kept a lookout for the appearance of the "gaffer"—whilst the rest of the gang sat or stood idle; and when under the eyes of the gaffer their efforts were such that the slowest manoevures of a new Corporation brigade man were swift motion in comparison.[99] Here is where the government advisers dealt out the successful blow—and it would appear premeditated—the great blow for slowly taking away human life, getting rid of the population and nothing else, by forcing the hungry and the half-clad men to stand out in the cold and in the sleet and rain from

99. Presumably a reference to the work practices of labourers employed by Derry Corporation.

morn till night for the paltry reward of nine pennies per day. Had the poor pitiful creatures got this allowance, small as it was, at their homes it would have been relief, it would be charity, it would convey the impression that their benefactors meant to save life, but in the way thus given, on compulsory conditions, it meant next to slow murder.

With every hardship and so small a recompense, the man who got work at the lucky nine pennies per day still considered it a great favour and thought himself happy at earning even so small a sum when at the same time the yellow Indian meal was bought at two pence per pound. Oh! the thought then of the nine copper coins worth of Indian meal as the means of providing a supply for the twenty-four hours and thus to keep life in a family of perhaps five or six (and in this calculation we are forgetting if not omitting the Sunday).

There were private laws made by the "committee" men and those who had the distribution of the relief; amongst their law acts was one that any man possessing a four-footed animal—not a dog or cat—one which could be sold at fair or market, was in consequence debarred from government aid as long as he had such. The absurdity of this enactment is manifest, for the result was that very soon a great many were brought to the same level of poverty; then the want and suffering became general with few exceptions. Every conceivable means was resorted to for getting something, anything, to support life, by soliciting on trust, by borrowing even in the smallest quantities from those who had a little to spare from day to day; if unsuccessful in entreating at one house, people would try another and another, and at last some neighbour would be found who would through pity share [their food] as a loan; during the while the hungry family were praying for the successful return of the messenger that they might get something in the shape of a repast for the day. Things and substances never heard of before to support human life were of necessity resorted to; in fact any substance which the palate did not completely rebel against was used to alleviate the pangs of hunger.

Many affectionate parents reduced themselves to mere skeletons from the too oft repeated act of withholding from themselves the necessaries they were so much in need of and giving them to their silent helpless children, thereby feeling great comfort in the act but unawares that feebleness would steal upon them. So overcome would they be from a weakness caused by want of food that apparently strong able-bodied men, on managing to get into a neighbour's house without any business whatever but to while away the time and be relieved, to be out of sight of the distress if only for a few minutes, would sit on a seat and soon fall asleep from exhaustion, and on attempting to get home again would have to lay hands on a wall or a fence to keep from staggering—with, as the saying is, a multiplicity of stars before their eyes.

It may not appear strange to medical men, to those who know the frailties of the human system, that in persons reduced to this extremity, this weakness in the frame, the cheek bones became thin and high, the cheeks blue, the bones sharp, and the eyes sunk, arising from the deprivation of nourishment at the same time the legs and the feet swell and get red, and the skin cracks. All these signs were visible, strange as the recital may appear to people of the present day who do not know or think of such; what an unthankful being man is when full.

In order to lend their help in providing anything edible, poor women would go miles to the seashore to attend the ebb-tide for the purpose of picking up shellfish or seaweed or other substances growing upon the rocks, and these were carried home to the helpless and hungry creatures left behind; [there would have been] no one to console them in their crying, a chair having been placed across the door to prevent the small ones from crawling out, and an elderly one having had the charge of keeping the younger ones from getting into the fire until the mother came home.

To home! yes home, she would return cruelly laden, a self-inflicted cruelty, burdened with everything she could gather up, so much of all sorts that, judging from its weight, even a man would be unwilling to undergo the same. So great was the expectation and such the necessity that part of the cargo was eagerly fastened upon and at once eaten raw; part was chosen for immediate cooking such as shell fish, and the little ones went to work while the mother rested and partly refreshed herself so as to prepare for another trip at the proper time in the same direction. As a proof of the efforts and the struggle made in those days to allay hunger, heaps of shells and green mounds can be seen at a long distance from the seashore, and can be traced in many places to the present day marking the spots and the only vestige where human habitations once stood close beside.

The misery was such that hunger, sickness and death were felt and seen everywhere, nothing to support the living, no means of burying the dead. At the death of a person, some feeling neighbour or two went about and gathered pieces of board and formed a rough coffin. Often some five or six charitable neighbours took upon themselves the task to carry a dead body thus roughly coffined to the grave a distance of more than five miles; as they were too few for the task, they would rest at intervals as they went along, one man despairing and another encouraging them to persevere, and calling and asking any one coming in view or forcing those they met to give a lift for some distance, and rest again.

After a time another means for relieving the distressed was opened, trifling though it was the distribution of quantities of the Indian meal in small measures and that per a scale, that is per number in a family taking ages of every one into account. In this as in every thing in which Government has had the distribution, those who had hands on it took good care to benefit themselves, either by withholding in part, or lessening the supply to which families were entitled. Store-keepers were appointed, relief circles were formed, and committee men were appointed; some voluntarily took it upon themselves, and the committees met on fixed days to hear grievances and give directions.[100]

The "committee day" was a day for the gathering of the people and so they did. On this day "relief tickets" were given out according to information received personally or through other channels of cases of pressing necessity, and in many cases favour was instrumental in bestowing upon some who were not in most need. On such days the house of a "committee man" was besieged from early morning by parties beseeching and applying for relief, and he in his own charitable way of thinking did not think it wise to have his own services go for nothing, or at least without some profit in recompense in some way; he felt justified in sending one and all of them who were able to do anything to work for him in his garden, his barn, his grounds or his outhouses, and if the thought occurred to him, he seemed unmindful or unpitiable [sic] of the hungry stomachs which through shame they tried to hide or

---

100. An act of parliament in the winter of 1845 empowered local notables to form relief committees for the distribution of government aid. These committees established 'relief funds' for which they then sought subscriptions. Concerned to encourage 'local responsibility', government matched individual contributions but generally did not match donations from charities. Committees used these monies to relieve distress by providing food in return for labour on 'works of public utility' such as road-building. In extreme cases, they also distributed food and clothing gratis. The 'Relief Committee of the District of Fannet' was established for the parishes of Clondavaddog and Killygarvan in October 1846. The chairman was Thomas Batt Jr, a Rathmullan landlord. Sir James Stewart, the Vice-Lieutenant of County Donegal, reorganized the county's relief committees that December. A new committee was established for Killygarvan, and the reconstituted Fannet Relief Committee became responsible for Fánaid (Clondavaddog) alone. Chaired by Henry F. Letham, a resident landlord, the committee members included John Sproule, secretary, and the Rev. William Baillie D.D., treasurer. For these committees, see N.A.I., Relief Commisson 3/2 2/441/41 [Famine Relief Commission: Incoming Correspondence (Kilmacrenan) Co. Donegal 1846–7] 7200; 1991; 20457; 10375; 10156; 12230; 8852; 13525; 16551.

would not speak of. While he was getting work done to satisfy himself for his supposed goodness he was preparing leisurely before he started to the place of meeting. Unknown and unthought of by him, it was an act of great charity to have these poor people removed beyond the sight and smell of his hot victuals during the time his meal was being prepared for him. Poor hungry beings only too glad to be at his command for the time, by their ready compliance and by forced efforts beyond their strength they would be trying to please in the hope that by so doing his influence might be gained.

At last he is ready and starts in much haste, wishing to leave all behind him. He does not much care for the company, but is followed by a crowd to the place of meeting and that was the Petty Sessions house at a distance of three or four miles. The Petty Sessions house serves the two purposes at this time, but the [every day] duty of the magistrates is far the least, so very few attend with the exceptions of the Petty Session's clerk and three or four policemen there to teach a stray donkey the benefit of the act against wandering on the public road. On the days the relief committee meets, the doors are closed. But occasionally a side door opens to admit some one in authority who by this device escapes the attention of crowds outside. Inside, they consult and issue tickets - but on every occasion the supply of Indian meal at their disposal is unfortunately not enough to meet the pressing demand. The day's work of the gentry over, they are on the way to disperse, but how to get away, for not a tithe of the expectant multitude outside get the expected "token", that is a ticket or as they called it a "line" for as much as a morsel?

It may then be easily imagined how the pangs of the already hungry parent, waiting all day, made his wants, his grievances, known as much as the language in his power lay, but thus disappointed and returning home in the evening hungry, vexed, and with no word of consolation on his lips, only to view the sad scene, the agonizing scene of the family before him still more hungry. Oh! can we imagine his feelings, his sufferings?

On leaving the place and gaining the outside, a rush is made at the committee men, the skirts are nearly pulled off their coats at the attempts to get some words from them. It is with the greatest difficulty that they can make their way, every one asking, "Can you do nothing for me your honour?" or "your reverence", for we must not forget that the "soggarth aroon" felt inclined to go there too and, though his influence was not the greatest, still he went there, and in the jostling and

PUBLIC
MEETING

To the Gentry, Clergy, and Inhabitants of the Barony of
KILMACRENAN.

A Public Meeting of the Inhabitants of the Barony of KILMACRENAN, will take place in RAMELTON, on MONDAY, the 21st inst., for the purpose of taking into consideration the condition of the Working Classes, on the approaching season of destitution, arising from the entire failure of the POTATO Crop, and the *utter want of any public employment.*

It is a well-known fact, that Thousands of Families are depending on the Potato alone for their support, and that resource having totally failed in this district (not having any regular employment to depend on,) the prospect for the ensuing season is deplorable These facts having been taken into consideration, it has been deemed advisable to hold the above Meeting for, by a late Act of Parliament, the Lord Lieutenant is empowered to grant a sum of Money to any locality, to be expended on Public Works, on their Meeting, and forwarding a Petition to the Castle. Resolutions to this effect will be submitted to the Meeting.

☞ The co-operation of the Magistrates, Clergy, and Gentry, is respectfully solicited.

Ramelton, September 7, 1846.

S. MADDOCK, PRINTER AND STATIONER, LETTERKENNY.

John Harley of Rathmelton, a nail-maker, had this notice posted throughout north Donegal in September 1846. The local poor-law inspector complained to the constabulary that Harley was a 'troublesome person' and that the meeting was likely to produce 'much excitement if not worse consequences'. The resident magistrate remonstrated with Harley 'as to the impropriety of such a proceeding'. No meeting took place as a 'baronial meeting' ordered by the Lord Lieutenant to approve relief works was held in Letterkenny on the same day, drawing a large crowd of demonstrators.

pulling his garments also got their share like another.[101] From one and another comes the lamentation "I am here all day"; "How can I go home now, for I did not leave as much as a spoonful of food behind with me Molly and the children, and I did not tell you that before as I thought you would do something for me, after keeping me here all day, and how can I go home wanting?" The manner of the consoling replies to such appeals are in the shortest words: "Nothing can be done for *you* this day"; "Come back next week and we will try". Good encouragement indeed for an empty stomach, to live, to do or to die during a week.

The "committee men" [were from] all denominations, but it so happened that our meek Doctor of Divinity of the established church, the man of learning and of other enticing qualities spoken of in the last chapter, was honorary chairman and had the greatest control.[102] Other committee men were entrusted with small sums of money and at their discretion divided them among those supposed to be most in need, and if they had not the necessary goods to give in lieu themselves, they were watchful to find out a friend who had and put the money in his way. The applicant for relief presented himself at the committee man's dwelling, got an hour or so at some job, then was supplied with the desired ticket drawn out in favour of some petty shopkeeper at some distance, and having reached that place, would have to await his turn. All this circuitous way of doing good was more like hard labour or convict punishment.

The benefit of relief was abstracted from the fund in many a way: part of it was given away in the shape of wages to a few, who felt it rather humiliating to carry a bag of meal. Those who had the distribution employed favourites to build fences, make drains and improvements, beautifying the approaches to their dwellings. Many parts of the jobs left unfinished then remain so, as never since was any attempt made to complete them, showing clearly and well where the money then came from. This was the way in which a great deal of the relief fund being entrusted to those worldly minded men, was smuggled and converted into other uses. Yet such men were looked upon as *good* men because they gave employment—for their own benefit and with the charitable money bestowed by others, in America or Australia perhaps.

Such imputations may seem to the reader rather harsh when we refer to men who should have better feeling towards the weak and the hun-

---

101. Fr Daniel O'Donnell.
102. Baillie was treasurer, not chairman.

gry. Yet such was the undoubted fact and therefore it is no way trespassing the rules of charity to relate the same. Nor could it be given half in its true light as to how the poor were treated and despised as if they were beings of quite a different creation. The satiated never understand the emaciated.[103]

One year succeeded another with little or no improvement, the ingatherings from the harvests always being small and consequently every succeeding summer experienced a scarcity of food. Some who were always trying to persevere against the difficulties made efforts year after year to put down crops, with only a faint hope of reaping any harvest. It was when hopes were lost in the attempts to cultivate the potato that other green crops were tried: the Swedish, the Aberdeen, and the White Globe turnips were for the first time cultivated; also more ground [was] laid out under cabbage, carrots, parsnips, beans and peas. Cabbage was already known but cultivated only in small quantities in gardens (and used for cow feeding more than anything else); now it was used as an article of food with only water and salt to qualify it.

Many people from their experience of the seasons, between hope and despair, became negligent and drifted from bad to worse, selling everything they could dispose of for the merest trifle to any one who could afford to buy or to exchange them—until the Workhouse, the last game of all, or (through the well wish of some friends abroad) the Emigrant ship, shut them out of view of their native country for evermore.

Others and they were not a few disappeared. Some made their way to all parts of the kingdom never returning. Some went to England and Scotland, returning after a lapse of years only to see their homesteads gone, their friends and dear ones dead, or if not dead, their whereabouts could not be traced. Off they go again.

Arising from death, emigration and dispersion to all parts, the population soon dwindled away. And indeed I hope it will not be any way uncharitable to say [it, but] with the multitude also disappeared many turbulent and indifferent persons and characters who were only a disgrace to the good, the honest, and the well-doing, and if there was poverty, there was peace too.

103. Direct translation of the Irish proverb 'Ní thuigeann an sách an seang'.

RELIEF IN SHIPWRECKS

In the year 1846, the signs and dread of want had set in, but 1847 and 1848 might be called the beginning of the years of Famine, and in the spring season of each of these years there came ashore partly wrecked one of those large ships trading to and from America, and strange enough too, they followed each other about the same time of the year into the same bay, and nearly into the very same place.[104] "Large Americans" as they were called by the people, and each of them laden with flour in bags, Indian meal in barrels and Indian corn in bags. The Indian corn was a new sight, but the people soon found out how to make use of it. The inhabitants were easily led to believe—and the fact is that it would take extra-human argument to have convinced them otherwise—that it was by the will of Providence on their behalf that these vessels were so driven ashore at the very time and place where wanted; reasoning from this would mean that the people were relieved from the scruple which they might otherwise feel of appropriating to themselves whatever they could get.

This tempting means of relief came at the time when all were ready for it, that is in the spring, and the old and the young were attracted late and early to the scene of the wreck. At ebb-tide the ship sat clean and dry on a level sandy beach; at full tide her situation was a long distance

104. Presumably the first wreck was that of the barque *Zulette* of New York in April 1847. The ship had been bound for Rathmelton with a cargo of Indian corn, flour and meal. It was dismasted in a storm and drifted into Mulroy Bay, where it became sanded up on Donaghmore Strand on the south-east of the bay. The Carrigart coastguard secured the cargo, which was brought ashore for auction. A press report is consistent with Dorian's memory of the event: 'the country people collected in very great numbers, and became so violent that the auction was suspended, and, in defiance of constabulary and coastguards, they forcibly took upwards of one hundred bags of Indian corn, and even compelled one of the purchasers who had his grain in boats for Milford, to deliver up the food, they declaring "that Providence had sent them the supply, and that when in great distress a wreck with provisions was sure to happen on their shore". The military from Letterkenny were sent for and the people are still in a disturbed state.' For this report, see *Ballyshannon Herald*, 23 April 1847.

In first week of the following month, the *Emily* and the *Messenger*, both bound for Sligo, ran aground in Downings Bay; the *Emily* was carrying tea, sugar, flour and spirits, while the *Messenger* was laden with 130 tons of Indian corn. Crowds plundered some of the corn before the authorities could intervene. Soldiers of the 38th Regiment were involved in guarding the salvaged cargo from 8 May; a store in which they had lodged corn 'was entered on the night of the 10th and almost two and a half tons stolen therefrom'. A 'large assemblage of the people' insisted that the remaining foodstuffs be sold in the locality on terms dictated by them; by 13 May, the Indian corn had been sold in small quantities. For correspondence on this incident, see N.A.I., Outrage Papers 1847/7/143, Glenties, 15 May 1847, B. H. Holmes to Under Secretary. For press reports, see *Ballyshannon Herald*, 7 May, 28 May 1847.

from dry ground. But the shore and the surroundings were night and day covered with human beings trying by every means to get anything they could recover in the shape of provisions out of that great three-masted ship. Whether they succeeded in getting anything or not made no difference; still they hung about in expectation, and some days of a valuable season were thus passed over (those who had forethought to put in as much seed [at that season] as they were able had the satisfaction of being rewarded next autumn with the greatest produce, the greatest yield, witnessed for many years before or after, whilst those who neglected found out their great mistake).

As I said, the large ship was nearly dry at low water, and the Coast Guards with swords and pistols, the Constabulary with guns and bayonets—this force and all of them together—could not save the cargo from being carried away. Assistance therefore was called upon from another quarter: the Redcoats soon appeared on the scene. A detachment of soldiers one bright morning came dashing down the hills with their glittering arms and wild head gear, a strange sight indeed in such a place, and a stranger sight to those who never saw a soldier in uniform before. Robinson Crusoe in his solitary confinement could not have been more in dread of the overpowering of the natives than were the people at the first sight of the "Red Soldiers". The women, the young people, and the old men were mightily frightened, but as these strangers showed no wildness beyond that occasioned by their dress, and as hunger is the greatest weapon for taming either the bold or the timid, so the country people gradually ventured to come closer to the Redcoats, and they were greatly relieved to find in them not the enemies they supposed, but on the contrary soon learned that they were far from being harsh or the worst of men. Under the Redcoats were concealed hearts like other people and, far from being harsh, to their credit be it that they were far more humane, had more compassion in them, and felt more for the starving people, much more so, than the tyrannous, sneaking, place-and promotion-seekers, dressed though they were in the Blue and Green uniform.

Part of the cargo was discharged at each tide and as soon as possible and conveyed to the beach, which act in itself gave work and wages to a good many hands and especially to the owners of boats and boatmen while it lasted. The men employed in this work brought the stuff ashore and the military and the police tried to watch and guard it; the Coast Guards being more aquatic in their nature kept watch on board the ship. The task of watching on the shore was not an easy one as the crowd was immense and restless, continually pushing and advancing forward to get their hands on a bag or a barrel. From the ship it was taken, directly stolen; between the ship and heap it was stolen; and out of the heap—if once a bag or barrel got its way through the first rank of the crowd—farewell! To follow it was in vain for the people shuffled and jostled in such a manner, and they stood so closely packed that nothing could be seen; so valuable was the prize thought to be that it was shifted from two to two and away to the rear. The Indian corn got [in this way] was boiled in the husk and eaten, the same proving a sweet and pleasant food.

Part of the cargo brought ashore was placed in large heaps on the dry sandy beach, and close to these were erected tents for the accommodation of the military who kept watch and guard as before a camp, pacing up and down as soldiers do, and in so doing the Red-coated-man showed the honour, the royalty about him, that once he turned on his heel, look back he would not do. The eager crowd, soon learning his manoeuvres in that part of the drill, as soon took advantage, and no sooner did he "face about" than two or three courageous fellows leaped at a bag and it was instantly conveyed off and hidden in the crowd.

The soldier proudly and manfully returning to his "starting point" saw that all were apparently right, the people standing quietly; he was not supposed to count bags or barrels and the people were so pitifully calm—but just viewing where to make another pounce as soon as the opportunity offered, and such was the silence that the only word audible at all would be in the vernacular, *Bannaght Fadrig go ro aga*, "The blessing of St Patrick be about him, but he is the good man", and "The curse of St Bridget on the sneaking policeman, see how he watches us, looking sideways all the time"; "May his neck get stiff"; "Let every body keep eye to him for he is a bad man".[105]

There was one night memorable for the inhabitants; in the midst of darkness, the country people attempted a very hazardous sally on the provision heap and managed for a little to overcome the sentries. But in a short time with the reverberation of the discharge of two or three muskets the whole body of armed men were on foot, and such cracking of musketry and flashes of fire were never heard or seen in those lonely hills before. The multitude soon dispersed, and what is better to relate, not one individual was known to get the scratch of a bullet—all being fired in the air. The very fact of no one being killed or wounded on that night of great danger and great terror showed a proof of Christian

---

105. *Beannacht Phádraig go raibh aige*, St Patrick's blessing on him.

humanity, showed good feeling in all from the officer to the private, otherwise someone among them might have had the wickedness, the ill-feeling and the cruelty to fire low, and so sure would human life have been sacrificed.

Whether the act to take the property at this time was condemnable or not, there were certainly many who kept the breath of life and their little families together by means of the benefits thus derived, and what added more gave them the chance of saving some seed which otherwise of necessity they would have been forced to consume. As I said, the following year was the only one good for a number [of seasons], and to the few persons who persevered in planting the potato the following year gave them a start which they learned to keep up, and it came to pass that those who were comparatively poor, who really had nothing to spare in the good times, those who might be called the lower class, were the first to creep up in the world, while those who fancied themselves the "genteel folk" as rapidly drifted downwards and for obvious reasons.[106] The latter class of people, unwilling to make any narrow shift or to be seen connected with any mean action, held aloof looking on at the sudden changes, the desolation around them, consuming all they possessed and conjecturing to themselves that it was the end of the world, relying too much upon that old saying, "that before the end, man's food or the seed thereof was to rot under the sod".

And so in reality the very appearance of a potato field in the first years was something awful: in one night, smitten with the blight and changed from the natural green to that of polished black, the real resemblance of death; today the crop green and in blossom, tomorrow dark, withered, and an unpleasant and offensive smell, which could be felt at distances away.

Not alone was man frightened at the sight of the surrounding fields then laid desolate, but also the elements above seemed to show signs of vengeance. There appeared in the skies unusual signs and strange phenomena: in addition to much thunder and extraordinary lightning, there were close and instantaneous flashes of fire, wavering, hovering over certain places; in addition to these realities, there were exaggerated stories of balls of fire falling in many places. To add to their other sufferings and from close observations and wild rumours, the people got horror stricken—men lost all energy, all activity, merely creeping about like so many bundles of clothing. Their belief was that the fire from the elements did the damage, for it was always plainly seen the day after.

106. In other words, the autumn of 1847.

Not alone I say was man terrified at the sight of the fields, the shadows of death, but deaths, real deaths, were everywhere and it was, as I said before, with the greatest difficulty they could be coffined or carried to the grave, and the graveyard itself was in complete irregular mounds of sod and clay.

It is therefore no way surprising that in a few years families became extinct, their dwellings were swept away, and arising from this, tenements and places changed owners, all but the graves—the graves, the families of which, no descendant, no tenant is now to be got, cannot be traced, and there they are, green mounds, walked over, unknown and forgotten.

This was the time too that the cities and towns began to increase, arising from the numbers of persons finding refuge and any sort of employment in them. So also the miserly, the narrow-living class of people, those who were little thought of before, creeped up in the world and became possessors of land such as never was in the tribe or family before. In whatever light this tide in the affairs of men may be looked upon, the change of ownership was productive of no good in social life in the hereafter, for there was always some relative or other who claimed a better right, and it could not be said, speaking honestly, that these changes in property were always accomplished by fair and honest means. On the contrary some did undermine and injure their poorer neighbours and got property without paying a farthing. The poor people or their relatives were bereft of their rights, and seeing it pass into strange hands could not have much love towards the newcomers, but they were powerless to resist. They might harbour revenge and still have their eyes, their hopes on the old place, and in after years when despairing of justice they might perhaps, in the mad fury of vengeance, have recourse to unlawful acts of violence or something of that sort. It is forbidden to man to do these things, but "to err is human" and therefore very often a district and a people may get a bad name from some sudden recent act of violence in their midst, the cause of which is unknown to the generality; it may have been slumbering for many years, and then the oppressor or the descendants of the oppressor, the cruel man in his day when he could act cruelly, will be the first to preach against oppression, injustice and cruelty. Oh! the hypocrisy, the wickedness of some who are under the mask of a false face now; if their history was made clear to other human eyes and if they themselves were stripped of their outer pretended covering, they would be really astonished to see that they are not the saints they pretend to be.

The clergy were the only tribunal the suffering party could appeal to, and they tried in many cases to bring about restitution and reconciliation, and in this and in trying to pacify the complaining parties they kept matters calmer than otherwise they would have been. Yet even with the respect in which they were held, those families who had the gain, gave fair promises only until in the end such claims were forgotten, as the remnant of the claimants disappeared. The property acquired fraudulently in this manner succeeded well for a time with some, but such people were not looked upon in the light of being just men, and there was always the foreboding thought that some evil would befall the man or the family, "not wishing ill to the innocent". And if evil befell, there was not that general feeling of sympathy which would otherwise be [the case] but rather a whisper would circulate that "he was one deserving a certain visitation"; "but it was a pity that the innocent should suffer so, for the crime of his father"; "his father was not good"; "he was blamed for turning out Widow So and So"; "he has all the lands held once by So and So, and never paid a penny for it"; "got it in the bad times"; "how could he have luck?"

In those years of distress as harvest succeeded harvest the yield of production was not equally bad, nor in proportion to the tillage. One season would give something to cheer, and another would be miserable in the extreme. One neighbour would be a little reprieved by some lucky stroke of fortune—his field escaped and was not so bad as others. To add to the misery many of the summer and autumn seasons continued extremely wet so very little turf could be saved for winter fuel, and then cold and hunger were twin companions.

After the first dreadful shocks went past and a few years were weathered over, those who remained and intended to stick to the old sod saw plainly that to depend on the potato as a feeding crop meant starvation, and they therefore turned their attention to the cultivation of other crops as a substitute. The next in point of nourishment to the potato, taking the yield into account, was the Swedish turnip. A man possessing a good field of Swedes flattered himself that there was no fear of dying of hunger so long as they lasted, and some farmers cultivated it to such an extent that they could sell large quantities to their poorer neighbours. Glad and thankful in being spared in life, when so many had died, glad in having his native hills surrounding him, the father would sit down with his family, showing every sign of comfort, to a quantity of boiled turnips out of the pure spring water, with no spice to qualify them but a grain of salt and pepper mixed to accelerate the passage to the stomach, living in hopes of a better next year which surely did arrive. Many did survive to see more comfortable times, but as many and as many more, as I have repeated, went to their graves for want of nourishment or by diseases brought on by unusual diet; or, no doubt, from the effects of a broken heart, seeing the hardships in their homes and the weeping and longing for their sons and daughters, their loved ones, once their pride and hopes for old age but now away from them in the opposite hemispheres, glad to get there, to render the service which they could not do at home, and no one can measure the distance of the broad Atlantic speedier and better than a father whose child is there.

It is true the children did not forget home; their letters and relief were regular but that comfort, good as it was, was not sufficient to balance the intensity of grief which the parents suffered, and real relief for them was only found when the earth covered them over and a sorrowing friend settled and tramped the green sod overhead. Years passed on, the same vicissitudes recurring, some few persons mounting a step higher in the scale of worldly comfort, some at a standstill, some drifting downwards in the face of all exertions, whilst self-preservation was the predominant thought with all men. Friendship was forgotten, men lived as if they dreaded each other, every one trying to do the best for himself alone, and a man would rather deny the goods he possessed than make it known that he had such or that he was improving in the world.

It may be readily understood that during these years of extreme trial, debts were contracted and rents were neglected for the very good reason that the people were unable to pay. Rent above anything was nearly if not altogether forgotten. But after the first trials and terrors had somewhat subsided and the minds of men had become a little collected in facing the dangers to which they had now become somewhat hardened, a new scourge just then appeared on the scene, one equally terrifying but whose strength and severity could not be prevented. And this scourge appeared in the person of the *Landlord*.

CHAPTER 11
The Landlord Extermination

Land for tillage along the coast was for many years before the Famine
so scarce in proportion to the population that every spot was cultivated,
places where now no one would think of, that is the highest ground, the
hillsides, old bogs, the bare sandy soil. Not but that there were large
tracts uncultivated in other places, but these were removed from where
the people were thickest. In the thickly populated parts, wherever the
ingenuity of man could put in a seed those who had no land were glad
to get the liberty [to do so] and to give some price in return. It may be
asked how could those who had no land be able to meet the price of it
for a season's crop. Well, in addition to those who partly subsisted by
fishing, there were others within easy distance of the shore who laid out
their accounts for making kelp, and in many cases the fisherman was
also a kelp-maker. They gathered up the seaweed, summer and winter,
and when the proper time arrived, they burned it; for many years it was
the only industry along the coast, bringing a very good price then, sometimes as high as £6 per ton of twenty-one hundred weight.

... The seaweed out of which the kelp is made is of two kinds, but
the rods or as they are called by the natives "*slat mara*" are the part
reckoned best.[107] These are gathered after a storm or cut off the rocks in
calm weather in winter or summer, but principally in winter or early in
spring, and are placed on the tops of rocks or other elevated ground for
the purpose of drying, and addition after addition is put on until a considerable quantity is gathered in one place. Such heaps are called

107. *Slata mara*, sea-rods.

"cocks", and from the quantity a man has collected in this way he speculates on what he may be worth in summer, and no matter what the cold or hardship may be, such was not felt so long as the "cocks" are increasing, and from the number engaged at such the coast in many places is studded with them. Some were very large and some small according as some were thrifty and some not. About the beginning of May, the seaweed in leaves, "float wreck" as it is called or "*leagh*", is eagerly expected and regularly at every tide it floats into the bays in very large quantities.[108] This is gathered with the greatest speed and exertion, and carried away by assistants to a distance to be spread out and dried, and so diligent would they be that their food would be brought to the shore and a man might be seen up to his middle in the waves and taking a bite of nourishment at the same time. All the material thus gathered up became perfectly dried and shrivelled up, and a person unacquainted would think there was no substance at all.

It is then fit for burning. A dry day with a good breeze is chosen for the burning, and a rude kiln is for the time constructed about two feet wide, less in depth and any length according to the quantity of the stuff intended to be melted. The sides and ends of the kiln are fenced outside with sand or clay as may be convenient to exclude the air. A small fire is kindled in one part of the kiln and tufts of seaweed are thrown upon it. This is continued until the burning extends the whole length. Then tuft after tuft or a handful is thrown on wherever the flame appears; the object of this is to keep the flame from appearing, for strange as it is if the flames put forth all would run to ashes, whereas by being kept constantly smouldering it will run together like pig iron in a furnace, and when cooled and become solid it is of a dark greyish colour. By its colour they also can know of its purity, as from similar material may be turned out good or bad kelp. This depends upon handling.

When it is considered that the kiln is sufficiently full, they turn to the process of what they call "raking", that is two or more take up iron instruments with wooden handles and commence mixing from one end to the other as long as it is soft. By this process the stuff is made to adhere more closely, to become more solid and firm, and during this process the man who wishes to add to its weight can hide a fair share of stones or nice gravel in the same. This is cheating of course; nevertheless it is done but on the supposition that it cannot be prevented, kelp is rated at 21 cwt. to the ton. It is afterwards split up into pieces of convenient sizes and carried to the purchaser or agent, who in turn sends it to the chemist.

108. *Leathach*, broad seaweed, sea-wrack.

The kelp-maker may be blamed for adulterating his kelp, but from one evil arises another. The kelp-buyers or agents were unscrupulous avaricious men who extorted their customers to an unreasonable extent. They always had money and goods either of their own or their employers on hand, and lent to such people only in time of need on conditions that every sixteen shillings meant twenty shillings worth of kelp. The seller was therefore of the opinion that the agent was well-paid, having so much interest in so short a time and his commission besides, and considered that anything to make weight was good enough. Nor could the real amount of adulteration be discovered until it got into the hands of the chemist when the solid lumps were broken up. He calculated his profit on the quantity of iodine extracted per ton, but there were many other compounds as well, the prices of which was supposed to meet freight and other expenses.

New discoveries, foreign competition, and dishonesty at home brought part ruin upon the chemical works in Glasgow and elsewhere, and the promoters who yearly distributed thousands of pounds along the coast were forced to turn their capital into something else. The kelp-trade, though still carried on, is not so much nor near so lucrative as formerly. There are only a few buyers and prices at their own option. Thence from the ocean and in the ocean was the poor man's treasure, and it was with difficulty that the owners of land further inland could reserve for themselves as much pasture ground as would keep their few cattle alive. There was hardly such a thing as land changing ownership by way of tenant. If by chance a man got an opening for removal to what he considered a better place, and such might happen through deaths and want of heirs, the nearest relative was objected to by no one and then he set his own to public auction, and then competition went up. Men without capital went in debt to the full amount and underwent heavy interest, putting themselves under a burden for the remainder of their days. The auction day came; "a hammer's man" was appointed, the biddings went up but very often the highest bidder did not reap the reward of his earnestness. Perhaps after paying an instalment of the money by purchase, family ties and the interest of the bailiff had to be tested, and at last another man got it. These transactions were at this time carried on unknown to the landlord as much as if there was no such a one; his power was not much dreaded, he was known to be somebody existing, and that was all. No record can be given of the number of years previous to the setting in of the years of the Famine that no dread of the landlord entered into men's minds [sic]. The people knew that there was a higher power, but to be slaves or in slavery they knew not. They called their own what they possessed, paid their rents when they liked, and in most cases just as they liked.

If a man held land, he had in himself chief control, no one for to interfere with him in his disposal of it. He divided and subdivided it as he thought fit. But such methods were not wise in the end as it would be better if there was a certain restriction, because the subdivision ran to a ruinous extent. Men lived to a good old age in those days and spent their latter years, not in wearing out the bones till they fall to the earth as nowadays, but in giving advice, superintending and feeling happy at the prosperity, the success of a son, or a grandson, or it might be a worthy son-in-law. The old man, the father was the owner—the tenant; the receipt if such could be produced was in his name, the son or the daughter at their marriage got of the land as best they pleased him, and were subtenants and were accountable for a proportionable share of the rent. Next the grandson got a share and was likewise accountable for his addition to the general purse when the time arrived. But the old man always reserved a share in his own name till death, which was wise as even in his feeble days he was well cared for, as he could leave to whomsoever he wished. Few could divide money as they had it not, but any one having land could divide it and following up this old system, field after field, piece after piece, was divided and subdivided, until at last one man might have fifty or more pieces in a townland, either by bequest or by purchase, and seven or eight persons might be connected in the amount of money in the one receipt, the whole perhaps less than £5. Those plots of ground varied in size and of every shape possible, and to point out or define the property large stones or other marks were set up here and there to mark the boundary. This was the Rundale System.

As to calculations of land in acres, roods and perches, most of the people hardly knew what such terms in value meant, as all calculations were made by them in what they called "sums". A "sum" meant a quantity of land sufficient to graze one horse or one cow or six sheep; and as six sheep were equal to a "sum" the latter showed an easy method of reducing [fractions] to the smallest extent, all of which were understood; and a quantity of land might correspond to that of "one foot" of sheep, so ridiculously small did the subdivisions go, but the money value as rent or for purchase corresponding to each was far better known than the value of an American dollar coin …

If all who were connected in a joint receipt came to an agreement to meet the demands of the landlord, they met at a certain time and put their respective sums of money into one purse, but if one held back, the rest were forced to do the same for that day anyhow, but it made no great difference until by consent they collected themselves again. The landlord who was owner of the greater part of the district was called the Big Landlord, the head landlord or *"Tierna-More"*, and they knew him from his family name and nothing more.[109] Of course there were many petty or minor landlords, but the head landlord lived far away in London or in Dublin, and either of these places in their calculations were equidistant with Boston or New York. He had an agent, it is true, living on a selected part of the property about fifteen or more miles distant who seldom came to see the tenants but acted through his bailiff, and the bailiff by his underlings. The agent always got as much as paid himself and was a J.P. and associated with the upper class.

The head bailiff pretended to be a man of consequence; he had about him an air of pomp and pretended influence and power, could speak two languages, and was a fair scholar. He was of the people, lived among the people, knew them all young and old, many of whom were his relatives in some way or other, and as far as authority on his part and submission on the part of the people went, he was almost himself landlord, agent, and bailiff. He could bestow gifts which cost him nothing, a piece of land or a piece of bog for turf cutting which some other one would have to do without, but in return he could accept to himself many other as valuable gifts, either in money or goods. He was also a county cess—and when that time came, also a poor-rate—collector, so that most of all the coin having any circulation in the place necessarily went through his hands, and from being constantly among the people he had every opportunity of seeing anything worthy to be made a present of, and to mention it was enough. If any man bestowed upon him either money or goods, such a one was then a favourite with him and had a chance of escaping when another suffered. Invitations and good dinners were no bad stakes to gain him over, and as for christenings, he was at so many, that it did not at first occur to him to take a list alphabetically arranged he quite forgot the biggest half of them. These were the rogues and the fools who tried to have him on their side, the rogues who meant to gain from him, and the fools who thought it a matter of honour if they could prevail upon the bailiff to come to their table. There were others who kept "the breadth of the road between them", who had no love for him, would not flatter him, but whatever degree of hatred they carried they were bound to keep it hid. Such were not

109. *Tiarna mór,* great landlord, here referring to Nathaniel, 2nd earl of Leitrim.

unknown to him though, and at such he had his private spite; they need not, neither did they, expect any favour. He would compel them to pay rents either by threats or incessant warnings, or by the process of distraining warrants, be the same authority legal or not, and in all cases costs attended the papers.

It was a long time before the people began to understand that the real landlord was content with whatever he got, for while some did pay and were forced to pay regularly, many others, the favourites, were years in arrears, and at last the disclosure came out that nearly all were on the same footing as far as the rent book was concerned when the years of famine, the distress came on.

The years of scarcity set in when news spread that the good old landlord had died, and soon after a new landlord by hereditary law came into possession of very extensive estates, and this one among the rest.[110] This new landlord at first start seemed amiable enough and continued so for a little while, but soon he began to show signs of his power and authority and set about framing new laws, new rules, new everything, hitherto unknown to the people who hardly knew what a landlord rule was; most, in fact nearly all of them, had not even seen their real landlord before. So seldom did the old man visit this part of his dominions that only one or two aged men could relate seeing him once passing on a tour with other gentlemen, and that they recollected him as being pointed out as wearing red velvet breeches and knee-buckles. Complaints are made against absentee landlords, but here the people were never so contented as during the time they never saw their landlord.

The heir did not follow the footsteps of his predecessor in this respect, for immediately he set his mind on explorations, visited every place, made himself acquainted with the tenants personally as well as their means of living. No sooner was he in one place than he removed to another throughout the estates, left everywhere rules and regulations behind him which had to be strictly obeyed, fulfilled to the letter, and put into execution before his return. Not a hill, a plot of ground, a nook or a corner in his broad lands but he knew from maps and personal inspections and observations.

Among his first acts were what in the country phrase is called "squaring the farms", and the same if justly carried out would be beneficial to all, as thereby their tenements were concentrated and each one had his own piece, and it also gave the chance of enclosing and of

110. William, 3rd earl of Leitrim (1806–78); his elder brother having died in 1839, he succeeded to his father's lands and title in 1854.

improving the land, which could not be done during the rundale division. This encouraged and pleased a good many of the people, never thinking of what was to follow—the increased rent. Yes, first a "new cut", then a new rent; next, improvements by the tenant; and next, increased rents.

While the new allotments were beneficial to some and ruinous to others, if considered in other ways it was the easiest method, the most quick way, for the scattering of the population where villages had stood, scarcely more than one, or at the outside two, dwellings were left standing on the old site, so that all other [households] had to remove within a certain time, and so the landlord by his authority or the tenant on whose lot the houses were situated had to turn out all who had not farms to go to. This was a war upon the cottiers.

In all cases everyone in a townland had to give up possession before the surveyor came to the ground so that he could do as he liked, and the good or ill luck of everyone was in a manner a lottery, and let the quantity or the quality be what it may, whatever was laid out for a man, by that he had to abide—there was no alternative, take or go without, and in most of the townlands, the hills, the bogs, and other large scopes were cut off under the name of "reserves", or as the people called them "wastes", and these were the landlord's immediate own and no others.

The mountain grazing is cut off, the straight lines marked off, and then the surveyor's part of the work is done: all the tenants in a townland march along with the bailiff to the rent office to hear the new arrangements. The new allotments being cut out and as many as hold receipts, it is needless to say coming to an agreement, these alone are put in possession as new tenants in different parts of the townland, and in many cases favour and bribery had much to do with the location of the lot. It was then that the influence of the bailiff was courted and for his intercession as far as it could go, and now was laid the root of bitter and lasting hatred among neighbours. One man got his share in the best part of the land, just where he wished it, and the bailiff was blamed for doing this. Some other poor insignificant persons were sent to the uncultivated outskirts, some on the bleak mountain side, and so on, and the bailiff and his favoured party were blamed for this. No matter where placed, each one had to go to his lot—no appeal—all settled at the stroke of the pen. The tenant entitled to the largest quantity of land had a choice of sitting unless he wished otherwise; that if a nearly equal lot but of better quality lay convenient, according to the rule made, he could not be prevented from taking it, but all others had to remove dwellings.

This soon scattered the villages, for the work of removal began as soon as possible, being as I said limited to a certain time, and the people also considering their own interest put up a cabin or part of one and removed thither as soon as they could. These rebuildings and removals were allowable for the tenant only, the conditions being one farm, one smoke. Those who had no land allotted to them, subtenants and cottiers, were at the mercy of the landlord and tenant, and they knew their doom, but still most of them remained there until the strong arm of the law and the crowbar brigade came round, threw them out on the street, and demolished their dwellings.

Some wise enough to know what the end would be took the precaution to escape beforehand, others who knew not where to go to had to sit there: on the appointed day, the sheriff, the agent and bailiffs appeared and if there was any apprehension of a resistance they were accompanied by a strong guard of police. In any case and in every case, more or less of the police were present. The bailiffs entered, caught hold of the old man and old woman, and removed them apparently carefully to some distance from the walls. The collection of whatever necessary household utensils inside was next removed to the nearest place—the dungheap—the fire was then put out, and the final operation was to stick a few crowbars, here and there in the walls and to let the roof fall in. The trained bailiff knew as well where to stick the exterminator's needle as a physician to point to the heart of his sick patient, and so a stroke or two brought down the roof. The shelter was thus destroyed, and those who had a shelter a few minutes before were now sitting weeping besides some cold wall. The night is drawing near, they collect some fuel, make a fire, surround it, erect some covering to break the cold, spend a night or two in this way, eventually having to find a better shelter elsewhere. This was eviction made easy—this was eviction without lamentation—eviction without sympathy—eviction on the plea of giving to other men their rights. The people who had no land to get and from whom nothing was to be gained in the shape of rent being all got rid of in this way without much talk and without much trouble, and no cry of any injustice for the reason that they did not possess anything, and no more thought about them. It was just removing the dead, as if for the benefit of the living.

The surplus thus removed out of the way, the landlord then fixes his determination to subject and to govern the tenants who meanwhile were making every effort for the improvements of their holdings. The landlord for the better fulfillment of his objects in view appoints, at a very small pay, a regular but lazy ragged army of bailiffs, men chosen from the lowest scum of society, unscrupulous, unmerciful beings, and these were scattered in every direction: some as mountain bailiffs, some bog bailiffs, some shore bailiffs, but each and everyone excelling the other as to who could best watch their employer's so-called property, and all these were subject to and at the command of the rent bailiff. Tis true most of the bum bailiffs were always of the lowest type of humanity, but a few were constrained to accept of this miserable occupation, urged by the thought of the oppression or cruelty exercised towards themselves or relatives a short time before, so that there was therefore a grudge and no way to exercise it but by this stroke of getting under the protection of the landlord and having the power at their back; the farmer who thought so little of getting a cabin lowered found to his grief that though he had crushed, yet did he not kill the worm, and that the one he thought as little of was now in a position to persecute and torment him and ultimately turn him out. If former cruelty be any palliation for a spirit of revenge, it is to be feared that some kept it in view. Such is humankind and the time is yet to arrive when men will forget injury and for the same return good.

During the years of Famine, the value of land was forgotten, [none] cared about it—many tenements were deserted and these deserted places after a little while fell into the hands of others in such a way as "we take but do not care", and any one who ventured upon any additional land got it without much trouble—merely for a trifle or oftener for nothing at all—but as soon as the people began to draw breath a little after the great scourge, they saw that land was the only means for living, and so the desire for it became more and more intense—and hence arose disputes and ill-will among neighbours and even among the nearest relatives, for those who lost when they could not help it being now sorry could not regain from those who held it. And those who attained land then held on, heedless of the sorrow in the breasts of others; not only that but they were anxious to get more. Hence bitter feelings were manifest between father and son, neighbour and neighbour, one without protection striving to recover, the other having the landlord at his back, not only holding on but trying to become more firm and to add more. The "Big Landlord" was soon found out to be a man of that nature and character, to be dreaded, he having now all authority in his own hands, and times with its customs had so changed that it was through him and by him that any one [had to apply for] the least or any quantity of land, and he set his face at once against the incoming tenant giving any compensation whatever: he was the only sole owner and master, and the tenant was to understand that he alone permitted him to be there, and these contemptible minions of the landlord who sought to acquire more land were made use of to cover the deeds of the ambitious man.

Self-interest and greed overcame some who should give better example and from them the malady spread to others, and so the meanest bailiff was flattered, was pampered, for the purpose of some paltry gain, to such an extent that the underminer would court friendship with them, bestow gifts publicly and give bribes privately, so that this otherwise degraded set imagined that they were something, and to serve their benefactor, if opportunity offered, they knew where to unloose or to tighten the screw.

After the late divisions [of the land] the tenants were in spite of themselves within limits; a straight line and in nearly all cases a fence formed the boundary between man and man, and between them and the landlord's part, "the reserves", and everyone must now keep inside of his lines. Formerly where a man's cow or horse or other animal had liberty to graze, now on it they dare not tread. It is the landlord's, and the bailiff is watching it or, if he is not openly in view, he is supposed to be hidden behind a rock, and if the hungry beast is tempted to glide on, he comes on it so suddenly that before the brute feels the enjoyment of one good bite, down comes the yellow staff of the detective bailiff across the animal's back, and it is taken prisoner from the spot for the serious crime of trespass, and turned on its way in the direction of the Pound, or else the owner has pity on the beast and claims it, saving it from abuse, but pays or becomes accountable for the trespass money. This trespass money and the fines go to pay the bailiffs, and the more of this he returns shows his diligence in his master's employ, but it does not follow that there is any check on him to return all.

Instances arose in which the tenant who was sued for trespass, believing himself not entitled to pay, would let the case go to the Bench, but this only made matters worse for him for there was one bailiff in particular against whom it was useless to go to law. No cross-examination would make any change in him. He stuck to the one point, the one phrase, "on his master's property", and to add more force "far, far from the dispute" meaning disputed property, so that the magistrates had no other alternative but decide in his favour.

The neighbour who feels too kindly towards his beasts, who permits or attempts to trespass too often, is noted—unknown to him—as troublesome, in fact as a dishonest and it may be added a disloyal man, and his crime after some time leads to the belief in another, until lastly comes that terror of terrors—he is served with a Notice to Quit for simply incurring the wrath of the landlord, and other misrepresentations meantime are put forward, and at next Quarter Sessions ejectments are found against him and the time is not long until out he goes.

His piece of land then lies "waste", but it gives more employment to the bailiff and more cause of dread to the adjoining tenant till perhaps through similar faults his turn comes, and out he also goes, and when piece after piece are added to form a "landlord's waste" sufficiently large for rearing of bullocks or fat sheep, the landlord then stocks the same with a breed of foreign cattle for himself; appoints a herd, the same having also the authority of a bailiff; a cottage is built for him, he is supplied with arms and ammunition which he carries about with him as a sign of protection, and in the course of time a police barrack is established convenient. The work of eviction, though bad enough, did not as yet come to that alarming extent which was afterwards experienced, but in every case where a man was turned out and the farm laid waste, a bailiff had to watch whether it was under stock or not. It was the duty of the herds as well as the bailiffs to watch the "reserves", the "waste farms", the bogs, the shores, timber, seawrack, hares, rabbits and all wild fowl.

If any man persistently enters, takes, or otherwise uses to his advantage any of these or anything derivable therefrom without payment and a written permission from the office, he is liable to ejectment and suffers the penalty thereof. Each of the low dependents of the landlord is also supplied with that handsome piece of furniture—a crowbar—of a light and handy make, which can be carried anywhere, and this insignia was often exhibited whether wanted or not; the bailiff when suddenly called upon carried the crowbar, being of the opinion that it was part of the uniform, not knowing what duty was before him. This often happened when a sudden express came to him from higher quarters. The higher quarter is the head bailiff, residing in some central position, and he is the only one privileged with communications in writing, and he issues orders as he gets them, as to him all the rest are subservient.

He gets word of what is going to be done and on what day the sheriff, the agent, and the police are to be at a certain place. Word is sent by him then to each of his minions around, and next day they prepare and hasten to the place of action. The sheriff and his force on the ground, those heartless hounds, linger around and are waiting for the command of general formalities, the final execution, when they enter and go to work ...

In cases where there are pretended excuses for lessening the severity of the landlord, the acts of throwing out are performed by these ruffians with a certain degree of apparent vengeance, to show that their feelings correspond with that of their master's so as to distinguish the crime as deserving of punishment, such as wilfully violating the laws and interfering with the majesty of the landlord, whereas in the first series of evictions, the turning out of the cottier, his treatment was apparently more lenient as far as rough handling was concerned. If these poor unjustly condemned and now evicted creatures have to a certain degree provoked the wrath of the landlord, that is if they do not at once submit, if they simply oppose him to the last and give some trouble, then the edict goes forth that no other tenant on the property dare shelter them even for one night. Their nearest relatives must silently pity them.

The scene of an eviction always attracted a crowd merely to look on, and as the people are collecting, the executors of the strong arm of the law seem to be incited with madness and are busier at work, and no sooner do they go through the process than they steal away, more like demons than men who had committed murder. Murder though it was in reality, but sanctioned under the name of law. Not long until this terror ran so high, that it came to pass that a father dare not and would not shelter his son, nor a brother another, as the same fate would befall themselves. When the crowbar brigade disappears from the scene, the crowds soon after disappear and the forsaken, destitute people are left alone—yes, alone and forsaken, with the wide sky overhead, no other covering; a neighbour may for the moment be moved to tears but dare not put a roof over their heads for fear of incurring wrath and the same fate at the hands of the landlord. Night of this trying day is approaching and nature is yearning for that natural rest, no matter how sore and broken the heart may be. Then the sheltered side of a wall or a fence or maybe a large rock presents itself for relief, and a few dry sticks and other fuel are collected and a fire is kindled—which is not hard to do from the many broken timbers scattered about; again a few doors and boards are put together to form a kind of hut, and the friendless human beings, no way now dreading ghost or fairy but sighing and sorrowing—to rest they go.

In this pitiful extremity, days and nights and by some members of the family weeks perhaps are spent, and adding occasionally to the covering, making some alterations as the wind and weather change. One or other of the family day after day disappears, finding work and food in some distant part of the country. The old couple are left behind, and if

they are very old and supposed to be harmless may find shelter by permission with some other who is not on the same rent roll from which
they have been expelled, but the greater number of the evicted are
forced to go away, go to beg or go to the Workhouse, and the grave to
them would be preferable to the latter.

The cruelty of the laws against those evicted became so severe that
neither brother, sister or other relative dare recognise each other in their
distress or mention the act at all on pain of suffering the same fate, and
so the unfortunate people had to remove as speedily as they could to
other places beyond the pale of their late governor and tried to work for
life while it lasted. But with those who were suffered to remain, to add
to their hardships, anxiety and misery, their rents were increased and
there was no escape from [having to] pay on the appointed day.

The terror in itself was such that at the word of the bailiff so many
would be at the office on that day, be the state of the weather what it
may, that the agent and his assistants could not possibly receive all, but
only a fraction of what were in readiness. Little did they in their heated
apartments care for keeping men wet, cold and hungry, standing in a
gateway or the street from morning till night, expecting to be called and
get relieved of their savings. And many who had long distances before
them would have to retrace the same journey on the same errand next
day and if the bailiff could relieve he got a warm mouthful for his pains.

This hardship was endured because the bailiff "had warned", and
for fear of worse, that a name might be called in his absence. Not only
increased rents but other new taxations were laid on, namely a tax on
seaweed, whether got on the top of the wave or cut off the rocks. The
tax for seaweed was of two kinds—the higher tax one pound sterling,
paid for the best quality, that is that used for burning into kelp, and the
lesser tax was for permission to gather at a certain season an inferior
quality for manuring the land, the same land from the produce of which
the rent was paid. This tax was five shillings, but a kelp burner had to
pay the two rates. And lest any man might escape and use the seaweed
or not, everyone was forced to pay the "shore-money". Tax must be
paid and permission granted for the use of a certain quantity of bog, laid
out by the bailiff for cutting turf on, and the same plot could only
remain in possession for a stated part of the year and must be left clear
before a certain date.

The mountain pastures which the landlord could not easily turn to
his own use immediately, he let to the people through his agents from
the first of May to the first of November to graze their cattle and sheep,

their paying so much per head; such animals were branded and numbered so that no fraud could be attempted. Immediately a stray or a hungry sheep, made its way to smuggle among the branded ones, it soon found itself inside the cold walls of the Pound, for the eye of the bailiff was upon it and the brute is forced for a time to live on its fat or gnaw its wool. This grazing for which payment was forced upon the people as a separate tax should by right be free to them, but now from the method of registration and the amount paid, the landlord at once knew the circumstances of the people with regard to stock.

Office rules innumerable were laid down and these were printed and posted up and distributed, and so sure as any tenant violated any of the rules, so sure his name was Walker. The most trivial cause, the slightest excuse, even the cutting of one surface sod, was enough in his new statutes to lead to eviction.

To be always prepared in case anyone committed an offence meantime, the landlord left no one unserved with a Notice to Quit before the first of May in each year that he might immediately have recourse to the law. The fact of these "white messengers" of the law, the forerunners of nothing good, being distributed once a year wholesale was certainly no cause for any great encouragement to the struggling man holding a piece of land. Well might he indeed have courage to make any improvements, floating under the banner of a six-months lease, not knowing but November of that year might see him preparing for the wide world. The serving of these notices became so regular that the dread which was at first naturally felt began to abate a little, like everything that becomes common, but though the dread was not so severely felt it saved no one from the danger, and all toiled on as usual. But as the month of November set in, some families were then made aware of their doom—to be turned out. The cause could only be conjectured at in many cases, and it was a matter of the greatest secret with the bailiff, for he gave no hint to anyone as to who was in danger until he got the ejectment served, for fear any one might try to evade the law for a short time. In due time the course of the law was taken and very few were the resistances offered, as it was useless at any time. But some were of the opinion, and that opinion still survives, that until a man is first turned out he should not be punished for offering resistance, but the law speaks otherwise, and they are severely punished in both ways.

At one time one poor ignorant man, when his turn came to get outside like many another, tried to hold his citadel, that is the four walls and the roof tree around and over him, and so tried to keep the officers of the law from entering, and prepared himself for a defence inside the door and armed himself with that destructive and formidable weapon, the one he was best acquainted and trained with, an old spade, declaring at the same time that he would hit the first man who attempted to enter. No one of the crowbar brigade was so courageous as to venture and there was a short parley. There was the agent foaming, there was the sheriff losing time, what was to be done?

Without waiting to hear of the determination of a full council of war on the plan of attack, a young half-fool of a policeman lately liberated from Phoenix Park and thinking to walk into honours by showing his military tactics for the first time and before the eyes of his superior officer, screwed on his bayonet and "forward" put in his head.[111] The bayonet was knocked aside by the defender, and on the next move, the adventurous policeman got the weight of the old spade just above the ear, which was the cause of leaving him a bandaged-head barrack charge for many a day after, and at last he got a few pounds compensation. It was said that the landlord gave him a gratuity of one pound for his bravery.

Poor Shemus, besieged though momentary successful, was unable to follow up his victory, being overpowered by discipline and superior numbers, and he was therefore forced to surrender, was taken prisoner, and securely handcuffed and conveyed to the county gaol to await his trial for rebellion and attempted murder; bail of course was refused. After some time the trial came on and he was too poor to employ counsel, but said a few words in his own defence, his English being very poor. He tried to do his best and he gathered up as much as to give them to understand that he thought it no harm, no crime, as he was only trying to hold his own right, so long as they did not get in, and that he was trying to keep out those who were not his friends: he did not know or care who they were and, what he thought the best part of his defence, he gave them sufficient warning when he "hit the spade with the policeman". The administrators of the law in their wisdom saw that there were fools on both sides, took a more lenient view of the case, and awarded poor Shemus only nine months hard labour inside the walls of the county gaol at Lifford for his experiment with the spade and the policeman. The spade was taken as a trophy of war on the first occasion and produced in court, but there is no record of what became of it afterwards. Shemus survived his confinement and his acquaintances gave him the title of Shemus of the Spade whenever his name was mentioned.

111. The headquarters of the Irish Constabulary was in the Phoenix Park, Dublin.

The experiment and punishment of Shemus was a caution to others who from henceforth, and when their turn came, submitted quietly, knowing that to act otherwise would be useless. The evictions continued year after year and seemed never to end so long as this landlord might live; he seemed never to be satisfied with turning out the people, and not for non-payment of rent in all cases, for he made no distinction between those who were able to live and the miserably poor. If one or the other dissatisfied him, no favour was given for creed or class (he could not be charged with a religious bigotry but, if anything, a hatred for mankind generally), and once he thought that his laws were disobeyed, or if a tenant at all presumed to have any or certain rights but what he as "lord of the soil" controlled, if once the least dispute got up, no intercessions could save the tenant, no petitioning, no recommendations of character, once he was entered for the court of law. And thus did he continue and had every sign of continuing the work of extermination, till his death, which came upon him suddenly when he little suspected it, and all at once he left his riches, his splendid dwellings, his broad lands, and all his possessions behind him to fall into the hands of another.[112]

The evictions then ceased as his successor did not follow in his footsteps in that respect; on the contrary he reinstated any who were able to become tenants anew, but for some time he persisted in exacting the high rents, though afterwards he became more moderate, and even if he did appear a little overbearing it could be easily overlooked, as it was slight in comparison to what the people were accustomed to, and so after many years of terror and trials they returned to a comparative state of ease and freedom.[113] Not however without traces of the stamp of slavery, for so downtrodden, so browbeaten, were they by suffering for more than a quarter of a century that they entirely forgot the dictates of manhood, and the landlord's myrmidons were the only persons thought of, flattered, and overflowed with gifts and promises.

On account of the many and severe restrictions put on those who were not dispossessed, such ground-keepers lost energy and that characteristic of manliness which their forefathers exhibited and boasted of, this arising in the first place from the great dread of the landlord or, which amounted to the same thing, being trampled upon by his underlings and, secondly, from hunger and hard work. A man with a rising family, while they were young and at his command, did the best he

---

112. Referring to the assassination of the 3rd earl of Leitrim in 1878.
113. Robert, 4th earl of Leitrim (1847–1892).

could and fought the battle fairly through the sea of misery—until the boys arrived at the age of exercising reason and became conscious of what they were doing, and for whom they were working; when they saw that their hard work, their early risings, the improvements they helped to make on the piece of land, the crops they helped to raise, all or nearly all going to the benefit of the landlord, and that withal they lived upon nothing better than Indian meal for themselves and went barefooted for the long summer months yet at November they could hardly afford to spare for themselves the price of a pair of shoes. Seeing all this and considering there is no prospect before them for bettering their condition, it is no wonder they make up their minds to leave father and mother, and as some find passage money for America, some can only manage a few shillings, and with these few on some fine day or early morning, they are off unknown to father and mother, make their way to the nearest seaport for the land of the Scot, and farewell to friends and to Old Donegal. Another and yet another are privately soliciting from some relative in the land of the setting sun, the Great America, for to pay their passage, and if successful off they go. The old father oppressed with years, with sorrow, must remain with the younger members of the family, tilling and toiling, reduced from the plough to the spade and preparing for the November demands! Yes, what! the rent!

That great unlost sight of overhanging cloud never to be banished from the mind, never to be forgotten, always oppressing the brain, from the month of May till November and from November till May: the rent—the rent. The state of living of those householders, or if we may choose to call them farmers, was such that they were bound to deny to themselves the best of the very produce brought by the land and cultivated with their own hands and through their sweat, but they were as much a stranger as far as consuming or using the same. If there were two fields of potatoes for instance, neither of which were very good but one was of a better quality than the other, the better ones were left in store untouched, to be sold for a higher price, and the smallest and watery ones were reckoned good enough to be used by the family along with Indian meal. If a man held a cow or two, all the benefit the family derived from them was the buttermilk, mixed with a plentiful supply of water—no talk of butter as that commodity was sold and the price carefully laid up for a certain day.

It was at Halloween or such "set times" only that a good-natured mother ventured to run the risk of giving to the family "a taste" of butter, but at all other times the youngest only, the pet of the family, had the best chance of coming near to the churning and the smallest quantity on the point of a spoon was spared to satisfy him.

The thrifty housewife did not forget that she also had a task to perform, and she too did her best to increase and contribute her share to the sinking fund and, as much as possible unknown to the husband, she might in the day of need come upon him unawares with the amount of her savings, and for this end she was not tired of rearing poultry, not for home use, Oh! no, but to serve another purpose, turn the profits into money for the day of reckoning. All the eggs were saved, brought to market and sold to the man who gave the highest half farthing, and on the same evening the members of the family were very well pleased with the sight of half a dozen or more salted but rotten herrings, or some other kind of salt fish brought home by the old dame. Why all this thrift, these savings, these denials? All for "going to make up the rent", and at November on the rent day the father returned home glorying in his stars that his rent was taken and that he had another year on the old sod, but he kept to himself the thought that he would be wise and watchful and not anger landlord or bailiff.

The above named were the better class—bless the comparison—many others fared worse, had to live on soft potatoes and turnips for a part of the year and then the Indian meal when the hot weather set in, and nothing to add to the potatoes or turnips except salt and pepper, and very many were for nearly nine long months on the Indian meal alone, the latter of course got its full complement of water. [The less fortunate] though toiling for the landlord in the sun and in the rain, without shoe or stocking, might after all not meet the demands within their own bounds. Where are they to get the necessary addition then? Oh! there was still a little remedy, the little ones, the strongest of the family were always at service, in the Laggan or elsewhere, some of them little boys not of the age to leave the petticoats, undergoing a six months indenture for a few shillings.[114] A day labourer at ten pence per day employed in building fences for the landlord, without food or drink in addition, might be thought reduced low enough on such pay, but his poverty was not equal to the man holding a piece of land, as the day labourer was sure of his pay and had no other anxiety and, as for work, he cheated as much as he could, and he wrought within hours [sic]; not

114. The Laggan, a fertile and predominantly Protestant district in east Donegal where children from the poorer Catholic districts in the north and west of the county were hired as herds, labourers and domestic servants for terms of six months to a year; west Donegal people came to apply the term to areas in west Tyrone and west Derry where children were also hired.

so with the small farmer, he had the worst of tax masters—himself—he worked hard, late and early, and his pay was much less, that is its equivalent, for he had no pay at all.

As I said above when speaking of the allotments of the townlands, the people getting into possession then deemed themselves secure, and to work they went for to improve the land as best they could, on the fickle faith depending that such was theirs. Old fences were levelled, stones gathered and removed, new soil broken in, drains made in wet ground, crooked fields made straight, thistles, briars, and shrubs rooted up, a strong wall to shelter the dwelling from the prevalent storm. It was no unusual thing to see the man and members of the family together in the clouds of the night long after the setting sun at such work.

In addition to the severe toil late and early improving the land, there were certain times that this work could not go on, that is while the crop was growing, and this spare time was devoted to the building of a dwelling house, and so in the course of time the cabin was turned into a neat dwelling, also some outhouses were constructed, the street surrounding was dried up and the place had a little air of comfort; the tenant began to feel a little proud in viewing his surroundings.

Oh! fickle faith, Oh! foolish toil, for he is soon curbed, and his short experience of comfort is soon put an end to. In August or during the months that everything is in bloom, down pounces upon him the agent and his bailiff—that agent being most likely a discharged army pensioner, a captain of course, a Captain Rock or a Captain Slack or other idler who knew as much about farming as do the Finns or the Esquimaux [sic] who spend their light of day standing over a hole cut in the ice expecting to catch a seal or a walrus.

A land agent of this description is in one respect not unlike the Esquimaux, for the so-called captain on his tours as valuator of land, on his first visit to a poor man's farm, his object is to find out a hole or a spring of clear spring water, on the discovery of which, say a well, he sits down, takes out his flask, unscrews the apparatus, and by a qualified mixture quenches his thirst. After partaking to his satisfaction of the pleasant medicine for eye-opening and brain purifying, he is then truly in a condition capable of doing his master's duty and we might say justice between man and man. He calmly takes a view of the poor man's farm, and before expressing any opinion he meditates for a little, the appearance of his cheeks showing he is in good health, and he now divides but in a lesser degree with his companion part of the medicine, thereby testifying his good nature, and then consults his maps as to acreage, arable and pasture, never [having seen] the same ground before, nor having the least knowledge of what he had taken upon himself to do; ignorant of its original state, the change it had lately undergone, or by whom, or the amount of sweat and toil and hardship it had cost the present occupier to have his fields brought to that fair state of cultivation.

No, by no means, any consideration of this sort is entirely discarded; it is his master's interest he is now to consider. Neither has his companion any courage to thwart him in his designs, and so this one-sided valuator at once jumps to the conclusion that this farm is too cheaply rented; everything helps to convince him for on looking around he sees that the tenant has got some sheep, a couple of cows and a heifer and of course he feeds pigs, and away in the distance in some corner half hidden among briar bushes is another useful animal—an ass—whose existence would not then be known as it could not be seen by the visitors but, hang to it if the unfortunate animal had the instinct to keep from braying so loud [sic]. Whether this action, this expansion of the lungs on the part of the brute, arose from the unusual sight of the strangers and as a welcome for them, or the fact of its being neglected or forgotten too long on its piece of tether, is difficult for us to decide. But from whatever cause, the voice of the ass is rather much re-echoing on this very day when it is not wanted, and no prayers or curses either on the part of its friends can make him stop it, rather the more it is cursed, the more it increases in vigour.

The agent performs his theory and, all things ruminated upon with respect to the farm, it was not very hard to come to a conclusion: the tenant lived comfortable, his land had been very cheap for many years, and therefore one third more additional rent for this time was "not out of the question", "cheap enough still".

When well-rested and nourished and notes taken, they prepare to move on, but the bailiff lags behind: he is in no great hurry, he looks like one who had forgotten something, he wants to whisper, to give a word of consolation on the first opportunity to the man whose heart is quickly beating, and the bailiff conveys his "say" as if hidden and confidential—for the man to not be afraid, that he spoke well for him, in fact did as much as he could, and the end of the consolatory story is that "others would be worse than him", but for him to say nothing, and so by false pretences he gets a few words put into the man's ears but giving more to understand by looks and gestures, and the other returns as many good prayers and blessings on the false friend as time can permit until he is out of hearing, but the efficacy of such stolen prayers before the time for fructifying is reversed.

This same land is saddled with an additional burden of rent but before the present occupier got it to cultivate the greater part produced no crop, part being taken from the uncultivated bog, part taken in from where the mountain heather grew. More drains were made than was in reality necessary in order to hide the stones, and when all the stones could not be hidden in drains and fences, they were then made up in pyramidal heaps to take up less space, the stones carried on the back or on the arms or on hand barrows between the father and his rather weakly son, whose youth only encouraged him against such hard unnatural work, but on returning home at night sure enough with his soft hands blistered and shoulders painful. The increased rent is now their reward; this is now the kindness shown to them for their hard slavery by the self-made qualified land valuator—the landlord's own agent—the man at the spring. If a hard-working miserable tenant escapes on this first visit at less than the one-third additional rent, he tries to content himself that as now the land is in a fit state to give produce, and that between one thing and another he can manage for a while longer, and says nothing, keeps his mind to himself until the rent day comes, and hurriedly goes to the office like one who has found a hidden treasure, and the landlord is the only one who is entitled to it. After depositing more than he was worth, for perhaps he had to borrow some, he gets a written slip of paper in exchange for his money, but as for praise or thanks, for being so good a collector, he has full time to bestow as many of such as he likes upon himself.

Some other unfortunate man is doubled in his rent, and may be part in arrears at the same time, and he tries to explain to the agent and bailiff his want of means, his utter impossibility of being in a position to meet such a burden, but all his language is to no purpose; pay he must or he knows the consequence—out he goes. Maddened between hope and despair he strains every nerve, exhausts every source, to pay one year's big rent—but before parting with what he is reluctantly forced to do, knowing it to be not his own, he makes use of the same arguments as to his inability, praying for some or any abatement, but all in vain, he has no effect, cannot penetrate in the slightest the deaf ears against him. Where he tries now to intercede for himself is in the rent office but he dare not say much, be his eloquence what it may, he is not able to say much, when the command is given, "Out with the money" or contra; the money turns out, it is hastily taken from him, he is handed a form of receipt to calm the feeling in his throat, and no longer wanted but too long killing time, the bailiff quickly shows him the door, and he gets outside without being much hurt at the heels if he is any way quick in lifting his feet, and as much thought of as if he had been infested with a pestilence, and another is immediately called in. "Come be quick", "Off hat".

The following year he pays only one-half year's rent; it is taken from him and not a word said as now he is showing signs of getting into the net; what pleases the office best, he gets into arrears from which he cannot recover, and this is the excuse which was wanted. The third or fourth year finds the man in extreme poverty, not able to pay anything and, as the saying is, indebted to king and country, but the landlord got all he could get in money and now finds his way to take the land to himself after first going through the process of law—that familiar English word "ejectment", the best understood word in the English language, understood by young and old who had not a second word of English, and the landlord covers his doings under the legal term, "ejectment for non-payment of rent".

The landlord seems no way careful about his money so far as law costs are concerned; on the contrary he is very friendly to the lawyer, for should it happen that the tenant who sees he cannot do better and imagines that he will keep down his displeasure is willing to walk out peaceably and proffers to do so, no matter for all that, his flag of truce is of no use to him, the lawyers must get their fee, as it might be considered in some measure a sacrilegious act to throw down the dwelling or to scatter the inmates unless the Chairman at Quarter Sessions first gave his sanction.

At the time of the scattering of the villages, it was no way uncommon that a man was driven entirely to the outskirts, the parts never before cultivated, or to a mountain bog, wet and wild, for which no one heretofore cared about, its value being so little and it being held in common by everyone, but even in such a wilderness a stretch is laid off which someone would take to himself. The poor man whose lot it is sees his difficulties and considers what is best to be done; he knows, wild as it is, that he is still among his native hills, he musters courage and to work he goes, but he must commence on a scale, if not on a level, at least similar to the settlers in the prairies of the western states of America. He first builds a sod cabin or sometimes, more convenient, cuts one out of the clean turf bank, and this for warmth is far the best, and there he goes to reside, makes a few roods of cultivated ground at the start around this dwelling place. The rent is at first very small, in fact nominal in order to entice him to work, as on no other condition could any one fasten thereon, and he is apparently forgotten for a few years; his family is getting stronger and assisting him and they go on cultivating farther and farther. They make a narrow-gauge road, cover it with heather, stones and gravel to take them with dry feet to the open country. They seem at last to get saucy enough to take a notion of improving their uncomely dwelling and the sod cabin is exchanged for stone walls, and in the course of time, nothing less will do them, they get it limed and whitewashed, and they enjoy then the additional comfort of two glass windows.

Now they are at their height. It is now near the time for the emissary of the landlord to pay them a visit. The agent is some day passing at the distance and he makes the discovery, he unintentionally casts his eye abroad, and in the far view—What? white walls attract his attention. To explore this unexpected oddity in the surrounding waste and wilderness, of course he cannot refrain and he therefore finds out the pleasant "pad" and makes his way towards the white-washed walls, on reaching which there is nothing about them in reality strange, but Oh! what a fine farm, what a neat dwelling house, so very very comfortable, and how quiet a place to live in. The tenant ventures to approach, the agent seems astonished at the surroundings, and he questions as follows, "Do *you* live here? Are all these fields held by *you*? How far does the boundary go?" and at last, "How much rent do *you* pay?"

During this interview the tenant is bareheaded, his hat in hand giving truthful replies in his best English till coming to the question of rent, and then he is stunned; he forgets his English, to answer he wished he would rather not, and the rapidity of his own ideas bewilder him, and to evade he sees he cannot; he knows his predicament, and all at once appears to his mind, his own doom; he gets confused, he is no way quick in answering this last question, mutters a few unintelligible words, and, "Your honor this was a poor place when we got it"—"not much rent".

The agent knows well the cause of his unwillingness to answer, but he assumes the demeanour of a judge in the judgement seat and pretends to be ignorant of the existence of such a man at all on the estate, and for documentary evidence simply asks to see the receipt to convince himself, and on seeing it he seems more astonished, his countenance changes to signs unfavourable; he seems to doubt even the office memorandum: "it must be a mistake". The bailiff is called on to explain, and he knows no more than that was the man's receipt, that was the rent he was asked to pay. But his answers too seem unsatisfactory, and "it must be the error of somebody and the thing must be looked into". Nothing further is said on the subject that day, but sure enough the tenant's heart, hopes, and mind are upturned, the dread sets in, peace is taken away, for "everybody knows it was to no good end that the agent spent so long a time in the hill that day", and what evil star was it sent him round that day. So sure as the dread hung over the family, so sure at a certain time before November, the same bailiff turns round with haste and authority flying in his skirts to warn the man for the amount of his new rent, quadruple the sum in pounds sterling he paid before, and the old receipt of two pounds rendered useless. If it be any consolation to him, his neighbours try to persuade him that he is not the worst off yet, considering how others are situated. This is another reward for sweat, toil and privation, for the task of turning up and converting into arable the ground never before cultivated, and worth what is allowable for the haunts of the snipe since the Creation or, maybe more properly speaking, since the Flood, but to add to the tenant's uneasiness of mind his thoughts tell him that he is found out, that he is now under the same broad rule as other people.

The rents of all must be met at November and at May in each year, but the November gale is not the worst as it is the expected plentiful season and anything which can be spared then goes to make up the rent, but there is a deep dependence on the few shillings brought home by some members of the family to complete the amount. These poor creatures, so much welcomed home now, have been at their service since May and put up their time in the wet and cold, before the rising and after the setting sun, late and early and now too glad to get under the old walls, to turn out their earnings, not one penny of which was spent by them, but kept carefully to assist father or widowed mother, to stop the gaping mouth of the greedy landlord for a time. So careful would these poor creatures be of their earnings that for days before leaving service they would be thinking of the best and safest way to carry it home without it being lost, and it would defy the art of a London pickpocket to find out where they had it concealed on their persons, and on the journey home if the distance was considerable they had no call to use any of it, for the masters and mistresses were always so kind as to put into their kit as much bread as was enough, and some to take home.

November being sailed over, May at once appears in sight, but hopes are held out that a pig or two must be sold if no disease or accident sets in, or a heifer or a few lambs or sheep, and as the last resource the few potatoes which were stored expecting to be exchanged for Indian meal to pass part of the summer, and the price added to meet the present and pressing demands viz. rent, poor rate, and county cess, and in all justice, while the distribution is going on, if a few shillings can be spared, the husband and other members of the family who earn it well are entitled to give to the shopkeeper a few shillings for corduroy and moleskin to enable them to appear in covering above the beggar, and so all the money which could be collected has vanished before it got much time to rust.

The month of May draws nigh and very soon after all the resources are gone. From that time nothing but Indian meal, yes the yellow Indian meal, must be looked to; some of this is first got by paying ready money, but the greater part is got on trust, and this is the only food for the summer, three long months. No other remedy but [getting it] on trust, and the poor man is glad to get it. The meal monger gives freely to one whom he expects to have some means of paying at the right time, taking good care to stipulate what price he must get at or about November, and so he for one increases his fortune rapidly by charging exorbitant, incredible interest for the loan. Like the landlord, the meal monger had his way and what could a hungry family do? It was no way disputed that fourteen shillings worth of meal at or after May became twenty shillings owing at November. This brings us to another consideration: in calculating increased rents, this extortion seems to be forgotten, the poor rate seems to be left out, and where the people get poor, the poor rate is sure to increase ...

We can take the above short but too true description as a specimen of the sufferings of the downtrodden peasantry of Ireland, for what happened in a part [of the country] must have happened elsewhere, wherever tyrannical landlords held sway, where no feeling of humanity, nothing but slow murder went on year after year, an iron rod hanging over the heads of poor struggling and (as some in their ignorance or levity of speech might call them) ignorant men. If guilty of the term in its full meaning, it was beyond their power to remedy it, yet they were men, weakened by hunger, maddened by oppressive tyranny, and still one after another suffering patiently. The father wandering along the road weeping for his children now in a foreign land, whom he expects never to see, his wife, the companion of his bosom, now prematurely grown old, banished from her own once happy hearth but now sheltered at some stranger's fireside, so quiet and so lonely that she can hardly make herself known even to a friend: she is sitting crouched in the darkest corner of the house to make way for the members entitled, and must also bide her time to get the use of the fire to cook her lonely meal, and while thus suffering and in poverty, bearing it patiently, their piece of land, their former means of support, the spot they loved so much, now yielding nothing but grass, now occupied by the brutes, now the footpath of fat bullocks ...

The questions naturally arise, What is man? and, What is life? What can be the cause of all this? Is it a punishment for our crimes? or those of our forefathers, or is it to purify souls here by suffering to prepare them for a happy eternity hereafter? Would that the latter supposition was so. Would that men would take it in that light. If we have the real feeling to thoroughly understand all these sufferings, we might well ask humanly speaking, how was it that man could govern flesh and blood so as to submit to such slavery, that in the whole world, the Celtic Irish and they alone could do so—instead of reaching into deeds of revenge, as the man guided by nature alone would mean to do. And the answer can only be accounted for and traced to the teachings of and consolations given them by their clergy; their own submissiveness to the advices given; their expectations in a future world; their thoughts on the shortness of time; and in short their love and fear of the Invisible—the Great Supreme Ruler—and each and all of these things taught to them in and from their infancy and which they could not learn to forget, and it was these and these only thoughts kept them within bounds and enabled them to suffer.

It is true some attempts at revenge have at intervals been resorted to and perpetrated to a certain extent; these things we are told are not right, we say so, but let a man ask himself, and where is the man among us who is not daily looking for revenge, if his honour or his property is invaded upon? Who is the man humanly speaking who could not allow a certain latitude when poor suffering creatures, poor humanity like himself, are driven to despair to commit deeds which otherwise they would abhor or never think of? Where or in what country under the sun would not the people openly face death and danger to resist such tyranny?

It is not too much to repeat, then, that it is through the influence of religion, through the salutary lessons taught in youth, the fear of the unseen Creator, the words of comfort from their spiritual directors, the consoling words of friends, that the persecuted man keeps within bounds, suffers patiently, expecting his reward in the world to come, and supported by these thoughts, lingers out his remaining years until at last he is stretched in death, and his good-natured neighbours lay him in the grave, with the last words that can be said of him "a good honest, hardworking man in his day", "one who saw better days", "one who was never known to do harm to anybody".

It is therefore unmistakeably true that those who are so willing to malign the Irish peasant and who are aliens to them know not what they say, or by their malice cannot understand the real character of the people they mean to blacken. One way they could be taught to do so is by exchanging their position in life, and it would then soon, very soon, come to pass, that the treacherous and varnished hypocrite would change colours, and instead of suffering patiently as the downtrodden Irish did for years in oppression and cruelty, he would at once cry treason and proclaim force as the remedy.

If those with the tongue of the serpent, those with the cry of manufactured Irish crime constantly on their lips, were only forced to experience a tithe of such sufferings, they would themselves be the first to [have recourse to] the means of violence, regardless of *consequences.*

CHAPTER 12
Observances on the Divisions of the Year

After the many revolutions and changes which have occurred in the ways of the people, the introduction of the English language, its prevalence at the present time, the decay (or rather the misuse) of the ancient musical Irish language, it is a consideration worthy of note that the commemoration of certain days, the commencement of the seasons in particular, are preserved and almost held in religious veneration, though many if not all are in name and in meaning traditions descended from the ancient pagan Irish.

They divided the year into four quarters, each called "*Raigha*", that is to say: "*Raigh-in-Arr-agh*", corresponding to the spring quarter; "*Raigh-in-Sow-ru*", corresponding to the summer quarter; "*Raigh-in-Fow-war*", corresponding to the autumn quarter; and "*Raigh-in-Giev-ru*", corresponding to the winter quarter.[115]

The first day of May was the beginning of the summer—[or rather] of half the year, for summer was a general name for so long as the good weather lasted, in other words till November. The first of May then was called by them "*Bealtaine*", or more commonly "*La-bal-ta-ne*", "la" meaning day, that is the first day of May. We read that Tuathal, king of Ireland in the first century, instituted the "feast of *Bealtine*" at a place then called Uisnagh, now called Usnagh in Westmeath, where ever after the pagan Irish lighted their druidical fires on the first Day of May. *Beal-*

---

115. *Ráithe an earraigh*, spring; *Ráithe an tsamhraidh*, summer; *Ráithe an fhómhair*, autumn; *Ráithe an gheimhridh*, winter.

taine, that is *"Bil-tin-e"* or *"Tin-e-bil"* which is the goodly fire, and *Beltinny* from *Bilt* or *Birt*, the root of which is *Bi*—two goodly fires.[116]

Down to the present day some relics of the old druidic fire, the superstitions of May morning, still linger among the peasantry, as it is not at all forgotten or uncommon for some withered old hag in a country townland who has herself nothing to lose and as little to gain beyond satisfying her evil intentions to hover about and take from a fire lit on a May Eve a cinder of whatever description, and on the May morning before the rise of the sun [for her to] be the first person at the village well—the well in most cases being common to all living near—and with the charmed cinder go through the performance of "burn the well", simply dropping the cinder into it.

From whatever motive impelled it is not easily guessed, and it is hard to say that the trace of original sin would demean itself so much, would trickle so far through such obscure channels; but yet by this superstitious act of coveteousness, [the old hag] believes she will secure to herself "the year's luck". If the cinder cannot be conveniently got, a handful of nettles will answer the same purpose.

Such foolish unmeaning acts are fast dying away for the plain and simple reason that it is not in many places that a burnt-skin old crone can now be seen, resting on a crooked stick, having her old head enveloped in a piece of blanket, as the island has got rid of nearly all of such species, and there is hardly anyone to perform or to instil the idea any more. So the younger generation who on a May Eve set fire to a whin bush or burn a heap of straw at the present time do so for amusement, and never think of any charm which was attached to the ceremony in years gone by.

May Day is also welcomed in on the previous eve by the display of a twig or green branch of any kind of tree, placing it if possible on the chimney top, or if not, on some part of the roof, or over the door, or on some conspicuous spot before the door. This is called the May Tree—*Cran-Baltine*.[117] If it is difficult to get to the house top any eminence before the door serves as well, and although the practice is not entirely forgotten and is carried out in most places, no one can assign any reason for such foolish observance further than that when one person sees his neighbour do so, he also thinks it is right, or in other words, he does not wish himself to be odd.

116. *Lá Bealtaine*, May day, date marking the beginning of summer; Tuathal, an historical figure whose career is difficult to disentangle from pseudo-history: see Ó hÓgáin, *Myth*, pp. 409-10.

117. *Crann Bealtaine*, May tree, May pole.

A simple, honest and innocent countryman well-known to the writer some few years ago tried to give an explanation of the May Tree. The dwelling house was indeed not too lofty, and he had a bush in the chimney, and if there was any benefit to be derived he intended to have a share, for he had another large whin bush in full bloom stuck on the manure heap just before the door, observable to every passerby. He was asked by one of two clergymen who were going the way what was his reason for sticking up and having a green bush in his chimney, and it being long after May Day too, or why put up such on May Eve at all. His name was Hughdy Hazelton, and Hughdy replied that he was a little puzzled to answer in that, and did not rightly know, but that he thought the clergy ought to know, but that as far as he knew that it was "to keep up the faith". It is unnecessary to say that the last expression was the cause of much loud laughter then and for a many a time long after whenever rehearsed, and one of the clergymen getting rid of his fits exclaims, "Well done Hughdy. Easily kept up faith, if that is what is wanted—a whin bush".

If we be justified as surely we may to laugh and mock at the foolish idea of a countryman and his May Tree, how then are we to excuse the display of an offensive banner or flag instituted to commemorate hatred, held up in honour of a usurper, in honour of faith begotten by the will of man, or if we suppose again the carrying about and wearing a primrose in honour of a Jew? Really is not one act as equally ridiculous as the other, and if any difference, the latest invention is much more so, for that was instituted in the so-called darkened period, and this in what is termed the enlightened period, or rather the last half of the nineteenth century. The first is styled superstition and yet does nobody harm, the second is called veneration and apt to create, and intended so to create, ill-feeling.

"*Loon-as-na*"—August. One of the Tuatha-De-Danions' kings, that is Lewy of the Longhand, established a fair or a gathering of the people on the first of August at a place on the Blackwater in Meath, between Navan and Kells, in which games and other pastimes as well as marriages were celebrated and continued down to times comparatively recent. Moreover, the Irish-speaking people all over Ireland still call the first day of August "*Lah-Lugh-Nasadh*" which is pronounced "La-loon-as-na", that is Lewy's Fair Day.[118] In consequence of the Old and

118. *Lúnasa*, August; *Lá Lúnasa*, first of August, date marking the beginning of harvest. Lugh was a central figure in a cycle of mythological tales first written down in the medieval period in which the *Tuatha Dé Danann*, the bright tribes of Dannon, overthrow their oppressors, the Formorian giants.

New Style, and since the introduction of the New, the *two* days are kept in commemoration, and so with all the fixed days, and one is called "Ure"—"*La-baltaine-Ure*", that is New May Day, and the first of August "*La-loon-as-na-Ure*", "*Ure*" meaning new; it is a peculiarity in the Irish language that the adjective comes *after* the word it qualifies.[119]

Preference is now given to the New, but the Old, the eleventh day, is not forgotten. The writer of this was told by an old man who was present at a fair in a backward part of the country and in county Donegal that when first the New Style was attempted to be made known to them, the method taken to do so was that a man with a hand-bell, a "bell-crier", walked the streets, shouting in a loud voice that the first of May of that year was ten days earlier. Some made the news a laughing sport, the people could not understand his method of explanation, and gave the man the benefit of being a fool, but at last the crier was brought to a standstill by a rough countryman who had a sheet in the wind, telling him that he was a "lying fool" and with an appended salutation, "Your body to the devil, you son of a woman! Who is going to believe you? Where to did you send the other Ten days?" This gives an idea of how recent the New Style came to be known in backward parts of the country.

The first of August is also welcomed in as the day on which the fresh products, the earth's granary, are opened up, as it is then expected new crops are fit to be used; the potatoes are first dug not earlier than this day, except in a case of extreme necessity, as a man would look upon himself as reduced in the eyes of his neighbours in the olden times; but of late years this rule is much departed from, as the earlier they can be got at, no one now thinks it any shame.

In any case the first of August is the termination of a long, perhaps hard summer, and the season of enjoyment and plentiness is supposed to set in for the weary and hardworking husbandman himself and the labourer after many months of hope and toil, so that everyone who has a crop to fasten on makes it a point to open the new [?clay] or as they say "bleed the crop" on the first day of August. To fulfil the observance of digging on the first of the month, some would do so at a loss to the green crop, it not being in perfection, but then they withhold hands for some days after till nearer ripe. Others who felt the summer rather long but who had not the power like the "bell-crier" to bring the first of August any nearer, took to the method of pilfering their own, [taking] the potatoes from the roots while the stems remained lest they might be

---

119. *Lá Bealtaine Úire*, new May Day; *Lá Lúnasa Úire*, the new first of August.

seen till [i.e.before] the appointed day. Many who still believe in the Old Style think it is not lucky to dig the clay till the eleventh.

Samhain—November. The first day of November is called *Samhain* and it also has the New and Old day. "Savin" or "Saw-an" which is explained "*Sam-hoo-fhui*", that is the end of *Samh* or summer, and like *Bealtaine* it was a day devoted by the pagan Irish to religious and other festive ceremonials. Tuathal also instituted the "Feast of *Samhain*", so that on the first of November the people of this country, following up old traditions, still practice certain observances which are undoubtedly relics of ancient pagan ceremonials, having descended through the space of eighteen hundred years, and in all probability will continue for many years yet to come; such will depend upon the inclination of the people and the custom of the locality, no one having any cause to interfere, such things being harmless in themselves and no trespass upon any law.[120]

The observances and the apparent solemnity at the [festive] time of November are greater than at any other season of the year. It is the time of the in-gathering of the crops; it is the time at which, if there is any cause for rejoicement [*sic*] for the tiller of the soil, he may be allowed to do so. At this time the farmer can calculate almost to a certainty his returns and is satisfied or discontented as the case may be. In any case, the feast of *Samhain* cannot be forgotten, though some might be in grief and many might rejoice or the contrary. Every family gathered under its own roof, those who were at service now arrived home, and such used to be the case that all would try to rejoice and be thankful, but times and customs are much changed.

Fruit especially apples are greatly indulged in at this feast, no matter how provided; the opportunity is not lost when the "apple woman" goes round, as a supply must be laid up. The apple dealers make a profitable return for some weeks before Hallow-eve, as they get double and treble the price in other goods. Nuts are also got in the shrubs, or bought up, and are consumed to a large amount so that many a one who never tastes an apple or a nut for the remaining months of the year make all efforts to have a fair supply at this time. The nuts are not all consumed or intended to be consumed in eating: by no means, for they serve and are reserved for another and most important affair—that is to say the marriage destiny—which is made to appear in the following manner.

120. *Samhain*, November; *Oíche Shamhna*, hallowe'en, date marking the beginning of winter.

An assembly sits round the cheerful fire in some house where they are permitted with full liberty to act as they please; the assembly is mixed with the old, but is principally composed of young people. The hearth is well swept and dusted and a clean space made as near to the burning fire as possible; then the nuts are placed in pairs at regular distances from each other, no two being allowed to touch or come too close. They are turned round several times until perfectly dried; then someone who is well up to all the courtships going on in the neighbourhood and the names points out each pair to represent a young man and maiden who may perhaps be both present and listening, but in their bashfulness give only a smile, do not interfere, and silently give consent, but with smothered breath quietly expecting their good luck in the turn of events. A light is soon applied and the nuts easily catch fire. If the flames touch or unite—marriage is sure to follow, and the length of time and union and extent of happiness of the intended are foretold from the intensity of the light, or the length of time and degree to which it unites, and other happiness besides. Should there be any sign of repulsiveness, which is eagerly watched, such as no regular concentration of united flame, or one [flame] jutting in an opposite direction, it is read as a dislike, or no marriage at all; or if they meet but suddenly separate, it denotes widowhood or a disagreeable marriage.

The stealing of cabbage stalks on Old Hallow-eve was intended for a similar purpose, by placing one over the door and that night dreaming of the future partner in life, and the first who enters in the morning, answering to the sex, bears the name of the intended. The man who felt angry, the man who boasted most of doing harm and of preventing his cabbage being taken, was the very one came off worst, for someone in his own family would assist in doing it; [such a one would sit] and watch but withal the cabbage stealers would by some ingenuity take it unknown to him, and all he had to do in the morning was to stamp and foam and curse a while until he would cool.

A pretty rough man, apparently very determined, sat one night with dog and gun watching his garden; the boys were silently outside the fence, but there was some danger in entering; to withdraw the old boy, two or three of them sets fire to some old straw before the byre door, and his own son shouts out the cows were a-burning; he ran immediately on seeing the light, but on returning his garden was robbed.

The stealing of cabbage is nearly done away with now as "the law came so near hand"; "the Bench" and the old farmers have got too much law in their heads of late, and if a few young persons ventured on a cabbage garden they would be sure to get, in the country phrase, a "white horse", that is a summons for their freedom. While these pastimes were going on by the youth, a few of the old neighbours would meet and make up a "reckoning", put their sixpences together and make themselves jolly with a drop of the "*isquebaugh*"—the water of life.[121]

November is the season in which fairies are believed to be more at large than at any other time of the year. Stories are told of innumerable multitudes of them, meeting in certain places in regular military order, as well cavalry as infantry, and armed in like manner with miniature swords and guns; after a regular pitched battle, one side overcomes the other, one division is made to retreat and finally make their escape to the nearest bush or hawthorn tree, or to some precipitous rock, which immediately opens as if by lightning rapidly to receive the fugitives, the gentry; they disappear, and nothing more is seen or heard of them except the clinking of arms for a few minutes after disappearing inside the rock or under the hawthorn bush. The triumphant division or victorious army march off to some distant hill or other hallowed spot in another direction, and after a halt and some consultation they also disappear.

All this has been witnessed by some Darby or Pat or Micky who "saw it with their *own* eyes", whose veracity cannot be doubted, or some other equally credible person who then unintentionally and involuntarily but unavoidably happens to be passing close to or in view of the place and the affray going on at the time: he could not shut his eyes, how could he for he was making his way home all speed to join his family, and it was on a Hallow-eve night; he was overtaken by the darkness, and just as he was trying every means he could think of, by speaking aloud to himself or by singing a part of a song, to keep the fairies from coming to his mind as he had to pass "*Carrick-a-teigha*" or the Fairy's Rock and if there was only one blind hole in the path he was sure to put his foot into it and to stammer; he just happened to get confronted with the sight of the "squad" and got such a dreadful fright.[122] Oh! save him from seeing the like again—but he did not talk much about it, as "they say it is not right to tell".

The truthfulness of the story is never disputed, never for a moment thought to be otherwise than as related. And why? Because the man who saw it was "never known to tell a lie", and why should the man be

121. *Uisce beatha*, water of life, whiskey.
122. *Carraig an tSí*, rock of the fairy mound.

belied? Forbid it! Neither do the persons who repeat such stories wilfully intend to tell a falsehood, they merely rehearse it because they give credit to the rehearsals of others, and all taking signs for convincing proofs and give in words what may certainly in imagination deceive either themselves or some other. But to give more force and make the story (if it is an old one) more impressive, it is told as in the name of someone who is long dead, and it is a fixed point that "no one should speak ill of or belie the dead", and such a one surely actually saw the contest going on and no less than the traces of blood on the field of battle next morning. "But the man is now dead, and it is not many to whom he told it, as everybody knew him not to be a talkative man anyhow, so that only he saw, he would not have said it. And that is as true as I am telling."

In contradiction to these seeming truths it is curious enough that an old man in the neighbourhood, more courageous than many others, and having the additional advantage of being "half top heavy" and after withstanding the first shock on having a field of fairies brought suddenly before him and not being too rapid in his movements, he blew his nose, rubbed his eyes, and stood. His brains got time to cool down and he mustered courage to enter the field, made a rush at the fairies, and found nothing to oppose him but strong thistles, by which his hands were sorely pierced; mixed with the thistles was a multitude of upright stalks of a more friendly nature, the "bineweed" waving to and fro with the breeze.[123] It is necessary to say that this man for one ever afterwards cared little about the fairies, but was wise enough to keep his experience to himself and let others have their own opinion, as he knew his story would be no proof against the many.

This is the season too—Hallow-eve time—that fairies are more given to sport, as the passerby can hear the sound of music coming from some steep rock, or if a man in the dusk of evening is looking for some stray animal he experiences their tricks by going astray and wandering about himself, and then he hears their laughing aloud at him in his difficulty. "Will o' the Wisp" who ranked as a fairy chief often drew the people from their firesides to peep from the house corners of their dwellings, witnessing his pranks and his exploits in jumping from marsh to hillock, and thence backwards to or near the same place, then halting at the foot of the fairy rock, then for a time invisible, again seen by some eager eye in the far distance who in a state of excitement points out to the rest, and again seen in a different spot, but all the time watched with awe

---

123. *Recte* bindweed.

until the crowd got tired watching and wondering and in a prayerful manner they slowly retire to rest, everyone as they go along giving a version of what was seen.[124] Strange to say, that poor harmless "Will" has unaccountably disappeared from the bogs and marshes wherever and whenever drainage set in, and the vicinity of bogs and marshes were his favourite places of resort. Although "Will" was often seen performing thus his pranks, he was never known to do any harm to anyone, but then it was not known what amount of harm he had in his power to do, and it was not known that any one was ever willing to interfere with him. Enough it was that he was of the fairy tribe, and that it was well known that some of that tribe had a certain spite against the human beings. "Will", it was said, was banished out of heaven along with the fallen angels, but being too good to be sent to the lower regions, he was therefore privileged with getting a burning wisp to give him a glimmer of light till the Day of Judgement. At November too the fairy wives, or as they were called "Ban-teighe", are to be seen in certain "genteel places" such as green mounds, round hillocks, or in the proximity of hawthorn bushes, wandering about in the dusk of evening; their haunted and hallowed spots were also well known.[125]

Every townland has its hallowed spot or spots, and strange to say a man gets afraid of the invisible in his native townland as soon as the darkness sets in, but if he happened to be out late and in a strange place no such dread sets in, no trembling, no sweat, no supposed stiffening of hair up on end until near home, and all these have to be battled against.

These foolish stories, at first made to frighten children, are so impressed upon the mind and afterwards grow up with them as they became adults that in after life they could never be eradicated. Granting that all these things are foolish in themselves, how can we account for the strange sensations which come over flesh and blood, arising from the thoughts of the invisible, when from the effects of fear the whole body quivers and sweats from head to foot, without seeing or hearing anything but what is in the imagination alone?

The "Ban-teighe" were diminutive little creatures in the shape of women, lean and famished and extremely thinly clad, who glided about unmolested and unmolesting, except that accidentally and suddenly coming in close quarters to "someone having the breath of life", and then as suddenly there is the well-known shriek, and a bound and a leap

---

124. Will o' the Wisp, *ignis fatuus*, meteorological phenomenon observed over marshes and bogs; it is caused by the spontaneous ignition of methane gas produced by dead plant matter.

125. *Bean sí*, fairy woman, banshee.

of an incredible distance to the nearest hallowed spot, and as speedily an opening of the rock or chasm at the foot of a tree and the fairy woman disappears.

The great dread of the "wee-woman" with the red petticoat and the thin cloak is that she is supposed to have a control over new-born children before they are baptized, and has been known to steal infants from their mother's breast and leave instead pieces of black oak or some other inanimate substance, and it is the look-out for such that is the chief object of her predatory excursions in the evening. At other times the same image is seen along the seashore where someone is sure to meet death by drowning, or if she is not really seen, the mournful cry, the silent wail of the "*Banshee*", (*Banshee*—contracted from *Banteighee*, fairy wife) is heard by one or by several, and a sudden death in some shape is near hand. But as it is known that her greatest mischief consists in the much dreaded act of stealing babes, the midwife is not at all reckoned worthy of her vocation unless she possesses the power in herself of keeping the "gentlewoman" at a distance from the house, and for this end she must be initiated in certain knowledge known only to the craft.

The messenger who goes for her [i.e. the midwife] must be a man or boy of the lucky type, and no red haired man is lucky, and no female is lucky of any colour on any account. If she rides on horseback, and this must be so if the distance is anyway considerable, she sits so that the left arm and shoulder must be to the front, and her right arm at liberty. If she walks she must have one arm thrust under the right of her escort, and thus her right is again free. As she arrives at the dwelling she circumscribes the house, and in so doing delays some time at each of the corners, repeats certain incantations known only to herself, then enters, and if there be none already over the door, which she at once examines, a horseshoe must immediately be placed there, which act is recognized to be the best curative against the approach of the "fairy", who may come that far and no farther; she dare not pass under the "blessed iron". No ashes, no coals are to be removed from the hearth to the outside of the house for a number of days until all is quiet. As I said, strange the agitation, the ebullition, which fear and fear only sets the body in through the imaginary thoughts of ghosts or fairies, but equally strange that at the same time that people believed most in them it never occurred to them that at the same time and in the same place—the thief, the man who attempted to get his neighbour's goods unjustly, or the person who was determined on doing what is bad, never experience the sight of a ghost or fairy, never the dreaded one, no, but the "breath of the human" is what they dreaded, and to escape such lay their art and ingenuity.

A certain amount of gain was made by trafficking in the supernatural power of the fairies. A belief was instilled and fostered by some professed old witch in a village; when I say professed, I mean understood as such, who made it an easy matter to prevail upon the minds of the young—to the effect that a certain spot near at hand was haunted and hallowed by the fairies, or as she was pleased to call them the "genteel folk", and that the so-named places were visited by them at a certain hour in the night of Hallow-eve, but not till that particular hour, and that therefore no one need be afraid if they meant to conform to the rules for gaining or regaining or continuing in favour and friendship with the fairies for the remainder of the year. That consisted only in the simple task of providing, unknown to any other person, some gift and leaving it for them, and such to be a present of the first and best products of the earth in whatever shape a person may prefer, either in food or drink; but the conditions were such that no two persons were to go together. To fulfil the obligation, it is known to everybody who ever saw a stalk of corn growing that the fairies are jealous of and appropriate to themselves the tip top grain on every stalk of oats, and it is therefore very easily explained that as oats are turned into oatmeal bread and are sure to be in every dwelling on that particular night, a piece of that ingredient well greased with butter (salt or fresh), or two or three pieces cemented together by butter, the same is an acceptable offering and sure to satisfy the wishes of the fairies, especially the Queen.

The ignorant young dupes so easily deceived are anxiously waiting for the darkness to partially set in, or as much of it as will enable them to go unperceived to fulfil the promised requirements, and therefore with breathless anxiety they hurry off to the spot for depositing this gift, taking care if any one is there first to give time for him or her to leave unperceived if possible, and each one lays his present carefully and cleanly down, scarcely able to look around through fear, thinking the time too long though only the work of a few minutes while engaged in the act; so benumbed and overclouded with imaginary ideas would each one be that two persons could be nearly side by side unperceived by each other.

The retreat homewards is performed mechanically; part of the time walking backwards, scarcely knowing when the foot was laid down; and the darkness increasing too, they consider it an age in thought, though really only a very few minutes, and the idea of the expected reward being the main instrument in supporting them from fainting and falling. Each one arrives at his home and slides in heated, sweating, and breathless for some time, and during the remainder of the night, no fee or earthly reward could induce them to visit the same place a second time.

Not so indeed with the old crone, her time for gain, her hour for reaping the reward of her well-conceived tricks is drawing near, and she as stealthily goes round within a few paces of the doors of the villagers to see that all are at their meals, which is generally at the same hour, and when all the members are sure to be within doors. Hallow-eve is a night on which everyone, even the greatest "door-blinder" (a term applied to those who visit their neighbours frequently) considers it a point in decorum to persecute himself so much as to stay within his own dwelling for a considerable time after supper in order that his neighbour may have a chance of doing justice to his good things as he did himself. This opportunity is appreciated by the old hag and gives her sufficient time to gather to her dwelling the rich supply laid out for the fairies and which she is not in the least afraid to appropriate to herself.

The hard oatmeal bread preserves for a long time; it is therefore reserved, and the more perishable stuff is the first fastened upon and consumed. But in any case for many a long winter's night and day the deceptive old being, who generally lives by herself, can enjoy a good skinful of the choicest food at the expense of her immediate neighbours who have not the least thought that she is so well supplied with samples from their tables. Her old windpipes are also thoroughly refreshed by the quantity of butter coming in contact with them, also by the assistance and application of that precious ingredient, the content of some flasks or crockery bottles of poteen whiskey. By no means must this be forgotten, cannot be forgotten, because the fairies—the genteel folk— are the greatest friends to the whiskey smugglers, also if deserved, the greatest enemies if they are not kept in remembrance at the appointed time; that obligation is satisfied by leaving a "taste" of the beverage, so their allowance falls to the lot of the old hag.

While this so fraudulently obtained supply of provisions subsist, she is in a perfectly fit state in every department of her machinery, has a welcome for everybody, is ready at all hours to lecture and enlarge on fairy tales, and consequently her cabin during all the long winter nights is the only place of resort for the younger inhabitants who have already been beguiled by her, and so they go hear her rehearsing stories oft repeated, or new ones invented, of the "goodness" and "badness" of the fairies. Where seen, by whom seen, and what occurred.

Stories invented, or repeated, descriptive of the manner in which Paddy Micky was saved from drowning; how Jemmy Neddy was extricated from the "worst part he could go to" in a dangerous bog, in the "black darkness" of the night; and how "Mary Brinney" got astray in the mountain by happening to come across or just place her foot on a "stray sod"—each of them saved by or through the interposition of a friendly fairy. But this the rescued parties did not know then, did not suppose otherwise, than that it was some neighbour who gave the helping hand until they were left on safe ground. It was after the sudden disappearance of the friendly companion that the mind of the rescued began to clear up and to reflect, and then it was plain to him that a fairy and none other saved him, "for by the hedges" how could it be otherwise, and this thought increasing to the "fainting point", yet no one fainted all out until at the very doorstep, at the step, or just inside the house where care and Christian hands were near.

Countless stories are told of the rewards derived by the wise, and therefore fortunate, poteen manufacturers, who through their forethought acted generously to and remembered the fairies at a trifling loss to themselves, but in return got from them timely warning of danger, to remove and to hide the stuff; this done by signs which the smuggler knew, such as the apparent moving in the distance of a party of police, but really in advance, some friendly fairies in police uniform, and this was to give sufficient warning. Or else the tramping of feet or the clinking of arms in the distance, though nothing could be seen; still the trained smuggler understood the least hint, and immediately took advantage and speedily removed everything, every mother's son went to work with a will, so that when the real enemy, the real "still-hunters", the men of the Revenue Police with panting breath and forced steps, put in an appearance, they were just a shade too late, they were in time enough to find a deserted nest and the "bird" gone; the wise smuggler could silently laugh at the vain search of the police, musing within himself and whispering to some friend, "Who could he be that would inform upon him, but thanks to his stars, they had little for their pains this time. Perhaps it is wrong to blame anybody, for the black boy himself could not beat the Revenue".[126]

Others who followed the same trade but, in their unbelief or else forgetful of this duty, not reserving a supply of the "first shot" for the "genteel folk", were often taken by the police by surprise and lost all and with narrow escape to their own persons. In some instances the

126. From *An boc dubh* or *An fear dubh,* the black man, meaning the Devil.

fairies themselves from excessive anger did not await for the arrival of the police to execute, but took revenge into their own hands and destroyed the brewing in spite of all exertions: either the contents of the still took fire accidentally and all was lost, in addition to some hurt or burns to the owner or they punished in a more deceptive manner, such as everything going on apparently satisfactorily, the pure and bright liquid being allowed to flow into its customary receivers before the eyes of the man, yet it did not in the least add to the keg, so that the owner was grievously vexed, and had every reason so, to see his toil go for nothing, for to his astonishment when all was over he [would find that he] had only a few drops and while thinking over his loss, which he could not now remedy, he could at the same time hear laughing and giggling not far from him, but could see no one, and all this for the non-fulfilment of the fairy tribute.

Should a person be found dead on the road, on the hill, or anywhere outside, the greatest dread prevailed for a long time after, as the ghost of such a person would be often "seen"; if a death by drowning, their cry was often "heard". Such persons were not really dead just then, as they were only "taken by away by the fairies".

Such stories and similar ones being repeated so often and so long after the Hallow-eve, they took such hold on the recollection of the young people that again at the expiration of nearly twelve months the old crone on the approach of the next commemoration had only to hint the idea or perhaps invent other stories equally impressive, and her wishes were sure to be attended to, and she reaped her *reward*.

CHAPTER 13
Poteen and Smuggling

What I am now going to relate regarding the manufacture of poteen is true and beyond contradiction. The three parts of a still in working order or, as they are called, the "instruments" are—the still (or body); the head; and the worm. The foreman or man in charge who is in most cases the owner stands with patient yet anxious look after the head has been put on and secured. He oversees every movement and attends to the degree of heat necessary, examining every part where steam might escape, expecting every moment the concentration of steam into liquid and then comes the first shot—the foreshot.

He gives orders to be executed, but does nothing himself. The happy moment has arrived and he will surely see what his labour has produced. No, however much he may long for the pure malt, he does not yet venture, nor are the visitors or neighbours who may chance to be present more highly favoured, although their gaping visages show well the painful strife that is going on within. A good supply is first taken up by the owner, or someone authorized by him, in a wooden vessel or bowl, carried to the foot of a rock, and is laid there for the fairies. Whatever may have been the origin of this custom it was as yet carried out. This being done, the man at the worm is still attentive to his part of the business, and the next duty is to take up small quantities and dash it into all the corners where a fairy might be concealed.

The precious liquid is now flowing freely and many a longing eye beholds it. Thirsty tongues lavish praise on its beauty and marvellous colour. Someone present makes a computation and a guess, there will be so many gallons produced: he is sure though not to be below the mark. This is echoed and re-echoed by all—indeed, the yield could not be less. This blarney was all intended to puff up and gratify the man at the worm, and if possible to soften his heart that he might the sooner set about a distribution and deal out liberally. The happy moment is greatly desired and everyone present draws near to say something, or at least to show himself lest he might be unnoticed. For one cause or another known to himself, he prolongs the time as much as he can. Perhaps the flow is too strong, and a call is made for more water to cool the worm, or the fire is too great and must be lessened—take away coals—lower. In this way, owing to pretended mishaps of one kind or other, a good deal of the best finds its way into the keg. The flower of the "barley bree" was thus saved for the present. All things returning again to order and to his satisfaction he makes a search in one pocket for some article and not finding it there, he tries another but all in vain. He then asks if any one saw the "whipper", the "penny whipper", which at last is found with some difficulty.

Many dry spittles have been ejected during all this time, but now the signal—the long-wanted signal—the penny whipper has appeared. This was a small tin vessel—equal width, mouth and bottom—and is usually carried in the pocket, capable of holding a glass or something else. He now begins to distribute and everyone present gets a full penny whipper handed to him. Some make the contents disappear with lightning rapidity, so rapid and with such a sudden jerk that a person unaccustomed to the sight would imagine that the penny whipper had also disappeared in the action.

Some, no doubt really delighted with the flavour, begin for to consult for their still greater happiness and extol the strength of the produce, "uncommonly strong", "never in my life tasted better or anything like it", "takes one's breath away", "so strong I can hardly drink it". Such ejaculations were frequent. But what was worse, some of the guests would continue thus whilst sipping the glass, thereby detaining the worthy and coveted measure to the great detriment of others, and so causing cruel water to fall from many a mouth. The patience of the distributor at least gives way, and that he may get on with his business and get possession of the instrument, he is forced to say "up with it man alive", "shame for you", "will you try another?". The last four words have the desired effect, the whipper goes up, and the contents—oh! where are they? Alas they reached the oesophagus without touching the tongue or teeth. Then there is a shake of the head, a closing of the eyes, and a tightening of the lips, and a simultaneous out-stretching of the arm reaching back the whipper when (apparently breathless) he says, "Yes, I think I will be fit for another"—"that is no sickening stuff, in fact, I find it doing me good already, for I had a headache since yesterday, but it has suddenly disappeared". Another dram of course must now be given to make the cure complete. He quaffs off number two, and before long the action of fire and spirits combined tell on his eyes, which appear to be not steady in their sockets.

No one is forgotten, although some get a preference either because they are held in greater respect, or because they come sooner to the front themselves. Everyone drinks to the health and the great good luck of the honest "black-strapper", and "may she never run dry", "that a buttermilk rumpy (a policeman) may never see her", "and good luck and prosperity to the rest of the stuff, for surely the owner deserves it, as he never had his heart in a glass of whiskey and he is nothing the worse for that, nor never will". No man was ever anything poorer for parting with a glass of whiskey.

Among the visitors there are some who do not forget themselves and who have a moderate amount of shame and bashfulness; they silently and stealthily disappear after [?finishing] their first go, but there are others who are not so—those hangers-on who have the intention of getting a good gorge. These linger on and, of course, the whipper goes round for several turns. Fear soon leaves them and Revenue men are things of fancy. To make some recompense for the good things received they lend a helping hand such as carrying water &c. as long as their legs can support them. Mishaps do occur occasionally: being too top-heavy, the head comes splash into the drain or pool of water. It matters not; equilibrium is again restored at the expense of a laugh. The distilling and drinking goes on till near day-break, when all is *run* and the keg—the fruit of all labour—is then removed by trustworthy hands to some secure retreat.

Everything is removed in order: still, still-head, worm and other utensils are consigned to their hiding places, perhaps the waters of a lake, or some deep bog-hole. A few lighter articles are carried off, and all traces of the lately working still-house are obliterated as far as possible.

The keg I have said is removed—but not so fast. Its presence is required a little longer. There are many whom we have not yet introduced who claim a potation. Can we forget those who have titles to it for various reasons? Those who lost their sleep and sweat in connexion with it? From the dark and stormy night on which the barley was steeped to the present; the lifting it again under similar circumstances; the malting of it, which consisted in spreading it out in a chamber under ground; the turning of it at regular intervals; the drying of it on a kiln; the grinding of it at a mill, or it may be by the more tedious and laborious means of two handstones, and then at last—its conversion into the precious liquid now produced. These cannot be forgotten. And time is come for them to enjoy the beverage which they have all conspired in making. Therefore before the precious keg is transported to its lonely hiding place underground, it is brought to the front and made to yield a liberal share. Enough is drawn forth to supply the demands we have mentioned, besides something more to treat the neighbours and friends who are called in to join in the merrymaking. Old friendships are renewed, and "healths" of all descriptions are drunk round. Everyone must taste from the other, and if any one cannot do so, he must take the glass in his hand to show his good feeling. In offering a glass there is always a shake of the hands and another just before drinking: "Your health", "Your own health again", "And that every day *you rise*". Often times however a person finds himself in a predicament of having a glass in each hand, and to shake hands with another is not at all easy, yet it must be managed somehow.

The host is really annoyed with the number of manifestations of friendship and gratitude. From the wink of the eye to the vice-like grasp of the hand no token of feeling is forgotten. "The left hand is nearer the heart"; "here it is"; "this is more than I deserved but I knew you would not forget me"; "that is just what Molly said, that I would have to rise again, when I was about to go to bed and I was just falling asleep when the tap came to the window but I knew at once what it meant"; "I always knew you should have luck for man alive you never put your heart in it, once you got it to hand"; "here is good luck to the rest, I have this, and that the Guager may be far from us". Some wit says holding up the glass, "Men and women, healths to you all", and fixing his eyes upon the glass, "if this is a ghost, that it may often appear to us", and sure enough his share of the ghost never more will.

The good man of the house is heard to say from time to time "Pooh! Pooh! My boy! Your *own* father's son, it would ill become me to forget *you*. Here is your own good health, and the good health of *them whose bones* are in the *clay*, for many a drop of "darlint stuff" we both had together when you were little worth—I mean when the world was no trouble to you—here man alive take the top of that—do—take it—it's good—don't be afraid of it—nothing ever came through my hands but what was good. Shame for you but we never saw anything about but what was decent since you were a little fellow in red petticoats, and that is not so very long ago, and we hope you will continue so. If you follow in your father's footsteps, it would be a sorry day that any dispute would arise between you and one belonging to me. But where is the use in talking, you are not up to "ould times", sure the rising generation will never be like the ould people for the *raison* that wains now are ould men, aye *gorsoons* that you wouldn't take from the sheep market are more ould-fashioned and long-headed than our grandfathers—rest their bones—were when they were grey.[127] No matter *avick*, the ould times were good times, plenty to eat and plenty to drink, and everyone good about it.[128] Oh! I don't know if ever you heard your father tell the story about the christening in Billy Raffles. It was on the night that young Billy was born—did I say born, Oh! no but I mean christened, but it is all the same. Anyhow we drunk it out for three days and three nights— you are laughing. Oh! but on my oath we did and I can't go beyond that, and on the third day Darby Longbow fell over asleep—stiff with drink—and it was no wonder for by the hokies, no man could tell how much he had drunk. What stood to him was he had a very strong con- stitution, man aye, when Darby was at himself he could carry a weight would break the back of the *garran-bawn*—the white horse.[129] One time he was so blind, the strong whiskey you know, had just taken a hoult of him, when he sat down to eat—and plenty of all sorts we had—no stint—to tell the truth—and lots of butter, fine hard butter, cut in big slices too. What should Darby do, but by the high and low, he fell to at the butter and ate his fill, and you know, no one cared what the other was doing, and I suppose he mistook the butter for slices of bread. At last as I was telling you he fell asleep over a *piggin* of broth which was given to him for a cure, but before he had appropriated much of it, he was over—by the toss! stiff over and by the hokey you might as well try to lift the *Royal George* as rouse him.[130] They just dragged him to the one side out of the way and there he lay as stiff as starch for twenty-four

127. *Wains,* colloquial form of wee ones, meaning small children; *Garsúin,* young boys.

128. *A mhic,* my son, my man.

129. *An Gearrán Bán,* the white horse, a mythical horse that figures prominently in folk- lore.

130. *Pigín,* pail. On 29 August 1782, when the British Channel Fleet was assembling at Spit- head for the 'Relief of Gibraltar', the *Royal George*—a 100-gun ship—capsized and sank at anchor; Rear Admiral Kempenfelt and some 900 people, including many women and children, drowned. For this incident, see W. L. Colles, *The royal navy: A history from the earliest times to the present* (London, 1897–1903) vol. III, p. 540.

hours as true as if the watch was set, and as soon as he opened his eyes, his first words were "Where is the broth?". Many a time I heard my own father tell that same story and a great deal more, but this big head of mine can *mind* nothing but, *ahone!* he is gone now and, not because I say it, he had a good wish for you.[131]

"Well my son, don't be vexed because I mention your father, you know we must all die. Look at your own little fellows rising up, they will soon be a help to you; that boy Tom is a fine young fellow and just the picture of his grandfather, like two fresh herring: my soul to happiness but he is. I never see him and many a time I look at him, but he brings to my mind the right *ould sort,* the brave *ould* fellow himself— your hand in this *fist*—and now my boy give me your left hand. "Here is my left hand and if it was better, you would get it." And never say, you have not a good friend, as long as ould Hughdy is at your back. Don't be afraid. I'll stand to you. Your hand again. Here is *"Slainte-ne-Erin, agus Kondi Wee-oigh".*[132] "Good health to *All* Ireland and the County Mayo". "Oh! *massagh, slainte wore wigh,* every day the sun shines on you, and what you have not today that you may have tomorrow."[133] The long night thus passes till early morning in conviviality. The women are in a corner of the house by themselves, and enjoying themselves as those of their sex in such cases usually do. There is an unbroken series of simple and ridiculous stories of old times all come to the fore—courtships, personal looks, their marriages, fortunes or misfortunes in life &c, till at length the sun has come on them apace.

The stock in hand is small and must go along with the rest—the last half glass is poured out, and not only is it much needed but also highly prized for the very reason that it is the last. This passes round all hands, and the time has come when of necessity they must separate, each for his own quarters. Where they throw themselves is of little consequence, and their first view of Phoebus is also the *last* on that day. The luminary of the sky shines as usual, but on their vision he does not intrude. It is late in the evening when most of them are in a state to rise and many there are whose heads do not afford to leave the blankets.

We left "John Barleycorn" after reducing his volume in a place of security and well hemmed in by a strong cylindrical vessel—the keg— one of McDaid's best make, well hooped and coopered. Here he might remain at his ease and defy all poachers on the hillsides if he were

131. *Ochón,* alas.
132. *Sláinte na hÉireann agus Contae Mhuigh Eo,* the health of Ireland and the County Mayo, common drinking toast.
133. *Maise, sláinte mhór mhaith,* well, great good health, common drinking toast.

allowed. But no, this he was never intended for. Necessity soon calls for him and he must come forth again.

Not many days pass by when a woman might be seen trudging along wrapped in a long cloak peculiarly made for reasons known to herself, who is undoubtedly unevenly balanced for she is visibly reclining on one side. We luckily understand why. Beneath is concealed a large earthenware jar in a bag and she is making all speed to the house where she expects to get her cargo of recently distilled poteen.

... The first introduction over, she discloses her mission and in a trembling half-smothered voice asks if all is sold or if there be still a chance of her getting a few quarts. Silence, a solemn silence ensues. The reply is so long withheld that a person of another type would be insulted. Not so with the Shebeen Woman, she is used to it; she only coughs, several times, and patiently waits for an answer. The father looks at the son, next at the wife and both in return at himself. This dumb language carries with it a world of meaning and conveys the idea "shall we or shall we not?" This is the question. Silence reigns supreme all the time and none but a Shebeen Woman could sit so long in expectation. She has however become somewhat callous, and remains there when another would be on the way home full of wrath.

After a little, conversation again opens in this way: "Well, there was that person and this person, and so many persons looking out for it— you would wonder—you would hardly believe me when I tell you that some gallons of it were bespoke of before the barley was *steeped*. Yes indeed, I may say when I had it in the "stook", but then my friend they knew the reason why, they know who makes the "good drop" and I tell you moreover, my decent woman, that I never made a better "drop" in my life, not since water was first put over my head and that is a good while ago, than the few gallons I have in the keg at the present day. It is not much of it I have altogether, and I do not see any reason you should not get a share, for we never saw any of your bad pay yet, though I have the price of some out that I never expect to get on people I took to be honest."

While the owner of the poteen is thus attempting to hit the right vein, the woman with the jar is trying to find out a pocket at her side, from which at length she abstracts a parcel of rags well tied with woollen threads and, after the operation of unravelling and breaking of threads, an opening is made and a few silver coins turn out. The appearance of the silver very soon has the effect of changing the countenances of the lookers on, and at once comes forth the words—"Well, I am in a hurry to sell it, for I know it will not lie long on my hands, and to tell you as a friend, I intend to give the "tin pot" another trial before long if I am spared, for the Assizes are coming on and the "black boys" will be away for some days; but if you get any of this you will not leave the house until the strength of this is proven before your eyes."

Turning to the son, "Charley *avick* are you there yet, man go away with you, quick, what is keeping you, and get us the keg, but mind Charley what you are about, and see and meet Linkum, he will watch the glen for you and do not forget to promise him that I will give him a good Wet, but don't depend to that altogether, don't have your eyes in the back of your head, take your time till it is near dark." While Charley is absent, the worst thing said about the stuff is that it is strong proof spirits at the scale she is going to get it, that is to say that it is engaged at the strength of five-and-two, as strong as ever was tasted. Charley is on the mission, but in no great hurry; he spends a few minutes with any one he meets, he is looking for a pig that strayed from the house, or the pony who breaks every tether, and they appear to be up the glen for he is always looking in that direction, as if all stray animals went that way. He never goes straight for the keg but makes a circuitous route and it is astonishing how unusual daylight hangs around so long.

The Shebeen Woman lingers on; the keg arrives after dark, and a few scouts are turned out to keep watch, the test instruments are brought forth. But the best test for the strength of the liquor is a taste on the lips, and everyone pronounces "strong and good", "no two sayings in that". At long last she gets the quantity she desired; at the appointed place she is met by one or two assistants who, tired enough of their watch, assist in taking the burden home.

Poor silent "John Barleycorn" went through a great deal of changes and sufferings but it is not all over with him yet, for as soon as he arrives at the abode of his late [i.e. new] mistress, he must undergo the five and two operation, and this consists in putting two glasses of water into every five of whiskey, well mixed in some vessel and then filled into black glass bottles or bottles of any or every description, and then stowed away in hiding places but never too far away. Some stuck in the house thatch, some under the clay in the garden, or anywhere least expected.

Poor unfortunate John is thus scattered; each time a detachment from him appears above ground its fate is to be annihilated, never to appear anymore. A conspiracy is often formed against him and he is banished to new regions. Half a dozen or more meet at the shebeen with a few shillings to pay his passage, and as long as the coins last there is no mercy for John. The black bottle is produced and the contents measured out by means of an old pewter vessel which from many years standing is dinged at the sides, the bottom also stoved in and if there be a hole in it, the same stopped with butter or potato starch. There may be a notch or two, a split in the rim, but this is unthought of, this is no loss to the seller: the measure is there in full size but it is impossible to be filled. She knows this well and though she pours over, and each time she goes through the same performance she holds measure and liquid over a deep plate, and the flow over is caught, and goes to the next measuring, of course to the benefit of the landlady, nothing lost.

The pewter vessel as above is called a naggin full "British measure", but often a tin measure for a naggin is made by the still-maker, and it is equally just; and sometimes a measure is made of the cow's horn, nor [is it] any way clumsy [for it] can be carried or stuck in the breast; or by an agreement with the contracting parties an egg-shell serves the purpose. In the measurement of the liquid there is a certain gain arising in this way, but it is not the worst cheat nor the gain greater until the party gets heated and more water is added to the contents of the bottle; the consumers do not know the difference, it is always good until the money runs out, and then it is a great deal better when half-mixed and got "on tick" by one or two who can be trusted, until next turn round. So between "tin and tick" the party get a fair ballast to keep their heads on the pillows till morning.

It is needless to say many were the attempts made by the authorities to suppress illicit distillation and although these checked the progress of the manufacture yet they never succeeded in bringing about the total abstention desired. Here and there, where suspicion cast a piercing look, it became necessary to cease the operation and often for a lengthened period. But the time came around when a venture could be made again. Perhaps the art is forgotten. Well nigh, alas! but not entirely. Someone is always to be found who can and who indeed is inclined to look back on earlier days when he was engaged in the pleasant and profitable occupation, and it is now his glory to instruct his younger and more ignorant brethren.

Something must be done: there is an excuse for a trial. There is a demand in the near future and as yet there is not wherewithal to meet it. The crime if crime it be finds thus an excuse, and the skilful old smuggler entertains the idea of once more hazarding a trial—if he succeeds he bridges over the impending difficulty, and little does the rack-renter know—or care—what is the source of the income [he receives] ...

The ruling powers thought that smuggling [*i.e.* illicit distilling] should be put down at any cost, and to effect this a detachment of cavalry was stationed at some twenty miles distance from our scene.[134] Their reconnoiterings when on duty were so uncertain that no one could for a moment guess whither they were going or when they might change their line of march. A lookout was therefore of little value. Often did they swoop down like eagles on their prey and made sad havoc—fearful spills—recovering however what was good for themselves, for each one carried a bladder which he always took the liberty of filling with pure stuff when a seizure was made. But who could blame him? The animal heat should be maintained, and the spurs used on the return journey. Alas! yes, the spurs were not idle then as the poor horses could often tell. Rough roads, hedges or ditches, it mattered not, nothing impeded their direct route except water. Some interesting anecdotes might be recorded of these jovial bacchanalians after plunder. On one occasion the first of the party tried his horse at jumping over a bog hole, but the poor jaded animal was not just then fit for it and began to rear and spatter. At last he plodded his way across. It was merry sport for all those horsemen as they looked on with interest. But shall I say it—the next performed the same manoeuvre, and each afterwards in turn till the whole number—ten—got to hard ground. This they did while one turn of the rein would save the unnecessary trouble. But it did not end here, for they then dismounted and washed and cleaned the animals, and this they did in style, for the last rubbing was that of the handkerchief. It is unnecessary to say that the bladders proved useful between times during the operation. And it is also worth relating that a smuggler, not very far out of sight, embraced the opportunity and saved his utensils and all that could be removed of his stuff.

When these roving representatives of the ruling power went on their foraging expeditions, nothing save what was on a precipice could escape them. No obstacle seemed to impede their way, difficulties were only romantic; in a word, they might be expected wherever their horses could carry them. Still let it be said to their credit, they were not after all cruel or revengeful. No, they passed things over as lightly as possible, went through a form of law and, what was uppermost in their minds, they forgot not that "we owe justice to ourselves as well as to our masters". They did little work themselves, and always had with them one man

134. Referring to the activities of the Peace Preservation Force in the late 1810s.

called a "stave-breaker" who was kind enough merely to knock the hoops off the vessels, leaving the staves untouched. And these could be easily put together again. As to the malt, they scattered it about roughly so that it was easily gathered up again.

At their approach, the chief instruments—the still and worm—might be with difficulty removed, but the pot-ale or malt which could not be easily carried off remained to be scattered, which being done they scampered off again. No sooner were they out of sight than things were gathered together and filled up again as well as possible, and the fire was lit on the same spot as it had been before.

Everything comes to an end. The world is one of changes—changes of place—changes of business—changes of fortune &c. So it was with the Cavalry. They were changed as to place. People were not sorry to see them away, but were somewhat disconcerted to see Revenue Police sent as their substitutes.[135] The object of their lives was to scent, seek after and thoroughly eradicate distilling. A barrack was erected for them in a central part of the parish, containing when all told twelve men and a serjeant. In fact every parish could soon boast of its barrack. It is a question whether the Government gained or lost by supporting so many men to try and put down smuggling ...

In our own district an officer who had but recently resided there as a private gentleman lived close to the barrack. He was a man that stood by his colours, for he took a liking to command and called the men to march by night or day as he felt inclined. It was amusing in the extreme in those days to see twelve men marshalled and armed with gun and bayonet, cartridge pouch, handcuff pouch &c., setting out in grand array to forage. At first they marched in military order. When they came in proximity to or in sight of suspected places, the command was given to disperse, and suddenly they all separated, each going his own way with full liberty to search inside and outside any house, in a word to ransack any place where concealment was likely to be. The would-be Wellington took his position on a height commanding as much of the view as possible so that he might see how the work progressed. We do not wish to be considered a thought-reader but we are certainly mistaken if that officer did not flatter himself as to what his manoevures would be now as an army general, or indeed if he did not in imagination see an army pass before him in review. Such is the weakness of human nature. We have seen men, aye, and men without a great part of an army at their backs do great and wonderful things. But we are not astonished, for we know

135. The first revenue barrack in Fánaid was erected in Croaghan (Massmount).

well that man is ever anxious to display a little before others, however ignorant or weak. It is only a natural weakness which comes out very strong in the Indian who wears his piece of riband.

A day such as the above was a holiday, but a very important one to the people all about. While the police hovered in sight everyone was watching them and eyes were just peeping out at them from various holes and corners, some more anxiously than others as they could observe them treading on dangerous ground, yea perhaps after passing over the enchanted spot several times, or nearing the malt hole. At some distance a crowd may be seen who are now blessing another dutiful officer as he approaches nearer and nearer to the hidden object. But in spite of all their wishes and prayers the Revenue Man heedlessly pursues his course and very soon the golden rays of the sun shine gloriously on a still wormed up from the earth. A shot is fired and like a flock of vultures descending on their prey, the whole party make a rush to the spot to see the prize. Never did bills of vultures dive deeper in their quarry than the points of the bayonets do now into the tin vessel. The lucky finder gets his reward. He now mounts the now useless lump of tin upon his shoulders and marches thus in triumph to the barracks. There is yet however a solemn ceremony. The inspector holds an inquest on the offending article and after pronouncing judgement, it is kicked outside the walls of the yard—a scarecrow ...

But where on earth was the malt-house? or was it on earth at all? It was in a place where no one but an old smuggler or a well trained official would dream of. Some kept it underground, and the very crops grew over it, or again under the public road where people unwittingly passed over it. The malt-house might be under a thick wall of dry stones with an entrance by the top of the wall. It was the pride of the smuggler to boast that he had a malt-house for so many years which no Revenue man ever found out. A curious place was under the floor of the kitchen, with an entrance by the fireplace, or by a trap-door under a bed. If there were more houses than one together, a double wall could be made between them and here was a first rate malt-house. Sandy soil answers well for the purpose. Brushwood or some such thing was laid at the mouth of the hole and this was carefully covered over with sand. A small peg was thrust in the ground near the spot for a landmark. This could be found by groping. One of this description might remain undetected for years, until perchance an unwary policeman passing over it would suddenly sink shoulder deep among sticks and sods, giving him for the moment a sudden shock.

The poor Shebeen Woman was another object for alarm. She also had her own manoeuvres. Quick as lightning she placed herself at her [spinning] wheel, quietly slipping the jar beneath her garments with her basket of wool alongside. The rest of the family instinctively made their escape, they slid away and she was left alone save probably the companionship of a child, a little girl of the family. The last mentioned was taught to keep at the fireside and to attend to the calls of the Visitors, for the policemen after making a search were in the habit of asking a drink, milk or water, and the little servant for the time being was ready to attend, so that the woman at the wheel was not interrupted at her work, but rather continued spinning and singing like a Mavis as if she was double paid.

Whilst the Revenue Men were thus searching after and occasionally finding and destroying in one part of the district, the smugglers of the other part were not idle. Why would they? They sympathized undoubtedly with their unfortunate neighbours, but no one could blame them for availing themselves of an opportunity. Scouts were always on the look out, and the police were always seen by some of them leaving the barracks. The directions they took were soon passed along. On one side, it was notice of danger; on another, security from the motions of the still-hunters—Jamey or Philip would catch it. They could not miss, but they might have time to save the vessels.

No wonder that many of Her Majesty's force were supple and swift, especially those on duty in backward districts. They should be like mountain hares. Many a time on a sudden and unexpected arrival of these gentlemen a chase was the consequence—it was for life or death, for forfeiture or for possession. But in most cases if the smuggler got a fair start in advance, his safety might be calculated on, and the only effect would be to expand the chest of the pursuer—good exercise, no doubt.

Most of the smugglers who heeded not danger were young men, strong, stout, and healthy, often barefooted on these occasions, with a piece of cord tied round the leg below the knee, ready for a race if necessary, and if not taken unawares, farewell to the policemen. There were young men of the Revenue force who prided themselves on being very clever runners. Yes, they could catch anybody. But let some of the young smugglers of 22 or 30 with trousers tied up and in bare feet get before them but a distance of two bounces, and I never yet saw the official who could overtake them. He might as well follow a bounding stag.

The men wearing R.P. on their foreheads were men and not beasts. They were not all inveterate haters of the poor smuggler and I hope we have not insinuated it. On the contrary in more cases than one seizures were saved by timely hints given by these same parties. The R.P. were Irishmen and for the most part sons of struggling farmers, and it would be impossible for them not to have a share of that sympathy, compassion and tender feeling which finds a place in every Irish heart. If the smuggler had a good-looking daughter or sister as the case might be and the policeman himself was well behaved and good looking, he would think it no harm to speak to her on the road, to or from market, or it might be at the market. To ruin her father or brother afterwards was not his wish, save when compelled by his duty to do so. But there could be not much harm in slipping a word to their relative who of course was sure to act as instructed for their good.

Sometimes when in hot pursuit and gaining ground on those he did not wish to make prisoner, someone advanced in years say, he would accidentally if not intentionally stumble and fall roughly on the ground, thereby hurting himself or straining his foot. The time lost in recovering gave the pursued a chance, lengthening his distance and securing his escape. For at that time, unless a prisoner was taken in the act and detained, there was no further prosecution.

The professional smugglers were all well-known both to policemen and magistrates. But that made no matter; nor did they deny it. So long as they were not caught they were safe enough. There was a good chase one day between a policeman and one Pat [?Green]. The former was keeping close on the track and shouted out, "I will catch you Pat before the devil catches you!". "I hope not, Sir," said Pat, and he made his escape good.

There was a motto of these smugglers: "Hide well and watch well". Still they had confidence in some of the J.P.s who by the way had no special dislike to a drop of home manufacture and who were supposed to be lenient.[136] Indeed, there was not a few of them whose presence on the Bench was hailed with delight. These gentlemen all had stables and anything delivered there was of course just delivered to the coachman. There is no use in telling who it was meant for. Now a kindness deserves a kindness, and men are men and always will be. The decision of a smuggler's case at a court was always looked to with interest by the people, and everyone was glad if he got clear. The magistrates were forced sometimes to decide against him contrary to their feelings, as they knew that he was an honest innocent man in every other respect. Should an old customer be put forward charged with the crime, the presiding

136. Justices of the Peace.

chairman, a resident in the place and well up to the law would shift every point, and if the case appeared doubtful, or if there was any variation on the part of the witnesses for the prosecution, the smuggler got the benefit of the doubt.

In some cases he was marched to gaol for three months or a fine of £6, but even in gaol he was not treated like other prisoners: there was no hard labour, and he could reduce his term if able to pay cash at any time, as time and money were in proportion. Often the money was collected by friends and he was set at liberty.

The third method introduced by the Government for the overthrow or the destruction of smuggling was a surprising one—viz. placing a steamer filled with armed men along the coast. The "Black Boat" as it was called was something to be wondered at by those unconcerned, but the poor smuggler saw no great reason to wonder except that it did not sink under the load of maledictions heaped on it. These cruisers seemed for a moment to sound the death knell of smuggling. There was no place safe from their surveillance. Whether a still-house had its entrance by land or water was of no consequence. To carry on operations now a person should go to the moon. Heretofore those who lived near the coast could often bid the police defiance, but alas! those days were of the past. The steam cruiser coasting along could see the least sign of smoke from the creeks, was regardless of wind or tide, fled from one creek or bay to another, and often landed the men by means of boats on little islands or on promontories whence they proceeded to scour the country.

This was very effective, so much so that when it ceased the very art [of distilling] was forgotten in many parts along the coast, and one thing only remained—to learn it again. Coast Guards very rarely interfered then, except when the chief boatman had a dispute with some neighbours upon whom he wished to be revenged.[137] The people never had much dread of the Coast Guards as they came four or five strong in a body in a boat, made a "sudden sally", and as suddenly retreated. They were not so military looking as former enemies, and the smugglers had little to fear if it went to a hand-in- hand fight—an occurrence frequently taking place. A shower of stones often put them to rout, and a prisoner has been frequently rescued by the crowd. They were armed of course, but four or five men had little use in opposing a band of strong determined country fellows armed with spades, forks, clubs and stones ...

137. The coastguard service developed as a civil branch of the British Admiralty, monitoring the movement of all shipping. Between the 1820s and 1860 a network of about ninety purpose-built coastguard stations were built around the Irish coast, including ones at Rathmullan and Sheephaven. There was also a coastguard watch-house at Croaghross in Fánaid.

After the Revenue Police were discharged, the Constabulary got the by no means pleasing duty to discharge.[138] Up to this they had nothing to do with still-hunting. They went their rounds taking the calculations of hens, ducks and geese, dog and cats of the neighbourhood, spent a great part of the day at some business in a shebeen house, and acquired from some acquaintance in the evening as near an approximation as might be to the sundry animals in the place surrounding.

For reasons just given as well perhaps as for others, the work of still-hunting was one which a few of the Constabulary undertook very reluctantly. To their credit, however, let it be said that this applied to the minority. The majority were always willing to obey orders. Taken as a body they set about their task in good earnest, for though fewer in numbers than the former officials their visits were more frequent, their destruction was greater, their manner of searching more shameless and outrageous, and finally their manner of obtaining information was at once degrading and base in the extreme. They were always what they have been known too well to be—friendly and affable in conversation to nearly all, but—but—men whom it is better to listen to than address, yes, the very child was not safe from giving clues. The laws were also made more severe against smuggling.

Before the new office was conferred upon the Constabulary, their causes for "lipping" the book were trifling indeed. Perhaps it was occasioned by the arrest of a stray donkey on the King's highway, or by a summons for putting a pig quietly off the same; and in all cases the owner paid a fine and the costs of court; but now so diligent were they in their efforts to make a case that the sick bed or that of the woman in confinement offered no sanctuary. They would turn up an empty bottle on the palm of the hand—smell it—they never used snuff—and carry it away, and it was no fault of theirs if they did not afterwards make a case of it. Shameless as it is to relate it, the bottle was taken from under the clothes at the bedside of the sick woman, and the husband in the course of time paid the penalty. This was certainly doing duty with a diligence.

The country people would rather see a whole party of Revenue-men enter a village or townland than two of the men of the Constabulary or, as they were often called, "Peelers", "Peacemen", or when anger and detestation mixed "Pig-men", and so well the people might: the very dungheap was not safe from their ravages, and many a time the residents had a good laugh at their expense. It was amusing—shall I say sublime?—in the extreme to see some of their manoeuvres. The people

138. Referring to the abolition of the Revenue Police in 1857.

hearing of the approach of the police would strew straw or chaff on soft dungheaps or holes, and these fanatics in their hurry would dive knee-deep into the mire.

The Revenue Police in their search had passed on gradually, never remaining too long if they got nothing. Not so with the Constabulary: once *they* entered a townland, no one could guess what time they left, and very often if they pretended a light search in the morning, before night they would return to the same ground again ...

The inhabitants were fond of fishing and they could not be blamed for trying the skill of their enemies. The place was near the sea and I presume this suggested an idea. At all events they decided to see if they were behind the times of the Johnnies lately come from the [Phoenix] Park, who undoubtedly were smart young men and who in many ways fished with large nets. But the old line is the thing that tests the angler and there could be no harm in a trial. However the lake was small and a substitute had to be found for fish. This was tied to a rope and made to sink, the other end of the cord being fastened to a peg which was driven into the bank. This looked very much as if a still lay beneath the waters. To work then the policemen went, and I must say they showed that their muscles had well developed. Nor did more than one of them think of the unpleasantness of getting wet-shod, so eager were they to recover the booty.

At this time the neighbours stood at a distance, enjoying the scene wonderfully and they lightened the labour of love by shouting, whistling and singing. The job is nearly finished and the glory won; it is finished but, alas! they haul onto the beach the carcass of a dog with a heavy stone to its neck. Then they look around, but the boys in the hills are at their defiance and keep whistling and shouting to their hearts content.

The illustration given was derived from a method used by the smuggler for hiding the still where it was tied to a strong rope and shoved out on the water, the full length of the rope. Then by a sudden pelt it was upturned and immediately went to the bottom. The other end of the rope tied to a peg was then thrust an arm's length into the mud. The police by some means heard of the invention, and to secure their prey they walked round the dry bank carefully dredging before them with a staff or ramrod until they touched the rope.

Lastly and in conjunction with the constabulary came the most dreaded of all, the landlord, whose wrath was worse against the poor smuggler than any of the parties mentioned. His law was that any man on whose holding illicit matter of any description, or any such nefarious traffic, was found—whether concealed or in the process of working, came under the catalogue of eviction crimes.

One should think that the dread of eviction should put an end to it but no, it was soon found out that all landlords had no evil in their minds against it and did not care, and the smuggler took the precaution "to hide well and watch well", for he knew where the act was binding on himself and was sure not to be caught on dangerous property.

In order to evade the landlord code, the most hazardous places along the seashore were selected—places such that in darkness one false step was sure to hurl you over a precipice and leave you mangled below. Sometimes the machinery was set up in the boundary between two townlands so that the owner or perhaps the tenant could not be proven in case of seizure. The greatest security lay in the cliffs along the seashore; at night there was no fear of the police venturing here, and in the daytime, should they appear, there was a curragh or a boat lying near that the smugglers launched, but while they had the consolation of riding safe on the waves they had the unprofitable view of their late property burned, spilled and utterly destroyed.

What added much to the pain inflicted by the landlord's interference was that the property of the poor respectable smuggler should be seized and destroyed by one who was considered, and deservedly so, the meanest and lowest of mortals—the bailiffs. It was surely trying on the patience of the owner to stand by and look on at the detestable self-made constables, acting the part of Government men because they had the landlord at their back, and not to be able to say he owned it. It is not for us to say what his feelings were but we venture to divine that if home and family could be lost sight of, many ugly results would have followed.

It is wonderful the venture of a smuggler [sic]. We have known them, when hard pressed for a place, to run the risk in their own dwellings where they could be sure, if caught, that eviction and a fine or imprisonment would be the result; also for them to make malt in uninhabited houses from which the owners had been dispossessed and were then in hands of the landlord; no policeman of any coat would think of them as being used for such purposes.

We have traced the history of the art of private distillation in a locality where nearly everyone knew it well and, what is more, often practised it. We have left the place many years, but we are happy to know that the good old practice is not entirely forgotten and, were it not for private intervention, all the blue jackets that ever trod the soil as well as green could not put it down.

French brandies are very good and three stars outside of a bottle warrant genuineness, but we hope we are free to hold our opinion that home-made poteen manufactured from barley is, if it gets a fair chance, unrivalled for strength and purity and flavour; if our authorities knew more about it, they would be less opposed to it and more opposed to foreign importations. We hope that at no distant date the good old "barley bree" will be more universally known and that more latitude will be given to those who can make sufficient quantities, for at least their own consumption ...

CHAPTER 14
Hints on the Manufacture of Poteen

Having said so much on the use and abuse of poteen whiskey, the dangers attending it, and all the methods tried by the authorities to suppress it without however succeeding in their efforts, it may not be out of place now to give a few hints on the different stages the raw produce must undergo before it is converted into real poteen.

Of late years, the idea arising I suppose from some knowledge of chemistry and following the trade of adulteration in this as in all other commodities, a way was found to extract from molasses a poisonous whiskey which goes under the name of poteen, but which is no way to be compared with the pure stuff that is obtained from the barley. The inferior stuff comes under the name because it is partly run [*i.e.* distilled] in the same way and by means of the same kind of instruments, and it is therefore smuggled goods, but at best it is nothing but a poisonous and sickening drink, the smell of which would even discover itself, and besides it has the disadvantage that it cannot lie long; unless consumed immediately it loses all strength and turns into an unpleasant and nauseous quality of drink, very hurtful to the health.

The best, the real poteen, or as it is often called "the Mountain Dew", is got from the clean barley alone, and that too when the barley is properly prepared, because it requires knowledge and the nicest, cleanest, and most skilful handling from the very first turning the barley into malt; if not carefully attended to, it would soon rot or get a sour taste, and if one or the other of these things happened the yield would be small and bad, and any foreign flavour taken up by the malt would be conveyed to the liquid, let it be either taste or smell.

Of all the corn crops, barley when sowed in time is the earliest and the first that is ripe; the smuggler keeps this in view and tries to have the first of the season before any suspicion arises and before the fields are bare, or any suspicion sets in on the part of the people or of the police. The right old smuggler therefore lays out his accounts and makes all efforts to have a run or two before the still-hunting season really sets in while the police are patrolling the highways, capturing stray donkeys and getting the owners fined for allowing such to trespass on that sacred property "the king's highway", or else when not engaged in that, enjoying themselves in the heat of the sun, lounging lazily on the green hillocks convenient to the barrack ...

This then is the smuggler's opportunity and he tries to make the best of it; he is waiting day after day for the barley to be fully ripe; he then reaps it at once, puts it into stooks to dry, and in a very few days it is ready for the flail and is thrashed. He selects some of the best of the sheaves, taking care not to leave the ground bare on which it grew for fear of arousing suspicion, but leaves a few scattered stooks on the ground for a length of time. As much is taken as will fill a sack with barley and this is all that is wanted for that time, and so cautious is the distiller and everything done so quietly that his nearest neighbours are taken by surprise when they find out that on someday he is making preparations for a brewing.

The sackful of barley when cleaned and ready is taken away after night and thrown into some deep pond or in a quiet corner of a lake, and here it lies for forty-eight hours or a little more. It is then lifted in the darkness and with the greatest secrecy. The barley was innocent while dry, and no excise or revenue man dare meddle with it, but now by this simple act of dipping it in water, poor "John" throws away every vestige of loyalty and becomes one of the most rebellious of nature's gifts and is at the mercy of everyone.

So dreadful is the result of the transformation that from the hour it is steeped in water until the hour it is enclosed inside the human body any person and every person handling it, or within a certain distance, or in any way connected with or assisting at its manufacture, runs himself voluntarily under the standard of high treason, and if caught in the act is liable without mercy according to the law of a punishment either three months inside the strong walls of the county gaol, or the alternative a fine of six pounds sterling. This punishment is binding on the very smallest quantity in whatever state, either as grain or liquid.

A fitting hour of the night is chosen for taking or dragging the wetted barley out of the water, and the sack is left in some out of the way place until it strains and gets lighter; an hour arrives and the opportunity taken for transferring it to the malt-hole. Into this hole or "malt-house" the contents of the sack is turned, and the floor being smooth and as clean as possible, the wet barley is spread on it to a certain depth, say about six inches or less and as evenly on the top as can be, the operator all the time on his knees while doing so. Then the entrance is closed up for the night. Again for a number of nights regularly at about the same hour, or if possible twice in every twenty-four hours, someone who knows what to do makes his way stealthily to the hole. If it is indispensable to go in the day time, there is a lookout in the distance who by an understood signal gives timely warning if any suspicious person approaches. The one who enters the holes loses no time in going to his work, and he carefully turns over with his hands the "flooring" as it is called, commencing at one end and ending at the other, giving an occasional peep to the outside world and relieving his mind of any disquiet by a look at the signal.

This turning at regular times is necessary to prevent the barley from "growing", from running too much to the "sprout"; therefore the skill of the malt-man lies in keeping the growth at a regular state, not to prevent the sprout but not to let it grow too long. If it grows too long the substance is lost. The malster is glad to see a good stout bud, for on the beauty of the bud does he speculate on good malt and is satisfied. Arising from the heat in malting, the barley throws out shoots and roots, but would if neglected become in a very short time a solid lump and useless; it is therefore the business of the attendant to prevent this by constant turning and if the exertions of the attendant prevent it from long sprouts, he has a sure sign of good malt.

When he is satisfied that this process is properly done, [the barley] is again filled into bags, which can be easily conveyed to a rudely constructed kiln; if a lime-kiln is convenient it serves the purpose. It is then dried and this is done late in the evening and during the night, one or two being in attendance, occasionally turning the malt and attending to the fire while a staff of watchmen are on the lookout at certain points. When properly dried it is taken away and concealed in some dry place, very often the same malt-hole again as it may be thought the safest place. As long as it is kept dry it is all right, but now it must be ground.

If the mill-owner is agreeable a time is appointed to get this part of the work done. The mill-owner by running the risk is fairly paid, and he therefore fixes the time and is in readiness to let on the [mill] water and turn the mill when he gives the consent for the stuff to appear; a very short time runs it down. If he is afraid to venture and refuses, then recourse must be had to the hand-stones at home. This latter piece of mechanism is supposed to be an invention of the Danes (and that period being in the opinion of the people just as far back in the history of the world as was wanted, for everything which could not be traced was— "in the time of the Danes"). In any case, the hand-stones or miniature millstones are of ancient date and must have been used before water power was thought of, and they are shaped in the same form and made of the same quality of stone as those now used in country mills. It is a very fine exercise turning one of them, as the person engaged at such can work himself to perspiration point at his pleasure and to his satisfaction, and when he feels exhausted another may take a turn. Tradition locally says that such were used by the Danes to grind down the heather which they converted into gin, but unfortunately that secret was lost, so the story says, for that the last man of the Danes was suffered to be put to death before he would disclose the secret. To go to work with these "grinding stones", they are placed on a clean cloth on the floor, and a handle, a piece of wood, is put into a hole in the uppermost or revolving one, and the rapidity or work or number of revolutions depends upon the willingness or strength of the arm of the operator. Another person sits near and supplies with his hand small quantities of the stuff to be ground, letting it drop gradually in imitation of the hopper into the hole on the top, and another person is busy in gathering up the mealy part as it escapes from between the stones, viz. the flour like or ground stuff, now white and fine, and puts it into a clean bag.

It may lie concealed for another while, but the malt is now ready for the brewing and every following day is watched to get an opportunity for fixing the "hob", that is a place for the fire and for the still to sit on. The whereabouts and the doings of the police are carefully noted such as whether a fair or market day is drawing nigh or a court day, which might lessen their ranks. Any of these would be considered a fitting time and opportunity for wetting the malt. If such days did not appear in view, a day of the week was chosen such that the finish would come off on the afternoon of a Sunday and a Sunday night. The police were supposed not to come out on that day to still-hunt—but they soon learned. Some who were unconcerned, the apparently pious, would say that Sunday working was not lucky, showing their religious scruples, while perhaps they would do worse themselves; others would say, it was no harm, as the man was only trying to make the best of his own, but prevented by law. The smuggler cared not if he escaped the police.

The place for setting up the implements, in other words constructing a still-house, was well considered and not hastily pitched upon. It must be such that a good supply of water be as near as possible, either a stream or a well of water. If a river runs near, so much the better, as out of it a simple watercourse is made about six inches deep, and through this sufficient supply runs to the very top of the still by an ingenious winding and can be turned on or off as it is wanted. A place is chosen as much out of the way of any traffic as possibly can be, say at the entrance of a cave, or under a steep rock or high bank, in order to hide the smoke, and the fire is placed so that at night the reflected light would run in an opposite direction from any road or pathway, and a screen of sacks hanging from pieces of sticks is placed before the fire to prevent reflection. In many cases outhouses and even dwelling houses were used for the purpose ...

The implements at the brewing stage are the still for heating the water to pour on the malt; a large wooden vessel called a keeve, but properly called a vat; and a few hogshead barrels and tubs.[139] The vat is a very large wooden vessel, made somewhat like a tub and bound with strong hoops; being large and therefore difficult to hide or get into any house, the smuggler knows as much of the cooper trade and is so skilful that he can knock off the hoops, tie up the staves in bundles, carry them everywhere, and when the vessel is wanted again put them all in their proper place.

Two pieces of dry stone wall are made about two feet high with a space between them about two feet wide for the fire; this is "the hob" and the still is placed upon it. It is put up without rule or measurement, and yet the still sits level. Exactness is necessary so that no heat may be lost and that the bottom of the still gets a uniform heat. The vat is placed at a convenient distance and in it is fixed a false bottom, a few inches higher than the real bottom. These boards are perforated and over them coarse straw cut short to prevent the holes from being stopped up. This acts as a strainer ...

When the water in the still is at the boiling point, part is lifted, taken out and put into the vat, and a quantity of the malt is put in and mixed up with a long pole called a "dirty stick" to form a mash; more water and more malt is added, and always kept stirring until the vessel is full. It is then covered over and left for some time to malt and mix, and after

139. Keeve (Eng.), a tub or vat, especially a vat for holding liquid in brewing or bleaching.

a while a plug is drawn from the bung-hole, at the very edge of the bottom [of the vat], and at once the liquid begins to flow.

The liquid is of a greenish colour, very sweet, thick and glutinous; it is a very pleasant rather sweet drink, not intoxicating, and is called "wort". If the wort continues flowing freely and gently it is a very good sign of quantity [*sic*], and bucket after bucket of hot water is spread round upon the top to keep it trickling and until all substance is drawn. This goes on as long as the wort carries the sweet taste; when it comes near the end of that state, it is often tasted until pronounced as water or worthless. Should the wort cease flowing or flow very irregular, the vat is then said "to sit", and in such cases there is no remedy but to empty all out again and this is great loss of time and a very considerable loss to the stuff. In fact the smuggler considers it a ruin for that time. When the wort is sufficiently cooled, the hogsheads are then filled, and a quantity of barm and boiled hops are put in, and some distillers cut up soap in slices and throw into the mixture. They don't know any reason, but that it "cuts it".

After a little then, the hogsheads begin "to work", that is ferment, and the liquid begins to boil and bubble and the surface is covered with froth, and the contents expand so much that the hogsheads would overflow if not watched. When it works strongly in this way a man must sit to watch, and when he sees one ready to overflow he prevents the same by whirling a stick rapidly in the top. He will consider it no lost time to have to do this, for he has every sign of being repaid by the quality of his stuff when this is the case.

It is reserved for the man of experience to put on the barm, for the whole secret is in a proper mixture of this. It is the barm and hops which cause the wort to rise, and strange too, the first quantity put on must do, must be sufficient, and it is hit or miss as no addition afterwards is of any use. If the contents of the hogsheads do not rise at the proper time and to a good "head", hopes are lost as to the quality, and the yield is sure to be small and bad. After a certain time the contents of the hogsheads will settle down of themselves; the liquid is then of a clean beautiful brown colour on the top, and by placing your head over one, a peculiar sharp sensation is felt in the nostrils, and a good draught of this good "top pot-ale" as it is called has the effect of intoxicating much more so than the same quantity of porter or ale.

The hogsheads lie for some time in this state before being disturbed again, and the longer they are let lie the better and, no person perhaps in view, someone who takes a liking to have a drink of the "pot-ale" circles round and round like a thief, ventures at last upon the still-house, feeling some reasons to be afraid of the owner as well as the police; still the thirst overcomes him, he knows there are no small vessels to drink with, and to dip his head in is rather a trying experiment, so he provides himself with pieces of straw or reeds and with these he speedily sucks up to his satisfaction, escaping as soon as he can from the scene. Another who is promised against drinking whiskey comes in and takes his drink of the good "pot-ale".

The top part of the vessels (until about half-way down) are the best portion of the stuff; the sediment at the bottom is a thick whitish gluey substance, and the best of this is taken up for "new barm" and is preserved carefully, or it may be that a neighbouring smuggler is just waiting to get a share, who in return lends to another and so on. Nothing denied, nothing hidden that one can give the other. At the commencement of a season it is difficult to get the barm and one may have to go to the next parish for a supply. The smugglers were very neighbourly in this way, for no one would refuse or deny an article belonging to the trade and would give each other all the assistance and all information.

The "pot-ale" is let lie as long as it is thought safe to do so, and as I said the longer it could be left in this state the better it would yield whiskey, and also for strength and purity. But unluckily, through dread, haste is taken for safety sake, and there is then a loss as to quantity and quality. Long ago before the still-hunters came to be such near neighbours, seven or eight days were thought short enough for "cutting" in the pot-ale state. Now scarce twenty-four hours if danger is apprehended, so that it is impossible to have it so good, being as the smugglers term it "only scalded".

The pot-ale then undergoes the operation of "singling" and at this stage all the implements are wanted, viz. still, still-head and worm, the three parts being mechanically joined together, through which the stuff must pass. There are also in readiness a number of kegs to hold the liquid, which on coming off this time is of its pure water colour.

The still is placed in position on the hob as before and nearly filled to the shoulders with the "pot-ale"; the vacancy above the shoulders, necessarily left for space for the formation of steam, and when coming to the boiling point the head is quickly put on and the worm is as speedily fitted to and placed in its proper position.

Formerly all three were made of copper; now still and still-head are made of tin, and if destroyed the loss is not so much, but the worm must be copper, and in case of pursuit the worm is the first article carried off or saved at the greatest risk. These three articles are made to fit neatly into each other. The head is inverted on the still, and has a long arm, thick at one end and tapering to a thickness or point which fits exactly into the thick end of the worm. The seams at their junctions are carefully sealed up by a simple kind of cement, made from blue-clay of an adhesive nature and well mixed with other substances, among the rest horse-dung, to make it more adhesive, so that no steam can escape at the joints and nowhere except at the point or end of the worm.

... One end of the worm is fitted into the point of the arm of the still-head, and except this small part, the rest is hidden in a large barrel or cask full of cold water, and cold water must continually flow into it to the level, or else carried to it. Many a smuggler could not explain or give reasons for many things which they use; they know from experience and that is all, and they keep up to every point; however it is no great amount of knowledge to say that cold water is necessary for converting the steam or vapour arising from the still into fluid on its passage through the worm, otherwise it would escape in steam or smoke at the point of the worm. Indeed the first jet always appears in vapour. The worm is of a special form and placed thus erect, the smallest end of it jutting out at the bottom of the barrel, under which a hole is dug large enough to hold the keg, and its open bung is just under the worm.

It is amusing to see with what speed and accuracy the distiller can fit all the implements at the first attempt, which to an inexperienced hand would appear difficult. The cask or barrel must be placed so as to fit the length of the still-head arm and that part of the worm which joins it; neither must it be placed too high or too low, for that would disarrange the joints and also the proper place where the point must protrude. Often a weight must be placed on the head, a stone for instance, to keep it from blowing up, but the why and the wherefore—the power of steam, or the conversion of steam into pure water by means of simple instruments and simple agencies, the smuggler knows naught. He just does as he saw his father doing, he knows from experience what he is doing, but the strength of the power he is ignorant of.

Attention and care must be bestowed to the fire that the heat may be rising gradually; if it is too high, too much of the stuff would escape in steam, and the smuggler knows it is to his loss; equally as bad as if not worse, too great a heat would run the pot-ale too thick and of a milky or whitish colour, so discolouring and destroying what is already good and taken in. Again, less heat than is required would slow the working; still this is the safest for the purity of the liquor and, when brought up very gradually, the steam on its passage through the worm is converted into what is required and so appears beautifully clear at the point where it drops into the keg placed to receive it.

This production is called the "singlings", and two or three "penny whippers" of the "first shot"—or as they call it "foreshot"—would produce a reeling effect upon the head and body. The singlings gradually lessen in strength, but the pot-ale is run down as long as it is thought worth anything, which can be easily known by the taste. Of course, nearly all in the still could be passed into water, but as this would be useless; no labour or time is to be lost beyond what is necessary.

Immediately then the head is dexterously thrown off, no other article having any cause to be removed. What remains in the still is called "burnt pot-ale" and is let run into the tubs and other vessels and is carried away for other uses. Everything is carried on in haste now as it is now near the wind up, the still gets a clean washing, is put on the fire again and the last process draws near.

The "singlings" is poured from the kegs into the still, the fire renewed and stirred up, the *three* pieces of machinery put in position again. The first appearance of liquid is the long-wished for "doubling", the real precious stuff—the isquebaugh—the life water—the throat scourer—the much coveted "poteen", the first keg of which, the best, is hastily taken away and hid. The second best, is taken up and if time permits and no danger, an inferior quality is also put in a keg to be mixed with singlings again at some future time.

In the years long ago when time was at the smuggler's disposal, the "doubling" was in some instances put up again to convert it into extra strong stuff for to satisfy the tastes of certain people who were able to pay for it, and gave instructions to do so; this was called "double refine".

The refuse of the malt, called "grains", is the best feeding for cow and pig, so that a smuggler's cow had a "skin". The "burnt pot-ale" is the most wholesome drink for cattle, but as it would be dangerous to store too much the owner is willing to divide with the neighbours and all is carried off at once. The doubling is taken away to be consumed by man, and it requires no words to prove what the use or abuse of the same leads to.

I have often heard the smuggler characterized as a man of lazy and drunken [?habits]; this most certainly is not so. It is not by being drunk he could run before a policeman. No man earns his reward, his profit, at a dearer price—hard work while he is engaged, want of rest and sleep and anxiety, while others do not feel anything of the sort, and as for intemperance, he is the last to indulge in that! It would be cruelty of course to deny him a taste of his own, but his chief aim and object is to convert his own produce to bring better value, and if he succeeds, that he may be able to meet his *demands.*

CHAPTER 15

Prevailing Customs at Marriages, Births and Deaths

Most novels have a plot ending in marriage. Perhaps there is no occurrence of human life that presents so much matter to writers of fiction, for whose career of courtship and marriage is without some romance? Had we the pen of Dickens or Scott we might set forth as interesting stories as they, but we remain content to tell our own experience "in a round unvarnished tale".[140]

MARRIAGES

There were three ways of bringing around the sacred bond of wedlock: by abduction, runaway and contract. In spite of the protestations of the clergy who used all their influence to the contrary, elopements and abductions were by no means uncommon.

The *abduction* case:— It was not surprising to hear in the morning that such a man's daughter was taken. This was usually owing to a disparity between the families in some respect, generally in regard to pecuniary inequality. Here the would-be groom might fear a rejection of his claim if he went straight forward and proposed. Or it might be that he had not the necessary courage to do so. His usual resort in such a case was to consult his friends about the prospect of his plot and work accordingly. Lo! in the dead of night the old man's house is surrounded, there is an entrance, and the prize is carried off. In such cases every pre-

---

140. Charles Dickens (1812–70), English novelist; Sir Walter Scott (1771–1832), Scottish novelist.

caution is taken that no one be harshly treated. The maiden was especially well cared for, and the old father was offered what was considered the gift of gifts, the medium of reconciliation to cool his temper, and help him to sleep soundly; a bottle of the best five and two was also presented, to not forget the old woman.[141] To this he was heartily welcome, but off the young woman should go. In the meantime she is borne away on the arms of strong men or placed on horseback with an attendant at her side, and landed safely, although bathed in tears, in a secure place among strange faces, soon to be introduced to a young man whom she never saw, or if she did, to whom she never spoke in her life. Her state was now pitiable. All present tried to console her. Some of them cared something about the transaction, some cared little, and many cared nothing except in so far as it concerned themselves—to get plenty to eat and drink, having got which all appeared in a state of jollity.

That night was spent in merry-making, in lecturing and in explaining many quaint topics and how good can come from evil, &c. &c. "The priest says this and the priest says that", "his advice is always good", "surely but there is no harm in all this, everything will be all right yet". Next morning the news spread rapidly that Biddy or Kate So and So "was stolen", but where the intended couple were, that was a mystery; in any case, though bitter animosity might arise, and a brother shed tears and feel sorry for parting with his sister, no person would think of obstructing the marriage, for when it was once known that this took place the young woman in question would find it difficult to get a match again, and the young bachelor was in as awkward a position, slighted and neglected and jeered at by the girls. Nor was there such a thing unknown as *stealing the stolen*. The young girl, not feeling at ease, would find means of communicating with her chosen friends, and then by a bold manoeuvre and her willingness they carried her off. There was then the commotion among the friends of the abandoned one who wished to have him settled at once before the story got circulation. I have known a man in his bachelorhood thus left desolate [whereupon] his friends hawked him about during the night, opened and solicited three doors [i.e. families] before they got a welcome admission. The girl in the fourth took pity on him where he did not expect it, and next day there were hastily celebrated two marriages, and the whole affair hushed up.

The parents of the stolen one [would normally] feel very uneasy; still they could not better their condition. But those who were anxious to

141. Presumably a reference to premium legal whiskey.

gain friendship with both parties and who accordingly kept secret the "locale" of the hidden pair, brought word that all was right, that the old couple might make their minds easy and had just better come to an agreement when everything would be smooth. By the influence of arguments, promises, or if necessary threats, the old fellow was forced to give in, to encroach upon the results of his hitherto hard life's toil, and to promise such terms in cash and chattels as would relieve his daughter for the present in bondage.

Much depends on the amount, followers or "backing", whether the old father will put on an obstinate face and remain firm. But whether successful or not, the ambassadors let him know that the marriage shall go on, which is fact, and time is left to overcome him for the rest.

The *runaway* case:— Runaway marriages were of more frequent occurrence and after all were more to be enjoyed than the former. They took place in nearly every case at the fair or market. In such cases, it was usual for the parties to lay the plot beforehand. This was considered the best opportunity; no suspicion was raised for they were dressed of course for the fair. They could thus spend the day with their friends till darkness set in when their escape became easy. They now eloped with two or three confidants to a friend's house somewhat about.

Next morning they quietly got married. Then proceeded the outbursts of displeasure and dissatisfaction among the relatives on both sides. One party would say, "it is no match", neither giving any "face" or inlet to the new member of the family. The other priding themselves on their honour and dignity would say, "it is well known that one of our family never demeaned themselves by joining such people or their stock", "no harm to the boy", "he may be good enough and is so as far as we know". These paltry objections arose more than anything else from the fact that the friends wished to save themselves the expense of celebrating the wedding, and still more to keep free from promising anything by way of a "portion".

So in a manner disowned, the young couple had to make the best of a bad matter, or a good one we hope, and start in life for themselves. When a beginning was made and things going on well, they were not so neglected, for all of a sudden they who were so bitterly opposed to the match at first relented and began to assist the happy pair. The late castaways began to feel the comforts of life and henceforward all was as merry as a marriage bell. As their prospects succeeded so did their friends increase, which is true at all times in this deceitful world.

The *contract* marriages:— Those belonging to the higher sphere of worldly life rarely had resort to either of the above methods. No, they could ride in saddles and pillions to public places, had a different view, and signalled the same by bombastic shows, though it did not necessarily follow that their engagements proved more happy. Such should be the case frequently where the intended spouses often had never seen each other before, and as a consequence were each ignorant of the faults and frailties and temper of the other. Negotiations were carried on by the friends on either side and when an agreement was come to, the young man was told to prepare and visit his intended father-in-law. Soon he, all blushing, was on the road with a few friends, well supplied with the native beverage to spend a pleasant evening.

... As coming events cast their shadows before, the news of the approaching one was soon scattered far and wide. The second night was a famous one and went under the name of "bottle night", a very significant term. All friends who were glad to hear of the successful issue came in pairs with a black bottle full of "the best". As there were black bottles of various sizes, none dare appear on any man's knee but the largest. That night was spent happily at the bride's house also, whether the groom was present or not. But he made it a point to be there some hour before day, unless the preparations necessary for the happy day necessarily called for his attention elsewhere.

On the third morning the groom invited all his friends, taking special care not to forget any couple whether married or single, but especially the single, who had come to see him with their bottle, for to omit or to forget any of these would cause ill feeling. The bride's friends did the same and that was without doubt a busy morning between invitations and preparations. Those who had not good dresses were hurrying to and fro, borrowing cloaks, hats, bonnets &c.

It might be thought how were the groom's friends and bride's friends to be known for the purpose of invitation. Well, that was not so hard, for on bottle night the party declared himself by first drinking to one or the other. The wedding came off on the third day and close upon evening, and by a previous arrangement both sides met at a certain place: the groom with his party marching two and two, male and female, started at a certain hour, and when the bride who on her side tried to keep up equal numbers did the same, and from the time they came in sight of each other, they appeared more like enemies in warfare. At that time there was no law prohibiting the use of old flint guns— Queen Anne's muskets and gunpowder—and once they came in sight of each other, it was tried who could burn most powder. They then met and by a manner of salutation the "best man" on each side, that is the companion of the groom and bride, each hastily distributed a measure of whiskey to everyone on the other side. As the drink fell down they fell into rank and marched in regular procession to the church or residence of the clergyman. In this procession the bride and her "best man" walked first and the groom and his "best maid" came next. The best man on each side was supposed to be kind to the people along the road, and to be able to meet emergencies he had an assistant or two carrying the whiskey and he distributed it as he went along, keeping an eye to stock in trade lest he might run dry and would so be ashamed if he could not do the "decent thing" by meeting with a decent person.

There were many decent persons to be met with, for any one who went to the trouble of giving a "crack", an explosion from an old musket or pistol, was sure of his bucket; all he has to do was to appear, but sure enough an odd one required a deal of "forcing", did not expect it, but wished well to the couple. An odd one came in the way "accidentally" after spending a good part of the day in the forge or the shop ...

The ceremony over, they muster for the homeward journey, and now the newly married couple walk in front. The best men and their maids come out; now the real firing from old carbines and pistols commences and an incessant blasting goes on along the road, for the wedding party spared their powder until now. They are in no great hurry home, for it is not a bad thought to give the people at home time to cook and provide all things wanted, so after a little consultation a public-house is invaded and by a reasonable delay evening sets in; they arrive home after dark. It falls to the lot of the newly married man to supply all the drink, and his best man sees to his interest; in other words he has charge of the keg. The bride's father gives all the luxuries in eating and of course house accommodation for that night.

The "best men" had the privilege of freedom from all charges in any "reckonings" and were pursers in such cases; they had the supervision and distribution of everything, free access everywhere, and a talk with anybody or everybody, and they tried to satisfy all claims as to neglect. The rejoicings at such "high life" weddings were not complete unless there was a fiddler or piper or both, and music, singing and dancing went on till clear "daylight in the morning", and part of that day. A good vocalist was very useful in giving his accomplishments and was sure of "many good healths" and a "health every day". While the singing and dancing went on, it was a saving to the whiskey, and when there was no apparent scarcity in the supply the honour of the groom was sustained. By curtailing the supply they might weather it out, but there could be danger.

But before the break of day it was thought that a little recompense should be made in return for what they [*i.e.* the guests] got during the night. "We know there is plenty"; "we know there is no scarcity, but that says nothing to us". The "best men" would be at different ends of the house with their plates receiving the collection, a certain rate having been fixed for the "reckoning" to purchase a parting glass in honour of the man who did so well for them during the night. They would give him the honour, but they also expected their money's worth of what was forthcoming. Somehow or other it was often managed that the stuff would not be too far away. This being got, it would be as hastily distributed and swallowed. They get their money's worth and, daylight setting in, they jog on to their homes, those better related going arm in arm for strength's sake.

The first Sunday after (except the marriage happened too late in the week) was Outgoing Sunday, although the day of exhibition was kept back if one of the company had his or her dress not complete, but on the next Sunday all appeared in their gayest attire and met as on the first day but in a more quiet way and manner, but [the wedding party] would be sure to be late going to their place of worship, entering so that all eyes could be upon them—the old who might momentarily forget or foolish enough to be diverted from their devotions, and the young who forgetful of everything had their eyes riveted on the parade of white veils and fancy dresses.

Immediately on leaving the house of worship they all marched to the public-house, and here the last gift was bestowed, the parting of the "shilling" for reckoning, and this having been distributed to the satisfaction of some and to the dissatisfaction of others, now all scattered different routes homewards, and the event was at an end. Without enlarging on the moral of such exhibitions of vanity it must be admitted that more sin, more scandal, follows in the train of such unions than in that of the Runaways, who are afraid to be seen but who in afterlife very often are more happy, more prosperous.

BIRTHS

When there appears such a sign as a descendant of Old Adam appearing on earth, the father of such is coerced by a combination of women and forced to leave his dwelling for a time, take refuge in a barn or in a neighbour's house, if convenient, and thus without grumbling he surrenders house and property until all are well. Care was taken before hand at the advice of the mistress that the cupboard was not empty, that a plentiful supply of strong drink was laid up, some hidden and some near at hand, and a trusty neighbour woman or a relative got the secret of the whereabouts it was stowed, and before long in order to soften the hearts of those present as well as pass the time, freedom was made in such a way, one "taking a drop of hot punch" and another preferring "a taste raw" as a better cure for relieving "wind" from the stomach; the women wrought themselves up to "half blindness" and then every-one, be they wrong or right, trying to be officious or in the midst of a quarrel among themselves, pushing and jostling and collisions on the floor, everyone maintaining she was in the right.

The critical moment over and all tears dried up, word is sent to the father to come in to see his "own picture"; "his very picture and that is no lie". Oh! just as like him as "two herrings"; "no one ever saw him but would know him", "just look at him, his very eyes and nose that of his father's". Under such circumstances the likeness must be wonder-fully apparent when so easily discerned by those who could hardly see each other. Nevertheless he was made believe it, that was enough; nor did he scrutinize much just then, as his mind was wavering on the beams of rejoicement not knowing which side to turn to, a visit to the mother or a look at the baby, but in any case he gets a bottle by the neck and lets down "one" to try its strength, and then begins a wholesale distri-bution; he must see everybody and everybody must drink from him, not only those about him but his neighbours, men and women, must be invited, so that in a very short time, a bed is the easiest thing procured, for a stretch in any corner or along the wall is quite pleasing.

Fortunately there are always one or two who make up their minds to keep their senses about them so as to be able to see and attend to press-ing events. After the first night there is a party of volunteers, young girls, who sit up "watching" till the day of the christening. This watching goes on for two or three nights or perhaps longer if there is any danger of the child getting weak or sick; meantime preparations are going on for the feast. The girls sitting up try to have their own merry making and to this end attempt a little feast for themselves, but seldom do they enjoy it in peace for there is always someone among them who betrays the camp and opens the gate for a batch of young lads, who are prowling about till the dead of night and suddenly burst in, and if there is less peace there is more fun, no danger of falling asleep anyhow, and no fear of a fairy till morning.

The christening comes on as soon as convenient, and first there must be a selection made of Godfathers and Godmothers, at the choice of whom more than one or two must have a vote, for very often the voice of old Granny must be consulted. This point is settled; then there are many couples, friends, whom they cannot "shut their eye upon", "could not leave behind", and others whom they wish to form friendship with who are invited.

All are glad of course to get the invitation, and all attend who are invited, but unlike the marriage gatherings they do not come empty handed: every couple has a present in some shape, and with a great deal more of good things than they could make use of themselves. This act of kindness on their part though well understood does not hinder the "man of the house" from going to unnecessary expense in providing all things in decency for the comfort and enjoyment of his guests.

A party of the best pedestrians carry off the babe to get the baptismal rite performed, and on returning, it would not be a bad consideration to get something for the women to help them for *they* must feel tired. So a short call at the public-house, if it does not shorten the distance, at least serves to pass the remainder with less pain. Arriving home, everything is on the point of readiness, those who were dispensed from the toil of walking were waiting and all fall in to enjoy the good things. At first there is great quietness, except the rattling of plates, spoons &c., a little bashfulness, and a forcing of some to fasten on eating or drinking, but soon bold "John Barleycorn" begins to show his pranks, and speedily as an electric shock, the voice of one is hardly discernible above another, there are rising and sittings, outstretching of arms, changing places, "shake of hands", "good healths", "good healths again", "good health every day", "ahoi! good health to you in the corner, you are too far from me to reach hands", "here pass that on and drink my health", but above all *"Slante-van-a-tee"* (good health to the woman of the house), not forgetting *Far-a-tee* (the man of the house), the one we are getting this by.[142] He drinks in return and "your own good health", and it is not because I say it—"You are welcome there"; "I don't know who to put before either of ye".

The night goes on, the drinking goes on, singing is not forgotten, and a space is cleared for dancing a "reel" or "jig" or "hornpipe", when someone remarks that it is near day, "time for the famous reckoning". Immediately the silver is collected and a despatch party is formed who lose no time in drumming up the owner of a public-house, who may be

142. *Sláinte, a bhean an tí*, good health, woman of the house; *Fear an tí*, man of the house.

sleeping over the quilt waiting for them, or a poteen-distiller if he is known to have it. A distiller would get preference so as to "put the money in his way", but in any case the drink is got, and hastily divided, no one forgotten, yet an odd one after getting his due wanted a word with his friend and so placed himself that he could not be passed over, "and in truth, though I got my share, I'll drink this from you as you bid me, a bad day that I would not", and at last when all is ended the curtain falls.

DEATHS

There is one thing certain which I may mention in favour of the people in rural districts in Donegal, be their station in life what it may, they always respected the old people. As the saying is, man's life is shortened, and very few persons are to be found now in comparison who can count an equal number of summers as men did some fifty years ago. For many years before the old men became bedridden, they were dispensed from doing any work, they could rise and walk about as they liked, visit their friends and neighbours, where they were always welcome, glad to make their way to the daughter's abode, and proud to see their grandchildren.

Of course they never lost sight of instructing and giving advice at their homes, and always saw what was amiss and lent their help, feeble though it might be, to set some things right. Their advice was always taken; nothing was done unknown to them, from the sowing of a particular crop, the field in which it should be sown, any contemplated transaction, the bargains, selling or buying to be made at fair or market—the old man is consulted and all was guided by his directions.

When at last he was unable to appear out of doors, all care was bestowed upon him—the daughter came hurriedly, regularly with some novelty to please the "ould man" and felt satisfied at smoothing his bed or his pillow. The son if on a day from home saw something which in his imagination might please the old man and so brought it home. If a son was so profane, or so forgetful, as not to pay due attention to his parents in their last days, not only his relatives but his neighbours would consider it the worst of crimes, and he would be detested by friends and neighbours. Seldom did the like occur, but an odd one perhaps undeservedly got the name for neglect of father or mother and would find himself on the road without perhaps any one to salute him. It was never known of the daughter to forsake or forget her father, and strange too I have found through experience and observations that more affection is carried on between father and daughter, while the son is more attentive to the mother in the last days.

Death comes, but it comes gradually and of course it is not to be expected that there is to be great grief at the end. They may feel lonely for a while in seeing the place vacant where the old man lay so long, but that soon passes away. They rest satisfied that they did their best and therefore feel their consciences at ease for the "fair play" given, and for carrying out his last wishes.

By the "outside people", the deaths of infants and of very old persons were not much taken to heart. There were certain to be crowds of people at such "wakes", many of them for no other end than that of smoking, burning and consuming tobacco, listening to and telling stories, having some little sport at someone "who was not made for mocking at", some hasty tempered fellow whom a prod of a pin or a pull of his hair behind his head, would set him in a blaze. A barn might be cleared for the young lads where they might play tricks of different sorts, as they got leaders to open up for them, such as "tug of war", "stiff hough", or the play of "boot-about", and being thus far removed from the scene of where the dead lay, they were at liberty to pass the time as they thought fit.[143] When middle-aged persons, or persons whose families claimed to be among the respectable, died—or if any person young or old died suddenly—the general feeling at their departure from this world was a general show of real or apparent mourning on the face of everyone, whether relative or stranger.

When trouble of this nature came to any family, every other one as they entered always attempted to give words of consolation, and if any thing else was talked about it was conveyed in whispers or very low tones, but the general subject for rehearsal was in praise of the departed. Someone knew something that no other body knew. Everyone as they entered, and before saluting anybody, first uncovered the head and said some prayers for the good of the soul lately gone. Two nights was supposed to be the duration of time that a corpse should be "waked"—

143. 'Stiff-hough', probably a test of hardihood similar to that known as *Tóin chrua* (Hard arse): 'Four players were involved. Two of them took hold of two others, one each, by the neck and legs and struck their posteriors together to find out which was the harder': see S. Ó Súilleabháin, *Irish wake amusements* (Cork, 1997), pp. 52–3. 'Boot about', or in Irish *Thart an bhróg*, was 'probably the most popular and most widespread wake-game of all'. It involved a pass-the-parcel type game played by people sitting in a circle waist-deep in straw and a leader. As the players surreptitiously passed the shoe around, they threw straw and poked the leader to confuse him. The locating of the shoe ended the first half of the game. The player holding the shoe then had to undergo a punishment—smearing soot on his or her face and being thumped on the back and required to guess how many 'horns' (represented by fingers held up) were on the person thumping them; for a full description, see ibid., pp. 118–22. For an important reassessment of the meaning of wake-games, see G. Ó Crualaoich, 'The "Merry Wake"', in J. S. Donnelly, Jr, and K. Miller, eds, *Irish popular culture, 1650–1850* (Dublin, 1998), pp. 173–200.

"kept in"— but often the time was three nights as they were not sure of the hour of midnight on the first night.

When the hour of dissolution drew near, the sick person was surrounded by the nearest relatives and friends, some of whom might have been sitting up for many nights before, trying to comfort. And when relief was out of the question, all they could do was to sit or stand mournfully looking on, or praying for his happy departure. No disturbance was given until it was well known that the soul had taken its flight, and then a regular piercing wail went up from young and old. The utterance of a feeling neighbour present would be that the grief of the daughter would "pierce a rock". After a while quietness is restored, possibly through sobbing and sighing and possibly exhaustion. Some present try to give consolation and explain the foolishness of such rashness as *all* must die. Then it would be decided at what time of night he departed.

This hour of the night was fixed, approved of, if some wise person gave a close guess at the length of time before or after that he heard the "cock crow"—the crowing of a good cock is always close on midnight, but sometimes they vary—or "the height of the moon above the western horizon"; or guided by what time someone who had an almanack said the moon rose or set the night before, or a very close guide was got from the position of that collection of stars called the "Clusters", how far they were round, what hill they hung over. When neither of these invariable guides could be heard or seen, the length of "half-penny candle burnt" was a close guide, "for there was no wind upon it" from the time it was lit, unless the tallow was bad and that it "ran too fast". Finally, it was decided to be either before or after midnight. If before the wake was "short", if close upon or after midnight the wake was a "long" one. This was what led to the three nights sitting up. When sad events of this nature took place, their reckoning as to the hour was calculated from tokens as above, for as to clocks or watches, they might as well be in Geneva or Birmingham or "Germaniee" for all the use they were to nearly everybody at this time.

Lest I might be understood as speaking disparagingly of the people, there was indeed one man in the neighbourhood who had a watch who always in public attracted many eyes towards him, having an appendage to the watch suspended from the left leg of his trousers' pocket. This protuberance consisted of half a dozen watch keys and as many signets, and connected with the fair-sized chronometer by means of an iron-linked chain. It was on going to his place of worship that old Hughey was often met, and the oftener he was asked the "time of day", the oftener gladness showed in his countenance. He was always delighted to be asked what o'clock it was, and the passerby never forgot the query, not indeed for the knowledge they wished to gain but for the sake of putting Hughey through the performance and get a sight at the "ticker". It gave him pride to be asked the time of day, but he was in no great haste replying as it took both his hands to bring the instrument to view. The outside tossel was easily caught, but then some manipulation was necessary to fold up the waistcoat, and the instrument placed on the palm of the hand, a look was first given at the sun's place in the sky, and then "one-two-three, every figure counts, five minutes you see", "it is therefore such an hour, and so many minutes", and "I am sure the watch is right". When too many would walk past in rapid succession, query after query "What o'clock?", and he takes out the watch, places it on his hand, twists the chain round his wrist, and the person walking close by gets a lecture on the workings of the watch, and he demonstrates that "she" would not lose a minute in seven years. Whether from nervousness or other cause arising whenever he pulled out the "ticker", he also protruded his tongue and hung it to one side of his mouth. No one disputed the correctness or genuineness of the machine and everyone seemed satisfied by having a look, and then he was saved the trouble of counting the fives from a fixed point, for it's easy adding one as he goes along, knowing from which one he started.

But as regards the hour at which a death occurred, in order to be on the safe side and to be independent of any talk on the part of any neighbour, it was considered dishonourable to send away a corpse before the time appointed. Immediately after the death word was sent round to as many of the neighbours as did not hear it, and if asleep turned out of bed. I have known neighbours who were not on very good terms for some time beforehand visit the afflicted, and this would be the first act towards renewing friendship, which would be lasting afterwards. So some one or two from every neighbour's house got up and slowly, silently and mournfully stepped in and kept watch till morning.

Next morning it became generally known, and all who dwelt in the inside bounds of the townland kept the day as a holiday, no outside work was done by any one, and if a man was working in the field, whether friend or foe, on hearing the news, instantly dropped his spade or unyoked his horse, no matter what time of year, either seed time or harvest, and no work was done until the corpse left the boundary of the townland on the day of the funeral.

The first outbursts of grief having subsided, the next thing considered was to provide necessaries for the "wake" and to appear with open hand in what was rightly called "spending", that is smoking tobacco, eating and drinking. The great waste in eating and drinking was reserved for the last night and day, but the tobacco was wanted and wasted at all times, and therefore willing despatches were brought to the front, and an explanation given to them of the number of pounds of tobacco and dozens of clay pipes they were to take as first venture, and when more was wanted it could be got. There never was any deceit in the payment of such things, and so the shopkeeper gave all things asked and kept his account, and as soon as the messengers returned, tables were in readiness, the tobacco and pipes set thereon, and two or three persons set to work, to cut up, spin fine, and fill up the pipes, to have a lot in readiness, and every man, young or old, on entering and getting barely time to sit down or look about, got a pipe stuck in his fist and forced to take it, whether he was in a condition to partake of the weed or not. The men at the tables were busy filling and had their attendants unceasingly going round, giving out the full ones and taking in the empties.

There was some whose constitution could not afford them to be continually smoking, but there were many who went for the purpose of doing so and got every chance. If some had the modesty to refuse, it was only a momentary put off, for the next messenger forced and forced over again, and the same salutation repeated "smoke", "take it man", "why don't you smoke?", "here you must take it", "don't spare it", "is it sparing it you are?", "plenty of it here". An odd one who had it not in plenty at any other time of year took the opportunity of doing good to himself. There were some few such persons, not indeed that they were unsuspected, but their fault in this was considered simple and forgiven, and as the pipes came round, they took everyone offered to them but somehow their pipes got stopped, and they had to go to the trouble of picking out, but the tobacco never went back again. If a chance was got, pipe and tobacco disappeared in the pocket.

"Many little makes a mickle", so between petty pilfering and breaking, the pipes ran scarce before morning and the plates lay bare of the clay machines. The request came round, "Boys hand in the pipes, there is plenty of tobacco here"—but the pipes were not forthcoming. It was laughable to see the man who wanted to smoke, and could not be supplied on this account, presenting himself at the table and producing his own "black duhdeen". "Here fill this, it will keep myself going", and everyone who sat near him knowing that at the same time he had no less than half-a-dozen in his pocket.

"To cover shame" another despatch was sent off before day and awoke the shopkeeper, a new supply was got which could not be done without as the strangers were expected, and some of them early in the morning. The next thing got and sure to be got if not already in the house was a sackful or a certain quantity of oatmeal, and a few stout, clean and healthy young girls at the directions of some tidy woman were set to the task of baking and hardening the large cakes or as they are called "*bannocks*".[144] The fires in the "wake-house" were not enough, the nearest neighbours "had to be troubled", and a number of fires were surrounded with irons and thin cakes the size of a neat riddle, the largest and thinnest being considered a cleverness on the part of the baker, the girl.

When the "white-loaf" began to be commonly used, it threw the girls out of trade, for when a quantity of it came home fresh from the oven, there was little toil in making divisions of any number of "thripinny" or "six-pinny" loaves; a woman would without using a knife at all tear up at once as many as covered a table. "It was good enough to pass time, but it was no eating" without a little sprinkling of the oatmeal cake, and a table was hungry looking unless a "*bannock*" was *entire* at the end of the table and one at the fireside, and to this day some people prefer the "hard-bre-ad", "what they got in youth", so that the custom may be a long time yet before it dies out.

A sufficient supply of bread for a start being provided, also butter, the manufacture of the tea was then put in motion, and no great science was exercised in the art. Teapots were not thought of at all, for all the instruments of that description in a parish in those days would be of no use. Instead of these worthless little toys, more "wide-hearted" vessels were used, that is to say two or three of the largest pots that could be got, and these were well scoured and cleaned, and covered with a wooden lid or a large wooden dish, and when the water was at the boiling point, a quantity of tea, measured in proportion to the gallons of water was, at the superintendence of some woman who saw the like done before put into each pot. When the mixture was pretty well stewed, it got the quantity of sugar and milk at the fireside, and when poured out of large jugs that had been dipped into the pot, it was ready made for use.

During the time that the women were busy in measuring out the tea into large bowls, some three or four men kept carelessly hanging about,

144. *Bonnóg*, scone, cake of home-made bread.

inside and outside the door, sentry-like lest anyone might step out, and at a signal from the servitors that everything was ready, then the hauling and pulling and dragging began. They commenced at or near the door and missed no one. It was not, "Will you come", but "you must"; "rise" "rise" was the only cry, and if any one refused or begged to be excused, it was no use, for then two fastened upon him, and unless he could part his arm from the sleeve of his coat, his body was forced to follow. "Shame on you, what makes you so strange"; "Come on". "If the man who is under board tonight was on his feet, he would be glad to see you, and would not begrudge what you are going to get". In this manner did the eating and drinking go on for a full day and night, and also the morning of the funeral day, up to the last minute, doing very little good to many who received it and on the other hand much loss to the parties who gave it, for the shopkeeper had to be met in his bill.

On the day before the interment took place a "funeral warning" was sent out to all parts of the parish, and sometimes into other parishes if the connexions of the parties so extended. To ensure accuracy in the transmission of such messages, a number of the most trustworthy young men were called together into a room before the relatives of the deceased, and a certain district was appointed for each "warner" with special instructions where and what houses to call in, and the exceptions they were to make if any.[145]

Certain houses and dwellings were forcibly fixed on the memory for fear of forgetfulness, and some other odd houses were as strictly forbidden to be entered for the reason that at the time "uncle Ned was dead and buried, word was sent them and none of them attended". This was the way the people felt, if word was sent to a house and no one representing the family appeared, that simple act of forgetfulness was kept in recollection for years by the party supposed offended, and on the other hand if another one who knew well enough did not get the customary notice, he would not attend, and would be sure to rise the question again at the first meeting with one of the family, "Why he was forgotten?", "Would surely attend if he got the word, but he was afraid, something stuck in his mind there was something against him".

If the burial took place on a Monday, there was then another method for giving the "warning". On the Sunday before, some man was deputed who could put on a bold face, who was not afraid his voice to

---

145. The practice of sending out 'warners' (in Irish *fir fuagartha*) in this manner appears to be have been almost unique to Fánaid; for an account see R.B.É., 740 (S. Ó hEochaidh, 10 Eanáir 1941).

be heard, and he stood upon some elevated position, outside the place of worship, and shouted out at the top of his voice that "Jamey Harry Duggan of Ballywaters is to be buried tomorrow". This practice was permitted years long enough by the old whims of clergymen, but as time changes so with this: the young clergyman already spoken of thought a more becoming method could be used, and so by means of one simple but imperative admonition he got the people to give himself *word*, either orally or if possible written on a slip of paper, and he at the fitting time let the congregation know the wishes of such a one, putting for ever since a stop to any or everyone from exercising their vocal powers on such occasions.

The young men who were chosen for "warning" performed their duty faithfully. They started together but soon separated for different circuits, each one carrying a good *blackthorn* stick—a stick being useful in the first place as a protection against strange dogs, but in addition to this there was some other unexplained reason to the carrying of the blackthorn, for it was always the quality of stick used on such occasions. While engaged on their mournful journey, they entered every house as instructed, turned round immediately on the floor without giving time to the housewife to get fully into a fright, and proclaiming their errand, off without any further talk, and on to the next dwelling. No delay, no talk, no time to answer questions till out of reach. Their appearance even in the distance distinguished them, for they took the privilege of all nearways over fields and cultivated ground and trespassing wherever they could find footing, no one interfering with them.

On returning, these messengers of grim countenance met again at the house of the "people in trouble" to satisfy them as to their having acted up to instructions, and then a good guess could be formed of the size of the funeral, for it was expected that every family warned was to be represented by someone whether man or woman, boy or girl. Men of middle age, half worn, or beyond the state of doing a hard day's work, always attended the funerals. Sometimes two came from one house, to show greater respect nominally but for another gain personally, and a procession of the equine animals were not wanting: the old man prepared a saddle and pillion, and he and the old woman mounted, he from getting a hold of the mane and dragging himself up and she from a "mounting stone" convenient, gathering up her tail ends to fall into the pillion and off they dodge to the funeral.

At the funeral of married persons, there was no regularity kept by way of marching; on the road was a closely connected crowd as far as they were forced to extend, walking so close as to injure the heels of some who did not keep eyes open, the *corns* being forgotten as the heels were the undefended points, the only regularity carried out was that all the women walked in the front, the men in the centre and the horsemen brought up the rear.

The coffin was always made at home, and on the evening before, a man sitting sideways on horseback could be seen, and tied to the horse's sides as many white deal as were required to make the coffin, and much worn at the edges depending on the distance they were dragged on a rough road, and on the arrival of the material for the "last suit", a carpenter—a friend if it was possible—set up a temporary bench in the barn, put the boards into shape, and spared as much timber as turned out a "cross" as well, the working or ornamentation of the cross depending on the timber left, and also the willingness of the carpenter to do so.

The carrying of the "cross" fell or should fall to the lot of the nearest relative, but the dying person might bestow it in his last words to another, and then often disputes arose about conferring the honour. The coffin enclosing the dead was always carried by four on "handspikes", two men fore and two aft, to the graveyard, no matter the distance be five or ten miles, and willing hands were always so ready that no one was kept under weight for more than a few minutes.

With unmarried persons, the young boy as also the old bachelor got a "boy's funeral", and the boys walked two and two and carried the coffin in regular turns. The first rank on being relieved fell out, stood on until falling into the rear again, and so on. The girls were at once taught the same drill and at a "girl's funeral" or, as I should say, at one unmarried.

At the funerals of the unmarried, whether boys or girls, married persons might attend for want of a substitute and many always did so, but they walked in the rear and did not or would not be allowed to interfere with those in the ranks. On the day of the funeral as may be understood, people came from all parts to attend it. In this part of the country there is no hour for starting, no consideration of the distance men have to walk or what time they will be home. Some of course were tired waiting, and some were late in coming, which could easily be accounted for: the first left his work undone, and the latter felt that all things would be right, and in addition to those who looked out for time and their own interest, a look out from the family in mourning was for "Paddy Faddy" or "Ned Billy", and "don't know what is keeping them". "We can't go till they come". The hours of the day were passing by but not lost idly inside, for during all this time eating and drinking were going on and at intervals some two or three newcomers were shouldered to the tables. Observations as to the sun's declination are often taken by many, and when it is decided by a majority that without doubt the sun is long on the decline, then by a mutual consent some three or four go abreast and try to impress upon the members of the family that it is near the time, if they have a mind to go that day.

Some little preparations are made for the move but not all yet, it is only to please some parties, "time enough"; "it is the last day we can have him and little enough we spend some of his own".

Men by being tired sitting, tired in waiting, gave signs of their uneasiness and move to the outside, and many expressing their views that it is time to start. Some friends hearing the amount of such mourning, make so bold as to approach the chief mourners, or those in command and say "now it is long enough we must go", and then the simultaneous bursts of crying goes up, which lasts for a considerable time, as preparations are slowly made for the removal of the coffin. If relief it be, at least it is considered such that all must get time to "cry their fill" and when tired out, hoarse and sobbing, some four go about "taking out the coffin", still the crying continues and increases for a good distance from the abode. By means of consolatory advice, by hugging and shaking, or through the intervention of a friend, one after another ceases the wailing, and the mixed crowd of men and women move on.

Times long ago the priest used to come to the house, perform some duties there, and then he was chief guide, but for many years past, through some wiser regulation, he fulfils his duty by meeting the funeral somewhere on the road and walks some distance before it, with someone or two who force themselves on his presence, confident of the power of their tongue in describing the state of the crops, the appearance of the weather, or it might be the faults of their neighbours, not knowing what to say.

The graveyard reached, the funeral service over, the grave is then to be opened, but this is not long in doing through the willingness of some sturdy young fellows who work with spade and shovel time about, and when the grave is opened and the coffin laid down, [those who have] opened it cover it up, and the last sod is settled down and the cross fixed at the his head. While the grave is being filled up, there is sobbing and half audible mourning going on, but when all is covered, and the crowd ready to leave, a loud and piercing lamentation goes up and a clapping of hands, lasting until again exhausted or until forced to leave the place by being dragged, The covering for coffins is a neatly tied-on clean sheet, as white as washing can do it. A clergyman once thought he would introduce a sign of mourning and got cloths for that purpose which were to be got at the sexton's and left with him again, but the idea soon fell through. The people could not become reconciled with the idea of covering their dead with "Moor cloth", and so the "white sheet" is always used.

Soon after arriving at the graveyard most of the people dispersed on their way home, but the relatives and some other friends hung about for to accompany the mourners as near to their homes as could be. On the way home a call was made at the public-house, with the idea we suppose of consoling the sorrowful, and herein was found the best medicine for drowning grief. This custom was of long standing and could not be avoided, for the reason that one was indebted to the other, and there was a sort of pride attached to the amount of money collected at a "reckoning", for on it rested the numbers of friends and well-wishers, everyone of whom could be named at home, as well as if a list was made out, and the family who then felt satisfied were unthoughtfully running into debt at the death of every such friend.

Of all men living, the public-housekeeper was the only one who felt less grief at the death of any man and would be the last to shed a tear, especially if the person had a large connexion and if any person of respectability had a lingering illness, no one made more inquiries about him. I often thought what a fit candidate he would be for a public executioner, but luckily such was not wanted in his part of the country ...

The publican was one of the first outside the family always to hear of the death of any one, and he told everybody, and if he knew it to be the means of a good game for himself, he at once made it his business to go to the wholesale to renew his stock, and get an additional permit added to the Gauger's Book. He was in the best of tune with everyone of the day of a funeral; for want of time, he seldom went to the house, but always met it at such a place as to be seen by everyone, and then went part of the road but was the first to return. From his experience and the other observations he took that day he could form a good idea of what was coming to him and so mixed and qualified his drink in proportion and had seats and tables in readiness for an emergency.

His place was central for the greater part of the parish; he had a yard and some stabling accommodation, but not enough to serve all on every occasion, and to supply the want, he had a number of iron rings fixed around the garden wall for to tie up the animals. Inside, the owners find themselves comfortable, surrounded with the perfumes of whiskey which muffles the time, and the poor beasts are forgotten by their masters. Finding themselves thus cruelly treated, and pressed with cold and hunger, they rebel against the will of their owners, and one after another break reins and make way to the nearest corn field, or wander home, saddle and bridle lost.

The presence of all those expected to be seen at the funeral [was remembered], but the coin expected to be spent at the drink was kept in greater remembrance, indeed the latter in many cases satisfied the two obligations, for if a person was prevented from some special cause, his remedy was to send money with a neighbour, who handed it in, naming the party and all was right, and one man might thus be purser for three or four. The cost in the "reckoning" was generally one shilling and the amount carefully collected and announced and on this sum was estimated the number of friends—but there was no hindrance to lesser combinations after, and such was the case. The first [such meeting] was only a preparatory course and when nearly over friends met in different groups to talk over old subjects and renew friendship over the glass. We are not to suppose that any large amount of money was squandered in this way because at that time when the drinking custom was in full force, the whiskey was cheaper by less than one-half in price of what it is now, so that a couple of silver coins when wisely handled would spin out a good while, and give a good drink ...

The number of people returning from the funeral were not all to be met at the drinking stall, no indeed, there was a pioneer party before them, waiting patiently long enough—Pat and Ned and Mickey and Shemus, and not far distant were there a few very dry spittles, persons who had a cold or a cough, or a sore foot, or a tightened shoe and could go no farther—persons who knew that one in their family was obliged to pay and therefore they had a certain hold of a share. They were not going there as beggars, their brother or son was there before them.

Immediately after all had arrived, some two or three take up plates or hats for to receive the collection, and as payment is made, the people fix themselves into their seats. The money being collected, and in order to please all parties, it was customary for the collectors—afterwards distributors—to inquire "If any one preferred any quality of drink". The greater part of the crowd in all cases were for the "hard stuff", but someone wanted *"gin"*—"could not drink whiskey, promised against whiskey"—and another wanted "porter or ale", as he could take no whiskey outside of his own townland. Women had their choice too, some wanted "punch", or it would do just well enough to have a taste of sugar on a saucer to put on the "cold stuff" and mix it up with the finger, it agreed better and prevented headache.

Complaints were sometimes brought against the distributors, perhaps by those already stupified from what they got, the charge being that they did not divide equally the common property which they took in charge, and that they showed by their actions that they paid too much kindness to particular friends and neglected others who had as much right. Arising from the heat consequent on the expansion of the alcohol, "one word borrowed another" and such charges arising out of nothing, whether well founded or not, were often the beginning of what led to disagreements, and perhaps serious quarrels arising from amidst that of friendship. The custom was of long standing and of course did not often go to the extremes I mention, but in too many cases unfortunately it led to abuses, such as drunkenness, and high words either at the public-house or on the way home.

The then clergyman of the place began to form opinions different from that of his predecessors and threw out hints that he would put a stop to it. The publican thought otherwise, hinting and saying "that he should mind his own business"; "what was it *all* that passed but a few words among friends, when the *wee* drop was taken, and which he knew would soon be forgotten". "And that he was no better than the priests who went before him". This priest however was not to be overcome by such reasoning.

The "reckonings" at the public-house were put an end to, and indeed drinking spirituous liquors at all, coming or going by any one who attended a funeral is now and for some years past entirely put an end to, much indeed to the displeasure of the then poor publican who seems dissatisfied if any one enters to light his pipe, troubling him on his floor and nothing to gain.

If any friendship is to be shown through the medium of whiskey to the family in trouble it must be done at their homes, when all is over, and if drink then goes to excess it is removed from the view of the general public. This permissive clause, "leave to drink at home", if permission really was needed, was next to nothing so far as the interest of the publican was concerned, because only a very few could conveniently go to the house a second time on the same day, whereas the public-house was on the road for all. For this reason and grievously to the loss of the publican, his "reckonings" at funerals are almost forgotten by him, but as yet he cannot see any just cause "why any man is prevented from taking a glass of whiskey".

The Sunday Closing Bill has put an end to drinking on the Outgoing Sunday of the newly married couple, and how can the poor publican stand against spiritual and temporal powers now combined against him?[146] So that of all men living, the feeling of the publican and his downward state on the roadside are the most *Miserable*.

146. *Sale of intoxicating liquors on Sunday (Ireland) bill*, a bill introduced in the House of Commons in 1876 that required public houses in rural districts and small towns to close on Sundays. Obstructed by members of the Irish Home Rule Party and English Conservatives, it was finally enacted in August 1878; see E. Malcolm, *'Ireland sober, Ireland free': Drink and temperance in nineteenth-century Ireland* (Dublin, 1986), pp. 238–49.

Concluding Remarks

Many of the incidents and events sketched in the preceding chapters happened in the lifetime of our "Waterloo hero" who made such a figure in an early part of our story, for he lived some years after the suppression of his own teaching capabilities, even though defeated in this employment. He was always held in esteem by his old friends and acquaintances. One of them he visited, wrapped in his old martial cloak, supporting himself on his stick: when he dropped into a house, his old admirers as many of them as were near [at] hand hastened in to meet him. Their conversations then were not as in the years long and not long past—not of wars, not of battles, nor the strength of nations; no, their subjects were lacking words, more silent, and of a more mournful nature.

It was a rehearsal of their own sad experience of the past few years—the silence, the sadness, the desolation around, caused by the Famine, by the crowbar brigade, and by emigration; of the death of many of their near acquaintances, who were hurried away in a short time. There was the recollection of the immense population at one time, and their dispersion almost unawares. In these short intercourses, a few words on the landlord's oppression and tyranny were broached, but very cautiously for fear any word might escape to the enemy; no one was secure then, not knowing but that at the end of six months the wide, wide world might be his inheritance.

Had our "man of many battles" lived a few years longer, he could have an opportunity, if not of satisfaction, of seeing the third stage of education arising and progressing; for strange as it may appear to the reader, it is nevertheless a fact that the very house which was first used for the Church Education Society's teaching and which was instrumental in setting him aside, was in its turn converted into a National School. The method of teaching and indeed everything changed over again, and it is so still. In this last transformation everything is aimed at and everything is provided for to facilitate learning—from that of the Board's rules; the manager's rules; the teacher's time table; the teacher's competency; the monitors with pointers in their hands watching over and keeping classes in subjection—all the requisites desirable being at hand, books, slates, pencils, chalk, pen, ink, paper and so forth.

Everything is done by time and to time, and it is therefore the opinion of the inspectors—that is, those men who earn more but work less than the teachers—that nothing is wanted at the present time but skulls and brains, nothing to prevent any young person becoming a *Scholar.*

The End

Elizabeth Batt, view of the Binn *of Fánaid from Glenvar, c. 1845, watercolour (private collection)*

NATIONAL SCHOOLS IN FÁNAID, 1842–1880

SCHOOL	FIRST PATRON	ESTATE	OPENED	CLOSED
Ballymichael	Daniel O'Donnell, P.P.	Leitrim	1842	1878
Drumfad†	Patrick Hay, Presb. minister	Letham	1842	
Fanavolty	James Gallagher, C.C.	Leitrim	1850	1859
Doaghbeg	James Gallagher, C.C.	Leitrim	1851	
Tullyconnell	James Gallagher C.C.	Leitrim	1854	1865
Glenvar	John Ward, C.C.	Sinclair	1856	
Ballyhoorisky	Lord Leitrim	Leitrim	1864	1873
Ballyhork	John O'Boyle, P.P.	Irwin	1866	
Rosnakill	Francis Gallagher, C.C.	Norman	1866	
Ballylar	John O'Boyle, P.P.	Leitrim	1870	
Fannet†	John O'Boyle, P.P.	Letham	1871	
Cashel	John O'Boyle, P.P.	?Skipton	1873	
Tamney	William Skipton, C.I. rector	Norman	1874	
Croaghross	?William Skipton C.I. rector	Barton	1875	
Leatbeg	John O'Boyle, P.P.	Leitrim	1875	

Sources: N.A.I., E.D. 1/23-7 [Donegal Applications]; Annual reports of the commissioners of national education, 1834–1878.

† Drumfad National School was in Drumfad Lower; Fannet National School was in Drumfad Upper.

Note: closure dates refer to formal 'striking off'.

INDEX

www.ingramcontent.com/pod-product-compliance
Ingram Content Group UK Ltd.
Pitfield, Milton Keynes, MK11 3LW, UK
UKHW020004310125
454458UK00010B/617